# Voices
## of the
# Faithful

### BOOK 2

European Peoples

Central Asian
Peoples

East Asian
Peoples

rn African and
Eastern Peoples

Southeast Asian
Peoples

South Asian
Peoples

Sub-Saharan
African Peoples

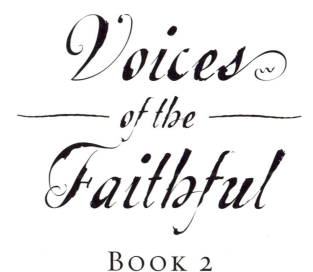

# Voices
## — of the —
# Faithful

## BOOK 2

COMPILER AND MONTHLY INTRODUCTIONS BY

# KIM P. DAVIS

SERIES CREATOR AND INTRODUCTION BY

# BETH MOORE

THOMAS NELSON
*Since 1798*

NASHVILLE   DALLAS   MEXICO CITY   RIO DE JANEIRO   BEIJING

Published in Nashville, Tennessee, by Thomas Nelson. Thomas Nelson is a registered trademark of Thomas Nelson, Inc.

Thomas Nelson, Inc. titles may be purchased in bulk for educational, business, fund-raising, or sales promotional use. For information, please e-mail SpecialMarkets@ThomasNelson.com.

Scripture quotations marked NIV are from the Holy Bible: New International Version®. © 1973, 1978, 1984 by International Bible Society. Used by permission of Zondervan Publishing House. All rights reserved.

Scripture quotations marked NASB are from the New American Standard Bible®. © The Lockman Foundation 1960, 1962, 1963, 1968, 1971, 1971, 1973, 1975, 1977, 1995. Used by permission.

Scripture quotations marked HCSB are from the Holman Christian Standard Bible. © 1999, 2000, 2002, 2003 by Holman Bible Publishers, Nashville, Tennessee. All rights reserved.

Scripture quotations marked ESV are from the English Standard Version. © 2001 by Crossway Bibles, a division of Good News Publishers.

Scripture quotations marked NLT are from the Holy Bible, New Living Translation. © 1996. Used by permission of Tyndale House Publishers, Inc., Wheaton, Illinois 60189. All rights reserved.

Scripture quotations marked CEV are from the Contemporary English Version. © 1991 by the American Bible Society. Used by permission.

Scripture quotations marked NKJV are from the New King James Version®. © 1982 by Thomas Nelson, Inc. Used by permission. All rights reserved.

Scripture quotations marked KJV are from the King James Version. Scripture quotations marked ASV are from the Authorized Standard Version.

Scripture quotations marked MSG are from The Message by Eugene H. Peterson. © 1993, 1994, 1995, 1996, 2000. Used by permission of NavPress Publishing Group. All rights reserved.

Quotation on September's introduction page is from Beth Moore, *To Live Is Christ* (Nashville: B & H Publishing, 2008), 104.

Other quotations on the months' introduction pages are from *Voices of the Faithful: Inspiring Stories of Courage from Christians Serving Around the World* (Nashville: Thomas Nelson, 2005).

ISBN-13: 978-0-8499-2071-4

CIP on file with publisher

*Printed in the United States of America*
09 10 11 12 13 QW 9 8 7 6 5 4 3 2 1

To the faithful brothers and sisters
in Christ
who lost their lives
while serving Him internationally
in 2008 and 2009

# Contents

# ACKNOWLEDGMENTS

Heavenly Father, this is Your book! You are behind every story. May You be glorified in every word printed and in every prayer lifted up.

To the readers of the first *Voices of the Faithful*, thank you for the many e-mails and personal conversations encouraging book two. May these stories inspire you to pray for the nations like never before and perhaps challenge you to participate in missions by going on a mission trip or starting a career as a missionary.

Hundreds of people are actually involved in a book such as this. Over 300 International Mission Board (IMB) missionaries wrote these daily devotions. They are unsung heroes of the faith who have dedicated their lives to following Jesus wherever He leads. It's not an easy task to be away from family and friends, English speakers, and comforts of a familiar culture. Thank you for these stories.

For the second time around, several faithful friends have been prayer warriors for this book throughout the entire process. Amy, Angela, Bobbye, Connie, D. Ray, Elaine, Eleanor, Gloria, Leigh Ann, Kay, Melinda, and Shawna have prayed on a moment's notice because they loved to do it. May God richly bless you for it.

Thanks to the people of Thomas Nelson Publishers who made this book happen.

The final editor, Jennifer Stair, came back for round two. Your hard work is appreciated.

Most of the prayers at the end of each devotion were written by Bobbye Rankin, Eleanor Witcher, Ed Cox, and Kim Davis. Praying for the nations is what this book is all about, so your role was crucial.

At the IMB, it took several people to assist in pulling it all together. Eleven regional representatives read devotions to make sure personnel security stayed intact. Clyde Meador and Wendy Norvelle proofread the book for accuracy. Dan Allen took care of business concerns. Elaine Meador looked at the manuscript and figured out how to make it better on short notice.

Last but not least, the IMB is grateful to Beth Moore for the vision of the series and for writing the initial introduction. And we're thankful for Kim Davis, who compiled and edited the book and wrote the monthly introductions. You will enjoy the touch that they bring to *Voices of the Faithful, Book Two.*

—*International Mission Board, SBC*

# FOREWORD

Being president of the International Mission Board of the Southern Baptist Convention has put me in a position to have a unique global overview of God's work around the world. Every day I receive reports, e-mails, and newsletters from our regional offices and from many of our missionaries—over 5,000 of them serving among people groups in 194 countries. I have gained an awesome sense of God's providence as He works through global events to fulfill His mission. He is even using war and ethnic violence, political disruption, economic uncertainty, and natural disasters to turn the hearts of a lost world to the hope that can only be found in Jesus Christ.

It is especially poignant to connect with missionary personnel and their families. Their ministry is not without hardship and sacrifice. Their witness often encounters resistant barriers and even antagonism. Many of them have left prominent positions of ministry and successful careers in America and embraced a different lifestyle, isolated from family and friends. They persevere and labor faithfully, compelled by a vision of seeing a lost world transformed by the power of the Gospel.

These missionaries are not planting their lives in foreign cultures out of desire for personal reward, recognition, or public acclaim. They are not motivated by guilt or the goal of personal fulfillment. They have a strong sense of God's call and serve out of a passion to see Him glorified among the nations and all the peoples of the world. They are the faithful ones.

These devotions are expressions of how God has worked in these faithful lives in simple yet profound ways each day. These "voices"

will inspire, thrill, evoke laughter, and bring tears. But they will also strengthen your faith and invariably stimulate a commitment to pray more faithfully and knowledgeably for those who labor around the world.

The first volume of *Voices of the Faithful* found an unexpected, massive response among readers interested in missions. It resulted in the extensive mobilization of intercessors praying for the nations. All royalties for books one and two support the work of the International Mission Board. I pray that the voices in *Voices of the Faithful, Book Two* may be heard as the voice of our Lord calling each of us to faithful obedience.

*—Jerry Rankin, President*
*International Mission Board, SBC*

# INTRODUCTION

With great joy, I'd like to introduce to you *Voices of the Faithful, Book Two*. The idea for this series sprang from a bumpy ride in a car on the other side of the world while Keith and I were in South Africa serving missionaries. Most bright ideas like these come to nothing. We get back home to the demands of our day-to-day lives, and if it ever dawns on us again, we wonder what on earth we were thinking. It's kind of like those three bold-colored saris that I purchased while I was in India. I got back home to Texas and wondered exactly where I thought I was going to wear them. Somehow they'd look a little awkward at one of our suburban malls. Maybe I could have gotten away with wearing one of them to my church on "Missions Sunday." After all, my fellow members there are like real family to me and have long since accepted my oddities. However, they'd have talked about me over lunch at the cafeteria, and I hate when that happens.

Turns out, this conversation couldn't have differed more from my temporary affinity for foreign dress on domestic soil. I find tremendous relief and comfort in some often-overlooked words recorded in Acts 5:38–39 as a test for things earnestly attempted in the name of Christ: "For if their purpose or activity is of human origin, it will fail. But if it is from God, you will not be able to stop these men; you will only find yourselves fighting against God" (NIV).

That's often the most obvious difference between a God idea and a really good idea. If God's behind it, you'd have a mighty hard time stopping it. The concept for this series of books didn't come from my heart or from Kim's. It came from God's. After all, it is He who "so loved the world that he gave his one and only Son, that whoever believes in him shall not perish but have eternal life" (John 3:16, NIV). By the time the first volume hit the shelves, we weren't left to wonder for long why He purposed it. Interest in world missions and in the lives of those who serve on the foreign field increased beyond what we had even hoped. Believers in Christ, who sincerely wanted to be interested in world missions but admitted they simply were not, testified to finding a resource that held their attentions. I think that's because it's full of stories. The real-life kind. And who doesn't love a great story? Why do we think Christ used the method of storytelling so prolifically in His teachings?

The art of any story is the truth that it paints. I pray you'll find this book chock-full of truth. I pray that every single entry causes words of Scripture to jump off the page and onto the pavement of authentic human experiences, causing you not only to see their lives differently but also to change the way you see your own. I want to give God room to do whatever He wants with the resource you hold in your hands, but these are a few things at the top of my list that I'm asking Him to accomplish:

*I hope you'll feel connected to brothers and sisters in Christ all over the globe.* We've got to ditch the "us and them" mentality. All of us in this generation who have trusted Jesus Christ as our personal Savior comprise the body of Christ at this strategic hour on the kingdom calendar. We need each other and, as Hebrews 10:25 tells us, "all the more as you see the Day approaching" (NIV). Translation? The closer we get to the return of Christ and to the prophesied "Day of the Lord," the tougher things will get. Check out places like Matthew 24 and 2 Timothy 3 if you want to see what I mean. But, whatever you do, don't lose heart as you flip through those pages. Christ built His church with the power of His own blood, and she is much stronger than she gives herself credit for. When hard times come, the key word isn't *survival*. It's *revival*. And there's got to be a coming together for genuine revival to take place.

It's as true today as it was in the generation of those first Christ-followers: A house united stands. A house divided falls. We usually think of the call to unity as the curative for disagreement. Perhaps the cry for unity is needed just as passionately for mere disengagement. We're busy with our own lives and simply unaware of what the other does. What the other *needs*. This resource could be a sizeable leap in the direction of full-throttle engagement that takes us across borders and across oceans.

*I also hope you'll be motivated to pray.* If you're like me, the more general I am in my prayer life, the less effective I feel, even if God is answering my intercessions in specific ways beyond my realm of vision. For instance, it's hard for me to simply pray for the leaders of our country to be wise. I am greatly helped when I have names and positions and needs I can lift before the throne of grace. Though God may be just as engaged when I pray in general terms for Him to heal the sick among His dear servants, I don't feel as effective in my intercessions as when I have some names and some details. I'm a relational person, and I often need real faces—even if they're sketched in words—and real stories to set my prayer life ablaze. If you're the same way, you're in good shape because you have some of those real lives and stories in the pages that soon follow. You're not just stuck with "God bless the missionaries," although He no doubt hears and responds to those simple words. You're going to get very specific directions to pray that can increase your confidence exponentially.

Whatever you do, never lose sight of the fact that your prayers matter immensely. The fact is, they matter *immeasurably.* When I wonder if my prayers for others are accomplishing anything at all, my mind often turns to Paul's words in the first chapter of 2 Corinthians. There you'll find these vivid realities:

> *We do not want you to be uninformed, brothers, about the hardships we suffered in the province of Asia. We were under great pressure, far beyond our ability to endure, so that we despaired even of life. Indeed, in our hearts we felt the sentence of death. But this happened that we might not rely on ourselves but on God, who raises the dead. He has delivered us from such a deadly peril, and he will deliver us. On him we have set our hope that he will continue to deliver us, as you help us by your prayers. Then many will give thanks on our behalf for the gracious favor granted us in answer to the prayers of many.* (2 Corinthians 1:8–11, NIV)

Day in and day out, whether on this side of the ocean or the other, we are surrounded by people who face situations they feel are "far beyond [their] ability to endure." As a way to unify His body of believers into a functioning whole, God has purposed that divine deliverance often comes as a direct result of corporate prayer. If you don't easily buy that, read the segment again. "On him we have set our hope that he will continue to deliver us, as you help us by your prayers." He loves nothing more than seeing two or three, 2,000 or 3,000, or 20,000 or 30,000 gathered on their knees on opposite sides of the globe in fervent prayer.

But don't miss the intricate beauty of this invitation. Not only are we invited to enter into someone else's struggle through prayer, but we are also invited to enter into someone else's thanksgiving. As Paul wrote, "Then many will give thanks on our behalf for the gracious favor granted us in answer to the prayers of many." My engagement with others does indeed cause me to take on some of their pain, but it also gives me untold opportunities to dance with thanksgiving over their joy. That's life in community. We who are believers in Christ need never be alone ... or lonely. The question is, how willing are we to get involved?

As I have the privilege to write this introduction to the second book in the *Voices of the Faithful* series, I have the wonderful benefit of having the effects of the first volume to draw from. I hope you'll be encouraged to know that numerous missionaries are reading the daily entries along with the rest of us. I have lost count of the many who have told Kim and me that the entry they wrote ended up falling upon a day of great need for them in the published version. Imagine it: they, in need of their own word from God, opened their own personal copy of *Voices of the Faithful* that day and, lo and behold, found their own story. Christ used the devotional not only to incite prayer on their behalf but also to affirm His tender, watchful, detailed care of them. And perhaps they found the courage to stay the course a little while longer. Don't you want to be part of that miracle? I do!

*Lastly, I hope you'll be motivated to cross your own river of fear and do the thing God has called you to do.* Please, please don't surrender to foreign missions because you know there is a need. Don't surrender to foreign missions because you know God's heart pounds thunderously for this lost world. The only ones among us who should surrender to foreign missions are those who are so called by God that resisting it is practically not an option. We're not all called to be missionaries like the ones we'll read about in the pages to come, but make no mistake: we are all called by God to do something specific and infinitely well-planned that will shine His great light in a corner of the darkness. "For we are God's workmanship, created in Christ Jesus to do good works, which God prepared in advance for us to do" (Ephesians 2:10, NIV).

Some of us are called into the public school system. Others, the political arena. Others, the justice system. Others, to the oppressed. The poor. The rejected. Others to those dying of their own intellectualism. Of their own affluence. Some are called to minister to children. Others to senior adults. Some are called by God into secular work (Joseph, Mordecai, Esther, and Daniel for starters). Others into vocational work. (Not so unlike Paul, but keep in mind, he had no idea how important he'd turn out. He often wondered whether he was making a difference, too.) The ways we could be called to serve God are as diverse as the people we'd serve. If you are a follower of Jesus Christ, you are tremendously gifted to do something that can make God famous in your sphere of influence, however big or small.

This I believe with all my heart: whatever you are called to do, you cannot—even under the best of circumstances—do it on your own. I don't care how talented you are. Or how educated you are. Fulfilling your calling demands the unhindered infiltration of the Holy Spirit of Christ working through you. Otherwise it remains a lovely theory. It also demands a death of sorts to self. We won't get to stay in the security of our own flesh and test to see if the work of the Spirit is worth what it would take. Until the return of Christ, at least one thing about discipleship will never change: we lay down our lives to find them. We'll never find them with one hand while we hold onto our back-ups with the other. "For whoever wants to save his life will lose it, but whoever loses his life for me will find it. What good will it be for a man if he gains the whole world, yet forfeits his soul? Or what can a man give in exchange for his soul?" (Matthew 16:25–26, NIV).

I see an epidemic of boredom in the body of Christ. I am convinced that one issue is primarily to blame: we are protecting ourselves right out of our callings. Right out of our God-ordained destinies. We are comfort addicts ... and we keep wondering why we never feel satisfied. I can't promise you that following Jesus wherever He leads will always be pleasant. Lord have mercy, I can't even promise you that it won't eventually kill you. I'd have to insult the memory of countless martyrs to do so. But this I can promise you: this life is like a vapor. In what seems like a few short moments, we'll have come and gone, and all we'll have before us is glorious, indescribable bliss. To fulfill our callings in the brief tenure we have on Planet Earth could conceivably prove the death of us—for a very little while—but to miss our callings out of fear is never to have lived at all. "I have come that they may have life, and have it to the full" (John 10:10, NIV).

Welcome, beloved, to the great adventure. I beckon you in Jesus' name to find your own ... if you haven't already. I am honored to be your servant. I am not worthy to tie the shoes of the men and women who will share their stories in this wonderful volume, but I am grateful beyond measure to be used of God to lace your lives together with theirs.

> *May the God who gives endurance and encouragement give you a spirit of unity among yourselves as you follow Christ Jesus, so that with one heart and mouth you may glorify the God and Father of our Lord Jesus Christ. Accept one another, then, just as Christ accepted you, in order to bring praise to God.* (Romans 15:5–7, NIV)

—Beth Moore

# JANUARY

## Prayer, the Priority

*Even if you and I don't get our words right,*
*if our hearts are right, God hears them.*

—BETH MOORE

Receiving a handwritten letter was not unusual in the early 1990s before the time of e-mail, but I did not recognize the handwriting. News from anyone back home was a treat, so I tore open the envelope and began to read. The letter writer introduced himself as David. He explained that God had called him to a ministry of intercession for missionaries. He quoted Scripture, gave encouragement, and again assured us that he was praying for us on a regular basis.

I didn't think too much about that letter I received during our first year as International Mission Board missionaries in South Africa until we got a second, third, fourth, and more letters from the same man. After 13 years as missionaries and four years of my husband working on staff at the IMB, we are still receiving letters from David telling us the ways in which he is praying for us and our ministries. Even after 17 years.

My husband and I met David in 2001 at a conference center in Glorieta, New Mexico. In appearance, he was totally unassuming. I probably wouldn't have noticed him in a crowd. He humbly introduced himself to us and explained that he had been writing us and praying for us. I couldn't believe I was meeting this committed prayer warrior. What surprised me even more was the fact that he went up to every missionary at that conference and told them the same thing.

We spoke to several of our colleagues. They all had been in correspondence with David. He prays for thousands of missionaries. Boy, was I glad to be on his list! Who knows what his prayers have accomplished all over the world. We were absolutely sure that God had powerfully worked through his prayers in our own ministry.

Faithful intercessors are hard to come by, but they are absolutely vital for kingdom work. God raises up people like David because He wants His people to have the joy of making a difference on earth. This month, you will read stories of how prayer makes a difference. Even when we aren't sure how to pray for the people groups of the world or for missionaries, God hears us and His Spirit helps us know how to pray. In one devotion, Joe says, "One of the great privileges of prayer is the ability to be a part of what God is doing. We may not know the people or the results of those prayers until we get to heaven, but what a glad day it will be when we meet them face-to-face."

This month, and in fact this year, God is calling you to a new journey of prayer for the nations, for missionaries, for lost people around you, and for yourself as you participate in kingdom work. He is giving you an opportunity to be part of what He is doing in our world today. Become a David.

—*Kim P. Davis*

# How important is prayer?

*"The effective, fervent prayer of a righteous man avails much." James 5:16b (NKJV)*

We received word that our translator could not go with us to an unreached city where we hoped to start future ministry. Feeling God's leadership to keep the appointment, we spent the travel time frantically practicing basic Russian and asking God to miraculously equip us to communicate. The meeting with the city leader was a challenge, but successful. It was over a year later, however, that we learned the true miracle of that meeting when the leader told us, "As I watched you struggle to communicate and saw your hearts of love, I began to question why a family would come from the West to the middle of nowhere to help me. There must be a God who loves me very much. I decided to make room in my life for Him." Dumbstruck and convicted, we realized that our initial prayers had been focused on our inadequacies, not on the salvation of this man. We had forgotten the most important thing!

We all understand that prayer is crucial to world missions, but we sometimes forget to pray or even lose sight of what to pray for. With millions lost with no access to the Gospel, our intercession must be daily. Countless lives hang in the balance! We need to ask anew for God to "teach us to pray" (Luke 11:1, NASB).

—RUSTY AND LORI, EUROPEAN PEOPLES

*Our Father,* TEACH ME TO PRAY FOR THE LOST OF THE WORLD AND FOR MISSIONARIES WHO FAITHFULLY SERVE YOU. MAY MY PRAYER LIFE BE RADICALLY CHANGED THIS YEAR, AND MAY MILLIONS COME TO KNOW YOU, THE ONE TRUE GOD. *Amen.*

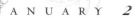
# Could you teach me how to pray?

*"Once Jesus was in a certain place praying. As he finished, one of his disciples came to him and said, 'Lord, teach us to pray.'"* Luke 11:1 (NLT)

A neighborhood Bible study started in Lucy's home. Lucy's 78-year-old father-in-law, José, showed up from time to time at the study hour, but he would always sit on the other side of the porch despite repeated invitations to join the group.

On those early Thursday mornings, José began to inch closer, but he never joined. The chronological Bible stories captivated the listeners. They asked questions and prayed for each other. Although only about seven or eight attended each week, they began to grow spiritually.

One morning, José arrived late. He sat a little closer to the group. The leader casually asked him to come over, and he did! There he was, sitting in the circle with all the ladies. As we finished, he asked, "I don't know much, and this is something I should know, but I do not. It almost embarrasses me to ask. Could you teach me how to pray?"

What a blessed time we had! Jesus taught His disciples to pray informally, which was unheard of in Jewish circles. We shared that talking to God is like talking to a best friend. Then each member prayed, and José joined in. I was reminded that prayer is not formal, but a close, personal way to speak with our Friend.

—K.B., AMERICAN PEOPLES

*Thank You,* LOVING FATHER, THAT YOU DRAW NEAR TO US AS WE DRAW NEAR TO YOU. MAY YOUR GRACE AND BLESSINGS SURROUND NEW BELIEVERS TODAY AS THEY GROW IN THEIR KNOWLEDGE OF YOU AND LEARN TO HEAR YOUR VOICE. *Amen.*

# A call to prayer

*"Who will not fear you, Lord, and glorify your name? For you alone are holy. All nations will come and worship before you, for your righteous deeds have been revealed." Revelation 15:4 (NLT)*

Echoing through the streets was the haunting call to prayer. I felt the heaviness of lostness, overwhelmed by knowing that millions around me prayed in futility.

I had climbed to the highest point of the city with my national friend and her family. It was a beautiful night to see all the lights of this massive city. While I was looking and thinking about how wonderful it was to live here, the calls to prayer began to ring out from one mosque to another. My heart was heavy, and I began to cry. I began to pray again for the city that God had called me to and that I loved. I prayed that God would exchange the peoples' hearts of stone for hearts of flesh and that they would instead sing prayers of praises to Him, the one true God.

After praying, I couldn't help but sing a prayer of praise knowing that one day every nation will bow before Jesus and acknowledge Him as Lord. Praises to Jesus are what I want to hear echoed across this great land.

In my own life, I couldn't help but evaluate my daily prayer life. Are my prayers out of habit or out of praise? The One alone who is holy deserves my sincerest prayers.

—MALLORY, CENTRAL ASIAN PEOPLES

*Break our hearts*, FATHER, FOR THE MULTITUDES LIVING IN TOTAL DARKNESS, DEPRAVITY, AND HOPELESSNESS. THANK YOU THAT YOU ARE NOT SILENT BUT ARE ACTIVELY DRAWING THE PEOPLES OF THE WORLD TO YOURSELF. MAY YOUR TRUTH BE SHARED AND EMBRACED IN DARK CORNERS OF THE WORLD TODAY. *Amen.*

# *Always joy and prayer*

*"Rejoice always! Pray constantly."* 1 Thessalonians 5:16–17 (HCSB)

The police followed us everywhere. My husband was called in for questioning about once a week: "What are you doing out in the countryside? We know you gave them Bibles! Did you teach them about Jesus?" The stress was intense. We finally were "invited" to leave our city by the increasingly hostile authorities.

We faced weeks of transition outside our country of service, living in a nearby country. Only able to get 30-day visas into our country, we went back and forth. Living out of a suitcase, there was no way to continue homeschooling or normal routine.

Finally, we felt we had the Father's direction and took a role reaching a city of about 4 million. As we unpacked our boxes, I was upset to discover that a favorite plaque had cracked during the move. Displayed on the plaque was 1 Thessalonians 5:16–17, both in English and our country's language.

My first instinct was to throw away the plaque. Instead, I mended it, although the crack was still clearly visible. It was a reminder that no matter what we're going through—persecution, moving, unstable lifestyles, unanswered questions about the future, political problems, or exhaustion—we are called to a life of prayer and joy.

—A WORKER WITH EAST ASIAN PEOPLES

*Father,* YOUR WORD REMINDS ME THAT JESUS ENDURED THE CROSS FOR THE JOY THAT LAY BEFORE HIM. CHRISTIANS ARE NOT EXEMPT FROM TRIALS, HEARTACHES, AND EVEN PERSECUTION. PLEASE DRAW NEAR TO YOUR CHILDREN WHO ARE SUFFERING TODAY, AND FILL THEM WITH YOUR PEACE AND JOY. *Amen.*

# In it for the ice cream?

*"[I pray that] you, being rooted and firmly established in love, may be able to comprehend with all the saints what is the breadth and width, height and depth, and to know the Messiah's love that surpasses knowledge." Ephesians 3:17b–19* (HCSB)

Thirty-four children didn't sleep the night before in anticipation of a day at an amusement park near Manila. We were taking the group of urban poor, where they experienced the Ferris wheel, roller coasters, and log flume for the first time with lots of laughter and delight.

While the kids were appreciative, their reactions to the experience differed. Some asked for nothing, while others asked for everything their eyes beheld! One 8-year-old girl wanted food, especially sweets, after almost every ride. She wasn't hungry; she was simply eager to enjoy foods she rarely ate. We wanted her to have a special day, so we indulged her.

As I was standing in line for yet another ice cream, I wanted to help this child understand that we desired to have a relationship with her that went beyond treats. It was then that I realized how God desires to have a meaningful relationship with me as well. I had to admit that many times my prayers sound very similar to this girl's wish list. I imagine that God simultaneously smiles and sighs as He indulges me out of His boundless love while recognizing that all too often I am focused on the ice cream also.

—JOE, EAST ASIAN PEOPLES

*Lord,* CREATE IN ME A NEW HEART, ONE THAT DESIRES YOU ABOVE ALL ELSE. DON'T LET ME BE SATISFIED WITH LESS THAN A DEEP, INTIMATE RELATIONSHIP WITH YOU. GIVE ME AN INSATIABLE DESIRE FOR YOU, YOUR WORD, AND YOUR PASSION FOR THE SALVATION OF THOSE PEOPLES WITHOUT HOPE. *Amen.*

# *Active prayer*

*"And you can join in helping with prayer for us, so that thanks may be given by many on our behalf for the gift that came to us through [the prayers of] many."*
*2 Corinthians 1:11 (HCSB)*

"Andy" and "Linda" were devastated by the news. Doctors said of their son, "Without surgery, he will die. But we do not think he will survive the procedure. There is little hope."

The church began to pray for the entire family. We did, too. During the risky surgery and the frighteningly long recovery, this family of new believers lived on prayer.

Throughout the surgery and the many days of wondering if their son would survive, Andy and Linda grew closer as a couple, and their prayer lives were strengthened. They reached out to God, and He reached back through His people who ministered to them.

My wife and I sat with the couple many times during the ordeal. One day, Andy and Linda said, "We hoped that others were praying, but we knew you were because we could see, hear, and feel it." Active praying sometimes includes being physically present where the prayer is being focused.

Being active in prayer allows people to see God at work and to experience how He can change lives. We don't always think we have the time, but praying for others in person is a great encouragement.

—JOHN, EUROPEAN PEOPLES

*Thank You,* HOLY ONE, THAT YOU ARE NEVER DISTRACTED OR ABSENT, BUT ARE ALWAYS PRESENT IN YOUR CHILDREN'S LIVES. YOU HAVE CALLED AND EMPOWERED BELIEVERS TO WALK ALONGSIDE THOSE IN NEED. HELP ME TO PRAYERFULLY ACCEPT THIS MINISTRY, CONFIDENT OF YOUR PRESENCE, POWER, AND ENABLING. *Amen.*

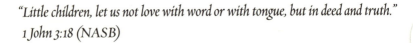
## A prayer full of love

*"Little children, let us not love with word or with tongue, but in deed and truth."*
1 John 3:18 (NASB)

"Mary" grimaced after the truck hit a bump. I reached over to squeeze her hand and slowed down a little. My friend had given birth to her sixth baby the night before, and I was driving her home from the rural hospital. Her sister was with us, as well as Mary's toddler. When we arrived, I carried the sleeping newborn to the mud-brick hut while the sister walked with Mary, waving off the children so they wouldn't bump into her.

Once inside, Mary sat on her bed while her sister rushed around to make sure things were arranged. In the hustle and bustle of children and family members peering at the new baby, I knelt next to Mary's bed and asked, "May I pray for you?" She said, "Yes, I'd like that."

In halting Sereer, I prayed for Mary and the baby. I also prayed that her family would love Him. I ended the prayer in the name of Jesus. I had concentrated so hard on praying, and my heart was so full of love for this family who didn't know my Jesus, I hadn't noticed the bustling noises had stopped. Mary's eyes glistened as she took my hand and said, "Thank you for everything."

God reminded me that the simple act of praying for someone opens hearts to His love.

—K.F., SUB-SAHARAN AFRICAN PEOPLES

*Father,* REMIND ME OF THE PEACE AND SERENITY THAT SURROUNDS ME WHEN I'M FOCUSED ON YOU. I ASK THAT YOU PROVIDE OPPORTUNITIES TO SHARE YOUR LOVE AND TRUTH WITH SOMEONE TODAY. HELP ME TO BE OBEDIENT. *Amen.*

# *Timely birthday prayers*

> *"Finally, pray for us, brothers, that the Lord's message may spread rapidly and be honored ... and that we may be delivered from wicked and evil men, for not all have faith. But the Lord is faithful; He will strengthen and guard you from the evil one."* 2 Thessalonians 3:1–3 (HCSB)

Have you ever wondered if your prayers for missionaries make a difference? One evening while I was home alone waiting for my family, I saw a man staring at me, just inside our front door. Thinking he was a neighbor who was coming in ahead of my family, I went to him with my hands outstretched in greeting. He pushed me roughly aside and said threateningly, "This is a robbery! Do you want me to kill you?" A second armed man came into our house at that point.

God gave me the words to say and the grace to respond. "I want you to know that this house and everything in it belongs to God. Do you know Him?" I asked. Tied and gagged, I prayed facedown on our bed, asking God to protect me and to have mercy on these men.

When my family returned, they were startled to find me tied up, but God's grace led them to respond calmly. The day before was my husband's birthday. Because his name appeared on the prayer calendar found in LifeWay's *Open Windows* devotional magazine, individuals and churches had bathed him in prayer just hours before the home invasion. Property was taken, but I was unharmed. Thank the Lord for faithful prayer warriors!

—LISA, AMERICAN PEOPLES

*Father*, YOUR OFFER OF GRACE EXTENDS TO ALL PEOPLE. I PRAY THAT THE WORDS OF TESTIMONY HEARD BY THE TWO MEN WILL CONTINUE TO RESOUND IN THEIR HEARTS. I ASK THAT THEY WILL RESPOND TO YOUR FORGIVENESS AND RECEIVE JESUS CHRIST AS SAVIOR. *Amen.*

# Walking with a purpose

*"He that saith he abideth in him ought himself also so to walk, even as he walked."*
1 John 2:6 (KJV)

Did you know that the word "walk" appears over 380 times in the Bible? It must be important to walk. To walk with God, walk by faith, walk in the light, walk uprightly, walk through the valley, walk and not faint ... the list goes on and on. God wants us to walk in an attitude of prayer every day, and He does amazing things when we allow Him to take us wherever He leads.

With God as our GPS, we walk and meet amazing people. We talk a bit, sometimes helping with a special need or crisis, but mostly we share hope in Christ and a smile. The best part is that we get to pray for the lost. As we prayerfully place Gospel messages in phone booths and at bus stops, we look back to see someone reading the material.

Walking, stopping, praying, and claiming an area for Jesus, even when statistics remind us that only 5 percent in our country are evangelical, God reminds us of the numerous neighborhoods in other areas that now have Bible studies and mission churches.

God likes for us to walk! Ask Him to show you where He wants you to prayerwalk, and get out there. Amazing experiences await you as you walk with God for His glory and pray for the people around you.

—R.C.H., AMERICAN PEOPLES

*Thank You,* JESUS, THAT YOUR LIFE PROVIDES THE ROLE MODEL OF MY PRAYER LIFE. AS YOU WALKED ON THIS EARTH INTERCEDING WITH THE FATHER, YOU TOUCHED THOSE ALONG YOUR WAY WITH REDEMPTIVE LOVE. HELP ME TO LIVE CONSTANTLY IN AN ATTITUDE OF PRAYER, READY AT ALL TIMES TO INTERCEDE IN FAITH. *Amen.*

## *I want to talk!*

*"Jesus asked, 'What do you want me to do for you?' The blind man answered, 'Master, I want to see!'" Mark 10:51 (CEV)*

Learning a new language has been exciting, challenging, and at times humiliating. Adult missionaries at language school have to become like children again, speaking on the level of 3-year-olds! Buying groceries becomes an exercise in humiliation when one can neither ask where a product is located nor understand the simple answer given. Particularly discouraging is not being able to share the Good News clearly with a national when the opportunity arises.

One day, my Bible reading was about Bartimaeus, the blind man. The words pierced my heart when Bartimaeus desperately cried out to Jesus, "Master, I want to see!" My soul cried out, "Master, I want to talk!" I wept from the conflict of my weak language capabilities and my passion to share His Word with others. Whereas Bartimaeus was blind, in Spanish I was mute.

I decided that I could at least pray for my lost neighbors. Later that day, my Christian neighbor visited. This dear woman is the product of prayers from missionaries who previously lived on our street. She came to tell me that her brother had gone to church with her as a result of the prayers of our family. She added that even our 6-year-old daughter had influenced her mother. God reminded me what He could do through prayer despite my mute mouth.

—MATASHA, AMERICAN PEOPLES

*Father,* I PRAISE YOU THAT OFTEN MY OBVIOUS INADEQUACIES, LIKE LACK OF PATIENCE, HAVE BEEN THE VERY THINGS THAT HAVE CAUSED ME TO DESPERATELY SEEK YOU. THANK YOU FOR REMINDING ME THAT YOU ARE FAITHFUL TO ANSWER PRAYERS PRAYED IN FAITH. *Amen.*

# Eavesdropper

*"Before they call I will answer; while they are yet speaking I will hear."* Isaiah 65:24 (ESV)

Most countries in Europe are multilingual, except France. In cities, it is common to encounter a French person who speaks English, but out in the country where we live, it is rare to meet an English speaker.

Each summer, college students come to Europe to pray. Sometimes they lead sports camps or English clubs, but unless they are fluent in French, all they can do in France is pray. This foundational work is not always rewarded with seeing immediate change.

On Bastille Day, we took the students by train to a festival. Throughout the day, they shared how the summer had been challenging since they did not feel like they had made a difference. We encouraged them that their prayers would not be in vain.

At the end of the evening, we boarded the train to return home. One student began asking us how to say different things in French. As we taught him phrases, we noticed that the French girl beside us was eavesdropping. She then laughed and began speaking to us in English! The student struck up a conversation with her and by the end of the trip, we were exchanging e-mail addresses so that we could meet again.

God used a praying college student, who didn't speak French, to help us begin a relationship. He graciously allowed the students to see how God can use them.

—ADELLE, EUROPEAN PEOPLES

*God of all wisdom,* YOU TOUCH HEARTS AS NONE OTHER CAN. REMIND ME TODAY, LOVING FATHER, TO TAKE EVERY OPPORTUNITY TO SPEAK TRUTH INTO THE LIVES OF THOSE YOU PLACE IN MY PATH. *Amen.*

# *A result of praying people*

*"I urge you, first of all, to pray for all people. Ask God to help them; intercede on their behalf, and give thanks for them."* 1 Timothy 2:1 (NLT)

A team of a dozen young, single professionals came to minister for 10 days in the countryside of our closed host culture. Their humility, sense of adventure, and godly devotion impressed us.

It didn't take long for them to be challenged. There were many opportunities to divert their focus, drive wedges in relationships, and thwart their willingness to follow the Father's lead. However, they were able to press on to the greater purposes of the Father.

This atmosphere spilled over to our children and me, who were left behind while my husband accompanied the group. That week, things went smoothly with our four young boys. I felt a surprising contentedness instead of counting the minutes until Daddy returned. My husband, too, experienced peace in the face of situations that normally would have been exasperating and stressful.

My husband learned that these volunteers had people back home praying around the clock for them and us. My husband asked, "Could you arrange for prayer for us 24/7?" The volunteers laughed, but upon returning to the States, they organized a monthly prayer group with as many as 50 people praying for our country and its people. Prayer is essential to the work!

—A WORKER WITH SOUTHEAST ASIAN PEOPLES

*Thank You, Lord,* FOR REMINDING ME THAT THE PRAYERS OF GOD'S PEOPLE AVAIL MUCH. HELP ME TO REALIZE THAT MY GREATEST PERSONAL NEED IS AN INTIMATE RELATIONSHIP WITH YOU THROUGH PRAYER. REMIND ME DAILY TO INTERCEDE FOR OUR MISSIONARIES AND FOR THE PEOPLE THEY CALL THEIR OWN. *Amen.*

# The power of prayer

*"and He who searches the hearts knows what the mind of the Spirit is, because He intercedes for the saints according to the will of God." Romans 8:27 (NASB)*

Team Day is a special day for ministry teams to get together for team building, prayer, rest, and relaxation. Most international Christian workers are members of a team, but our separate ministries often prevent us from spending much downtime with one another.

On this particular day, our team took a boat trip to a nearby island. At around 4 p.m., we boarded our small boat for the trip back across the bay to our hotel. "Dale" was sitting at the front of the boat when he saw a big wake approaching. In response, he stood up, hoping to brace himself against the impact. Instead, he was catapulted backward and hit his back against a chair. Thankfully, the damage to his back was only muscular.

Later that evening, I checked my e-mail and found a note from one of our stateside prayer partners. She said that she awakened at 4 a.m. to pray for me. Because we were 12 hours ahead, this was the exact time that we were on the boat. This was truly an experience of the Holy Spirit interceding for us, and I was overwhelmed with gratitude.

We can never underestimate the power of prayer. There is no way to know what could have happened. The Lord prompted this friend to pray for us. I am grateful that she was obedient.

—C.Y., EAST ASIAN PEOPLES

*Dear Father,* MY DESIRE IS TO HAVE A PREPARED HEART, READY AT ALL TIMES TO PRAY FOR YOUR SERVANTS AROUND THE WORLD AS SPECIAL NEEDS OCCUR. PLEASE HELP ME TO RESPOND IMMEDIATELY TO URGENT PROMPTINGS FROM YOUR SPIRIT. YOU, INDEED, ARE FAITHFUL. *Amen.*

## *Which of you has the power?*

*"For while I was passing through and examining the objects of your worship, I also found an altar with this inscription, 'TO AN UNKNOWN GOD.' Therefore what you worship in ignorance, this I proclaim to you." Acts 17:23 (NASB)*

Tumultuous times brought lost neighbors to our home to pray for peace. They believed in prayer, but they weren't sure which of their idols could help. We offered to pray to the one true God.

During this weekly prayer time, our neighbors had questions: "Who is this one God? Is He real? Does He care about us? Does He answer prayer?" This led to weekly Bible studies.

One evening, a devout idol worshipper asked us to pray for her handicapped daughter. After multiple operations, her daughter graduated from high school and had applied to the university. But the university would not accept her. Emma had one last chance to apply. "Please pray!" she pleaded. "Maybe God will hear."

Later, she came to our home and announced, "Emma's accepted! God answered your prayers!" Shortly after, she decided to follow Jesus. She said, "I stood before my idols, and I became so angry! I shouted, 'Which of you has the power to help me?'" Out of that dark moment, God helped her see that her idols were false. She longed for the true God and believed only He could hear and answer prayer.

—ROBIN, AMERICAN PEOPLES

*Father,* YOU HAVE CREATED US WITH A LONGING THAT ONLY YOU CAN SATISFY. THANK YOU FOR TURNING DARKNESS INTO LIGHT AND REVEALING YOURSELF TO THOSE WHO SEEK YOU. I ASK THAT THOSE WHO ARE IN BONDAGE TO IDOLATRY WILL HEAR THE TRUTH, BE TRANSFORMED, AND BECOME LIGHT TO THEIR FAMILIES. *Amen.*

# Claiming victory over evil

*"... and his ears are open unto their prayers ..." 1 Peter 3:12 (KJV)*

On a sweltering day, a group of us arrived to prayerwalk in "Zup," a town known for two ethnic groups slaughtering each other. The war had been over for several years, but the tension felt heavy as we separated into pairs. My partner and I trudged over hills and dusty roads, praying and reading Scripture with promises from God for hurting people. The heat made the walking laborious, but it was even harder to pray. The people eyed us with curious stares or scowling, suspicious faces. The spiritual opposition left me sapped of energy and inspiration. The whole day seemed wasted until we stopped in a field beside the river.

Suddenly, I felt the Holy Spirit prompting me to pray. With new liberty, we poured out our hearts, claiming victory over evil. I was in awe, not because of my feeble prayers but because of the Lord's burden for these people. A spiritual victory had been won.

We didn't return to Zup for three years. A young couple had moved there and excitedly told us how God had led them to start a youth center. They took us to the center, not knowing about our prayerwalking experience. With joy, I saw an answer to prayer. The building was located on the exact same field where we had felt that spiritual breakthrough. There is victory in prayer.

—PAT, EUROPEAN PEOPLES

*Oh Lord,* YOUR AUTHORITY FAR EXCEEDS THE POWER OF THE EVIL ONE. I ASK THAT YOUR LIGHT WILL PENETRATE THE DARKNESS SURROUNDING PEOPLE GROUPS OF EUROPE WHO HAVE HAD LITTLE OR NO ACCESS TO THE GOSPEL. CONTINUE TO BREAK MY HEART FOR THOSE WHO DON'T KNOW YOU AS LORD AND SAVIOR. *Amen.*

## *God bends down and listens*

*"I love the LORD because he hears my voice and my prayer for mercy. Because he bends down to listen, I will pray as long as I have breath!" Psalm 116:1–2 (NLT)*

As a new missionary, I felt incompetent. My language skills were lacking, and I was even less competent when it came to cooking, working in the field, and carrying things on my head.

One night, a distraught neighbor came to our lodging and yelled for us. He stood with his youngest daughter in his arms needing our help. We rushed to the medical clinic, but the clinic was closed. As the father ran to wake the doctor, I held the hand of the little girl. She cried, but I tried to comfort her, assuring her that her dad was coming right back.

I started praying out loud to the One who could help her. "Father, heal her body. Be glorified in this. Let her family know that You are God." When the doctor examined her, the diagnosis was cerebral malaria. We continued praying over her that night.

Two days later, a volunteer team came through town. When they heard about the situation, they came to the clinic to pray. One man, who spoke French, shared the story of Jesus with the father, who decided to follow Him.

The next morning, the girl was sitting up and laughing! The father was praising God. Even in our incompetence, God hears our prayers.

—MONICA, SUB-SAHARAN AFRICAN PEOPLES

*Miracle-working Father,* YOU AND YOU ALONE CAN HEAL THE BODY AND SOUL. I ASK THAT YOUR SPIRIT WILL HAVE FREEDOM TO WORK IN THE HEARTS AND LIVES OF DESPERATE PEOPLE WITHOUT HOPE. THANK YOU, LORD. *Amen.*

# *He hears our pleas*

*"He will show favor to you at the sound of your cry; when He hears, He will answer you." Isaiah 30:19b (HCSB)*

We arrived in the large city with hopes to start a Bible study within 10 days. After seven days, however, we had met no seekers and were frustrated by the lack of interest. My husband, Mike, prayed, "Surely in a city of 1.5 million, there is at least one person who wants to know You."

An hour later, as Mike walked into the hotel, the night bellman, "David," asked about a CD Mike was carrying. Mike told him it was Christian music. David said he had heard about Christianity and had studied the Bible a little, but he wanted to know more.

The next morning, Mike shared the Gospel with David, praying that seeds would take root. David said that he believed the Gospel was true. However, he wanted to talk to his father first, who practiced ancestor worship. If his father disapproved, David would still repent and follow Christ; but he asked us to pray that his father would be receptive to the Gospel.

The next morning, David had a big smile. He told his father that he was going to follow Christ. His father supported David and wanted to hear more about Christianity. David prayed with us and has now shared the Gospel with his whole family.

God heard our pleas and brought about His answers.

—ELIZABETH, EAST ASIAN PEOPLES

*Faithful Father,* OUR PRAYERS FOR THE SALVATION OF THE LOST ORIGINATE FROM YOUR HEART. THANK YOU THAT YOU ARE DRAWING SEEKERS TO YOURSELF. HELP ME TODAY TO PASSIONATELY SHARE YOUR STORY WITH BOLDNESS. *Amen.*

## Seeing the fruit of prayer

*"Unless the LORD builds a house, its builders labor over it in vain." Psalm 127:1a*
*(HCSB)*

I arrived in Mali with my family over 20 years ago, eager to share the Good News. Yet I soon became discouraged as I heard one person after another say, "What you share is the truth, but I cannot leave my religion."

Seeing prayer as the only recourse, I solicited prayer warriors in the States. These faithful servants spent hours on their knees pleading for the salvation of the Bambara people. Three churches were planted, and work began in villages not far from the capital. But churches were not planting other churches to reach the entire population. After 10 years, God called my family away from Mali. We continued to pray that God's Spirit would move among the Bambara.

Ten years later, my husband and I moved back to Mali and the Bambara team. Partnering churches in the States were "adopting" villages. I accompanied one such church to a village. As we shared the Gospel, a young man gave his heart to Christ. That night, he brought several of his friends to our meeting. Others came to Christ. The second night, 16 men trusted Christ.

A volunteer and I met with a group of women the next afternoon. After sharing the Gospel, 14 women believed. A church was born! The prayers from years ago are being answered.

—DIANE, SUB-SAHARAN AFRICAN PEOPLES

*Lord of the harvest,* I AM REMINDED THAT I MAY NOT SEE IMMEDIATE RESULTS TO MY RE-QUESTS. YOU ARE A FAITHFUL GOD WHO DELIGHTS IN ANSWERING PRAYERS. I ASK FOR A MIGHTY WORK OF YOUR SPIRIT AMONG THE BAMBARA PEOPLE. *Amen.*

# Expect the unimaginable

*"Therefore I say to you, all things for which you pray and ask, believe that you have received them, and they will be granted you." Mark 11:24 (NASB)*

"Gina" arrived at our medical clinic with her son, who needed stitches. We had seen her in the clinic before but had not shared the Gospel with her. After providing medical treatment for Gina's son, she insisted that we come to break the fast of Ramadan with her family. We agreed to come in three days to change her son's bandage and join her family for dinner.

The morning of our visit, I prayed, "Lord, may I expect You to do the unimaginable. Bring this family into Your kingdom. Open their ears and eyes to hear, see, and understand that You alone are God. Be glorified in this house, and may they believe and be saved today!"

We arrived at their home shortly before the call to prayer sounded to break the fast. After the meal, we went to another room that was soon filled with extended family members and neighbors. One of the women was named Mary. We asked if she knew about Mary, the mother of Jesus. We began to tell the story of Jesus. After sharing the Gospel, we asked if they wanted to follow Christ, and they all quickly replied, "Yes!"

Praise the Lord, this family and many in the village know Him now. He is faithful and hears our prayers, if we are willing to ask and believe.

—M.I., NORTHERN AFRICAN AND MIDDLE EASTERN PEOPLES

*Father,* I AM HUMBLED AND AMAZED AS I REALIZE THAT YOU ARE ALWAYS AT WORK, DRAWING PEOPLE TO YOURSELF. HELP ME TO EMBRACE YOUR HEART FOR THE PEOPLES WHO SURROUND ME AND TO PRAY BOLD PRAYERS OF FAITH FOR THEIR SALVATION. *Amen.*

## *Bringing calm to the situation*

*"Not to us, O LORD, not to us, but to Your name give glory because of Your lovingkindness, because of Your truth." Psalm 115:1 (NASB)*

Even before sunrise, long lines of people waited for hours for help from the volunteer medical team. Through many challenges, two things were always certain: we would see patients, and we would share the Gospel.

One morning, a mother approached me with her injured son, who was screaming and thrashing. She explained that her son was autistic and violent. Daily, he would hit his head and reopen the wound. Although he was just a little boy, it took four people to hold him down so that the doctor could treat him. The doctor felt helpless, wishing there was more she could do. Even a bandage would be ripped off immediately by the boy. Suddenly, the doctor began to sing "Jesus Loves Me" in Spanish as she treated the wound with tear-filled eyes.

As I talked with the family, they told me that they were Christians. We prayed with them. After we prayed, the doctor remembered they had brought some unused medicine for autism that could possibly help calm the boy. She gave them the medicine and told them that if it worked, to come back tomorrow, and we would give them more.

We prayed that night that they would return. The next morning, the uncle arrived. The medicine had worked! God heard us and encouraged us with answered prayer.

—BRENDA, AMERICAN PEOPLES

*Thank You,* LORD, FOR ANSWERED PRAYER AND FOR THE REMINDER THAT YOU ARE PRESENT WHEN I WORSHIP AND GIVE GLORY TO YOUR NAME. HELP ME LIVE TODAY IN ADORATION OF WHO YOU ARE. *Amen.*

# He puts authority in place

*"O LORD, You are my God; I will exalt You, I will give thanks to Your name; for You have worked wonders, plans formed long ago, with perfect faithfulness."*
*Isaiah 25:1 (NASB)*

The news wasn't good. We heard about a group of tourists entering our country who were detained and stripped of all religious materials before entering. The warning came loud and clear: "Do *not* attempt to bring any religious material across the border."

Big problem! The next week, we were to go to a neighboring country to pick up and bring 210 solar-powered, electronic devices back across the border into our country. These devices contained Bible stories, the *JESUS* film in audio, and the entire New Testament in the language of our people. We needed this massive quantity to get through the border. We considered dividing up the materials and making several trips, but we knew logistically, it was impossible. Everyone we knew was asked to pray about the situation.

After much prayer, we made our way to the border. After about an hour of friendly interrogation, we received a written release from the chief of security, who unbelievably was a Christian, to enter our country with all 210 devices. Of course, he did want to keep a couple of them for himself. This answer to prayer was living proof that our Father is faithful to accomplish His work and is bigger than any mandate or warning. He is a God who works wonders.

—A. AND A., NORTHERN AFRICAN AND MIDDLE EASTERN PEOPLES

*Your ways* ARE HIGHER THAN MINE, LORD, AND YOUR PURPOSES TRANSCEND ANYTHING I COULD ASK OR IMAGINE. EMBOLDEN ME TODAY TO DREAM BIG DREAMS AND TO JOIN YOU IN ATTEMPTING THE SEEMINGLY IMPOSSIBLE. *Amen.*

# Miracle in Moshawane

*"that your faith should not be in the wisdom of men but in the power of God."*
1 Corinthians 2:5 (NKJV)

My husband and I were scheduled to go to three weeks of training in another town, but before we left, I was asked to visit one of my Bible study ladies. Her 9-year-old son, Onkarabile (Own-kah-rah-BEE-lay), was very ill. When we arrived, he had lost the ability to walk or hold up his head.

We prayed over him and left. Finally, it was learned that the boy had tuberculosis. He was given medicine and sent home. A friend called to tell me that she didn't think he would live long. I was heartbroken.

Meanwhile, at the training conference, I was learning the chronological Bible storying method, a way of relating the great stories of the Bible in a culturally suitable manner, focusing on the power Jesus showed while on earth. Each night, God brought Onkarabile to my mind. One night as I prayed, I felt like I was fighting a battle for this little boy. I claimed the power of Jesus over sickness and disease. I don't know how long I prayed.

My friend visited the boy the next day. She called to report that he was holding his head up and smiling! She said, "You will see him again!" When I returned, we went to see Onkarabile, a living miracle. He walked out to greet us! My God has power over everything.

—JODY, SUB-SAHARAN AFRICAN PEOPLES

*Father,* YOU ALONE ARE ABLE TO HEAL BODY, MIND, AND SPIRIT. THANK YOU FOR YOUR MIRACULOUS POWER AT WORK IN SUB-SAHARAN AFRICA. I PRAY THAT MANY WILL HEAR OF YOUR COMPASSION AND TURN TO YOU AS LORD AND SAVIOR TODAY. *Amen.*

# *His plan stands*

*"I know that You can do anything and no plan of Yours can be thwarted." Job 42:2 (HCSB)*

Years ago when reading an account of Bible smuggling, I never dreamed that I would have my own adventure carrying God's Word in the form of audio and video materials to reach Muslims.

After obtaining over 100 disks, I began my journey. At the first checkpoint, the police searched the car. Each disk was examined, but the officer acted unfazed. He settled on one disk and began asking questions. This disk could have been cause for imprisonment. He asked me to play it, but it kept reporting, "Unable to read disk." As I prayed silently, the officer let me go.

Next, an officer stopped me at the domestic airport, searched my bags, and let me board my flight. I thanked God again. When arriving in an international airport, I was searched and told that it was illegal to carry religious materials in or out of their country. Feeling generous, the officer said he would let it go this time. I felt home-free as I flew to my country of service. However, upon arrival, new x-ray machines scanned my carry-on luggage. The officer immediately escorted me to his office. He confiscated all the disks to review over the next three days. I contacted all my prayer warriors.

Three days later the answer came: "Come and get them." I praised God all the way to customs and back.

—JAMES, CENTRAL ASIAN PEOPLES

*Holy One,* WE STAND AMAZED AS WE RECALL THE COUNTLESS TIMES YOU HAVE PROTECTED THOSE WHO PUT THEIR TOTAL TRUST IN YOU. I PRAY THAT YOU WILL CONTINUE TO GO BEFORE AND BEHIND, AND PLACE YOUR HAND OF PROTECTION ON THOSE WHO ARE TAKING YOUR WORD TO DIFFICULT-TO-ACCESS PLACES. *Amen.*

## Seeing and believing

*"And these signs shall follow them that believe; ... they shall lay hands on the sick, and they shall recover." Mark 16:17–18 (KJV)*

"Sister Wong" worked hard to achieve success. However, she felt empty, even after becoming a top leader in the Communist Party.

She suffered from edema without knowing what caused the swelling. During her illness, she thought of the Bible a friend gave her two years ago. When she opened it, Matthew 7:7, "... knock, and it will be opened to you" (NKJV) caught her sight. She was moved as she read the verse and cried tears of repentance. Miraculously, she was completely healed from her sickness and experienced the living God as her Savior.

She immediately shared her faith in God with her family, and all of them believed. Her neighbor, who was a Communist Party leader, had a handicapped son. With faith that God also would heal him, Sister Wong prayed for the boy. Now he is able to work at a company. Her driver's wife was healed of cancer through prayer. Through these miracles, Communist Party leaders believed in Jesus. They started a house church so that they could meet together.

Risking their social position and power, the church members continue to share the Gospel. Jesus saved them and gave them purpose.

—A WORKER WITH EAST ASIAN PEOPLES

*Dear Father,* WE KNOW THAT NOTHING THIS WORLD OFFERS CAN COMPARE TO YOUR MAGNIFICENT LOVE AND POWER. AS YOU WORK AMONG THE PEOPLE OF EAST ASIA, I PRAY THAT MANY WILL RESPOND AND BECOME MESSENGERS OF YOUR GRACE. *Amen.*

# A false fortress

*"You're hopeless, you religion scholars and Pharisees! ... People look at you and think you're saints, but beneath the skin you're total frauds." Matthew 23:27–28 (MSG)*

The village of 10 mosques was like a fortress with its cemented walls and steps. Known for its resistance to the Gospel, this Soninke village was the target of two teams hoping to prepare the ground through prayer. The first team made contacts and left behind the fragrance of Christ. It was now time for the second team to visit.

We visited the chief's brother and two wives. When we asked to pray for their people, we were told, "It's not time. We pray at 2 p.m., 5 p.m., 7 p.m., 8 p.m. and 5 a.m., but you can give a blessing." They took us to a very impressive mosque that had two special stones from Mecca embedded in the wall. We were instructed to place both hands on the stone and then pray. We explained that we were free to talk to the Father anytime and to pray open-handed.

We were then allowed to enter a large room, but first we had to remove our shoes. "You have to face east and bow down and get up like this." We again explained that God is everywhere, so it doesn't matter which direction we face. He always sees and hears us.

Without question, the people blindly followed tradition. I had to ask myself if I ever followed religious traditions rather than God alone.

—RITA, SUB-SAHARAN AFRICAN PEOPLES

*Thank You,* LORD, THAT THE FRAGRANCE OF CHRIST KNOWS NO BOUNDARIES, BUT HAS POWER TO TRANSFORM AN ENTIRE PEOPLE GROUP. I PRAY FOR COURAGE FOR SONINKE VIL- LAGERS WHO HAVE HEARD THE GOSPEL OF PEACE. PLEASE REMOVE CULTURAL AND RELI- GIOUS BARRIERS THAT HINDER THE ACCEPTANCE OF TRUTH. *Amen.*

## *Healed for His glory*

*"Is anyone among you sick? ... the prayer of faith will save the one who is sick, and the Lord will raise him up. And if he has committed sins, he will be forgiven."*
James 5:14–15 *(ESV)*

I was invited to travel to a small town about five hours away from the capital, where I live. At the end of my stay, I was introduced to a handful of believers from my people group. After worshipping, they invited me to lunch and gave fascinating accounts of their lives.

One man explained that he had been sent home to die of tuberculosis. His Christian neighbor asked if he and his friends could pray for his healing. The sick man was a devout Muslim and had sought healing through religious leaders and Islamic practices, to no avail. Believing that Christian prayers couldn't hurt, the desperate man agreed. After the group laid hands on the man and prayed, he was miraculously healed!

Later when medical authorities were sent to see if he had died, they instead found the man alive. Baffled, they sent him to have another chest x-ray. After evaluation of the new film, the doctor believed he had been given the wrong x-ray as there were no traces of the disease.

With a new lease on life, the healed man became a Christian and now takes the Gospel to neighboring villages. God answered the prayers of faith and raised the man up to become a witness for Him.

—A WORKER WITH CENTRAL ASIAN PEOPLES

*Lord,* WE PRAISE YOU FOR YOUR GRACE AND COMPASSION IN ANSWERING PRAYERS THAT ARE OFFERED IN FAITH. I PRAY THAT YOUR GLORY WILL BE SEEN THROUGH YOUR HEALING POWER OF THIS MAN AND MANY WILL RECOGNIZE YOU AS LORD, SAVIOR, AND GREAT PHYSICIAN. *Amen.*

# Praying for a thousand

*"For the vision is yet for the appointed time; it hastens toward the goal and it will not fail. Though it tarries, wait for it; for it will certainly come, it will not delay."*
*Habakkuk 2:3 (NASB)*

Sitting quietly in front of a beautiful water fountain, I prayed for 100 people to come to believe in our Lord before my husband and I retire. However, I felt the Holy Spirit telling me I needed to have the faith to pray for 1,000 people to come to know Him. I said that I did not know 1,000 people! Immediately, He assured me that He did. So I believed Him.

But after six months of prayer and off-and-on fasting, nothing was happening. Time was running out. Suddenly, within two weeks, our heavenly Father revealed His plan. We found ourselves training local believers to reach out and win others to the Lord. God showed us how to develop material into a Muslim-friendly format for our area. He even brought local believers to us whom He wanted to participate in this training.

Beginning with two small groups of believers, within six months our heavenly Father multiplied these into 27 groups and increased our new believers from one to over 550 new believers. Wow! Almost daily, new believers are entering the kingdom with new groups forming regularly. We are so excited to see what our Father is doing and how He will bring 1,000 into His kingdom.

—A. AND A., NORTHERN AFRICAN AND MIDDLE EASTERN PEOPLES

*Father,* FORGIVE ME WHEN MY FAITH IS TOO SMALL. HELP ME TO SEE THE PEOPLE AROUND ME THROUGH YOUR EYES AND TO EMBRACE YOUR VISION FOR THOSE WHOM YOU ARE DRAWING TO YOURSELF. CONTINUE TO MULTIPLY THE BELIEVERS IN THIS AREA OF NORTH AFRICA AND THE MIDDLE EAST. *Amen.*

# *Lazarus, come out!*

*"Now to Him who is able to do exceedingly abundantly above all that we ask or think, according to the power that works in us, to Him be glory in the church by Christ Jesus to all generations, forever and ever." Ephesians 3:20–21 (NKJV)*

Sometimes when we read stories like the biblical account of Lazarus, we forget that God is big enough to do things like this even in our world today! In one village, we heard about one believing family who experienced a miracle.

The father of this family was tragically electrocuted. After being rushed to the hospital, his wife and son were notified and the doctor pronounced him dead. The wife and son would not accept the doctor's declaration and discussed the miracle of Lazarus being raised from the dead. They decided to ask God to restore his life. As mother and son prayed, onlookers watched. In the same hospital room, other family members were beginning funeral preparations.

Suddenly, the husband coughed and opened his eyes! The wife and son joyously praised God. Many trusted Christ because of this man's miraculous resurrection that they saw firsthand.

Being a skeptic, I had to see for myself. At the village, I shook hands with the man. I interviewed friends and family who witnessed the event, all testifying how God did this amazing thing. God was glorified, and many idol worshippers came to believe in Christ because of this man's testimony. God is able to do more than we can ever ask or imagine.

—NELLIE, SOUTH ASIAN PEOPLES

*Lord,* YOU ARE THE SAME YESTERDAY, TODAY, AND FOREVER. THERE IS NOTHING TOO DIF-FICULT FOR YOU. I PRAY THAT AS PEOPLE OF THE WORLD SEE MIRACLES, THEIR SEARCHING HEARTS WILL BE TURNED TO YOU. *Amen.*

# *Sisters in Christ*

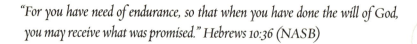

*"For you have need of endurance, so that when you have done the will of God, you may receive what was promised." Hebrews 10:36 (NASB)*

Ruby became a Christian at age 19, and shortly thereafter, she married a nonbeliever and moved in with her husband and his extended family. As anticipated, her life became very hard. Because her faith was not approved, she was not allowed to meet with other believers.

We prayed that someone in that household would become a believer also. Years later, God answered our prayers in a way that we did not expect. Coming from a neighboring country, Ruby's sister visited. Surprisingly, the sister began to share about her conversion to Christianity. Ruby had never told her sister about her relationship with Jesus, so it was with great joy that they discovered that they were also sisters in Christ.

In two countries where the percentage of believers is less than 1 percent, these sisters had both been drawn into fellowship with Christ. What a miracle! Now these sisters can encourage each other in their faith.

But God wasn't finished. Others in that family have since given their hearts to Jesus, including Ruby's husband. Sometimes we can be discouraged when answers come slowly, but God's timing is perfect.

—HEATHER, CENTRAL ASIAN PEOPLES

*Nothing* IS TOO DIFFICULT FOR YOU, HEAVENLY FATHER. I STAND AMAZED AT YOUR CREATIVITY IN ANSWERING PRAYERS BY BRINGING FAMILY MEMBERS TOGETHER AS ONE IN YOU. GUIDE ME IN PRAYING SPECIFIC PRAYERS, AND INCREASE MY FAITH TO BELIEVE YOU FOR THE IMPOSSIBLE. *Amen.*

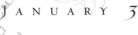

## Continuing to love

*"If you have raced with men on foot, and they have wearied you, how will you compete with horses?' ..." Jeremiah 12:5 (ESV)*

After meeting Isa for the first time, I began to visit him every time I was in his city. Over six years, we developed a good relationship, but he rarely wanted to talk about Jesus. Being a faithful Muslim, he was careful to keep as many Islamic rituals as possible.

After 10 years of marriage, Isa's wife was expecting twins. It was a complicated pregnancy, forcing her to be confined to bed rest. Isa confided that he was scared about the possibility of the babies or his wife dying. I told Isa that I would ask Christians to pray for the health of his wife and unborn twins. Finally, Isa's wife gave birth. When I asked Isa what I could bring them for a baby gift, he told me that I had already given him the best baby gift possible—prayer.

Isa has not yet made a decision to believe in Jesus, but I am praying for his continued progress toward Christianity. More often than not, this is how I see God at work, slowly and steadily. God never wants us to give up. He wants us to persist in praying and sharing Jesus, even when we don't see fruit, as that is His responsibility. So I continue to love Isa, believing that God is drawing Isa to Himself in ways I can't even imagine.

—MARTY, CENTRAL ASIAN PEOPLES

*Thank You,* FATHER, FOR USING YOUR CALLED-OUT ONES TO BE INSTRUMENTS OF GRACE AMONG MUSLIM PEOPLE. AS YOUR LOVE PENETRATES HEARTS, MAY STRONGHOLDS BE DEMOLISHED. I ASK THAT THE LIGHT OF THE GOSPEL OF TRUTH WILL BE CLEARLY UNDERSTOOD AND GENUINELY EMBRACED BY ISA. *Amen.*

# Reunions

*"... These are the ones coming out of the great tribulation. They washed their robes and made them white in the blood of the Lamb." Revelation 7:14b (HCSB)*

We often have reason to travel to the airport to meet visitors to Korea. Each time I wait for an arrival, I enjoy watching people. I've seen groups of tourists arriving for vacation, groups of Koreans returning from vacation, businesspeople coming for meetings, and military personnel. I even saw one man wearing a rainbow-colored wig!

Without a doubt, my favorite scene is the family reunion. I've seen grandchildren run to meet their grandmothers, husbands reunite with wives, and children reunite with parents.

As I witness these airport reunions, I am reminded of those I will see in heaven. I am looking forward to meeting friends and family who have gone before me, but I am also looking forward to meeting those for whom I have prayed, whether I know them personally or not. They may be a family member or a friend of a friend of a friend. They may be a member of a particular people group.

One of the great privileges of prayer is the ability to be a part of what God is doing. We may not know the people or the results of those prayers until we get to heaven, but what a glad day it will be when we meet them face-to-face.

—JOE, EAST ASIAN PEOPLES

*Father,* HELP ME TO LIVE MY LIFE INTENTIONALLY AS JESUS DID. THE UNDESERVED GIFT OF BEING IN YOUR PRESENCE WITH COUNTLESS MULTITUDES IN HEAVEN BRINGS JOY IMMEASURABLE. HELP ME TO BE A PASSIONATE, CONSISTENT INTERCESSOR AND WITNESS FOR YOUR GLORY. *Amen.*

# FEBRUARY

## God, Our Loving Father

*God loves the world. And the more He overtakes*
*our hearts, the more we will love the world.*

—BETH MOORE

As work on this book neared completion, I encountered major difficulties. Within a month's span, my brother found out he had stage four cancer, one of my best friends learned that she had cancer, my computer crashed, and there were other problems concerning another project. Honestly, I went through a rough patch, and there was nothing that I could do to resolve anything. It was completely out of my control.

In the midst of my very real despair over these situations, God brought Psalm 42:11 to mind: "Why are you in despair, O my soul? And why have you become disturbed within me? Hope in God, for I shall yet praise Him, the help of my countenance and my God" (NASB). Hope in God. That's what I've got to do. Hope in my loving Father and praise Him.

Our Father is worthy to be praised all the time. He is omnipotent, omnipresent, omniscient, mighty, strong, all sufficient, our Provider, I AM, our Banner, the Lord who Sanctifies, our Peace, our Righteousness, our Great Shepherd, the Lord Is There, the Lord of Hosts, the Most High, the God Who Sees, the Deliverer, Redeemer, our Shield, Everlasting God, Ancient of Days, and God our Rock.

He is our loving Father. No matter what we have done, no matter who we are, He loves us and forgives us. He is our God who shows us grace. I explained these truths to my grandfather for years. He would tell me over and over that he wasn't good enough. "I have done too many bad things," he said. I continued to quote Scripture to him, some that he had already memorized. It took him over 20 years to finally get it. About three years before he died, he received God's forgiveness, which resulted in him asking people to forgive him. My grandfather was far from perfect. He came just as he was, bowed to the Father, and received His love.

For those who didn't have a great earthly father, this concept of God's love may be inconceivable. But God does love each of us. "The LORD your God is among you, a warrior who saves. He will rejoice over you with gladness. He will bring [you] quietness with His love.

He will delight in you with shouts of joy" (Zephaniah 3:17, HCSB). It's pretty amazing that He loves us *and* delights in us.

God puts our broken and imperfect lives back together. The scars may still be visible, but He mends us. This month you will read stories from missionaries about the ways in which they and their family and friends have experienced God's love. Stories of His protection and provision are common. So are stories of His matchless love.

Do we sometimes take His love for granted? Do we often focus on our many distractions and difficulties instead of on our God who loves us? One servant states, "I think God is often saying to me, *I'm right here, I'm right here! Look at Me!*"

I can't wait for you to read these stories. You will be blessed as you spend time this month focusing on God, our loving Father.

—*Kim P. Davis*

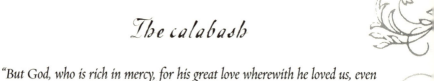

# The calabash

*"But God, who is rich in mercy, for his great love wherewith he loved us, even when we were dead in sins, hath quickened us together with Christ, (by grace ye are saved;)" Ephesians 2:4–5 (KJV)*

A calabash is a common household tool in Mali—a dried gourd cut in half and used as a spoon, bowl, or dipper. Over time, it eventually cracks or breaks into pieces, but Malians are so attached to their calabashes that they do not discard them. Instead, they stitch the pieces back together using grass and continue to use them.

Fatim's calabash was cracked, burned, and stitched—yet it was still useful to sift rice. When I offered to buy hers, she couldn't understand why I would want to pay for one that was battered and scarred rather than purchase a new one at the market. After she gratefully accepted the money, I explained, "This calabash is like me. A new calabash is perfect, but this one is broken. You took the pieces and sewed them together so that you could still use it. That is like my life. I was broken. My life was not good, but God loved me anyway. God put my life back together. This broken calabash reminds me that God loves me."

On the last day in the village, the women came to our hut to say goodbye. One of them had a small, mended calabash. Fatim told the others what those stitches meant and to remember how much God loves us.

—RITA, SUB-SAHARAN AFRICAN PEOPLES

*God, our Creator,* YOU HAVE FORMED US AND REPAIRED US WHEN WE HAVE CHOSEN TO FOLLOW OUR OWN WAYS. THANK YOU FOR YOUR MERCY AND LOVE. THANK YOU THAT YOU SEE US AS USEFUL IN YOUR KINGDOM. *Amen.*

# God keeps us close

*"I the* LORD *have called thee in righteousness, and will hold thine hand, and will keep thee, and give thee for a covenant of the people, for a light of the Gentiles."*
Isaiah 42:6 (KJV)

While prayerwalking in a market, God painted a precious picture in my mind as I observed a man walking ahead. He was holding the hand of his young daughter, who occasionally took a step to walk in another direction. The father, however, firmly yet gently held on to her hand, refusing to release her. He did not take long strides ahead of her but instead walked beside while gently pulling her along. This awakened my remembrance of how God keeps me close, never leaving or forsaking me, but steering me.

Moments later, I turned the corner and walked past another man who was standing with a teenage daughter. This teenager had her hand hooked inside the bent arm of her father. Wow! It was such a great reminder that as I grow with God, I learn to hold firmly on to Him because I recognize Him as my Protector and Provider.

On a day when it seemed like opposition was getting the best of our team, in the market I saw wonderful reminders of God's gracious love for all peoples. He is holding on tightly, using every opportunity to allow them access to His Word and His saving grace. Moved to tears, the meaning of my call was before me. As He steers me, He will use me to lead others to His arms.

—O.C.L., NORTHERN AFRICAN AND MIDDLE EASTERN PEOPLES

*My Protector and Provider,* YOU ARE THE FATHER FOR WHOM EVERY PERSON WORLD- WIDE LONGS. YOU HAVE PROMISED NEVER TO LEAVE OR FORSAKE US. WE ASK THAT MANY TODAY WILL HEAR AND RESPOND TO YOUR INCOMPARABLE LOVE. *Amen.*

# What's in a name?

*"And His name will be called ..." Isaiah 9:6d (NASB)*

Under the canopy of the rosewood tree, the Lozi women and I spread our outer wraps and sat in the soft, Zambezi sand. I told the story of how Hagar was chased away from her home by Sarah. Hagar knew she would die in the wilderness, but God saw Hagar and encouraged her. "You are a God who sees," she exclaimed, which is translated *El Roi.* I asked the women to go home and pray for God to show them His name.

That night, I thought, *How vain am I to believe that I know all the names of God!* I began to pray that the Lord would reveal a new name of His to me.

When I met with the women again, a woman who wholeheartedly follows Jesus said, "Last night I had a dream. I saw a wall that was slightly raised off the ground. Underneath the wall, I could see a man's feet walking back and forth. The man told me to read John 7:37–39." We excitedly looked up the verses and read: "If anyone is thirsty, let him come to Me and drink ..." (NASB) I just knew the woman would say that God's name was Living Water. But as she spoke again, she said, "God's name is 'God who cares for me.'"

Praise God for revealing Himself. He cares for us.

—SKY, SUB-SAHARAN AFRICAN PEOPLES

*Merciful Savior,* YOU CARE FOR EACH PERSON AND KNOW THEIR INTIMATE NEEDS. THANK YOU FOR REVEALING YOUR COMPASSION TO THE LOZI WOMAN. WE ASK FOR AN OUTPOURING OF YOUR GRACE FOR PEOPLE IN SUB-SAHARAN AFRICA. MAY THEY COME TO KNOW YOU AS THE GOD WHO TRULY CARES. *Amen.*

# *Look at Me!*

*"that the genuineness of your faith ... may be found to praise, honor, and glory at the revelation of Jesus Christ, whom having not seen you love. Though now you do not see Him, yet believing, you rejoice with joy inexpressible and full of glory," 1 Peter 1:7–8 (NKJV)*

As grandparents, missing grandchildren is probably the hardest thing we deal with on the mission field. However, thanks to computer technology, we are able to watch our granddaughter, Aubrey, grow and change. Almost every Sunday since she was a baby, we have connected by Internet and webcam for a Sunday afternoon visit. Recently, as we were praising her new accomplishments and gawking at her precious face on our computer screen, she looked at us on her computer screen, pointed to herself, and said in a rather frustrated manner, "I'm right here, I'm right here!" We were looking at her the whole time, but she didn't realize it because we were gazing *down* at our computer screen instead of looking *up* into our webcam that would have projected our eyes to her screen.

Later, I couldn't get her words out of my mind. I began to think about the distractions in my life and the times I look down instead of up. I think God is often saying to me, *I'm right here! I'm right here! Look at Me!* It is only when my eyes are focused on Christ that I gain a proper perspective on everything and fully experience His joy and peace.

—Cheryl, Sub-Saharan African Peoples

*Father,* I desire to stay focused on You. When distractions come, help me keep my eyes fixed on You, the Author and Perfecter of my faith. I pray the same for missionaries. Help them not to be more focused on ministry than on You. *Amen.*

# His love springs up

*"The flowers appear on the earth, the time of singing has come, and the voice of the turtledove is heard in our land." Song of Solomon 2:12 (ESV)*

In one of the most popular tourist destinations in the world where I live, visitors are impressed by designer stores, world-class museums, and famous sights. People come from all over to vacation in style. Six kilometers away in my neighborhood, however, it is entirely different. Gangs leave graffiti on the walls, glass litters the streets, and occasionally a trash can or a car is set on fire. There is a constant cloud of bus exhaust and cigarette smoke. My neighbors are immigrants who have come to raise their children in a better place and who are often struggling against negative stereotypes and racism.

As I was waiting on the train platform in my neighborhood, I noticed that poppies were in bloom, even in the gravel and concrete. I couldn't help but smile as I saw a clump of bright-red blooms waving back and forth in between the train tracks. It was a beautiful illustration of God's love. His love springs up and blooms in my dirty, rough neighborhood in the same way that the poppies persevere and thrive in the gravel and pollution. Looking through the hardship and ugliness of my surroundings, God can be found. He is not just in places of beauty. He is all around us, even during our discouragement and helplessness.

—L.E.W., Northern African and Middle Eastern Peoples

*Lord,* I praise You that the heavens declare Your glory, and the skies proclaim the work of Your hands. We ask today that in desolate and difficult places, the beauty of Your creation will encourage those who know You and draw those who are seeking truth to Yourself. *Amen.*

# *Finding joy in God Himself*

*"Let all who seek You rejoice and be glad in You; let those who love Your salvation continually say, 'God is great!'" Psalm 70:4 (HCSB)*

Kicked out and banned from returning, my family fled to a nearby country in Central Asia. We were devastated.

In the midst of this trial, the encouragement to "be glad" in Psalm 70 caught our attention. Initially, in my desperation to hear from the Lord about where and what He had next for us, I began to pursue His guidance above all else. In every verse I read, I sought to discover God's will for my family. The Psalmist, however, did not say, "Let all who seek *Your will* rejoice and be glad in *Your guidance*." He said, "Let all who seek *You* rejoice and be glad in *You*." My problem was that I was seeking and pursuing the wrong thing.

God's guidance is good and necessary for all who follow Christ. Yet it is much less important than seeking God Himself. I was missing out on who God is because I mainly was interested in getting an answer from Him. The joy the Psalmist speaks of is not found in getting what I want from God, but in God Himself. When I began to shift my focus to knowing and pursuing Him, I experienced peace, joy, and contentment in the situation. In the end, I did receive the direction I originally sought, but it was a blessed by-product of enjoying God.

—J.W., CENTRAL ASIAN PEOPLES

*Lord Jesus,* THANK YOU FOR PRAYING THAT WE MIGHT HAVE THE SAME DIVINE JOY THE FATHER GAVE YOU. HELP ME DAILY TO LIVE OUT THAT JOY, GROUNDED FIRMLY IN A RELATIONSHIP WITH GOD THAT NO CHANGE IN CIRCUMSTANCES CAN EVER SHAKE. *Amen.*

# God is bigger

*"For the LORD your God is living among you. ... He will take delight in you with gladness. With his love, he will calm all your fears. He will rejoice over you with joyful songs." Zephaniah 3:17 (NLT)*

As a new third grade science teacher, I moved halfway around the world and was homesick. I spent hours trying to plan interesting lessons, especially about natural disasters. I thought that my class, mostly boys, would love studying about catastrophes.

When I finished talking about earthquakes, I realized that many students were in tears! I had forgotten that we lived on a fault line. I prayed an SOS prayer to God. Then I asked the class, "Is God bigger than earthquakes?" They hesitantly replied, "Yes." I went down the list: "Is God bigger than a tornado ... volcano ... flood?" Finally, one student raised his hand and said, "I guess He would have to be if He holds the whole world in His hands!" Exactly! What started as a science lesson suddenly became a discussion of who God is and how He takes care of us.

Reflecting later, I felt like He was asking me, *If I am bigger than natural disasters, don't you think that I am bigger than the homesickness that is overwhelming you? I love you. I did not dump you in the middle of nowhere and leave. I am here with you.* I was reminded that I am never alone and that God, who holds the whole world in His hands, holds me, too.

—B.E.C., CENTRAL ASIAN PEOPLES

*Mighty God,* THANK YOU FOR REVEALING YOUR LOVE, PRESENCE, PROTECTION, AND PURPOSE TO THOSE WHO SERVE YOU AROUND THE WORLD. INSTILL IN THEM THE CONFIDENCE THAT NOTHING IS TOO DIFFICULT FOR YOU. ASSURE THEM THAT YOU TAKE GREAT DELIGHT IN THEM, AND YOUR PURPOSES WILL BE FULFILLED. *Amen.*

# Seeking solitude

*"Be still, and know that I am God; I will be exalted among the nations, I will be exalted in the earth!" Psalm 46:10 (NKJV)*

Listening, waiting, reflecting. That's what the conference speaker challenged us to do as we spent time in solitude with the Lord. We were sent out with a box lunch to spend three hours alone with God.

I settled myself near a creek, ate my lunch, and began to wait on God to speak. Stretching out on a blanket, I observed ants busily going to and fro. The ants worked hard carrying food. At the same time, I watched a small dragonfly on a stick. He occasionally moved but not more than an inch. Over two hours later, while the ants were still working, another insect swooped in from nowhere and was instantly eaten by the waiting dragonfly. Wow!

In that moment I knew that God was teaching me that there is a time to be busy and a time to wait on His timing when He will bring about what He desires. Continuing to reflect on this, I rolled over on the blanket and stared upward. A tree that had one dead, leafless limb was overhead. God continued to speak as I recalled John 15 and being connected to the Vine.

Jesus sought solitude with the Father. Seeking solitude can be a glorious part of our lives, too, so that He can speak to us.

—CANDY, CENTRAL ASIAN PEOPLES

*Loving Father,* MY GREATEST NEED IS TO KNOW YOU. THROUGH SILENCE, SOLITUDE, AND FULL SURRENDER IN YOUR PRESENCE, CALL ME TO YOURSELF AND HELP ME TO REALIZE THAT YOU TAKE DELIGHT IN YOUR CHILDREN. *Amen.*

# He carries our burdens

*"Come to Me, all who are weary and heavy-laden, and I will give you rest."*
Matthew 11:28 (NASB)

Heavy loads are carried on the backs of people living in the Guatemalan countryside, including firewood and large pots. In order to carry these loads, they use a leather strap and ropes to secure the load. The strap goes across the carrier's forehead so that all the weight is not on the person's back, but rather distributed.

This image of the burden carrier impressed a friend of mine to burn Matthew 11:28 onto leather straps as well as a picture of a man carrying a load of wood. I bought two from him and then mounted them, hanging one in my office and one in our living room.

As one who provides business and legal support for our missionaries, I sometimes find myself with many responsibilities. It is a heavy schedule, and there are many days when I feel like the burden is too much. Each morning during my devotional time, I see the strap in the living room and am reminded that the Lord will see me through the day. Each afternoon as I leave the office, I notice the strap mounted there, and I am assured that the Lord has fulfilled His promise. He is carrying the burden for me as long as I don't take it back upon my shoulders. The load is light for the Lord.

—GEORGE, AMERICAN PEOPLES

*Father,* I PRAY TODAY FOR OUR MISSIONARIES WHO ARE BURDENED WITH CONCERNS FOR THEIR CHILDREN, THEIR PEOPLE GROUP, OR THEIR MANY RESPONSIBILITIES. I ASK THAT THEY MAY TAKE YOUR YOKE ON THEM AND ALLOW YOU TO BEAR THEIR BURDENS AND GIVE THEM TRUE REST FOR THEIR BODIES AND SOULS. *Amen.*

## When in the deep waters

*"Give all your worries and cares to God, for he cares about you."* 1 Peter 5:7 (NLT)

I felt like I was drowning in the dark sea of depression. If I could sleep, all of it would pass me by.

Once, I had been so eager and optimistic! I was discipling several men, and God was working in exhilarating ways. But they had enormous difficulties as refugees. I couldn't fix their problems. On top of that was the stress of caring for and protecting my young family, language study, and ministry with other colleagues. I was overwhelmed and in way over my head! I couldn't be enough! I just wanted to hide in sleep, lost in my dreams.

But God's love is deeper than any ocean because He found me! God's voice came in the midst of the dark, suffocating water with a resounding, *I AM sufficient! You must trust Me! You cannot fix your friends' problems! Put all of this turmoil in your Father's hands. I can take care of it. I love you!*

Slowly, He pulled me to the surface. I inhaled deep, cleansing breaths into my lungs. God rescued, awakened, and renewed me! I was able to get help from colleagues, a counselor, and friends. God took care of every one of my concerns in glorious ways. He brought our family closer together. I learned that I must give God everything and trust Him with all my cares.

—TIM, CENTRAL ASIAN PEOPLES

*Father,* THROUGH YOUR GRACE, POWER, AND LOVE, YOU DESIRE TO TAKE ME FROM WHERE I AM AND BRING ME TO WHERE YOU WANT ME TO BE. DRAW ME TO YOURSELF, LORD, AND ENABLE ME TO COME HUMBLY TO YOU. THANK YOU THAT YOU ALONE CAN HEAL, RESTORE, AND USE ME FOR YOUR GLORY. *Amen.*

# Super-dependent on Him

*"At that time, when you call, the LORD will answer; when you cry out, He will say: Here I am." Isaiah 58:9a (HCSB)*

Being a missionary kid and now a long-term missionary, I never thought that missionaries were superheroes. It doesn't take long to realize how insufficient we are to handle all that life brings.

Newly married, my husband and I arrived overseas for service. Just when it seemed that life was settling down and our work was building momentum, riots broke out. From the roof of our building, we heard loud explosions and saw fire dancing on rooftops. Eventually the military arrived, locking down the city. Over the next six weeks, increased restrictions in the region caused our team to travel to a neighboring area.

Although displaced, we found some stability in studying language, until one afternoon, our hotel began swaying, then shaking violently, followed by the walls cracking and plaster falling. In the wake of a powerful earthquake, we found ourselves launched into a disaster relief project reaching out to millions of refugees.

I knew that whatever strength I used to think I had was only a mirage. Tenderly the Father spoke through His Word that I don't have to be a superhero! All power, strength, and protection are available to me through Him if I will but humbly cry for help and walk in obedience. Missionaries are just super-dependent people relying on a super-powerful God!

—C.S., EAST ASIAN PEOPLES

*Powerful Father,* WE ARE HELPLESS WITHOUT YOU. THANK YOU FOR ALLOWING US TO COME TO THE END OF OUR OWN SUFFICIENCY AND REMINDING US THAT ALL THINGS ARE POSSIBLE WITH YOU. *Amen.*

# *Choosing God's strength*

*"... My grace is sufficient for thee: for my power is made perfect in weakness ..."*
2 Corinthians 12:9 (ASV)

Looking in the rearview mirror, my husband said, "I hope that car can stop!" Immediately, a car plowed into the truck beside us. The truck crashed into our car.

When I became conscious, my daughter was crying frantically, and the book we had been reading was smeared with my blood. One driver fled the scene, another was taken to the hospital, but being a foreigner, my husband was taken to jail.

Still in a state of shock the next morning, the situation seemed overwhelming. The Father spoke to my heart saying, *You can go through this in your own strength, or you can choose to go through this in My strength.* As I felt the prayers of God's people, I desperately read God's Word and cried out to Him as I prayed for my husband, the policemen, and the other inmate in my husband's cell. For seven long days, my husband was in jail, but God had a plan. Javier, the other inmate, found new freedom in Christ and all the policemen received Gospel tracts!

There is no doubt that God was with us in the situation. His Word gave peace and calmness, He answered prayers, and He brought an inmate to Himself. Praise our all-sufficient God that when we are weak, He is strong.

—KYLEEN, AMERICAN PEOPLES

*Faithful Companion,* THANK YOU FOR GOING WITH BELIEVERS THROUGH TURBULENT TIMES AND FOR HELPING US TO LOOK BACK AND SEE YOUR FOOTPRINTS AS YOU CARRIED US THROUGH. YOUR WAYS AND PURPOSES FAR EXCEED OUR IMAGINATIONS AND HOPES. I PRAISE YOU. *Amen.*

# My Anchor and Rock

*"Therefore, we who have fled to him for refuge can have great confidence as we hold to the hope that lies before us. This hope is a strong and trustworthy anchor for our souls. It leads us through the curtain into God's inner sanctuary." Hebrews 6:18c–19 (NLT)*

I have always loved studying the different names of God and how each name ministers differently to individuals. It is such a testimony to the completeness and perfection of God and the ways in which He reaches out to each of us on a personal level.

These verses in Hebrews in which God is seen as our Refuge and Anchor create powerful pictures in my mind. My favorite picture of God is as my strong and stable protection, the Rock that I can cling to and in whose shadow I can hide. Sometimes I need more than ever to see Him as the One who protects me and keeps me safe.

Lately, however, He has been my Anchor. The anchor of a buoy is deep below the water, attached to the buoy to keep it from being dragged off course. It doesn't shelter from the rough wind and waves, though. The buoy is battered during the storm, but the anchor keeps it in place. I have felt like a buoy lately. If not for the strength of the Anchor, storms and currents would have carried me off. Many times, I didn't understand why I didn't drift until I remembered that God is my Anchor. He is the One who is always there.

—KARI, SOUTH ASIAN PEOPLES

*Almighty God,* THANK YOU FOR THE KNOWLEDGE OF YOUR PRESENCE, WHICH PREVENTS ME FROM FLOUNDERING OR GIVING UP. HELP OUR MISSIONARIES TO FOCUS ON YOU TODAY AND BE ASSURED THAT, WITH YOU, ALL THINGS ARE POSSIBLE. *Amen.*

# *Loving God by loving people*

*"If we love one another, God abides in us, and His love has been perfected in us."*
*1 John 4:12b (NKJV)*

What do I know about love, and especially, what does it mean to love God? I've never married or had children, and though I love my parents and siblings, I've been praying that the Lord would show me what it means to love Him.

A few weeks ago, I was preparing to preach on biblical love in our local African church when I came across 1 John 4:12–13. These verses reminded me that God's love abides and is perfected in us when we love one another. When we love others, we abide in Him. In other words, God's love is active in us when we express that love to others. Those verses hit me like a ton of bricks. In the quietness as I sat by my bedroom window in the warm, winter sunlight, I broke down and cried as I realized that God was answering my lifelong prayer. He was showing me His love and what it means to love Him.

I thought of how I couldn't help but love my African brothers and sisters in Christ and the other people around me who need Him. I thought of the two local university students who were staying in my home and whom I'd grown to love like sons. God was showing me His love, and I was loving Him by loving others.

—Brian, Sub-Saharan African Peoples

*Thank You,* Loving Father, for drawing me to Yourself. As I spend time in intimate fellowship with You, hearing Your voice and receiving Your love, You prepare me to serve You. Make me a channel of Your love and grace. *Amen.*

# Scorpions

*"What father among you, if his son asks ... for an egg, will give him a scorpion? If you then, who are evil, know how to give good gifts to your children, how much more will the heavenly Father give the Holy Spirit to those who ask Him?"*
Luke 11:11–13 (HCSB)

Sitting among a group of missionary mothers, I heard them pray, "Please, Lord, protect our children from scorpions." In a dry desert, scorpions are unwelcome nocturnal visitors. One sting can cause serious illness or even death for a small child. Many of our families choose to sleep on traditional floor mattresses, so insects can be a problem.

Stories of answered prayer began to reach my ears. One mother heard her 3-month-old baby whimper. As she rolled over to pull him nearer to her, she felt a scorpion's sting. The arachnid had found her hand before it reached her infant.

When the children in another family roused in the night, they would seek their parents' mattress. One night, the father rose from his crowded bed and stumbled in the dark to his son's mattress. As he lay down, a scorpion stung him instead of the child who should have been there.

Another mother sighed with annoyance as she chased her toddler across the room to dress him. Ready to slip on his pants as soon as she caught him, a movement in a pant leg caught her eye. It was a scorpion, tail bent, ready to sting. She wept with thanksgiving that the little guy had learned to run. God watches over our loved ones better than we ever could.

—A WORKER WITH CENTRAL ASIAN PEOPLES

*Merciful God,* YOU HAVE DELIVERED ME AND MY CHILDREN FROM PHYSICAL HARM COUNTLESS TIMES. THANK YOU FOR YOUR PROTECTION AND FOR THE SALVATION YOU PROVIDE FOR ALL WHO BELIEVE. *Amen.*

# *God will provide*

> *"Look at the birds of the sky: they don't sow or reap or gather into barns, yet your heavenly Father feeds them. Aren't you worth more than they?" Matthew 6:26 (HCSB)*

"God will provide." That is the motto of Juana, who has learned to depend on God to supply all her needs.

Juana grew up with an abusive father who spent most of their money on alcohol. As a teenager, she put her faith in God. She later married Miguel, a new believer who is still learning about living the Christian life. When Miguel was laid off, Juana reassured him that God would supply their needs. A job working at a clothing factory became available for Juana, which paid enough for their rent only. Coworkers mocked her beliefs, but nothing would dissuade her that God would provide, even after losing this job.

Miguel didn't understand how this could happen or how they would pay their rent and buy food for their young son. He was embarrassed to let anyone know of their situation and kept it a secret. But Juana confidently believed in God's provision.

Two days later, a volunteer mission team bought groceries for Juana's family. They did not know of the family's situation. When Miguel came home, Juana smiled and said, "I have something to show you." She pointed to the bags of basic staples. "Where did it come from?" he asked with surprise. Without hesitation, Juana said, "God." Miguel now believes his wife's motto.

—JODY, AMERICAN PEOPLES

*Father,* I CAN TRUST YOU WITH ALL MY PHYSICAL AND FINANCIAL NEEDS. THANK YOU FOR THE STORY OF THIS PRECIOUS BELIEVER WHO PROVED HER TRUST. MAY YOU CONTINUE TO PROVIDE FOR THIS FAMILY. *Amen.*

# God's angels

*"The LORD is like a father to his children, tender and compassionate to those who fear him." Psalm 103:13 (NLT)*

A wonderful vacation for my mother while she visited us turned into a nightmare. An illness she contracted while visiting developed into a life-threatening condition upon her return to the States. Learning this, I left our three young sons with my husband and headed home. Things were grim when I arrived, but God began to heal her miraculously and lavish His grace upon my family.

His love continued upon reentry to my adopted land. Breaking my flight to obtain a visa had forfeited my luggage allowance, and when I returned to the airport to recheck my bags, there were two men from my host country waiting near the counter. They noticed my heavy trunks and offered to check in with me. That way, I could use their luggage allowance and not have to pay extra for my bags! Afterward, I asked if they had been intentionally waiting to help someone when they, baggage-free, could have checked in quickly and proceeded directly to the gate. "Yes," they replied, "and you are the lucky one!"

I've been tempted to call the numbers on their business cards to see if these men were mortals or heavenly messengers who buoyed me in the wake of a crisis. Regardless, I know they were sent to assure me yet again that I am precious to my tender, compassionate Father.

—A WORKER WITH SOUTHEAST ASIAN PEOPLES

*All-powerful Father,* WE PRAY TODAY THAT OUR MISSIONARIES WILL RECOGNIZE YOUR MIGHTY PRESENCE WITH THEM. HELP THEM TO SEE YOUR HAND AT WORK PROVIDING FOR THEM WHEN THEIR OWN RESOURCES ARE INSUFFICIENT. *Amen.*

# *He puts food on the table*

*"Therefore take no thought, saying, What shall we eat? or What shall we drink? or, Wherewithal shall we be clothed? ... for your heavenly Father knoweth that ye have need of all these things." Matthew 6:31–32 (KJV)*

Living in a country where the average yearly income is around $150 per person, I was wealthy compared to my friend who was struggling to make her paycheck last through the month. The cost of groceries was increasing, and the price of gas for our cooking stoves had just doubled. In this culture, if someone asked her for money and she had some, she must give it. I considered giving her some money, but I struggled in my spirit wanting this dear sister, young in her Christian faith, to look to God to supply her needs.

I listened to her share her frustration and need, then together we prayed, thanking God for His faithfulness. We asked God to provide for her. I left my friend that day wondering if I had the faith to believe that God would care for her.

The following afternoon, the phone rang. My friend was bubbling with excitement. "Something wonderful has happened," she said. "I walked into my apartment and on the table was enough money to see me through the month! I have no idea how it got there!" My heart rejoiced with my Christian sister. All praise was given to the Lord that day, both my friend and I convinced of His provision.

—M.P., NORTHERN AFRICAN AND MIDDLE EASTERN PEOPLES

*All-sufficient Father,* YOU EXHORT US TO DELIGHT OURSELVES IN YOU, AND YOU WILL GIVE US THE DESIRES OF OUR HEARTS. MAY YOUR NAME BE EXALTED AND YOUR KINGDOM BE EXTENDED. *Amen.*

# Green chilies

*"Ah Lord GOD! Behold, You have made the heavens and the earth by Your great power and by Your outstretched arm! Nothing is too difficult for You."*
*Jeremiah 32:17 (NASB)*

I didn't realize before coming overseas how often I would be cooking for large numbers of people. Each Sunday my team gets together to worship and share a meal, and whoever is host prepares the main course.

It was my first turn as host, in the dead of winter. White chicken chili would be perfect to warm us up! My shopping trip for the ingredients was successful, except for one vital item: green chilies! I couldn't even find a good substitute. It looked like I'd have to change my menu.

A few days before our meeting, a care package arrived for our team. It was filled with goodies for the kids and food items not found in our country. When everything was divided among the families, I ended up with two small cans of green chilies. All I could do was smile in awe of the God of the universe. He knew I was nervous about having everyone over and that I wanted the food to be good.

The Sunday school class gathering the food items months before to send to us didn't know exactly what we might need, but God did. He orchestrated everything from the packing of the box to its timely arrival. Nothing is too big for God to handle, and nothing is too small to escape His notice and care.

—A.E., CENTRAL ASIAN PEOPLES

*God,* THANK YOU FOR YOUR PROVISION, NOT ONLY FOR OUR NEEDS, BUT ALSO FOR OUR DESIRES. YOU ARE THE GIVER OF ALL GOOD THINGS. PLEASE MAKE YOURSELF KNOWN TODAY TO THOSE WHO SEEK YOU. *Amen.*

## The gun that didn't shoot

*"Yea, though I walk through the valley of the shadow of death, I will fear no evil: for thou art with me; thy rod and thy staff they comfort me." Psalm 23:4 (KJV)*

Unaware of the men following him as he walked to his university class, Ronaldo was startled when a gang surrounded him and demanded his cell phone and shirt. At first Ronaldo resisted, but when they threatened him with a beating, he gave them his cell phone. He asked, however, if he could keep his shirt because it had a slogan on the sleeve that read, "100% Jesus."

When the leader of the gang saw what was on the shirt sleeve, he became infuriated and pulled out his revolver. He said, "Let's see if this Jesus can save you now." The gang leader put the gun to Ronaldo's head and pulled the trigger. The gun misfired, so he pulled the trigger again, and again, and again, and then again. Five times the criminal tried to kill Ronaldo, but the gun never fired. Slowly the leader turned and walked away as the other members followed. He could be heard cursing the gun as they left.

As Ronaldo was relating this story to a Christian brother, he made the statement that God had not only saved him from his sins, but also from this gang. God rescued this young believer during a time of trouble and displayed His power not only to Ronaldo, but to evil men who must process what they witnessed.

—MONTY AND JANIS, AMERICAN PEOPLES

*Master Designer,* THANK YOU THAT YOU CREATED US WITH THE ABILITY TO REMEMBER SIGNIFICANT EVENTS. I PRAY TODAY FOR PEOPLE THROUGHOUT THE WORLD WHO HAVE EXPERIENCED THINGS ONLY YOU COULD ORCHESTRATE. REVEAL YOURSELF TO THEM AS THEY RECALL YOUR SPECIAL TOUCH IN THEIR LIVES. *Amen.*

# An unshakable foundation

*"Trust in him at all times, O people; pour out your heart before him; God is a refuge for us." Psalm 62:8 (ESV)*

Thirteen-year-old "Mei Mei" pondered some hard questions. As we walked through her town just weeks after a massive earthquake, she confessed her fear in the aftermath of the disaster. Like millions of others in the quake zone, she was living in a government-issued tent because her home had been destroyed. Her school had also collapsed, killing over 1,000 of her classmates.

When I spoke of One who could bring lasting peace and would never be shaken, the longing in her eyes was indescribable. Words of hope had been few and far between, and disaster has an uncanny way of focusing our attention on the eternal.

As I rode away from Mei Mei's crumbled city over landslide-covered roads, I saw Psalm 62 in a tangible way. God cannot be shaken. With God as my Rock and Fortress, I was drawn to what the Psalmist said should be my response: "Pour out your heart before him."

Even in times of crisis, I sometimes feel that coming to God with my struggles, needs, and wants is a selfish act. Yet He longs for me to pour out my heart before Him as the only One capable of being a refuge. It is glorious to know that even if the world crumbles around me, my God remains unchanged.

—KATE, EAST ASIAN PEOPLES

*Lord,* TRULY YOU ALONE ARE OUR REFUGE AND FORTRESS, A VERY PRESENT HELP IN TIME OF TROUBLE. WE PRAY FOR THOSE WHOSE LIVES HAVE BEEN SHAKEN TO THE CORE BY NATURAL DISASTERS AND PERSONAL UPHEAVAL. MAY THIS BE A TIME WHEN YOUR MESSAGE OF HOPE DEEPLY RESONATES WITHIN THEIR SOULS. *Amen.*

# A close call

*"You are my hiding place; You protect me from trouble. You surround me with joyful shouts of deliverance." Psalm 32:7 (HCSB)*

My friend Ladya asked me to accompany him on a business trip. Although I preferred not to travel at night, I felt that God wanted me to go to continue to share my faith with him.

As we drove, we laughed and talked, but I did notice that Ladya drove fast. With dusk approaching and a slight mist falling, I prayed diligently for our protection. Coming upon a line of traffic behind a slow vehicle, Ladya decided to pass. In the dark, it was not obvious that we were near the top of the hill with a blind bend just over the other side. As we finally passed the front car, a semitruck appeared, coming straight at us. Ladya swerved, narrowly missing both the oncoming truck and the car we were overtaking.

Silence. We drove a few more minutes before arriving at our destination. In the parking lot, I looked at Ladya, who was shaking as he tightly gripped the steering wheel with both hands. A few moments passed before he fearfully glanced at me and said, "Your God must want you to live."

Since then, Ladya has been seriously considering what I have been telling him about my loving Father. God can use a crisis or near-death experience to draw people to Himself.

—SCOTT, EUROPEAN PEOPLES

*Merciful Father,* THANK YOU FOR DEMONSTRATING YOUR POWER AND PROTECTION DURING TIMES OF GRAVE DANGER. I PRAY TODAY FOR THOSE WHO ARE CONTEMPLATING YOUR EXISTENCE AND AUTHORITY. MAY THIS BE THE DAY THEY OPEN THEIR HEARTS TO RECEIVE YOU AS LORD. *Amen.*

# Nothing is impossible

*"And looking at them Jesus said to them, 'With people this is impossible, but with God all things are possible.'" Matthew 19:26 (NASB)*

"Sanjay's" new faith astounded us. Even though we continually taught him that he should pray for others and trust God to work in their lives, our faith was lacking without us realizing it. When Sanjay told us that he and his wife had been sharing the Gospel with their relatives who had a severely mentally disabled son, we listened with awe. The son couldn't speak or do anything for himself, which caused the family to struggle with how to take care of him with no professional help. Our friends told their family that if they believed in Jesus, He would take care of them and everything would be okay.

When I heard this, I thought, *I can't believe he said that. Now they're going to become believers just because they want everything to be all right with their son, and then nothing is going to happen.* God challenged my unbelief with Matthew 19:26.

About a week later, Sanjay's relatives became believers. Within another week, we went with Sanjay to visit this family. To our surprise, the mentally handicapped son was walking around. He could do things for himself and could even speak some. It was amazing! What I saw reminded me that nothing is impossible with God!

—KEELIE, SOUTH ASIAN PEOPLES

*Father,* INCREASE MY FAITH TODAY AND HELP ME LIVE A LIFE THAT REFLECTS ABSOLUTE TRUST IN YOU. THANK YOU FOR SHOWING YOURSELF POWERFUL IN THE LIVES OF NEW BELIEVERS. I ASK THAT MANY WILL SEE YOUR WORKS AND TRUST IN YOU. *Amen.*

# *Finding purpose*

*"When my spirit was overwhelmed within me, You knew my path." Psalm 142:3a (NASB)*

In a city of roughly 20 million people, running through the park provides opportunity for reflection, renewal, and communication with God. One morning, I was thinking about why my friend "Bethany" had yet to come to faith. In fact, she seemed less interested as time passed. I had several questions for God, like, "What on earth am I doing here?" and "Why am I not making a difference for Christ in Bethany's life?"

As I rounded a familiar corner, I was met by a beautiful glimpse of the sun rising over the Bosphorus Strait. It was almost as though God visibly responded, *Look what I can do! I designed this sunrise just like I have designed the course of your life. Do you really think I'm anxious as to whether or not it will all make sense?*

That very evening, I met Bethany, three other national friends, a national believer, and two teammates for dinner. I listened in awe as our believing friend connected and shared God's Word with them in ways that my limited knowledge of language and culture would never have been able to do. The answers to my questions became clear. God led me on this path to proclaim Him, to grow me spiritually, and most importantly, to glorify Him.

—VIRG, CENTRAL ASIAN PEOPLES

*Father,* ALL YOUR PROMISES TO ME IN CHRIST ARE YES! THERE IS ABSOLUTELY NOTHING THAT EXCEEDS YOUR POWER. HELP ME NOT TO BECOME DISCOURAGED, BUT EMPOWER ME TO PRAY IN FAITH AND WALK CLOSELY WITH YOU. IN YOUR TIME, I WILL SEE YOUR GLORY AS PROMISES ARE FULFILLED. *Amen.*

# God accomplishes His purposes

*"... I will strengthen you, though you do not know Me, so that all may know from the rising of the sun to its setting that there is no one but Me. I am the LORD, and there is no other." Isaiah 45:5–6 (HCSB)*

"Rafael" was a tough guy in town, but he had Christian family members who faithfully served the Lord. He chose to make life miserable for his family's pastor, ridiculing and trying to humiliate him. Eventually, Rafael's bullying manner and lawless lifestyle took him to prison.

One day, a family member went to visit Rafael. Rafael bragged to his relative that he was the "king" of the prison. Because he had taken over the prison black market, the other prisoners came to Rafael to purchase whatever they wanted from the outside. He boasted that he could sell anything in the prison. "By the way," he said to his surprised Christian relative, "the next time you're at church, pick me up some of those Christian music CDs and tracts that you give out to people. I can even sell them in here!"

On his next visit, the relative took Rafael some CDs and Gospel tracts. A few weeks later, he visited Rafael again. This time the relative heard prisoners singing Christian songs from those CDs, and he met people who told him they had read the tracts and trusted Christ. As in the case of the pagan king, Cyrus, God sometimes uses nonbelievers to accomplish His purposes.

—JOE, AMERICAN PEOPLES

*Father,* I REJOICE THAT ALL ACROSS THE WORLD, YOU ARE USING CREATIVE WAYS TO EN-GAGE PEOPLE WITH THE GOSPEL. HELP ME TODAY TO RESPOND TO THE OPPORTUNITIES I HAVE TO SHARE YOUR STORY WITH THOSE YOU BRING INTO MY PATH. *Amen.*

## *God creates life*

*"In the beginning God created the heavens and the earth." Genesis 1:1 (HCSB)*

Moving from an Asian city of 20 million people to the rolling hills of the Black Forest region of Germany, my faithful mutt companion and I thought we had died and gone to heaven! Each day's walk was a new discovery of one more beautiful view designed by God. I was continually astounded at the beauty of God's creation and His sheer inventiveness.

On the other hand, I have stood in enormous cathedrals and marveled at men's abilities to build. I cannot even imagine the untold hours that went into sculpting, fitting tiny mosaics, painting frescoes, piecing stained glass, and painting the many decorations in these places of worship. Yet the churches in Europe are little more than museums full of tourists, instead of vibrant communities of believers. What man builds doesn't last.

What God creates lasts. The sun comes up every day. The flowers bloom each spring. Reminders that He is a continual presence are evident. A neighbor laughed at my delight in the surrounding beauty and said, "Why should nature remind me of God? I don't even think about that!"

Just as God created the nature around us, He also builds the church. I can't bring people to Christ in my own strength. He is the one who creates and transforms life that will last.

—JANET, EUROPEAN PEOPLES

*Lord,* YOUR CREATION STIRS A SENSE OF WONDER AND AWE IN THE BEHOLDER. I ASK TODAY THAT YOU WILL PLACE A HUNGER IN THE HEARTS OF THE PEOPLES OF WESTERN EUROPE TO KNOW THE DESIGNER AND CREATOR OF THE UNIVERSE. PLEASE PLACE IN THEIR PATHS A PERSON WHO CAN SHARE TRUTH WITH THEM. *Amen.*

# The care package that gave

"'For My thoughts are not your thoughts, and your ways are not My ways.' [This is] the LORD's declaration. 'For as heaven is higher than earth, so My ways are higher than your ways, and My thoughts than your thoughts.'" Isaiah 55:8–9 (HCSB)

When we came to South Asia, we expected to see God do a lot. We never expected that He'd use us to change the life of a man back in Tennessee!

When we arrived on the field, our friend, Mary, began to send us monthly care packages filled with goodies. Mary's postmaster often saw her mail the boxes and finally asked her why she sent packages halfway around the world. Mary told him about our work in South Asia.

The postmaster couldn't believe people would leave the comforts of home to serve God, the same God whom his wife had been telling him about for 10 years. He figured there must be something to it and decided to go to church with his wife. At the end of the service, he looked at his wife, who had a smile on her face and tears in her eyes, and knew that he wanted to follow God, too. He squeezed her hand, stood up on his shaking legs, and started toward the front of the church, but made it only about six feet when his knees buckled. With determination, he crawled the rest of the way. The pastor met him, and only then did he realize that his wife was kneeling beside him. The three of them prayed together, and he became a Christian!

—J.D., SOUTH ASIAN PEOPLES

Gratitude FOR YOUR ULTIMATE SACRIFICE, LORD JESUS, COULD NEVER BE ADEQUATELY EXPRESSED WITH WORDS. THANK YOU FOR LEAVING THE PERFECTION OF YOUR HEAVENLY HOME TO COME TO THIS EARTH AND DIE FOR OUR SIN. THANK YOU FOR THE TESTIMONY OF THOSE WHO FOLLOW IN YOUR FOOTSTEPS. Amen.

## A tenderized heart

*"There is an appointed time for everything. And there is a time for every event under heaven ... A time to weep and a time to laugh; a time to mourn and a time to dance." Ecclesiastes 3:1, 4 (NASB)*

"Ben died!" my friend, Sarah, wailed when she called to report the death of her unbelieving brother. I had known Sarah and Ben since living in a remote area years ago, and she was like a daughter to me. Not hesitating, I traveled to the village to be with my friend and offer condolences to the family.

Upon my arrival, Sarah and I embraced as she cried her heart out. We had been praying for her brother, but he was not open to the Gospel, even during his severe illness. What heartache it was for us to know that Ben would be separated from God for all eternity. As Sarah struggled with her grief, two women who had practically raised her began to scold her for crying. But nothing would keep me from continuing to mourn openly with Sarah.

What was the difference between Sarah and these other women? These women had no concept of eternal life, so they couldn't understand the tragedy of dying without Christ. I pray that one day they will all be free to laugh and to cry, to mourn and to dance, and that they will know God, our Comforter.

—S.F., Sub-Saharan African Peoples

*Gentle Father,* PLEASE SHARE WITH ME THE INTENSITY OF YOUR HEART FOR THOSE WHO DO NOT KNOW YOU AS LORD AND SAVIOR. HELP ME TO SHARE YOUR ANGUISH OVER UNREPENTANT SINNERS AND YOUR JOY OVER THOSE WHO LEAVE ALL TO FOLLOW YOU. BRING THE PEOPLE OF THIS REMOTE AREA TO CHRIST. *Amen.*

# One way

*"... I am the way, the truth, and the life: no man cometh unto the Father, but by me." John 14:6 (KJV)*

"Sister, how are you?" asked the woman I sat down next to before the university play started. Being a new missionary, I assumed that this woman was a member of one of our local churches and began to converse with her freely. She was very pleasant and mentioned her relationship with God many times during our conversation. As she spoke, however, I noticed an unusual brooch on her blouse in the image of an African man. I finally gave in to my curiosity and asked, "Who is that?" She excitedly replied, "Oh, I'm so glad you asked. This is the great prophet!" Then she launched into a discourse, which included everything from crystals and reincarnation to yoga and meditation. I listened quietly until she finished and then simply asked, "Ah, Señora, have you ever read the Bible?" She enthusiastically replied, "Of course, I'm Christian!"

Syncretism, or the attempted union of opposing principles, is real not only in South America but all over the world. There is great temptation to give in to the philosophy that all paths lead to God, but Jesus Christ did not believe in compromise or common ground when it came to sharing the truth. God will not share His glory with another. Jesus is the only way to God, the Father.

—LORRI, AMERICAN PEOPLES

*Sovereign God,* THANK YOU FOR SENDING YOUR SON, JESUS, TO EARTH AS THE ONE AND ONLY WAY TO YOU. WE PRAY FOR THOSE WHO DO NOT YET KNOW HIM AS THE EXCLUSIVE WAY TO SALVATION. OPEN THEIR HEARTS TO YOUR LOVE, AND HELP THEM TO UNDERSTAND THAT JESUS IS LORD. *Amen.*

MARCH

## Divine Appointments

*If God's behind it, you'd have a mighty hard time stopping it.*

—BETH MOORE

My flight from Richmond to Atlanta had been delayed by about an hour due to bad weather further south. I wasn't really concerned since I would still have 30 minutes to make my connection in Atlanta to Montgomery, Alabama, where I was to speak the next day at a women's conference. We finally boarded the plane but ended up on the Richmond runway for a while longer. I had carry-on luggage only, and I knew my way around the Atlanta airport, so I still wasn't concerned.

When we finally landed, the Atlanta airport was in turmoil. Apparently areas all over the Deep South were under tornado warnings. When I finally found my boarding gate, which had been changed, it was obvious that I was not going to get to Montgomery that night by plane. The flight had already been delayed twice and when I asked the attendant if he thought it might be delayed longer, he smirked and said, "Probably."

I called the conference organizer in Montgomery to let her know the situation. She and the conference committee were in the bathroom of the church. Tornado warning sirens were going off in their community, and apparently, the bathroom was the safest place to be (made sense to me). I assured her that I would get there even if I had to rent a car and drive through tornadoes. (I was picturing myself in a blue-and-white checked dress with Toto in my bicycle basket.)

While I was talking on my cell phone, a woman was waving at me, trying to get my attention. Finally, I paused my phone conversation and let the woman speak. She said, "I don't mean to be eavesdropping, but my husband and I are going to rent a car and drive to Montgomery. We would be glad to let you ride with us."

Hmm. I didn't know this lady, but she looked nice enough. Why not! I told the lady in Alabama that I was hitching a ride, hung up, and followed this couple down to the rental car stand. In case you're wondering, I did call my husband. He asked me if they looked like ax murderers, and I assured him that they didn't, even though I've never personally met an ax murderer.

As I talked with the woman, she said that she had overheard me say something about my flight from Richmond, and she asked if I lived there. When I said that I did, she shared that her daughter had married a young man whose father worked at the International Mission Board. It turns out that my husband's former boss was this father. We had a lovely chat in the driving rain for the two hours to Montgomery. They only lived one mile from the church, and they wouldn't let me help pay for the rental car.

Out of the thousands of people stranded at the airport, God prompted this woman to offer me a ride. That's just how God is. His Holy Spirit guides us into divine appointments, often totally unexpectedly. It happens on the mission field, too. I remember one such appointment when my husband and our national partner shared Christ with a young man with AIDS. The man accepted God's grace that day and gave his life to Christ. Three days later, someone came to our house to say that the young man had died. He was now in eternity with Jesus.

God's Spirit directs our paths. If we will follow His voice, amazing opportunities will be opened to us. This month, you will read astonishing stories of dreams, "coincidences," and opportunities that only God could orchestrate. Nothing is too difficult or impossible for the Lord.

—*Kim P. Davis*

# Divine appointments

*"I will indeed bless you and make your offspring as numerous as the stars in the sky and the sand on the seashore." Genesis 22:17a (HCSB)*

When my husband and I were newlyweds, he taught me how to scan the seashore for shark's teeth. At first, I wasn't that interested, but after learning the art, I was hooked. What used to be difficult to find became more obvious with practice. And what excitement came for my husband and me when I found a tooth!

Likewise, the Father desires to teach us to recognize His divine appointments. As I stood in front of the bus stop one day, I felt a tap on my shoulder. "Can you help me?" asked a young man who was visiting our city to see art. Living one block from the art district, I told him to get on the bus with me, and I would show him the way.

As I began talking with this young man, the Father gave me an opportunity to share the Gospel and God's love for him. With tears running down his face, he gave his life to Christ on the bus as we prayed.

I never saw him again after he got off at his destination. When I was getting off the bus two stops later, I joyfully looked back to see all the people who might have heard our discussion. God gives us divine opportunities, and He is thrilled and we are blessed when we recognize them.

—S.P., EAST ASIAN PEOPLES

*Heavenly Father,* TRAIN ME TO RECOGNIZE YOUR DIVINE APPOINTMENTS. GIVE ME COURAGE. I PRAY FOR THOSE WHOM I WILL ENCOUNTER. MAY YOUR SPIRIT ALREADY BE DRAWING THEM TO YOURSELF. *Amen.*

# *Directing my paths*

*"Trust in the LORD with all your heart, and lean not on your own under-standing; in all your ways acknowledge Him, and He shall direct your paths."*
*Proverbs 3:5–6 (NKJV)*

Proverbs 3:5–6 have been my life verses for many years. I can recite them, sing them, and mop to them. Even though I truly try to live by them, I sometimes forget that the verses say, "He *shall* direct my paths." They don't say, "He *might*." It is a promise I can count on—always!

I am a planner who likes to have all my ducks in a row. It doesn't matter if I am writing a lesson plan, organizing a training seminar, or preparing for a volunteer team; I make a plan. My plans keep me focused and help me accomplish my goals.

I believe God is the ultimate plan maker. In these verses, He gives me an action plan that will work in every circumstance: (1) Trust Him completely, even when my ducks aren't in a row; (2) Lean on Him totally, even when I think my plans are great; and (3) Acknowledge Him fully, even when I'm tempted to take the credit for plans that wonderfully accomplished their objectives.

God's directions are infinitely better than mine. He will steer me on the right course at the proper time. I choose to believe His promise to direct my paths wherever I am. I choose to follow His action plan that enables me to understand and follow His directions.

—SYD, SOUTH ASIAN PEOPLES

*Promise Keeper,* HELP ME WALK IN INTIMATE FELLOWSHIP WITH YOU TODAY. THANK YOU THAT EVERY PROMISE IN SCRIPTURE IS AVAILABLE TO ME. PREPARE MY HEART TO RECEIVE AND RESPOND TO THE GREAT TRUTHS YOU HAVE PREPARED FOR ME. *Amen.*

# The right direction

*"Commit your way to the LORD; trust in him, and he will act."* Psalm 37:5 (ESV)

Samson is a humble man who listens to God's voice and is obedient in sharing the Gospel. One day, he felt God leading him to go to a town several miles away. Having no money for transportation, he walked through the bush. At one point, he stopped to ask if he was headed in the right direction. The man he spoke with was courteous and surprisingly spoke his dialect. After talking for a while, Samson simply presented the message of salvation and the man put his faith in Christ. Afterward, the new believer suggested that Samson go to a nearby village to share the Good News. What a divine appointment! Because Samson listened to God's voice and obeyed Him, he had the opportunity to witness not just to one man, but later to many others who also gave their lives to Christ.

Samson is our student. Our role as teachers in an academic setting has given us the opportunity to learn valuable lessons of faithfulness and obedience as we have labored side-by-side with our students. Their commitment has often reminded us of the importance of listening to God's voice and being obedient to Him. I wonder how many divine appointments I have missed simply because I didn't listen to God's voice. As I continually commit myself to God's service, I must listen to and obey Him as Samson did.

—DENE, SUB-SAHARAN AFRICAN PEOPLES

*Father,* HELP ME SAY TODAY WITH FULL OBEDIENCE, "SPEAK, LORD, FOR YOUR SERVANT IS LISTENING." FORGIVE ME WHEN I FAIL TO HEED YOUR VOICE. I WAIT WITH A READY AND EAGER HEART FOR YOUR DIRECTION. *Amen.*

# Pretty feet

*"How will they preach unless they are sent? Just as it is written, 'HOW BEAUTI-FUL ARE THE FEET OF THOSE WHO BRING GOOD NEWS OF GOOD THINGS!'"*
Romans 10:15 (NASB)

Even though I live in a large city, it's still a challenge to meet women since public areas are predominantly full of Muslim men. However, one day while shopping, two store employees kept glancing at me. Eventually, one woman said, "You have really pretty feet."

Since moving to South Asia, I have had a skin allergy, and my feet haven't been pretty at all. In my head, I heard my mom saying, "Because you love telling people about Jesus, your pretty little feet remind me of Romans 10."

As the woman rang up my purchases, she commented, "Oh, we made you self-conscious." I giggled and said, "No, I am follower of Jesus and the Bible says, 'How beautiful are the feet of those who bring Good News.'" With a puzzled grin, she replied, "Maybe so."

Leaving the shop, I felt that I must give the woman the Good News. In my car, I had a hot pink bag containing a Bible and tract. I grabbed it and returned to the store. As I greeted her again, I said, "I had these in my car. This booklet is about Jesus, and this Holy Book is Good News. Would you like them?" As she took the Bible and tract, she kissed my cheek.

No matter the condition, God uses our feet to take the Gospel to the lost.

—PIPER, SOUTH ASIAN PEOPLES

*I ask today,* FATHER, THAT YOU GUIDE THE STEPS OF OUR MISSIONARIES. LEAD THEM TO THE PLACES YOU WOULD HAVE THEM GO. FILL EACH ONE WITH YOUR SPIRIT THAT THEY MAY BOLDLY FOLLOW IN YOUR FOOTSTEPS AND SPEAK YOUR WORDS. BRING SALVATION TO THE WOMAN WHO RECEIVED THIS BIBLE. *Amen.*

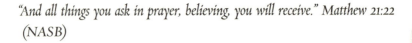

# The voice of the Holy Spirit

*"And all things you ask in prayer, believing, you will receive."* Matthew 21:22
(NASB)

The drug cartel had seemingly taken over the Mexican coastal city, and we didn't know how to reach the men with the Good News. With a small team of volunteers, we set out to prayerwalk and distribute the Gospel. We prayed outside each home, asking God to reveal to us men who were ready to hear His salvation message.

As we left one home, a group of drunken men began brawling in a neighboring yard. I quickly decided that we would cross the street and return later. We walked away, but my heart grew heavy with conviction. Had we not asked God to lead us to seeking men? I had passed by 10 men without ever considering their spiritual condition. If I didn't share the Lord with them, who would?

Accompanied by volunteers, I returned to speak with the group. Some made crude comments, but others listened. One man seemed drawn to us, and over the next two days, we were given repeated opportunities to speak with him. God placed him in homes we visited, and we saw him on the street and at his place of employment. A few days later, this man gave his life to the Lord and opened the door of his home for a Bible study location. How thankful we are for the sweet voice of the Holy Spirit, who guides us.

—SHERI, AMERICAN PEOPLES

*Blessed Redeemer,* THANK YOU THAT AN ENCOUNTER WITH YOU CHANGES A LIFE FOR-EVER. EMPOWER YOUR CHOSEN VESSELS IN MEXICO WHO KNOW YOU AS LORD AND SAVIOR. ENABLE THEM TO BE STEADFAST, OBEDIENT, AND DEVOTED TO YOUR WILL. *Amen.*

# Jonah and the goose

*"But Jonah got up and went in the opposite direction to get away from the
LORD ..." Jonah 1:3 (NLT)*

I love my daily walks around a nearby lake. It's my time to be alone with
God.

One evening as I strolled, I noticed a woman who was staring at
the quiet water. *Go speak to her!* I heard God say to my heart. *Are you
kidding, Lord?* I asked Him. *She'll think I'm weird.* I continued on my route,
unhindered. Every time I passed the woman, God kept impressing me
to speak. I developed a new excuse each time. *She wants to be alone!* or
*She'll think I'm a thief.* Then, *I don't know what to say.* Finally, *Lord, this is my quiet
time! I will not go to her!*

Suddenly, a huge, angry goose jumped into my path, hissing and as-
saulting my knees with its beak, pushing me back down the trail. Before
he could swallow me and spit me out like Jonah's whale, I retreated to
where the woman sat. I'm sure the goose smirked!

"Lovely evening, isn't it?" I asked. She looked up and shook her head
slowly, "Not really." I gently said, "This might sound absurd, but God
wants you to know how much He loves you." Tears spilled from her
eyes as she sobbed. I embraced her and prayed with her. Later, she left
with new hope. She told me her name, but all I heard was "Nineveh."

—JODY, CENTRAL ASIAN PEOPLES

*Father,* ALLOW ME TO SEE MYSELF AS YOU SEE ME, UNCOMFORTABLE AS IT MAY BE. I ASK
YOUR FORGIVENESS FOR MY WILLFUL DISOBEDIENCE. CREATE IN ME A CLEAN HEART, OH
GOD, AND RENEW A RIGHT SPIRIT WITHIN ME. *Amen.*

# Noticing the insignificant

*"... 'The kingdom of heaven is like a mustard seed, ... which indeed is the least of all the seeds; but when it is grown it is greater than the herbs and becomes a tree, so that the birds of the air come and nest in its branches.'" Matthew 13:31–32 (NKJV)*

While walking through a small village, two national brothers and I asked God to lead us to someone receptive to the Gospel. Soon, we saw two boys on the mountainside waving and yelling for us to eat mangoes with them. I thought, *We don't have time to eat mangoes with boys; we have to find who God has prepared us to meet!* But then the Spirit moved in our hearts, and we went.

Arriving, we realized the children had led us to the home of a large family. We enjoyed their mangoes and shared the Gospel. Afterward, the father commented, "How would we have ever known of Jesus if you hadn't come?" One of those who came to Christ that day was their adult son, an alcoholic. Through this man, almost 20 people now have come to faith in Jesus. In this village, three Bible study groups and one church have started.

Many times we pass by what seems to be insignificant. God's ways aren't our ways. His plans for us can be in the seemingly insignificant things of life. We just have to slow down enough to let God's Spirit work in our lives so that we can help nurture the mustard seeds.

—ARCHER, SOUTH ASIAN PEOPLES

*Nothing* IS TOO DIFFICULT OR IMPOSSIBLE FOR YOU, LORD OF THE HARVEST. REMIND ME DAILY TO ACT ON MY FAITH, AS INSIGNIFICANT AS IT MAY SEEM, AND WAIT ON YOU TO POWERFULLY MULTIPLY THE LOAVES AND FISHES. *Amen.*

## Passing the test

*"... I permitted Myself to be found by those who did not seek Me. I said, 'Here am I, here am I,' to a nation which did not call on My name." Isaiah 65:1b (NASB)*

The day arrived for my driving test. After two months of lessons, I was ready, after driving safely in America for over 40 years. I was encouraged by my husband, who had passed his test a week earlier. He told me that his examiner was very understanding of "mature" drivers. I prayed that "Mr. H" would be my examiner.

As we began, I silently thanked God that Mr. H was my examiner. He mentioned that I was the third American he had tested in the past two weeks. When I mentioned my husband's name, he remembered him. As we drove, Mr. H asked several questions that allowed me to use the Bible to answer. He asked, "Are you one of those born-again Christians?" We got into a serious spiritual discussion. After 20 minutes, we went back to the testing office. We returned so soon that my husband thought I had failed the test.

Mr. H told me that I had passed. Then I told him about my prayers that he would be my examiner. With tears in his eyes, he asked me to pray for him. He had hurt someone and wanted to mend it. After praying, we exchanged phone numbers.

As our friendship developed, Mr. H decided to trust in Jesus. He had not been looking, but God opened the way for his salvation.

—COLLEEN, EUROPEAN PEOPLES

*The prayers* OF THOSE WHO TRUST YOU, HOLY ONE, AVAIL MUCH. CONDITION MY HEART TO CONSISTENTLY COMMUNICATE WITH YOU. GIVE ME GRACE AND WISDOM TO SHOW AND SHARE YOUR LOVE TODAY. *Amen.*

# Offer of help brings friendship

*"I know, O LORD, that a man's way is not in himself, nor is it in a man who walks to direct his steps." Jeremiah 10:23 (NASB)*

With six days of language school under our belts, my teammate and I ventured out to an international agricultural fair. As we wandered around trying to find tickets, we saw a Muslim teenager carrying fresh bread. Through extremely broken French and Arabic, we asked her where we could purchase a ticket. With great hospitality, she adopted us for the day. We found tickets and then accompanied her to deliver the bread to her mother's house, where she picked up her purse and her English/Arabic dictionary.

"Fatima" was a bubbly girl who constantly chatted. We were led to various family members' homes. My teammate and I were soon separated for the majority of the afternoon. Fatima offered a late lunch with her family, postponing my plans for the fair. Leaving my teammate at the cousin's house, I was ushered back to Fatima's family home. And we had met her only an hour before!

The afternoon was a picture of the Lord taking over my plans and blessing me abundantly. I met new friends, got a lesson in culture, practiced language skills, prayed over a national home, and I received an intense reminder that this life is not my own.

—K.B., NORTHERN AFRICAN AND MIDDLE EASTERN PEOPLES

*It is evident daily,* EVER-PRESENT ONE, THAT MY WAYS ARE NOT YOUR WAYS. HELP ME KEEP MY HEART AND SCHEDULE OPEN TO YOUR GUIDANCE. I PRAISE YOU THAT YOU KNOW THE PLANS YOU HAVE FOR ME. I DESIRE TO OBEY. BRING FATIMA AND HER FAMILY INTO YOUR KINGDOM. *Amen.*

# Blessed interruptions

*"Peter went down to the men and said, 'Behold, I am the one you are looking for; what is the reason for which you have come?'" Acts 10:21 (NASB)*

*Oh no,* I thought when I noticed a man and woman riding up our driveway on a motorcycle. That morning, we'd finished our last session at our training facility, and I was exhausted.

"Hello! Can I help you?" I called down from our second-story window.

"We have come from a long way and were told that people in this place could tell us about Jesus," the woman yelled from our front yard. Okay, so how could I ignore that?

I asked the kids to seat our guests on the patio. I looked at the food our helper had prepared and noticed two plates of meatballs instead of one! There was a huge mound of mashed potatoes and a large fruit salad. I quickly prepared plates for this couple and called one of our national staff to join us for lunch.

Sitting with the couple, I learned that the wife had become a Christian years before, but there was no one to tell her more. They lived on a remote mountain top in a poor village. Two hours later, the woman was joyfully baptized in our fish pond. She jumped from the water saying that this was the best day of her life, and she was excited to tell her village about Jesus.

Blessed interruptions are gifts from the Father for His beloved disciples.

—Hope, East Asian Peoples

*Heavenly Father,* give me the ability to open my home on a moment's notice for your glory. Give missionaries many opportunities to welcome others, even when it's not convenient. *Amen.*

# It is worth it

*"Who knows, perhaps you have come to the kingdom for such a time as this."*
Esther 4:14b (HCSB)

Walking to the store, I noticed a young woman who unsuccessfully tried to ask directions from a man on the street. The Holy Spirit prompted me to catch up with her. When I did, I asked if she needed help. She replied, "Thank God, you speak English!" The woman was from a nearby Muslim country and had just moved to South Asia. She was looking for the store where she had purchased a refrigerator.

I could relate to her being in an unfamiliar place, so I spent the next few hours helping her find the appliance store, shopping for groceries, and eventually walking her home. When we arrived at her apartment, I sensed the opportunity to tell my personal faith story. Then I asked her if I could tell her another story. She attentively listened as I told the biblical account of Christ healing the demon-possessed man. I shared with her that the man in the story was alone. Jesus changed his life, and he was never alone again. I asked her if she would like Jesus to change her life, too. To my joy, she prayed and asked Him to change her. She sent me a text message later saying, "Thank you, I am praying to Jesus tonight!" If God had brought me to this foreign land just to tell this woman about Jesus, it was worth everything!

—MISTY, SOUTH ASIAN PEOPLES

*Lord of all,* YOU PROMISE THAT IF I ASK, YOU WILL SHOW ME GREAT AND MIGHTY THINGS THAT I COULD NEVER IMAGINE. EMPOWER AND LEAD ME TO LOVINGLY AND BOLDLY SHARE THE GOSPEL WITH SOMEONE TODAY. STRENGTHEN THIS FORMER MUSLIM WOMAN IN HER NEW FAITH. *Amen.*

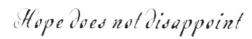

## Hope does not disappoint

*"and hope does not disappoint, because the love of God has been poured out within our hearts through the Holy Spirit who was given to us." Romans 5:5 (NASB)*

As the plane took off, I was anxious to transpose music on my laptop. I asked the stewardess, "May I use my computer now?" To my surprise, the lady next to me spoke English and complimented my Chinese.

I found out she had lived in Canada but had returned to China to run a factory. Trying to turn the conversation to spiritual things, I asked, "Did you go to a church in Canada?" "Yes," she responded, "but I am not a Christian." The subject changed, and then she fell asleep. I prayed that I would have another chance to talk and began working on my computer.

When she woke, she was intrigued that I was transposing music, so I offered to let her listen. "It's beautiful," she said. "What does it mean?" I explained that my music reflected that even when I have a bad day, I can talk to God, and He gives me joy. I then shared God's story from creation to Christ in Chinese. She asked a few questions, but I could sense she was ready. "Would you like to follow Christ?"

"I believe what you've said is true, and I want Jesus to save me." The plane descended as we prayed. I left the airport rejoicing in the power of the Holy Spirit and my hope in Him.

—GRACE, EAST ASIAN PEOPLES

*You are faithful,* FATHER, TO GIVE ME DIVINE APPOINTMENTS TO SHARE YOUR WORD DAILY. HELP ME TO EXPECT AND RESPOND TO OPPORTUNITIES YOU PLACE IN MY PATH. I WAIT EXPECTANTLY BEFORE YOU. ENCOURAGE THIS CHINESE WOMAN TO BE IN YOUR WORD DAILY. *Amen.*

# God's Detour

*"How narrow is the gate and difficult the road that leads to life, and few find it."*
Matthew 7:14 (HCSB)

Gripping their seats as the truck struggled on the road, the volunteers watched as the sheets of rain fell. None had ever been to Mali before, and only a Bambara translator accompanied them. Suddenly, the truck got stuck in the mud. When the men tried to push the vehicle, it wouldn't budge.

They had been trying to reach the village where a new church was growing. But as the sun set and the rain continued, they knew plans were changing. With no cell phone reception, they helplessly looked to their translator, who suggested trudging to the nearest village. Holding luggage above their heads, the team walked over a mile to a village. The villagers greeted the dripping strangers with hot tea, a warm meal, and a dry hut in which to spend the night.

A few days later, the team returned to share the Gospel. Six Bambara men accepted Christ. One convert said, "My grandfather was a Christian but was the only believer. When he died years ago, we lost the road to God. For months, we've seen your groups drive by our village. Your people were not thinking of us, but God was. He said, *Enough!* and stopped your truck in the mud so that we could find the road to Him again."

—SUSAN, SUB-SAHARAN AFRICAN PEOPLES

*Holy One,* GUIDE ME TO BE SENSITIVE TO UNSCHEDULED INTERRUPTIONS IN MY AGENDA, AND HELP ME RESPOND TO YOUR PROMPTINGS. EMPOWER BAMBARA BELIEVERS TO BOLDLY SHARE YOUR TRUTH TODAY. *Amen.*

# Drawing power of the Holy Spirit

*"There is salvation in no one else, for there is no other name under heaven given to people by which we must be saved." Acts 4:12 (HCSB)*

It was the first session of our evangelism training at a particular location in East Asia. We usually asked that believers invite nonbelievers to attend, but out of 25, there was only one nonbeliever in our first session.

As an example for the class, I shared my personal testimony of becoming a Christian before I asked them to write their own. As I finished sharing the Gospel, I remembered the one lady who didn't know Jesus. I asked her if she wanted to follow my Jesus, too. She exclaimed, "Thank you, yes!" The whole class was thrilled upon seeing the work of the Holy Spirit.

She then explained that her husband's family was Christian, but she was now going to be the first Christian in her side of the family. As we prayed, I realized that God not only desired to save this wonderful lady but also wanted to illustrate the drawing power of the Holy Spirit to the class.

In addition, I was able to emphasize that we should always give people the opportunity to receive God's gift of salvation. He wants us to be sensitive to His Spirit and to be looking for those He is drawing into His kingdom.

—JIM, EAST ASIAN PEOPLES

*Father,* MY HEART BURNS WITHIN AS YOUR SPIRIT SPEAKS. I WORSHIP YOU FOR DRAWING ME TO YOURSELF. MAKE YOUR TRUTHS IRRESISTIBLE TO THOSE WHO ARE SEEKING YOU TODAY. *Amen.*

# *Attentive to the Spirit*

*"Keep asking, and it will be given to you. Keep searching, and you will find. Keep knocking, and the door will be opened to you." Matthew 7:7 (HCSB)*

*Lord, please guide me today to the one who needs to hear from You,* I prayed as I entered the hospital where I worked as a volunteer. As I passed a hospital room, a young man was pacing. I felt like God wanted me to enter. With a smile on my face, I asked if he would like a magazine to read, my usual line to make conversation. He declined the offer as well as all other attempts to converse.

I started to leave, but the Holy Spirit impressed me to offer the patient a Bible. Silently I asked, *Are You sure, Lord? The administration can take my visiting privileges away.* But in obedience, I asked the man, "Would you like to read a Bible?" Surprisingly, he replied, "Yes, I would like a Bible." Taking my small Bible out of my purse, I handed it to him with the promise that I would return with one in his own language.

He told me that he was a European immigrant on a waiting list for a liver transplant, and he was running out of time. He believed there was a God and was asking God to help him. My husband later led this young man to Christ after more study in the Word, and after a week, the Lord gave this young man a liver transplant.

—DORCAS, EUROPEAN PEOPLES

*Father,* GRANT ME COURAGE TO RESPOND TO THE PROMPTING OF YOUR SPIRIT AND HELP ME BE PREPARED TO GIVE A CLEAR WITNESS OF YOUR TRANSFORMING LOVE. BLESS THOSE WHO ARE SEEKING AND RESPONDING TO YOU TODAY. *Amen.*

# *Following the Spirit*

*"Indeed, the LORD will give what is good, and our land will yield its produce.
Righteousness will go before Him and will make His footsteps into a way."*
*Psalm 85:12–13 (NASB)*

"My job is to take you around my village; your job is to tell your stories," the head man of the village informed the two volunteers and me. In the past, this village had been closed to the Gospel. At the top of the mountain where the head man had made his declaration, we sat on a cot, his relatives looking at us expectantly. So we began to share stories from God's Word.

After two stories, he asked if he could translate more specifically to his family. He started to retell the story but decided to tell the creation story. Before we knew it, he was telling about Abraham and continued through the Old and New Testaments. When he told about the death of Jesus, he stretched out his arms as he explained what Jesus did on the cross. Triumphantly, he yelled out, "And three days later, He was alive again!" Tears came to my eyes as I looked at the faces of his family and the boldness of this man. The truth that was shared that day was not because of my presence in that village but because the Spirit was at work in this man's life.

It is comforting to know that the Spirit goes before us and leads the way.

—ELLIE, SOUTH ASIAN PEOPLES

*Constant Companion,* THANK YOU THAT YOU GO BEFORE YOUR MESSENGERS TO OPEN HEARTS AND PREPARE THE WAY. ANOINT AND EMPOWER BELIEVERS IN SOUTH ASIA WHO ARE BOLDLY PROCLAIMING THE MESSAGE OF SALVATION. *Amen.*

# Airplane opportunities

*"Walk in wisdom toward outsiders, making the most of the time."* Colossians 4:5 (HCSB)

I sat down in my window seat for the last leg of my flight to Prague. Heading back after spending a week in Texas to be a bridesmaid in my best friend's wedding, I was exhausted and looked forward to sleeping the last couple of travel hours.

Years ago, a minister challenged me to pray for the passengers who would be occupying the seats around me and to share Christ if the opportunity arose. Since then, I try to interact with fellow travelers and share God's love. However, sometimes I'd rather reach my destination unnoticed.

As I debated whether to close my eyes or wait to see who would sit next to me, a girl set her bags down. We made eye contact and shared a smile. She looked about my age and had an unusually warm disposition.

Although my body ached for rest, the minister's challenge spurred me to introduce myself. Soon Petra and I were sharing stories about our recent trips, and I learned that she was a high school English teacher. We discovered that I live around the corner from her parents!

Not long after, Petra came to dinner. We had a great time. I praise God for His timely challenges, for being the ultimate networker, and for allowing me to meet this new Czech friend with a need for Jesus.

—NATALIE, EUROPEAN PEOPLES

*Lord,* YOU ARE THE ONE WHO OPENS DOORS AND PREPARES HEARTS TO BE RECEPTIVE. FORGIVE ME WHEN I IGNORE THE PROMPTINGS OF YOUR SPIRIT. HELP ME TO BE FAITHFUL TO SHARE YOUR LOVE TODAY. *Amen.*

## *A still, small voice*

*"And after the earthquake a fire; but the* Lord *was not in the fire: and after the fire a still small voice." 1 Kings 19:12 (KJV)*

What was I doing in East Asia? I'd watched good things happen, but I wondered many times if I was really making a difference. All I could hear were the shouts of the enemy telling me that what I was doing didn't matter.

Then I noticed something. The times when I actually stopped and let myself be still, there was a faint voice speaking to my heart. It was hard to hear, but when I let myself be still, I could hear it clearly. It was surrounded by peace, a strong peace beyond words. That still, small voice was saying, *This is where you are supposed to be.*

I knew with complete certainty that I could trust that voice. No matter how loud the shouts of the enemy grew, I knew I could listen to and believe God's Spirit. It was the voice of my Lord assuring me that He had called me to this place. Even though I didn't understand why He had brought me here or what all I needed to be doing, I knew that this was where I needed to be.

Trusting God to divinely appoint us to reach out to others starts with listening to Him. When things get rough, I remind myself that the shouts of the enemy aren't true. God's voice is truth.

—Peikou, East Asian Peoples

*Draw me to Yourself,* Lord, in silence, solitude, and surrender. Help me to hear Your voice above the clamor of the urgent and to respond immediately to Your divine direction. *Amen.*

# Alternate opportunity

*"Your ears will hear a word behind you, 'This is the way, walk in it,' whenever you turn to the right or to the left." Isaiah 30:21 (NASB)*

As I drove my truck from the Fulani village, the African pastor and I didn't know what to think. The village chief had seemed friendly at first, but we soon learned that he was a witch doctor and very much against our visits to share the Gospel.

Then I noticed a young girl on the side of the road waving to us. When I stopped, she asked, "Do you want to see another Fulani village?" "Sure," I replied, as she got in the vehicle. After 30 minutes of paths that had never seen a truck, we arrived. The men of the village were out with the cattle, but the chief and his three wives seemed excited about our visit. A week later, we showed the *JESUS* film in Fulani and the response was amazing!

"It's so easy to accept Jesus when you can hear about Him in your own language," said the chief's blind father. "Since we are Fulani, we thought we had to be Muslim." I assured him that Jesus loves the Fulanis, too.

God changed our original plans and opened up a thriving ministry in a different village. An African pastor now teaches in this first Christian Fulani village in the area, and the chief is eager to see other villages come to Christ. I have learned to watch for the unexpected.

—LIN, SUB-SAHARAN AFRICAN PEOPLES

*God of the harvest,* YOU ARE ALWAYS AT WORK DRAWING PEOPLE TO YOURSELF. REMIND ME TODAY TO BE FLEXIBLE AND PREPARED TO FOLLOW YOUR LEADERSHIP WHEN PLANS CHANGE AND NEW OPPORTUNITIES ARISE. *Amen.*

# A mountain encounter

*"O come, let us worship and bow down: let us kneel before the LORD our maker.
For he is our God; and we are the people of his pasture, and the sheep of his
hand." Psalm 95:6–7 (KJV)*

When my teammate and I agreed to trek throughout one of the mountain passes of South Asia to meet Muslim women, we didn't exactly know what to expect. By late afternoon, we were utterly exhausted as we came into a village. The locals took pity on us and invited us in for a cup of tea.

Judging from our surroundings, it didn't take long to realize that we were among the poorest of the poor. Though they didn't have much, their warm smiles assured us that we were guests of honor. As we visited, the setting was perfect for a story from God's Word. Using our guide as a translator, I shared one of the many stories of Jesus' healings. Afterward, we asked them how we could pray for them before we continued on our way. One of the young mothers replied, "Yes, please pray that we'll know how to get to heaven." Since we weren't exactly expecting God to drop this spiritual bombshell into our laps, it took us a moment to recover! My teammate told her personal spiritual journey and explained that the path to heaven was through Jesus Christ alone.

God is faithful to the ends of the earth. In return, He only asks that I be faithful in my walk with Him.

—SARAH, SOUTH ASIAN PEOPLES

*Father Creator,* THANK YOU THAT THE HEAVENS DECLARE YOUR GLORY AND THE SKIES PROCLAIM THE WORK OF YOUR HANDS. THANK YOU THAT ETERNITY IS ON THE HEARTS OF ALL PEOPLE. HELP MISSIONARIES TO CLEARLY SHARE THE WAY OF SALVATION TO SOUTH ASIAN PEOPLES. *Amen.*

# A timely delivery

*"Listen! Consider the sower who went out to sow ... Still others fell on good ground and produced a crop that increased 30, 60, and 100 times [what was sown]." Mark 4:3, 8 (HCSB)*

A volunteer team was partnering with us to plant a church in an unreached area of Zambia. As one group was prayerwalking, they met a young lady who was interested, but she didn't have time to talk, so the team gave her a tract.

That night, she read the tract in her home and believed the Gospel. She wanted to find the visitors, but they had left town. On the back of the tract she found an address for the North American Mission Board (NAMB). She wrote a letter explaining that she had accepted Jesus as her Savior and wanted to be baptized before she died from AIDS.

In the weeks of follow-up after the team left, we decided to send out letters inviting new believers to a Bible study. On the very day that we were writing the invitations, a letter arrived from NAMB. Enclosed was the note from this young woman. Excitedly, we sent her an invitation. She came, was baptized, and is now a faithful church member. Although she knows she will die from AIDS, she is filled with joy as a new Christian.

As the parable of the sower teaches, there will be some seeds that fall on good soil. Our responsibility is to sow the seed. God's responsibility is to open up hearts to receive the Gospel.

—WES AND LAURIE, SUB-SAHARAN AFRICAN PEOPLES

*Faithful Father,* YOUR TIMING IS ALWAYS PRECISE. PLEASE OPEN HEARTS AND EMPOWER THOSE WHO GO OUT TODAY IN YOUR NAME TO SOW SEEDS OF THE GOSPEL. I PRAY FOR A FRUITFUL HARVEST OF SOULS. *Amen.*

# Understanding from the Spirit

*"So will My word be which goes forth from My mouth; it will not return to Me empty, without accomplishing what I desire, and without succeeding in the matter for which I sent it." Isaiah 55:11 (NASB)*

Living in an Islamic country, one has to be creative in passing on truth. One time, I was speaking with two girls who wanted to work on their English skills. They asked me what I liked about living in their country. "This place has a strong biblical history," I replied. Seeing that they were intrigued, I asked them if they would like to study the Bible in order to learn about these places in their country. They both quickly agreed.

God provided an opportunity. At the end of our first lesson, I asked them if they would like to have a Bible of their own. With Bibles in hand, they left excited. Sometime later, one of them said, "I have been reading the Bible, but I don't understand what it means." We opened the Bible together and looked at the particular passage to which she was referring. After interpreting the passage, I explained that because I follow Jesus, He helps me to understand His Word.

How thankful I am that Jesus teaches me how to understand His truth and gives opportunities to share His truth with others.

—V., NORTHERN AFRICAN AND MIDDLE EASTERN PEOPLES

*Almighty God,* YOU ALONE CAN REMOVE THE VEIL THAT COVERS A HEART. PLEASE OPEN THE SPIRITUAL EYES OF PEOPLE IN CLOSED ISLAMIC COUNTRIES, AND REMOVE BARRIERS THAT HINDER THEIR UNDERSTANDING OF TRUTH. *Amen.*

# Dreams fulfilled

*"As soon as Gideon heard the telling of the dream and its interpretation, he worshiped. And he returned to the camp of Israel and said, 'Arise, for the LORD has given the host of Midian into your hand.'" Judges 7:15 (ESV)*

I rarely remember dreaming, and when I do, I usually don't remember the details. I haven't put much stock in dreams, until now.

Although my wife and I serve at a seminary in Ghana, we felt drawn to the villages to do chronological Bible storying. One Sunday, accompanied by our friend Joseph, we traveled to the Kasulyili village to worship at a small church. The pastor was surprised to see us and issued an invitation for me to preach. I declined, but he pressured Joseph to plead with me, and I relented. When Joseph introduced me, a young man stood and declared that he had been praying that God would send someone to show them how to reach nonbelievers. He told of his dream where God sent two people to the church, and God told him in the dream to listen to the people because He had sent them. The young man said, "Today my prayers are answered; the dream is fulfilled."

I told three Bible stories that they could remember and share. I urged them to go and tell. In Judges 7, Gideon was encouraged when God spoke to him through someone's dream. You never know when the Holy Spirit may have a word of encouragement for you, even through the dream of someone else.

—PASCAL, SUB-SAHARAN AFRICAN PEOPLES

*Give me eyes* TO SEE AND EARS TO HEAR WHAT YOU ARE SAYING TO ME, HOLY FATHER. MAKE ME ATTENTIVE AND OBEDIENT TO YOUR WORD THAT MAY COME THROUGH SOMEONE YOU PLACE IN MY PATH TODAY. *Amen.*

# *Obeying the nudge*

*"But you shall speak My words to them whether they listen or not, for they are rebellious." Ezekiel 2:7 (NASB)*

People use the illustration of picking up rocks to describe the work of a missionary in Eastern Europe. While this idea can encourage workers who daily face rejection of the Gospel, I confess I let the analogy dampen my excitement for witnessing.

One afternoon, I took a break from working in our business office to walk in the park. On my way back, I passed a young boy sitting at the park's entrance. The Spirit urged me to talk to him, but I resisted. *I have to get back to work,* I reasoned and continued on my way.

Yet as I walked, my thoughts remained with the boy. I turned and still saw him still sitting. In reluctant obedience, I walked back, my Bible in hand.

I met Pavel, a 15-year-old Czech who said he hated Jesus, although he could not tell me anything about Him. I shared with Pavel how much God loves him, even if he doesn't believe in Him, and how He wants all people to know His Son, Jesus, who died for him.

I don't know if I will ever get to talk to Pavel again, but I continue to pray for him and rejoice in the way God does not give up on me. He is faithful to use me for His glory, even when I am reluctant and weak.

—NATALIE, EUROPEAN PEOPLES

*Lord,* YOU PROMISE THAT YOUR WORD WILL NOT RETURN TO YOU VOID. HELP ME TO COURAGEOUSLY SHARE YOUR TRUTH. I ASK THAT YOUR WORD WILL PRODUCE A HARVEST IN THE LIVES OF PEOPLE IN EASTERN EUROPE TODAY, AND I SPECIFICALLY PRAY THAT PAVEL WILL TRUST IN YOU. *Amen.*

# Person of peace

*"If a son of peace is there, your peace will rest on him; but if not, it will return to you." Luke 10:6 (HCSB)*

Not one connection. I sat in the hot university cafeteria for more than an hour but failed miserably at starting conversations with students. Disappointed, I headed for the train station.

On the platform, I placed myself between two girls, beginning a conversation with the girl on my right. Between Yuki's questions and my answers, I told her that God loves the Japanese. She said, "You mean, even with our yellow skin and black hair and eyes?" I assured Yuki that all are precious in His sight and offered her a Bible and a chance to meet with her on campus.

Meanwhile, the girl on my left, Haru, was listening but not conversing. We all got onto the train together, but Yuki got off at the first stop. I was praying about how to approach the other girl, who was standing near me, when she said in English, "I would like to talk to you." I hurriedly gave her my card and asked her to contact me. Later that day, she texted me a message.

A month later, I finally had lunch with Haru and another student. As a result, these two women are studying the Bible with me. God encouraged my obedience by giving me Haru, a new person of peace. In my initial failure, God made a way through a divine appointment.

—NANCY, EAST ASIAN PEOPLES

*In spite of* THE DOUBTS THAT ASSAIL ME, YOU REMIND ME, FATHER, THAT YOU ARE PREPARING PEOPLE OF PEACE TO OPEN DOORS OF OPPORTUNITY. HELP ME TO BE SENSITIVE AND RESPOND DAILY TO JOIN YOU IN YOUR MASTER PLAN. MAKE YOURSELF REAL TO YUKI, HARU, AND THIS OTHER STUDENT. *Amen.*

# Planned and unplanned witnessing

*"We can make our plans, but the LORD determines our steps."* Proverbs 16:9 (NLT)

As an extrovert, most would think that witnessing is easy for me. That isn't the case. To keep me accountable, I schedule it in my busy week.

I was able to schedule three days dedicated to sharing the Gospel. It began with an early phone call from a volunteer team stranded at the airport. The airline went bankrupt while they were on a mission trip, so I had to purchase new tickets by phone. I arranged alternate domestic tickets and then connected with "Sharon" for the international tickets. When arrangements were finalized, I said, "Praise the Lord!" Sharon responded warmly, and I was able to share about the team. I told her I would pray for her.

The second day I helped a friend move boxes from a shipping company to his apartment. While we were loading the car, employees began asking us questions. We were able to give them Gospel tracts and exchanged phone numbers. A few hours later, a coworker and I asked two guys how to connect to a local Wi-Fi network. We again gave tracts and an invitation to meet. The third day, I shared the Gospel with the man who does our printing.

In my scheduled witnessing time, God provided unplanned witnessing opportunities. God arranges divine appointments; our job is to keep alert.

—ANDY, EUROPEAN PEOPLES

*Lord,* YOUR WORD COMMANDS AND INVITES ME TO MAKE DISCIPLES AS I GO ABOUT MY DAILY TASKS. QUICKEN MY HEART AND THE HEARTS OF OUR MISSIONARIES TO BE RESPONSIVE TO THE OPPORTUNITIES YOU PLACE BEFORE US. *Amen.*

# Ready for a witness

*"And let us not grow weary while doing good, for in due season we shall reap if we do not lose heart." Galatians 6:9 (NKJV)*

After a year of no breakthroughs, we packed up again to take the Gospel to an Amazon tribal group that had shown little interest in our message. A colleague and I rode the bus to a river port, hoping to hire a canoe to take us upriver to our destination. When we arrived at the port, there were no canoes. Mike had given a Gospel tract to a fellow passenger, so with our new friend, we walked with our packs about a mile in hopes of finding lodging for the night.

During our walk, I was able to share the Gospel message with the man, and just before our hike was over, he prayed to receive Christ. Even though he was not from our targeted tribe, we were very encouraged that God brought this man our way.

The next day, we hired a canoe and were able to be with our people group for a few days. Several men with genuine spiritual interest came to us, and we learned much from them about their beliefs and also shared some of ours. Once again, God encouraged us.

A few days later, a man and wife from our people group in another area were open to the message of salvation. God is faithful to bring the harvest in His time.

—RUSS, AMERICAN PEOPLES

*Forgive me,* LORD, WHEN I INSIST ON FOLLOWING MY PLAN AND FAIL TO WAIT FOR YOUR PERFECT TIMING. ALLOW ME TO SEE YOUR HAND AT WORK AS I FOLLOW YOUR GUIDANCE. FILL ME WITH YOUR SPIRIT AND USE ME FOR YOUR GLORY. BRING THOSE WHO LIVE IN THE AMAZON TO A SAVING KNOWLEDGE OF YOU. *Amen.*

# *Sports and God go hand in hand*

*"For You formed my inward parts; You wove me in my mother's womb." Psalm 139:13 (NASB)*

Often we believe that if we surrender to the Lord, we forfeit our hobbies or talents. My husband's father was a coach, so Mark was always involved in sports. One year, Mark was offered a contract to play semi-pro football. Although this was tempting, he was happy serving on a church staff. However, his love for sports never dwindled.

As a missionary in Poland, he and one of our colleagues were invited to meet with the general manager of the professional American football team in Krakow. After going to one of the practices and giving some feedback, Mark was asked to be the coach. He explained that he often traveled, but he would gladly assist when in town. Almost 30 years after receiving an invitation to play, he was now going to help coach a football team. He immediately set some team rules, such as no smoking or cussing, and Mark began to pray before every game.

These young men have been able to see a difference in my husband and our colleague. The team has had an opportunity to hear the Gospel several times. Several players are showing keen interest, including the general manager. Even after many years, God still uses the talents and interests He gives as we surrender totally to follow Him.

—SUSIE, EUROPEAN PEOPLES

*You knew me,* LORD, EVEN BEFORE I WAS FORMED IN MY MOTHER'S WOMB. SUCH KNOWLEDGE ASTOUNDS ME. THANK YOU THAT YOU USE THE TALENTS, SKILLS, AND KNOWLEDGE YOU HAVE GIVEN YOUR CHILDREN TO MAKE AN ETERNAL DIFFERENCE IN THE LIVES OF PEOPLE THROUGHOUT THE WORLD. BRING THIS FOOTBALL TEAM TO YOURSELF. *Amen.*

# God knows about location

*"And I, if I am lifted up from the earth, will draw all men to Myself."* John 12:32 (NASB)

People from around the world came to Germany for the World Cup tournament. The Evangelical Alliance in our city sought permission from the city to place a booth strategically where visitors could hear the Gospel. Every location requested was rejected. At the verge of giving up, God opened the door for the booth to be placed near the entrance to the main train station, where about 90 percent of the fans would pass. We could hardly believe it!

Each day from 10 a.m. to 8 p.m., the Gospel was disseminated through songs, skits, and preaching. Christians from South Africa, Latin America, United States, Germany, and even Iran shared the Gospel with hundreds every day. One day, a young Middle Eastern Muslim lady visited the booth. She was married, but on that day her husband permitted her to go into the city alone. My wife shared Jesus with her, gave her a Bible in her language, and prayed with her. This daughter of Abraham did not accept Jesus then, but she heard about the One who died for her. A few days later, God gave me an opportunity to share openly with a man from India.

During this event, people from the entire world heard about Jesus. Many rejected Him, but 160 decisions were made for Christ at that train station. God knows all about location.

—A.J., EUROPEAN PEOPLES

*Father of all,* WE PRAISE YOU FOR PROVIDING OPPORTUNITIES FOR PEOPLE AROUND THE WORLD TO BE TOUCHED WITH THE GOSPEL. ENCOURAGE THOSE WHO HEARD YOUR TRUTH AT THE WORLD CUP TO DESIRE TO KNOW YOU. BRING TO THEIR MINDS THE TESTIMONIES OF FAITH WHICH THEY HAVE HEARD. *Amen.*

# Willing to talk

*"And he was with them, moving about freely in Jerusalem, speaking out boldly in the name of the Lord." Acts 9:28 (NASB)*

Our first winter in Russia, I inadvertently shut off the heat to the apartments above us, causing my neighbors to be very cold. Early the next morning, the building handyman was at our door!

At the time, we had a really good reason for switching off the heat in our apartment. Even though the temperatures had hardly risen above freezing since October, our apartment was stifling hot. Evidently, the apartments above us weren't as fortunate. The handyman quickly fixed the problem, we exchanged pleasantries, and he left.

Several days later, I saw him outside my building, but he did not see me. God's Spirit spoke to my heart, suggesting that I take the opportunity to continue to build the relationship. Even though I was uncomfortable sharing in a language I barely knew, I found myself calling out to him. We had a brief chat, and I invited him to tea. In the cold of a Moscow winter, I learned an important lesson about being a bold witness. God daily presents us with opportunities to share His love with the people who cross our paths, no matter how difficult it is. Each day we meet people who desperately need the Good News of Jesus Christ. We simply must be willing to call out and start the conversation.

—MARC, EUROPEAN PEOPLES

*Holy One,* YOU ARE FAITHFUL TO BRING DIVINE APPOINTMENTS INTO MY LIFE. I CONFESS THAT ALL TOO OFTEN I AM DISTRACTED BY MY OWN AGENDA. REMIND ME, FATHER, TO JOYFULLY RESPOND TO YOUR GENTLE NUDGING. *Amen.*

# A blessing

*"You give him blessings forever; You cheer him with joy in Your presence."*
Psalm 21:6 (HCSB)

Driving through the back roads of my neighborhood, I was discouraged about my ministry. I craved iced tea and solitude. But just a few blocks from my home, an elderly lady struggled with several bags as she limped down the road. The Holy Spirit directed me to give her a ride, but I continued driving. When the Spirit spoke to my heart again, I reluctantly obeyed.

As the woman got in my car, she shoved her bags in my lap and told me to hold them. The bags were not filled with groceries but with rotten food from nearby Dumpsters. After she was settled, she reached over to hold my hand, thanking me for stopping. I noticed her fingers were black and slimy, her nails were overgrown, and she had several sores on her arm. The stench was strong. I lifted a silent prayer for her.

Upon arrival at her stop, I asked if I could pray for her. She said, "No, I will pray for you!" Placing her sticky hands on my head, she prayed a powerful prayer that God would fill me with peace and hope, and bless my family. She then gathered her bags and exited the car.

As I drove away, peace and joy overwhelmed me. God helped me experience His love through this woman when I was down and weak.

—TAMARA, CENTRAL ASIAN PEOPLES

*Compassionate Father,* YOU OFTEN CHOOSE THE WEAK AND LOWLY TO REFLECT THE DEPTH OF YOUR WAYS. HUMBLE ME BEFORE YOU AND BEFORE THOSE YOU PLACE IN MY PATH. HELP ME NOT TO MISS THE OPPORTUNITIES YOU GIVE TODAY. *Amen.*

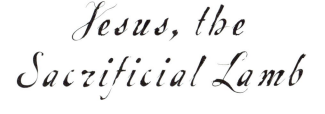

# Jesus, the Sacrificial Lamb

*Followers of Christ are called to live and love sacrificially.*

—BETH MOORE

*The Passion of Christ* by Mel Gibson gave many of us a glimpse of what it must have been like for Jesus to suffer and die so that we could have the opportunity to be restored to God. Honestly, I could barely watch the big screen as the actor playing Jesus was beaten brutally. Lash after lash was seared in my mind, and I openly wept with others in the theater at this graphic reminder of what my Savior voluntarily endured for me. I was physically and emotionally exhausted after seeing the movie, even though I had seen other presentations of His crucifixion and read the relevant Scripture passages many times.

My reaction to that vivid portrayal of the crucifixion reminded me of the reaction of a large group of Zimbabweans the first time they were exposed to the story of Jesus. My husband and I partnered with a local chapter of Campus Crusade for Christ to show the *JESUS* film in a high-density rural area outside of Harare, Zimbabwe, where we wanted to plant a new church. We had arranged to show the film under the night sky with the viewers sitting on the lower side of a rock hill. Not knowing how many people would show up, we recruited volunteers from the States to help receive any inquirers who responded to the Gospel presentation at the end of the movie.

Rain threatened the evening, but prayer must have held back the drops that night. Several hundred people showed up to watch the film even though we had only advertised by word of mouth. Evidently free entertainment or intense curiosity brought out seekers. The film was in the local language of Shona, and at first, the people laughed to see white actors speaking their heart language. But Africans love stories, and as they got into this one about the life of Christ, the laughter faded away. The people were riveted.

They began to gasp as they witnessed the miracles that Jesus performed. Later, the men and women thoughtfully nodded in agreement when they heard the Sermon on the Mount. But then they began to wail as they saw Jesus being beaten and crucified. They couldn't believe that Jesus, who had done nothing wrong, would be treated so harshly. Maybe they identified with Jesus because of their own suffering in a country where political violence is common.

After the crowd watched in amazement as Jesus was raised from the dead, the Gospel was presented. They listened carefully, and when we asked if they wanted to follow Jesus, hundreds came down the hill. We were not expecting such a response. Our team talked to every person who would wait. Later, the national pastor and our team followed up with each person. A church was born, and it began meeting in the open at the base of that solid stone hill.

When we realize what Jesus did for us, we can't help but respond. As you read the devotions this month and see Jesus, our sacrificial Lamb, may you be overwhelmed with appreciation and praise and challenged to daily live out a resurrected life in Christ.

—*Kim P. Davis*

# The Lamb

*"He was oppressed and treated harshly, yet he never said a word. He was led like a lamb to the slaughter. And as a sheep is silent before the shearers, he did not open his mouth." Isaiah 53:7 (NLT)*

I could hardly wait! Eleven young Bedouin men had invited me to go on a trip. When they came to pick me up, I noticed a solitary lamb and a load of firewood in the back of the truck. I knew that this trip would be an unforgettable experience and that the lamb would be our meal.

When we arrived and it was time to prepare the lamb for slaughter, I witnessed a graphic example of what our Savior did for us. The compliant lamb never struggled or made a sound. The innocent and unaware animal allowed the handler to lay it on a rock and take its life.

I thought of another silent Lamb, who *did* know what was about to happen. Jesus allowed Himself to be led to slaughter without defending Himself. As I contemplated the significance of the event before my eyes, God allowed me to share the story of the Lamb of God with these young men. I was able to tell them that Jesus gave His life because of His great love for all people of the world. As they listened intently, I explained, "Jesus became the Lamb to make a way for sinful man to live in a restored relationship with His Father, our loving Father." He sacrificed Himself for us.

—GREG, NORTHERN AFRICAN AND MIDDLE EASTERN PEOPLES

*As You watched* YOUR SON DIE, LORD, I CAN'T EVEN IMAGINE HOW YOU SUFFERED. YOUR LOVE KNOWS NO BOUNDARIES. YOUR FORGIVENESS IS AS FAR AS THE EAST IS FROM THE WEST. THANK YOU FOR THE INCREDIBLE SACRIFICE OF YOUR SON. *Amen.*

# Focus on the Son

*"And He said, 'Come!' And Peter got out of the boat, and walked on the water and came toward Jesus. But seeing the wind, he became frightened, and beginning to sink, he cried out, 'Lord, save me!' Immediately Jesus stretched out His hand and took hold of him, and said to him, 'You of little faith, why did you doubt?'" Matthew 14:29–31 (NASB)*

Conducting cultural surveys on the boardwalk was not what I expected. Two volunteers and I had been turned down 10 times by people who did not want to participate in our survey. Somewhat discouraged, I suggested that we sit and pray for a while. We found a place along the seaside to park ourselves and began to pray silently.

The sun was just setting, reflecting hues of red and orange on the water. I took my eyes off the horizon for a few moments, instead focusing on the waves and the wind that started to pick up. With the waves now crashing closer to us, I was afraid that we might get wet. I looked up again to see where the sun was; it had sunk below the horizon and was no longer seen.

I thought about how we sometimes take our focus off the Son and look at the stormy waves of life crashing all around. When we take our focus off the One who saved us, we begin to sink and drown in the cares of this world. Sometimes we doubt He is even there. The sun may have sunk below the horizon, but it is still there, just like Jesus.

—D.M.T., EUROPEAN PEOPLES

*Ever-Present Father,* TO KNOW THAT YOU ARE WITH ME ALWAYS IS WHAT I HOLD ON TO DESPERATELY. HELP ME NOT TO FOCUS ON THE TRIALS OF LIFE BUT ON YOUR SALVATION. *Amen.*

# Amazing grace

*"Indeed, we have all received grace after grace from His fullness."* John 1:16 (HCSB)

Some days there are too many words to comprehend in language study. I've been tempted to throw in the towel. Other days, when words make sense, studying is worth it. Perhaps I will be able to share my faith one day with potential new sisters and brothers in Christ.

Struggling with a new language heightens awareness of the once familiar. I see passages of Scripture or Christian songs differently because I have to focus on every word in an unfamiliar translation. Things I forgot have been brought to mind again as I study. What I took for granted has become precious again.

I grew up singing "Amazing Grace." In recent years, I had grown tired of hearing this hymn played on bagpipes every time somebody famous is buried. Then I encountered "Amazing Grace" in my new language. It can't be translated word for word and still fit the music. It had to be translated in concept, and those concepts deeply touched me.

"Grace so infinitely great. Grace I never earned. I found life though dead. Though blind, I now can see. Jesus carried the burden of my sin on the cross. He holds me fast through grace and brings me safely home. When I, before His splendor, shine like the sun, then I'll praise Him in eternity because I found grace."

—L4, EUROPEAN PEOPLES

*Compassionate Father,* AT THE EXPENSE OF YOUR SON, JESUS, YOU OFFER THE UNEARNED GIFT OF GRACE. ALTHOUGH WE DO NOT DESERVE IT, YOU BLESS US WITH SALVATION AND THE RICHES OF HEAVEN. I STAND AMAZED! *Amen.*

# His light

*"There are many who say, 'Who will show us any good?' LORD, lift up the light of Your countenance upon us." Psalm 4:6 (NKJV)*

Sunshine! Finally, after none for weeks. I stretched my arms in front of the window to absorb the Vitamin D. Light permeated the room. With only eight hours of daylight in winter, it felt so good. What an amazing influence the natural light has on my frame of mind!

Light is an appropriate analogy for Jesus in our world. Just as natural light promotes healthy living, the light of Jesus brings spiritual life and health.

In Ephesians 5:8, Paul says that we were darkness, but now we are light in the Lord! When we live in a spiritually dark place, we must be very careful to live each moment in Christ's light.

Christ's light brings clarity. It reveals stains that need cleaning. With His light, we can see the cobwebs and dust that need to be cleared away. Light gives us the ability to work on details and to repair what needs repairing. And with true, bright light, there is no need for artificial light. He's the source of energy that keeps us going. May we be highly motivated to live as children of the Light and to let Christ's light shine through us to impact others.

—D.D., EUROPEAN PEOPLES

*Father,* YOU ARE MY LIGHT AND SALVATION, WHOM SHALL I FEAR? YOU WHO TURN DARKNESS INTO LIGHT AND MAKE THE ROUGH PLACES SMOOTH, PLEASE SHED YOUR RADIANCE IN THE DISMAL, FORLORN CORNERS OF THE WORLD TODAY. *Amen.*

# In Jesus' name

*"These things I have written to you who believe in the name of the Son of God, that you may know that you have eternal life, and that you may continue to believe in the name of the Son of God." 1 John 5:13 (NKJV)*

The smell of eggplant and meat saturated my kitchen as "Elif" and I prepared lunch together. Because Elif is a former Muslim, we enjoy times of Christian fellowship in this country that is 99.7 percent Muslim.

As we headed to the table, my neighbor, "Hava," knocked on my door. God timed it perfectly! We invited her to join us, and she obliged. Hava watched as Elif placed her palms upward and prayed aloud, concluding with "In Jesus' name, amen."

Since praying in Jesus' name is countercultural, Hava pressed Elif on why she would pray in His name, since Jesus was in her mind a mere prophet. How could she pray in a mere prophet's name? That question alone led to a complete presentation of the Gospel, a message Hava had never heard.

Perhaps as believers who hear and use the phrase "In Jesus' name" quite often, we don't think about the power and authority that accompany it. When Elif was questioned about why she would pray in Jesus' name, her response began with three words: "Jesus is God." God alone has the authority, power, and ability to hear and answer our prayers.

—LESLIE, CENTRAL ASIAN PEOPLES

*Jesus,* THANK YOU FOR THE PROMISE THAT ONE DAY EVERY KNEE WILL BOW AND EVERY TONGUE CONFESS YOU ARE LORD. REVEAL YOURSELF POWERFULLY TODAY TO HAVA AND MUSLIMS AS THEY SEEK TRUTH. *Amen.*

# *Jesus is enough*

*"Philip said to Him, 'Lord, show us the Father, and it is enough for us.' Jesus said to him, 'Have I been so long with you, and yet you have not come to know Me, Philip? He who has seen Me has seen the Father ...'" John 14:8–9 (NASB)*

"Jesus is enough!" said our leader's wife. I have contemplated this statement many times since it was made. Was He enough when we had over 50 volunteers this summer come to our city? Yes. When I was absolutely exhausted and felt worthless? Yes. Was He enough when we found out one of our children had some issues, and we needed to make some changes in our lives to accommodate him? Yes. How about when one of our friends, who had been studying the Bible, told us that she had started dating a Muslim man? Yes.

Sometimes people see missionaries as spiritual giants who don't have problems like the rest of the world. That simply is not true. Living in another country with a different language and culture can set one up for failure, unless Jesus is enough. I have to purposefully make the decision either to deal with my problems by laying them at the feet of Jesus or handle my situations alone, which is never a smart idea.

For me, life has become a journey. There may be distractions along the way, and sometimes I take the wrong turn. But as I yield to Jesus, He gets me back on the right track. He's always there, and He is always enough.

—KIM, SOUTHEAST ASIAN PEOPLES

*Lord Jesus,* YOU DESIRE TO RENEW OUR STRENGTH AND EMPOWER US TO ENJOY ABUNDANT LIFE. ENABLE US TO CEASE OUR OWN PURSUITS AND UTTERLY DEPEND ON YOU. YOU ARE MORE THAN ENOUGH. *Amen.*

# The cheapest sacrifice

*"By this will, we have been sanctified through the offering of the body of Jesus Christ once and for all." Hebrews 10:10 (HCSB)*

Kurban Bayrami (koor-BAHN bahy-rah-muh), the "Sacrifice Holiday," is the time when Muslims buy an animal to slaughter as an offering to Allah. Afterward, the meat is divided between family, friends, and the poor. Some reasons given for the slaughter are to atone for sin, to remember Abraham's trial of almost killing his son, and to share food with the poor.

Before the holiday, I received a text message from a local grocer that read, "Come to our market for the cheapest sacrifice." They had special deals on live cows, goats, and lambs.

As I closed my cell phone, I thought of the sacrifice that was paid for me when God gave His only Son as the price for my sin. The sacrifice was perfect and spotless but not cheap. His suffering gave me access to God, and it was not cheap. His death on the cross was not cheap. Yes, my Jesus was and is the complete sacrifice for all mankind's sin. And it was not cheap.

As I thought of this costly sacrifice, it prompted me to question the kind of sacrifice I'm willing to give out of my love for Him. How often do I, as His follower, offer a cheap sacrifice? May I have a heart that refuses to give to the Lord a sacrifice that costs me nothing.

—LESLIE, CENTRAL ASIAN PEOPLES

*Father,* THANK YOU FOR EXCHANGING MY FILTHY RAGS FOR YOUR RICH ROBES OF RIGHTEOUSNESS. I WILL NEVER UNDERSTAND THE AWESOME PRICE JESUS PAID TO CLEANSE ME OF MY SIN. EMPOWER ME TO PASSIONATELY SHARE THIS MYSTERY. *Amen.*

# Mourning without hope

*"O DEATH, WHERE IS YOUR VICTORY? O DEATH, WHERE IS YOUR STING? but thanks be to God, who gives us the victory through our Lord Jesus Christ."*
1 Corinthians 15:55, 57 (NASB)

A few days before Easter, I was invited by a Shiite family to attend a memorial service for one of their great leaders who had died several hundred years earlier. Throughout the dimly lit rooms, the scent of perfumed "holy water" filled the air. Women of all ages crowded together on cushions, while two of the neighborhood's oldest women recited passages from the Quran. For three hours, the women mourned their loss by retelling the story of this leader's death, cursing his killers, singing dirges, weeping, and rhythmically slapping their laps with their hands. Some women even beat their bodies harshly, crying out in anguish.

My heart ached as I saw the depth of their grief and hopelessness. Their sorrowful memorial service stood in stark contrast to the joyful Easter morning my family would celebrate only a few days later. These Shiite Muslims mourn the death of their leader every year. Followers of Jesus daily rejoice in a risen Savior! Muslims mourn without hope because they believe death triumphed. Christians are filled with hope because Jesus triumphed over death!

I sat with my new friends and prayed silently that God would open their eyes to the truth and turn their mourning into celebration. May I never take for granted the victory I have because Jesus is risen.

—JOY, CENTRAL ASIAN PEOPLES

*Risen Lord,* YOU CONQUERED DEATH AND THE GRAVE AND TURNED MOURNING INTO JOY. I TREMBLE AT YOUR AWESOME HOLINESS. HOLY SPIRIT, INSTILL IN MY HEART A DEEP BURDEN TO SHARE YOUR VICTORY. *Amen.*

# Open their eyes

*"... for this purpose I have appeared to you, to appoint you a minister and a witness not only to the things which you have seen, but also to the things in which I will appear to you; to open their eyes so that they may turn from darkness to light and from the dominion of Satan to God, that they may receive forgiveness of sins and an inheritance among those who have been sanctified by faith in Me."*
*Acts 26:16, 18 (NASB)*

Christianity has been a part of Russia for centuries. Almost everywhere, one can see a colored, onion-shaped dome capped with a cross. On Easter Sunday morning, Russians even greet one another with the familiar "Christ has risen ... He has risen indeed!"

Whether we live in Russia or another country, our responsibility is to help those around us understand how our holidays, traditions, and Scripture point to Jesus. As we celebrate the Easter season, we can remind family, friends, and neighbors that Jesus' tomb remains empty to this day. And from watching us, others should see that having a relationship with the living God is more than just ritual and religion. True Christianity comes from asking Jesus to forgive our sin and following Him.

We cannot open the eyes of those around us, only God can. But we can pray, be a witness, and love others so that we point them to the risen Jesus.

—MARC, EUROPEAN PEOPLES

*Father,* THE LIVES OF YOUR CHILDREN ARE TEMPLES BECAUSE YOU ABIDE IN THEM. EMPOWER ALL WHO REPRESENT YOU THROUGHOUT THE WORLD TO LIVE IN SUCH A WAY THAT YOUR PRESENCE IS EVIDENT AND ABLE TO BE CLEARLY SEEN. *Amen.*

# Life-giving blood

*"But now in Christ Jesus, you who were far away have been brought near by the blood of the Messiah." Ephesians 2:13 (HCSB)*

She was thirty-something, attractive, but betrayed by her husband who infected her with HIV/AIDS and then abandoned her. I met Lettie within weeks of having arrived in the small town in North Africa. When Lettie became ill, there was no one in her family to care for her.

She grew weaker, and I feared she would die without Christ. As she approached death, I drove her to the hospital where they said she needed a blood transfusion, but there was no blood available. Two young men offered their blood for payment. Lettie asked why anyone would sell their blood. "After all," she said, "our life is in our blood." Our friend, Mula, who was at the hospital, said, "The blood these young men gave will help you feel better for a few days, but there is a blood that will heal you forever." Lettie responded, "Please, go and get that blood!" Mulu explained that this blood could not be purchased. It was the blood of Jesus Christ, who died for her. She told Lettie if she believed that Jesus is the Son of God and asked Him to forgive her sins, His blood would make her clean before God. Lettie prayed with Mulu that day to receive God's forgiveness, and she placed her hope for eternal life in the hands of Jesus.

Is your life in the hands of Jesus?

—L. LEE, NORTHERN AFRICAN AND MIDDLE EASTERN PEOPLES

*Holy One,* HELP ME NEVER TO LOSE THE SENSE OF AWE THAT THE BLOOD OF JESUS CLEANSES US FROM ALL SIN. ALLOW THOSE WHO ARE JUST NOW HEARING THIS ETERNAL TRUTH TO BOW THEIR KNEES BEFORE YOU IN CONFESSION AND ADORATION. *Amen.*

# Lamb of God?

*"The next day John saw Jesus coming toward him, and said, 'Behold! The Lamb of God who takes away the sin of the world!'" John 1:29 (NKJV)*

"Ray, have you ever heard of Jesus?" I asked the Chinese student who had come to London to get a master's degree. We had invited this new neighbor to supper, partly because we heard that he loved to play Ping-Pong, and we had a table.

When the topic of conversation made its way to Jesus that night, we could hardly believe that Ray had never heard of His name. So we watched the *JESUS* film together and gave him a Bible before he left, suggesting that he read John's gospel.

Later, I felt like we had come on a little strong, so I began to pray, *Lord, I don't want to push You on to Ray. If Ray is interested, have him ask about You the next time I see him.*

A few days later, I invited Ray over to play Ping-Pong. As he helped me set up, he said, "What did John mean when he called Jesus the 'Lamb of God'?" The Lord had answered my prayer. I spent the next few minutes giving Ray a brief history from Genesis to Exodus to explain the Passover lamb, and how Jesus was the sacrificial Lamb for us.

Ray hasn't made a decision to follow Christ yet. He has much to contemplate. What about you? Is Jesus your sweet Lamb of God?

—KENT, EUROPEAN PEOPLES

*Father,* THANK YOU FOR YOUR SACRIFICIAL LAMB, WHO PAID THE PRICE FOR OUR SIN. REVEAL YOURSELF TO THOSE WHO ARE HEARING YOUR NAME FOR THE FIRST TIME TODAY. OPEN HEARTS TO BELIEVE AND SURRENDER FULLY TO YOU. OPEN RAY'S HEART. *Amen.*

# A lamb cake for Easter

*"And he made from one man every nation of mankind to live on all the face of the earth, having determined allotted periods and the boundaries of their dwelling place, that they should seek God, in the hope that they might feel their way toward him and find him." Acts 17:26–27 (ESV)*

She walked in carrying a lamb-shaped cake for our Easter celebration. What a perfect introduction for the Gospel presentation! I asked the ladies gathered for English class if they knew why the traditional Czech Easter cake was in that shape. None knew the answer. So I shared with them about Jesus, the Lamb of God who takes away the sin of the world.

Evidence of a Christian heritage is plentiful, but many Czechs don't know it. This is the home of Jon Hus, forerunner of the Reformation, and Cyril and Methodius, missionaries who gave the Czechs a written language, the lamb cake to point to Jesus during Easter celebrations, and the tradition of baby Jesus bringing gifts to children at Christmas. With communism gone, the people are free to find Jesus again.

God has left familiar landmarks, not just in the Czech Republic, but everywhere in the world. Resurrection is all around us, in nature and in traditions, as a reminder of Jesus. His Son, the Lamb of God, came to sacrifice Himself on our behalf. Will we allow indifference to dim the signposts given by the Father? Or will we point others to Jesus while we live the resurrected life?

—KAREN, EUROPEAN PEOPLES

*Lamb of God,* DRAW THE PEOPLE OF THE CZECH REPUBLIC TO SEEK YOU. HELP THEM TO RECOGNIZE YOUR PRESENCE, POWER, AND UNIQUENESS THROUGH THEIR CUSTOMS AND THROUGH THE GLORY OF YOUR CREATION. PLACE BELIEVERS IN THEIR PATHS. *Amen.*

# Living the resurrected life

*"Come, let us return to the* LORD. *For He has torn us, but He will heal us; He has wounded us, but He will bandage us." Hosea 6:1 (NASB)*

Finally, an invitation to share our faith. My roommate and I had been befriended by a Muslim family, and they invited us to eat supper with them. They were preparing for their Eid celebration. We were interested in their customs and asked them many questions. This important Muslim holiday led our friends to ask about holidays we celebrate in America. We mentioned several holidays, but it was Easter that caught their attention, a holiday unfamiliar to them.

Even with language barriers, we told the story of Jesus and the miracle of Easter. As they sat captivated, we said that Jesus was the only sacrifice needed to clean our hearts and to give the promise of heaven. Immediately after our visit, we prayed fervently that they would continue to consider the things they had heard before we saw them again.

Later that night, I felt the Lord prompting me to look in Hosea 6. God spoke to my heart, telling me that He had heard my prayers for this family and for me. Even feeling torn from my own culture and family, He would heal my insecurities of living in a foreign land. He would heal me with opportunities to fulfill His purposes.

Even when we feel wounded, He will heal us so that we can live the resurrected life.

—J.J., NORTHERN AFRICAN AND MIDDLE EASTERN PEOPLES

*Lord our Healer,* AS YOU INITIATED THE MIRACLE OF THE RESURRECTION, YOU TAKE THE INITIATIVE IN THE EVERYDAY LIVES OF PEOPLE TO ACCOMPLISH THINGS THAT THEY COULD NEVER HAVE IMAGINED. I STAND IN AWE AND ADORATION OF YOU. *Amen.*

## *Evidence of His resurrection*

*"For behold, the* Lord *is coming forth from His place, He will come down and tread on the high places of the earth. The mountains will melt under Him, and the valleys will be split, like wax before the fire, like water poured down a steep place." Micah 1:3–4 (NASB)*

As we drove through miles of rubble in the mountainous earthquake region, we were saddened by the people who were evacuating for safer ground. Many had lost everything, and thousands had perished under the crushing stones that rained down from the mountaintops.

We found an elderly lady and her granddaughter picking pears from a tree beside the road. Her son and daughter-in-law had been killed in the quake. "The big foot of a god stepped on top of our mountain and shook it," she cried. When asked if she believed in the one true God, she replied that before the earthquake, the mountain contained hundreds of temples with idols, but they were all destroyed. She said the people will not replace the idols because the statues had failed to protect them. We shared that God loves all people, but He hates idols. His only Son died and rose from the dead as the sacrifice for all who believe in Him.

We helped her build a small hut and gave her water and food. We told her we had come to help because the living and Holy God sent us and that He loves her very much. She replied, "I believe He is the one true God because He sent you as the evidence of His resurrection!"

—C.V., East Asian Peoples

*Rather* than bowing to statues, Father, we tend to pour our time, finances, and energy into possessions and pleasures. Help believers to forsake all worldly gods and allow You to reflect Your character through us. *Amen.*

# A price already paid

*"Therefore, as through one man's offense judgment came to all men, resulting in condemnation, even so through one Man's righteous act the free gift came to all men, resulting in justification of life." Romans 5:18 (NKJV)*

"Ann" was my taxi driver one morning as I headed to the airport. We were having a normal conversation when she began to tell me that she was lonely and that her heart felt empty. She then asked if I could help her.

I began to share about God, but as I began to talk about His Son, Jesus, she quickly responded, "I don't understand." I thought that my language tones must have been off, but then I realized that she didn't understand because this was the first time she had ever heard of Jesus! I was reminded of my purpose in the large country. As I shared more, she questioned how much money this would cost her. She smiled when I told her the price had already been paid.

She immediately started coming to a Bible study my wife leads, and a few weeks later became a believer. When asked if she was willing to receive Christ as her Lord and Savior, she responded, "I am extremely willing!"

We're reminded daily of the countless millions who have yet to hear of the greatest price ever paid. But I am also unusually aware that I should never take for granted the price that was paid for me, as well. Jesus died for me! Hallelujah, what a risen Savior!

—J., EAST ASIAN PEOPLES

*Merciful Father,* WE KNOW THAT GOD'S WRATH AND PUNISHMENT ARE SIN'S JUST RE-WARD. THANK YOU FOR EXTENDING UNDESERVED GRACE TO ALL WHO ARE WILLING TO RE-CEIVE YOUR FORGIVENESS. *Amen.*

# A hug from a king

*"After this I looked, and there was a vast multitude from every nation, tribe, people, and language, which no one could number, standing before the throne and before the Lamb." Revelation 7:9 (HCSB)*

"God has sent you to help my people," spoke the Nkoya king as he wept with joy and thanksgiving. The king had given the team permission to teach the Bible among his people after a pastor, Mike, and other volunteers from Virginia shared the Gospel and prayed for him.

A few months later, Mike and more volunteers returned to visit the king. Upon their arrival, the king stood up, walked over to Mike, and embraced him. The action was unprecedented since kings from the western province of Zambia neither stand in front of their visitors nor touch them. The Nkoya king saw himself as Mike's brother, not his superior, for he also now worshipped the King of kings.

The transformation of the king and his people has made a significant impact in this remote area. But they were not the only ones changed. The pastor who shared the Gospel was radically altered, and Mike and his family moved to Zambia to plant churches among the Nkoya.

King Jesus also embraces us. His followers will one day stand before His throne, and we will stand with the Nkoya king and his people, receiving the tender touch from the King of kings.

—DAREN, SUB-SAHARAN AFRICAN PEOPLES

*King of kings,* WE WORSHIP YOU FOR HUMBLING YOURSELF, BECOMING MAN AND DYING ON THE CROSS, SO THAT ALL WHO TRUST IN YOU MAY LIVE FOREVER. GLORIFY YOURSELF THROUGH THE BELIEVERS OF ZAMBIA AS THEY SHARE YOUR GRACE. *Amen.*

# "Happy birthday, Boy!"

*"God, how difficult Your thoughts are for me [to comprehend]; how vast their sum is! If I counted them, they would outnumber the grains of sand; when I wake up, I am still with You." Psalm 139:17—18 (HCSB)*

A college student named "Boy" is a faithful encourager to fellow believers. His father died when he was only four. His mom struggles as a single-mother kindergarten teacher in Thailand. Boy likes to help volunteers who come to teach English to university students. As a result of the time he has spent with volunteers and missionaries, he's fluent in English.

His uncomplicated understanding of God astounds me. I once asked him if he was ever angry that his dad died. Puzzled, he responded, "You know all those verses that tell people to take care of widows and orphans? I always thought God loved me *more* than other people."

During a Bible study gathering, I asked what God had done that was special during the week. Boy quietly answered, "I've never had a birthday party, a cake, or a present in my life. My family is poor, and my mom works hard. She's never even said 'Happy Birthday' to me." Tears burned in my eyes as he continued, not complaining, just telling his story. "But one night this week, I had a dream. Jesus was standing in front of me with a birthday cake. He said, 'Happy birthday, Boy. I love you.' I woke up and realized that it was my birthday. I had forgotten it, but God hadn't."

Our Savior's thoughts are countless for each one of us.

—DAVID, SOUTHEAST ASIAN PEOPLES

*God of grace,* WHO KNOWS EACH STAR BY NAME, NOTHING IS TOO GREAT NOR TOO SMALL FOR YOUR ATTENTION. THANK YOU FOR GIVING US A HOME AND A FAMILY IN YOU. *Amen.*

# A lesson from bread

*"'I am the bread of life,' Jesus told them." John 6:35 (HCSB)*

Preparation of bread in Central Asia is filled with tradition, as I discovered during a bread-making lesson. I could hear my teacher instruct emphatically, "Don't leave any dough sticking to the sides of the bowl. Never knead it roughly. Love your dough. When leaving it to rise, punch your fist into the middle of the dough, kiss your fist, then touch your forehead as a prayer. Bread should never be dropped on the floor, turned upside down, or otherwise treated disrespectfully."

Unfortunately, I can forget these cultural "rules." Being friendly toward 5-year-old Bibimo while her mother was busy, I sat down to have tea and bread with her. I offered a chunk of bread to Bibimo, who politely refused. When I tore off a piece for myself, I clumsily dropped it on the floor.

Not realizing my cultural mistake, I smiled, but Bibimo gasped as she retrieved it and set it on the table, adjusting the bread right side up. Kissing her fingers, she reverently touched the bread, her brow furrowed in concern, worried that something bad would happen.

I thanked the Lord for not allowing anyone else to witness my cultural blunder. Still, my heart broke for this child with such ingrained fears etched into her mind. Freedom from fear is needed among the peoples of Central Asia, and only the Bread of life can offer it.

—C. LEE, CENTRAL ASIAN PEOPLES

*Bread of life,* YOUR DESIRE IS THAT PEOPLE WORLDWIDE WILL NOT HAVE A SPIRIT OF FEAR BUT OF LOVE, POWER, AND A SOUND MIND. OPEN HEARTS TO HEAR AND RESPOND TO TRUTH PROCLAIMED IN CULTURALLY APPROPRIATE WAYS. *Amen.*

# *The river is life*

*"Jesus said, 'Everyone who drinks from this water will get thirsty again. But whoever drinks from the water that I will give him will never get thirsty again—ever! In fact, the water I will give him will become a well of water springing up within him for eternal life.'" John 4:13–14 (HCSB)*

The Niger River is essential to the daily lives of the Songhai people. They fish, wash dishes and clothes, bathe, and use the river for transportation. But the river is dry for up to six months out of the year. Life becomes much more difficult for the Songhai during this time. Fish is expensive. The wells dry up, so the lines at the water pump are hours long. Everyone waits for the river to return.

*Isa* is the Songhai word for "river." What's phenomenal about this word is that *Isa* is also the Islamic word for Jesus! The Songhai people already know that the river is a source of life for them, but we long for them to realize that Jesus is the source of Living Water that never runs dry. No matter my circumstances, whether I'm waiting hours at the pump for water, if I face the loss of a job or the death of a loved one, or if I hurt for a sibling, Jesus will satisfy my thirst for Him.

The river can be completely dry one day and a week later, the children can be seen playing in the water while their mothers are washing clothes. How quickly and unexpectedly the river returns. May the Living Water come to fill the hearts of people just as quickly!

—SARA, SUB-SAHARAN AFRICAN PEOPLES

*Life Giver,* YOU ALONE CAN SATISFY THE DESPERATE LONGING IN EACH PERSON'S SOUL. AS THE SONGHAI DRAW WATER TO QUENCH THEIR THIRST, PLEASE REVEAL YOURSELF AS THE SOURCE OF LIVING WATER FOR WHOM THEIR SOULS YEARN. *Amen.*

# The peace of Christ

*"And the peace of God, which surpasses all comprehension, will guard your hearts and your minds in Christ Jesus." Philippians 4:7 (NASB)*

A bit uncomfortable due to cultural rules, I wasn't sure what to do when a man working in a shop began to talk to my friend and me. He began asking about Christianity. I realized his questions were sincere and answered his questions with biblical truths. The more questions I answered, the more he asked!

As I asked him about his Islamic beliefs, his eyes were filled with doubt and fear. I explained that even though he knows about the peace offered in his religion, he does not know the One who brought peace to the world. I shared much of the Gospel with him. Later, my husband and a friend went back to visit him, but he wasn't there. Another believer also visited him, but the man hasn't yet come to know Christ. But he is still asking and seeking.

The conversation that day caused me to think about the impact of peace in my life. Philippians 4:7 states that the incomprehensible peace of God will guard my heart and mind in Christ. Jesus does not give peace like Islam gives peace. He gives Himself! So when we are faced with life's questions, we know He is always on active duty to guard our hearts and minds from fears, doubts, confusion, worry, and all the turmoil of life!

—P.T., SOUTH ASIAN PEOPLES

*Perfect peace* PROVIDED BY YOUR DEATH ON THE CROSS IS PRICELESS, LORD JESUS. FILL YOUR MINISTERS OF GRACE WITH YOUR ABUNDANT JOY AND PEACE, SO THAT THEY MAY OVERFLOW WITH HOPE BY THE POWER OF YOUR SPIRIT. BRING THIS MAN WHO IS SEEKING TO CHRIST. *Amen.*

# Worthy of suffering

*"Then they went out from the presence of the Sanhedrin, rejoicing that they were counted worthy to be dishonored on behalf of the name." Acts 5:41 (HCSB)*

A local house church was broken up by police during their Easter service. Every door in the full room was blocked. There was yelling, tracking of names, and questions that demanded answering. Such meetings were deemed illegal because large, unauthorized meetings are seen as a political threat. After the initial public exchange, the lead pastor boldly but meekly asked, "Can we continue worshipping now?" The police of course silenced the idea.

Word travels fast through text messaging. When the pastor was released to go home, he began receiving texts from all over. Prayer networks were unleashed concerning this persecution. In one text message after another, a constant theme was reiterated: "Congratulations. You have been considered worthy to suffer for His sake."

In the following weeks, the believers were called in individually for questioning. Some were threatened. After a few weeks, one particular young man grew frustrated that he had not been summoned. He, too, wanted to testify to the Gospel of Jesus Christ.

Oh, that we would embrace Paul's words in 2 Timothy 3:12 that "all who desire to live a godly life in Christ Jesus will be persecuted" (ESV).

—C.A.V., EAST ASIAN PEOPLES

*I am humbled, Father,* TO PRAY FOR THOSE WHO COUNT IT ALL JOY TO FACE PERSECUTION FOR THEIR FAITH. SURROUND THEM WITH YOUR PRESENCE AND FILL THEM WITH YOUR PEACE AS THEY TESTIFY TO YOUR SAVING POWER. *Amen.*

# *His character on their faces*

*"... you received the word in much affliction, with the joy of the Holy Spirit."*
1 Thessalonians 1:6 (ESV)

Just saying "Jesus" to the three believing refugees made their faces light up. Having fled from their home due to war and genocide, they have seen more evil than anyone should. Now in a foreign land among a people who make it clear they are unwanted, these individuals live in the poorest, most violent neighborhood in my city. In the past five years, their lives have taken such a drastic turn that there is little hope things will soon change.

But they love Jesus. Despite their sufferings, His love still brings joy. Rather than using their experiences as excuses to become bitter, they have found that God is the only constant in a world of unknowns. They don't run to Christ simply to meet their material, temporary needs or they would have walked away years ago. Rather, they know Jesus as the One who loves in a world full of hate. They know Him as the Prince of peace amid streets where gangs, drugs, and racial tensions thrive. They know Him as the Bread of life when their pantries are empty. And despite being separated from loved ones, they know him as the One who is near.

I long to know my Jesus like these refugees, where even in my darkest moment, His name brings a smile. They have grasped the depth of His character.

—J.L.M., NORTHERN AFRICAN AND MIDDLE EASTERN PEOPLES

*Compassionate Father,* DRAW NEAR TO THOSE THROUGHOUT THE WORLD WHO ARE DIS-PLACED, SEPARATED FROM FAMILY AND HOMELAND. IN THEIR HOUR OF DESPERATION, MAKE YOUR PRESENCE POWERFULLY KNOWN. *Amen.*

# The Lord answers and delivers

*"I sought the Lord, and He answered me and delivered me from all my fears."*
Psalm 34:4 (HCSB)

"Mohammed," a young shepherd and devoted Muslim, decided to further his education. Every day he traveled to a small town to study at a vocational school opened by Christians from the West. Mohammed felt loved by these families and learned a lot at the school. He accepted a Bible from his teacher even though it was risky to have one.

One day when Mohammed returned from school, he saw a crowd gathered around his mother's house. They had found his Bible. The elders and religious leaders asked if he believed it. He said that he did, which infuriated the crowd. They beat him and locked him in a room. While in the dark room, Mohammed heard the elders plotting to kill him. He prayed and waited.

When the angry men opened the door, Mohammed sat quietly. They shouted, "Where did he go? He has escaped, but there are no windows." As Mohammed watched them, he realized that they could not see him, although he was in plain view. After the men left, Mohammed walked out of the room. The news spread throughout the village.

Mohammed said, "On that day, Jesus saved my life. I will never forget it!" We serve the Lord who answers, and He delivers us from fear.

—Nathan, Northern African and Middle Eastern Peoples

Father, truly You hide Your children in the hollow of Your hand. Thank You for working in miraculous ways among Muslim background believers. Continue to show Yourself strong to those You are calling out to Yourself. Amen.

# The Man in the middle

*"I know your works. Because you have limited strength, have kept My word, and have not denied My name, look, I have placed before you an open door that no one is able to close." Revelation 3:8 (HCSB)*

When "Ari" was 6 years old, she heard the village priest tell her mother that Jesus would take care of her little girl. Noticing a print on the wall of the Lord's Supper, Ari felt like "the Man in the middle"—the one she decided must be Jesus—spoke to her that day and assured her He would always be with her. Two days later, her mother committed suicide. Two years after that, her father died. Her grandmother reared her in a loving home, but the Bible was not mentioned.

All through her childhood and college years, Jesus guided Ari. She would always pray before making decisions and walked in obedience to what she believed Jesus wanted her to do, even though she could not understand the Bible.

Finally, she met a group of American volunteers and heard the full Gospel story. Ari was ready to receive Jesus as her Lord and Savior and be baptized. Before her baptism, she asked if she would be put all the way under the water. When we said that she would, Ari exclaimed, "I want to be totally immersed in Christ!"

He has put an open door before us to be totally His.

—MELINDA, EUROPEAN PEOPLES

*Almighty Father,* BEFORE THE FOUNDATION OF THE WORLD, YOU HAVE KNOWN THOSE WHO WOULD BECOME YOUR OWN. THANK YOU FOR NURTURING, PREPARING, AND CALLING PEOPLE TO HEAR AND RESPOND TO YOUR TRUTH. MAY ARI CONTINUE TO FOLLOW YOU WHOLEHEARTEDLY. *Amen.*

# Through the mud

*"Serve the LORD with gladness; come before Him with joyful singing."* Psalm 100:2 (NASB)

We met the national missionary as he stood by his skinny horse and cart in front of a repair shop, a lean-to with a workbench and a few tools. The cart needed some wheel work done, so the man waited in the partial shade of a tree.

The pastor we accompanied introduced us, telling us that the man helped with new churches in a remote area. We learned that when it rains, the roads in the missionary's mission circuit become muddy rivers. For a long time the only way he could get to his mission points was on foot. Often he would sink up to his knees in the thick mud. "I have diabetes," he said, "and sometimes my legs would get scratched and become infected when wading in the mud."

But if he didn't go through the mud, how would people hear about Jesus? Patting his animal, he said, "I'm really grateful for this horse and cart. Some Christian brothers sent money to buy the horse and cart for my ministry. Now, I can get to my mission points faster and without having to walk in the mud! Also, I can reach more places to share the Gospel."

No matter the cost, this man is compelled to tell others about what Jesus has done for him.

—YVONNE, AMERICAN PEOPLES

*God our Provider,* HUMBLE ME BEFORE YOUR THRONE. I AM REMINDED THAT I DO SO LITTLE WITH SO MUCH. HELP ME EMBRACE YOUR HEART FOR THE LOST AND NEEDY WITHIN MY REACH. BLESS AND EMPOWER FAITHFUL SERVANTS AROUND THE WORLD, SUCH AS THIS MAN, WHO HUMBLY OFFER THEIR ALL TO YOU. *Amen.*

# *Understanding a dream*

*"Jesus replied, 'This is the work of God: that you believe in the One He has sent.'"*
John 6:29 (HCSB)

"Farheen" was a student studying English to improve her chances for securing a job or going to America. One day, several Americans taught her class for a week. She had a conversation with one of the foreigners and heard the story of Jesus, the same story she had heard at a Christian school when she was a young girl.

That week, Farheen began to have dreams at night about Jesus. On the last day of class, Farheen sought out the foreigner and told her about the dreams. They agreed to meet outside of class. For the next three weeks, she continued to have dreams of Jesus calling her to follow Him. The third time she met with the foreigner, Farheen understood the message and knew that Jesus loved her, but she was hesitant. She said, "I believe in Jesus! But my family does not allow it." She would be disowned by her Muslim family for converting. The decision to either follow Jesus or reject Him was before her. She sat in silence for a few minutes, and with tears in her eyes, she asked Him to be her Redeemer.

Sometimes what Jesus asks of us is difficult, but we, too, have to make the decision to either follow Him or deny Him. What is He asking of you?

—B., SOUTH ASIAN PEOPLES

*Rewarder of the faithful,* YOU DRAW NEAR TO THOSE WHO COUNT THE COST AND CHOOSE TO FORSAKE ALL TO FOLLOW YOU. THANK YOU, FATHER, FOR SPEAKING IN SPECIFIC WAYS TO MUSLIM SEEKERS. COMFORT AND EMPOWER THEM TO COURAGEOUSLY FOLLOW YOU, AND ESPECIALLY GIVE COURAGE TO FARHEEN. *Amen.*

# Trial by fire

*"... our God whom we serve is able to deliver us from the burning fiery furnace, and he will deliver us out of thine hand, O king. But if not, be it known unto thee, O king, that we will not serve thy gods, nor worship the golden image which thou hast set up." Daniel 3:17–18 (KJV)*

"My family is looking for me!" said "Mary" with fear. Muslim women who come to faith in Jesus have little freedom to practice their faith. Of my three former Muslim friends, only one relates to her family because they do not know she is a Christian. Another has not seen her family for over nine years, while Mary is concerned about being "found out."

Do I tell them to be strong and face the trial, or remember what we've learned from our study of the book of Acts? "Whatever you decide to do, may it bring God glory," I said to Mary.

It was not by accident that I was studying Beth Moore's study on Daniel or that I was reading the story of Shadrach, Meshach, and Abednego. Perhaps God will deliver Mary from her trial, and her faith will be encouraged. Or if she chooses to go through the fire, her faith will be refined. The Lord may choose for her to be martyred.

Will she run away or face her accusers? Mary must make the choice. In the meantime, though I may spend some sleepless nights in motherly concern about her, I must entrust her to the One who loves her more than I and trust Him to help her through this trial by fire.

—C.B.G., NORTHERN AFRICA AND THE MIDDLE EASTERN PEOPLES

*Ever-Present Father,* YOUR PROMISE THAT YOU WILL NEVER LEAVE NOR FORSAKE YOUR CHILDREN BRINGS UNSPEAKABLE COMFORT. FILL AND EMPOWER MUSLIM BACKGROUND BELIEVERS WITH YOUR POWERFUL PRESENCE TODAY, ESPECIALLY MARY. *Amen.*

# *Shining the light*

> *"You are the light of the world. ... let your light shine before others, so that they may see your good works and give glory to your Father who is in heaven."*
> Matthew 5:14, 16 (ESV)

Living in South Asia introduced me to load shedding, which means that the government turns off the electricity at different times of the day to conserve limited energy. I quickly found out that one of the most useful things I brought from America was a rechargeable, crank flashlight. At least it offers a few minutes of necessary light when I have to see in the dark. When the light dims, I just recharge it.

Sometimes I feel like a little, rechargeable flashlight surrounded by looming spiritual darkness. My light begins to fade when I'm overwhelmed by the "lostness" around me. However, Jesus reminds me that it is He who has equipped me for this task, and He recharges me in my weakness with His light, which shines brighter than I ever thought possible. Jesus never calls us to anything He doesn't equip us for; He is always ready to use a willing heart and a joyful sacrifice. In Ephesians 5:13, the Bible says that when anything in the dark is exposed to light, it becomes visible. My prayer is to be a penetrating light set upon the foundation of Christ so that those blinded by darkness can see God and awaken from death into abundant life in Jesus.

Let Jesus recharge your light!

—ALAYNA, SOUTH ASIAN PEOPLES

*Light of the world,* ENABLE ME TO ALLOW YOUR TRUTH TO TOUCH THE DEPTH OF MY SOUL AND TRANSFORM ME INTO THE IMAGE OF JESUS. ILLUMINATE MY HEART WITH YOUR PRESENCE SO OTHERS CAN SEE JESUS IN ME. *Amen.*

# Her day of salvation

*"For He says: In an acceptable time, I heard you, and in the day of salvation, I*
*helped you. Look, now is the acceptable time; look, now is the day of salvation."*
2 Corinthians 6:2 (HCSB)

"Hi, I'm 'Jeanne,'" said the university student as she walked up to me during lunch. At university, students rarely approach this boldly, so I knew the Father was already at work.

The third time we met together, we went to the library to talk before our next class. Jeanne had been asking many questions about holidays we celebrate in America, so I had been describing Christmas, Thanksgiving, and Easter. Today she was to hear more about Easter.

I used a paper-folding method to share about Christ. When the paper was folded correctly and torn once, a perfect cross appeared, as well as pieces that when placed together, words in English and Chinese were spelled to share the Good News. Like all of my friends who have seen the cross appear from one tear, she was amazed and wanted me to teach her so she could do it herself.

As I showed her again, I explained how God loved her and sent His Son, Jesus, to die for her. Without Christ, she would be forever separated from God. She asked, "How do I believe?" After more discussion and prayer, Jeanne became a believer. The Father had prepared her heart for her day of salvation. He is preparing hearts around you as well. Go and tell.

—JOY, EAST ASIAN PEOPLES

*Lord,* YOU ARE ALWAYS AT WORK, DRAWING PEOPLE TO YOURSELF. YOU ARE THE TREASURE FOR WHOM EVERY PERSON LONGS. QUICKEN MY HEART TO EXPECT OPPORTUNITIES TO SHARE YOUR LOVE, AND HELP ME TO BOLDLY PROCLAIM YOUR WORD. STRENGTHEN JEANNE'S FAITH TODAY. *Amen.*

## Transforming power of Jesus

*"For the Son of Man has come to seek and to save that which was lost." Luke 19:10 (NASB)*

"Hannah" walked into our medical clinic and asked for a copy of Psalm 23 in Arabic. As we read it together, I shared with her how Jesus cares for us like a shepherd cares for his sheep. I went on to explain what Jesus did on the cross and how He rose from the dead.

"I need to know more about Jesus!" announced Hannah when she came to the clinic the next week. God was working in her heart through His Word and Spirit. I gave her the book of Luke and told her I was praying for her.

When she returned a week later, the gospel of Luke was already worn on the edges as she had read it over and over again. That day, she told us that she had placed her faith in Jesus as her Savior! A few days later, she came back to tell us that her husband and three of her friends now believed in Jesus, too!

Even through trials, she has continued to walk with a joy and light that only comes from knowing the Lord. Jesus has done so much for us. It is mind-boggling to think about His sacrifice. How can we not show anything but joy as we walk in His light and share His love with others?

—M.I., NORTHERN AFRICAN AND MIDDLE EASTERN PEOPLES

*Beckoning Father,* YOU INVITE ALL WHO ARE WEARY AND HEAVY LADEN TO COME TO YOU AND RECEIVE REST. I PRAISE YOU FOR DRAWING PEOPLE FROM NORTHERN AFRICA AND THE MIDDLE EAST TO FIND ETERNAL JOY IN YOU. EMPOWER THEM TO BE WITNESSES TO THEIR FAMILY AND FRIENDS. *Amen..*

# MAY V

## "Follow Me"

*For love of Jesus, they chose obedience over convenience,
answering a call from God.*

—BETH MOORE

After I became a Christian and a student of the Word, I have to admit that sometimes, especially in the early years, I would come across a verse of Scripture that would stump me. *Why did God do this?* or *Why did Jesus say this?* I would think.

I really was puzzled by Matthew 10:37–39: "He who loves father or mother more than Me is not worthy of Me; and he who loves son or daughter more than Me is not worthy of Me. And he who does not take his cross and follow after Me is not worthy of Me. He who has found his life will lose it, and he who has lost his life for My sake will find it" (NASB). In fact, in Luke 14:26, the language is stronger: "If anyone comes to Me, and does not hate his own father and mother and wife and children and brothers and sisters, yes, and even his own life, he cannot be My disciple" (NASB). I don't know about you, but when I first read this, I wasn't sure what to think. Surely Jesus didn't mean that I would have to hate my family in order to love Him with all my heart.

The Greek word for "hate" is *miseo*, which *Strong's Concordance* interprets as "to love less." In looking at the expanded translation of Kenneth S. Wuest of Moody Bible Institute, the word "hate" was made more clear: "If anyone comes to me and does not hate his father and mother and wife and children and brothers and sisters in the event that they become hindrances to his supreme love for me, yes, moreover also his own life in the same manner, he is not able to be my disciple." It was beginning to click. I was not to actively hate my family, but my love for Christ should extend far beyond my love for my family, if I was going to truly follow Him. Discipleship is serious, and Jesus gave the bottom-line to His disciples that there is a cost to following Him.

I never thought I would be tested in my discipleship. My husband went on a mission trip to Jamaica with our little church outside of Atlanta. I stayed home with our infant son, and honestly, I never worried about my husband. I was excited that he could go and be a minister of the Gospel to needy people. When he came back, he was so excited. He had helped build a church, witnessed to prostitutes and drug addicts, and experienced Montezuma's revenge. But that wasn't the only bug he had caught. He had also caught the missions bug. The problem was that I didn't have this bug, nor did I want this bug.

I'll have to give him credit: he didn't nag, coerce, or leave hints around the house purposefully. We continued to attend our missions-minded church, we hosted foreign missionaries in our home when they came to speak at our church, we watched hundreds of slide shows from exotic foreign fields, and we paid for car repairs for missionaries who drove the worst cars I've ever seen.

It wasn't until I picked up a book that my husband was reading called *The Great Omission* by Robertson McQuilken that my world was rocked. The book explained that many people were willing to go wherever God wanted them to, but they were planning to stay right where they were. Sure, I was willing to do whatever God might be calling me to do, but would I actually do it? That epiphany started me on a journey to catch up with my husband.

Now back to Luke 11:46 and Matthew 10:37. In 1990, my husband and I realized that through His Word, advisers, circumstances, and our personal times with the Lord that He was calling both of us to international missions. Once we made the decision, we were excited and headed that direction like gangbusters. To Africa or bust, and all that. But my extended family was not that thrilled.

As I was praying for my relatives and grieving over their first response, God brought those verses to mind. He did it very gently. Instantly, realization hit me that my love for God had to be supreme over my love for others. His call was indeed going to cost something.

We arrived in Africa in 1992, and over the years God gave us a missionary and national family. Eventually we also earned the support of our flesh-and-blood family members who had once questioned our sanity. Each missionary who wrote the stories in May was called by God to proclaim the Gospel to the people of another culture in a foreign setting. It's not always easy; in fact, sometimes it's downright difficult. As you walk with these faithful ones who have been called overseas to do His work, ask God what in the world He is calling you to do. You might be surprised.

—*Kim P. Davis*

# Hearing His voice

*"My sheep hear My voice, I know them, and they follow Me." John 10:27* (HCSB)

It was a good day for a picnic, so we loaded up our family to drive to a village to visit some shepherds we knew. It is always fascinating to see shepherding in action. Traditionally, the oldest son of a family becomes the shepherd when he is able to accept the responsibility. As the next son grows old enough, he becomes the shepherd, and the eldest takes on a different job. The youngest son usually keeps shepherding as there is nobody to take over for him. That was the case with our friend's youngest son.

Many shepherds allow their sheep to graze communally with other sheep. As sunset approached, we watched as the shepherds began the process of gathering their animals to go home. They each called out to their own sheep. The sheep then separated from the large group and followed behind their shepherd.

We were amazed and commented to our hosts. They told us that sheep are followers. If there is no shepherd, they will follow the goats that are also in the flock.

Jesus calls His sheep. He speaks to us from His Word and gives us the choice to follow Him. He leads us the right way. The goats, or influences of the world, also call. If we do not follow Christ, we are going to follow something.

—T.M., Northern African and Middle Eastern Peoples

Lord, my Shepherd, I choose to follow You. Speak to me through Your Word. Help me not to follow worldly influences around me. Allow lost people all over the world to hear Your voice and respond to Your call. Amen.

# God chooses the "nobodies"

*"Then he called his twelve disciples together ... And he sent them to preach the kingdom of God ..." Luke 9:1—2 (KJV)*

With a sinking heart, I looked at the group in front of me. Two were professional beggars—a father and teenage son who were new believers. Two were local teenagers who also had recently believed, one a social outcast, the other with a reputation for petty theft. In addition were teenagers from Holland who didn't speak the local language. To give out free New Testaments in the past, we had sent adult American volunteers with interpreters. Getting everyone in the present group to understand what they were supposed to say when they offered a New Testament was a challenge. How could we possibly send this group out?

I realized how Jesus must have felt sending out the disciples. They weren't an elite group, either. There was a despised tax collector, a thief who would later betray Him, one who would deny Him, and the whole group would forsake Him in His hour of greatest need. What faith for Jesus to entrust that weak band to be His representatives! What about us? How could He entrust "nobodies," with no special abilities, to do His work?

Over the next three days, the group never got the "script" right, but they gave away 750 New Testaments. God reassured me that all He's looking for is a willing heart. It's His work anyway.

—P.A., EUROPEAN PEOPLES

*I am grateful,* MY FATHER, THAT YOU ARE NO RESPECTER OF PERSONS. STRIP AWAY OUR PREJUDICES AND PRECONCEIVED IDEAS. TEACH US TO WORK SIDE-BY-SIDE WITH OTHERS. *Amen.*

# The ordinary

*"But He said to them, 'You give them something to eat!' ..." Luke 9:13 (NASB)*

I'm ordinary. I've had no grand conversion experience or a single moment of severe persecution. Even the word "missionary" doesn't fit me. My days are spent raising four kids, doing umpteen loads of laundry, and constantly restocking our small refrigerator.

So I was intrigued when God led me to the story of the feeding of 5,000. After reading the four accounts, I discovered that in all but John's gospel, Jesus instructs the disciples, "You give them something to eat." Why would God tell mere men to feed such a crowd? By no means did they have the ability to feed them! Yet they distributed what little, ordinary food they found, and Jesus did something extraordinary with it.

I was stunned. It was as if God had written that story just for me. I had felt deflated because I didn't have an exciting ministry and was overwhelmed by the surrounding spiritual poverty. All I had done was spend time with women, chatting over tea while gently speaking the truth of God. Surely nothing significant could come from that.

The Lord reminded me that while I may have ordinary abilities, His are forever extraordinary. He has the ability to do magnificent things through my life. Even if the "bread" offered is time and tea, I can expectantly watch how God will multiply it in the lives around me.

—CINDY, EUROPEAN PEOPLES

*Dear Lord,* I PRAY FOR CINDY AND OTHER MISSIONARY MOMS LIKE HER THAT THEY WILL DAILY RECOGNIZE THEIR EXTRAORDINARY WORK. PLEASE MULTIPLY THEIR SIMPLE OFFERINGS OF TEA AND TIME SO THAT LOST WOMEN WILL ENCOUNTER YOU, THE BREAD OF LIFE, AND EXPERIENCE LIFE-TRANSFORMING CHANGE. *Amen.*

# What can I do for Him today?

*"Dear friends, let us love one another, because love is from God, and everyone who loves has been born of God and knows God." 1 John 4:7 (HCSB)*

"Why does my house flood every year?" asked Tiffany, my Taiwanese friend. Thirty-five inches of rain fell the day the typhoon hit. Tiffany labored strenuously, throwing away ruined furniture and cleaning up mud after sustaining four feet of water in her house. On Sunday, she worshipped God and made cakes for two neighbors.

Later, Tiffany prayed, "Jesus, what can I do for You today?" She decided to make papaya cake and soup for two house-church families. When three relatives came to visit, she made two more cakes. While she was at it, she made enough soup and cakes for eight more church friends. As I helped Tiffany deliver the food, we met some of the unbelieving mothers of her friends. Tiffany demonstrated the love of Christ for His children, and these mothers noticed.

God heard Tiffany's tears, frustration, anger, and questions. By His grace, she chose to worship and serve Him regardless. In the aftermath of destruction and exhaustion, Tiffany offered to serve Jesus by ministering to His body, the church.

What can I do for Jesus today? That is a question to ask each morning as we live every day sensitive to His Spirit.

—KAREN, EAST ASIAN PEOPLES

*Mighty God,* TIFFANY SHOWS A MARVELOUS EXAMPLE OF UNBRIDLED WORSHIP. REKINDLE IN ME A SPIRIT OF SERVICE THAT MEETS THE NEEDS OF OTHERS ABOVE MY OWN. USE ME, LORD, TO DEMONSTRATE YOUR LOVE TO FELLOW CHRISTIANS AND NONBELIEVERS ALIKE. *Amen.*

# Humbling ourselves

*"Humble yourselves in the sight of the Lord, and he shall lift you up." James 4:10 (KJV)*

Squatting down to talk to tourists who had received a Bible and were sitting on the roadside curb, "Ting" felt very odd. In her culture, she normally would not lower herself in relation to someone else, but it was awkward for her to stand while they sat. *This is what Jesus would do. He would lower himself to meet people where they were*, she thought.

Truly, Jesus did humble Himself. He can work through us when He and others become more important than our own comfort. As Ting and the rest of us humbled ourselves physically, emotionally, and spiritually, God gave us opportunities to share His love, His Word, and how to know Him. Over 300 volunteers stood in the rain or blistering sun for hours to give Bibles and the Good News to over 37,800 people from a restricted country. God did the "lifting up" as 16 of these tourists made initial decisions for Christ on the spot.

Humility is not an action but an attitude. As we begin to voluntarily serve others, our focus is no longer on ourselves. There has never been a more perfect example of humility than Jesus. God lowered Himself to reach mankind. Meeting people where they are is the way to present true Christianity.

—M.M., East Asian Peoples

*Forgive me,* LORD, FOR MY PRIDEFUL ATTITUDE—WHEN I THINK I KNOW MORE THAN OTH-ERS OR THAT MY WAY IS BETTER THAN THEIRS. GUIDE YOUR MISSIONARIES TO BE HUMBLE AS THEY SERVE OTHERS AND GLORIFY YOU. *Amen.*

# *Getting my hands dirty*

*"Make your own attitude that of Christ Jesus, who ... humbled Himself by becoming obedient to the point of death—even to death on a cross." Philippians 2:5–6, 8 (HCSB)*

I halfheartedly pray for humility, perhaps because I don't fully understand it. God is helping me to get the picture, however. Our team retreat gave us an opportunity to make our plans for next year. One morning, the retreat speaker gave a challenging devotion about how Christians need to be the same person on the inside as on the outside, unlike the Pharisees.

As we traveled home from the retreat, we stopped at a prayer center. We met a lady who has lived in the area for a long time. She cleans the homes of difficult people and has a good reputation among Muslims, although she is a Christian. After meeting her, I wondered if I would be willing to be a servant like that. Could I humble myself and take the job of a house servant in order to share the Gospel with people?

It is not written anywhere that Jesus cleaned homes, but He healed, washed feet, and tended to the needs of those who were a lot less desirable than most. Sometimes, when we make big plans for our ministries and our lives, we possibly can forget what it is like to get our hands dirty. May we be servants like Jesus.

—A.D., NORTHERN AFRICAN AND MIDDLE EASTERN PEOPLES

*Jesus,* YOU ARE THE SUFFERING SERVANT, AND YOUR CHARACTER IS MODELED IN THE LIFE OF THIS UNASSUMING HOUSEKEEPER. PLEASE MAKE HER BODY STRONG AS SHE LABORS, PROVIDE HER EVERY FINANCIAL NEED, AND FILL HER WITH JOY IN SERVICE. *Amen.*

## Making wise the simple

*"The testimony of the LORD is sure, making wise the simple." Psalm 19:7b (NASB)*

"I want to partner with you to see these people come to Jesus." This was a bold statement from "Hope," a simple, uneducated woman from a farming village in the mountains. She had come to the big city to do what her parents expected: find a job, buy a house, and get married. But after she partnered with us, sharing Christ in a remote village area, her life goal changed.

Hope was terrified but compelled to obey His call. She left her job, sold her house, and postponed getting married. Yet the hardest thing she faced was believing that God could use her to reach this village. Only in God's wisdom could the task be accomplished.

Today, Hope is a picture of the Father's grace, mercy, strength, power, and love. She realizes more than ever that she can do nothing apart from Him. Without a doubt, Hope believes that God can do anything through anyone He chooses, and He delights in doing so. Because of her obedience, over 250 members of an unreached people now worship the one true God. We have seen our loving, Almighty God speak in miraculous ways through a simple, unassuming woman to establish His kingdom in a remote village in Asia. Praise His name!

—P.M., EAST ASIAN PEOPLES

*Lord,* IT IS HUMBLING TO BE USED BY YOU TO REACH THE NATIONS. THANK YOU FOR CALLING EACH OF US TO SHARE YOUR WORD, AND THANK YOU FOR YOUR MIGHTY WORK IN AND THROUGH HOPE'S LIFE. *Amen.*

# Living on faith

*"Jesus asked his disciples, 'When I sent you out without a moneybag or a traveling bag or sandals, did you need anything?' 'No!' they answered."* Luke 22:35 (CEV)

As I waited to board, I suddenly felt lighter by one wallet. I was about to travel to a distant island of an unreached people group. Because the ship only passes once a month, I couldn't cancel. With my ticket, passport, suitcase, and faith, I ascended the rickety gangplank.

I soon realized that the thief who stole my wallet also had my identity card and suitcase key. Yet during the three-day voyage, the Lord provided every need: a waiver on a required deposit, a bar of soap, and free first-aid for the gash on my toe.

As we passed ports with cell coverage, I sent messages to friends who lived at my first stop. Although the family was away, they arranged for a national to take me to their house where a full refrigerator waited. I had no idea how I could disembark with the generator I was bringing them, unable to hire porters. A group of traveling Bible school students came to my rescue. When my friends returned, we took my suitcase to a garage where it was opened easily, allowing me the first change of clothes in five days. With a temporary police letter in my pocket and some borrowed cash, I caught a small boat for the overnight crossing to the unreached island.

God provides when He says, *Go.*

—A WORKER WITH SOUTHEAST ASIAN PEOPLES

*Thank You,* JEHOVAH JIREH, FOR PROVIDING MY EVERY NEED AND FOR USING THOSE MOMENTS OF URGENT NEED TO TEACH ME BOTH PHYSICAL AND SPIRITUAL DEPENDENCY. HELP ME ABANDON MY PLANS OF SECURITY AND SEEK YOUR WISDOM ALONE. CONTINUE TO PROVIDE FOR YOUR SERVANTS OVERSEAS. *Amen.*

# Birthday in the bush

*"Our desire is for Your name and renown."* Isaiah 26:8b (HCSB)

When I was a kid, my dream was to be a schoolteacher, musician, or basketball player. Later, as a structural engineer, I had expectations of my future. By age 30, I wanted to have a significant corporate career, two kids, and be the kind of mother who planned birthday parties with clowns and inflatable bounce houses.

But at age 30, I live in an African hut, a far cry from that big, colonial-style house I pictured. The only ladders I'm climbing are not the corporate ones but the ones leading to hut rooftops. I'm not married but live in a 10x10 hut with a teammate who shares her cans of tuna with me. Instead of having two children, there's a village full of them around me. The only parties I'm throwing are the end-of-rainy-season celebrations. I turned in the keys to my BMW convertible to ride on the back of an open-air donkey cart.

Who knew that on my 30th birthday, I'd wake up in a world of Senufo Supyire people who don't know Jesus. I woke with a desire in my heart for these friends to know Jesus, not for any of my previous dreams. My birthday was not what I had expected, but it was beyond anything I could have imagined! His plans are far better than anything I could have dreamed.

—MONICA, SUB-SAHARAN AFRICAN PEOPLES

*Transform my desires,* LORD, SO THAT I CAN FULLY CELEBRATE LIFE. BLESS MONICA AND HER TEAMMATE FOR SURRENDERING THEIR DREAMS TO YOU. I PRAY FOR THE SENUFO SUPYIRE PEOPLE TO MEET AND ACCEPT JESUS WHO IS THE LIFE. *Amen.*

# *I can*

*"I can do all things through Him who strengthens me." Philippians 4:13 (NASB)*

People in the States often ask, "Do you like where you live?" Not always. Many times we can appreciate the beauty of the places where we serve and the people we live among. Sometimes we can't. On those days when my vision seems to fail, I call to mind Paul's confident claim in Philippians 4:13. God challenges me to make it personal.

I can live in this place *through Christ who strengthens me.* I can give up my personal freedom to dress as I choose and to go where I choose *through Christ who strengthens me.* I can deal righteously with people who constantly beg me for money *through Christ who strengthens me.*

I can be flexible when plans suddenly change and my expectations are not met *through Christ who strengthens me.* I can live in a world of uncertainty and violence *through Christ who strengthens me.* I can daily witness *through Christ who strengthens me.*

No, life on the mission field is not always easy. The struggles and annoyances we face are real. But joy comes from surrendering our frustrations to God. We give Him our weaknesses, and He replaces them with His strength. Then our vision is restored, and we can continue doing His work and sharing His love with those around us.

—C.B., SOUTH ASIAN PEOPLES

*Gracious God,* NO ONE ENJOYS STRUGGLES OR WEAKNESS, BUT I WILLINGLY YIELD TO THEM "SO THAT CHRIST'S POWER MAY RESIDE" IN ME. I PRAY THAT MISSIONARIES WILL COURAGEOUSLY FACE EACH CHALLENGE TODAY THROUGH CHRIST WHO STRENGTHENS THEM. *Amen.*

## His purpose for our family

*"He who calls you is faithful, who also will do it."* 1 Thessalonians 5:24 (HCSB)

In the busyness of everyday life, it's easy to forget the journey I've been on with God. My family came to Madagascar several years ago to build a team to engage the lost in a country of 20 million. With 80 percent of the population deep in the rainforest, the spiny desert, or along the coast, the work isn't easy. God has steadily called a handful of new missionaries to join us. We sense that we are on the verge of God doing something big.

Why should we be surprised that God answers prayer? God took my husband, who served in Russia until his first wife's death from cancer, and me, who lost my first husband to cancer, and brought our lives together. I had sensed that God was calling me to missions before I remarried, but how could I serve effectively as a single mom? God responded, *You be obedient to what I have called you to today, and I will take care of the rest.* In God's timing, I remarried, we blended our families, and we began seeking where God wanted us to serve. The lack of laborers on this massive island was brought to our attention.

We shouldn't be surprised that He, the same God who turned our broken lives into something beautiful, is accomplishing His purposes. He really does work things out.

—LuSinda, Sub-Saharan African Peoples

You, dear Father, are able to complete the good work You begin in us. Thank You for working out each need and allowing these two families to serve You together. Father, please bring abundant fruit to the good work begun in Madagascar. Amen.

# *He brings the fruit*

*"Blessed are those whose strength is in you ... As they go through the Valley of Baca they make it a place of springs; the early rain also covers it with pools."*
*Psalm 84:5–6 (ESV)*

My first year was over. Language had been studied, foods had been tried, and close friends had been made at the university where I worked. I headed home one day in the sweltering 110-degree heat. As the Saharan sun shone through my taxi window, I put my earphones conspicuously in my ears so that my taxi driver would ignore me. It seemed that every driver that week was determined to marry me for a visa to America.

Tired, hot, and sick of eating the same old bean sandwich every day, I felt brokenhearted. For a whole year, I had searched for people willing to hear the Good News, but it seemed no one was interested. They pray each day mechanically. I tell them that I am a Christian and believe in one God, but they are shocked because they have been taught differently. I tell them Jesus died and they say, "No, Judas took His place on the cross." My attempts at breaking through with the truth feel so ineffective.

However, God faithfully reassured me that I am called to labor and bring glory to His name while He brings the fruit. I am breaking up the hard ground, praying and trusting that someone will come and water it. And when the rains come, the harvest will be plentiful.

—A.M.W., NORTHERN AFRICA AND THE MIDDLE EASTERN PEOPLES

*I get so discouraged,* LORD! I WANT TO KNOW WHEN AND HOW AND WHY NOT NOW? I ASK YOU, THE ONE WHO GIVES US RAIN FROM HEAVEN AND FRUITFUL SEASONS, TO ALLOW DISCOURAGED CHRISTIAN WORKERS A GLIMPSE OF THE FRUIT OF THEIR LABORS. *Amen.*

# Glorifying God through incarnational pain

*"I cry out to God Most High, to God who fulfills his purpose for me ... Be exalted, O God, above the heavens! Let your glory be over all the earth!" Psalm 57:2, 11 (ESV)*

King David's cry in Psalm 57 is for God to save him, a request I relate to easily. I find myself almost daily seeking His help. But are my motives pure? I confess that most of the time, I am seeking help from the Lord with an end goal of self-promotion. David's heart motive was for God's glory. David's pain at the beginning of Psalm 57 is transformed into praise by the end.

In the missionary world, there is tremendous emphasis placed on incarnational ministry. In my own experience, studying about living where you minister and practicing the concept are very different experiences. My expectations of work on the field used to be glamorized. The reality has been anything but glamorous, however. I struggle with discouragement, the culture, and language. While living among millions of people, I often feel isolated. Few have shown interest in our message. For Jesus, incarnational ministry was much worse. Stepping into a sinful world, few understood Him, most rejected Him, and finally they killed Him. It wasn't pleasant; it was incarnational.

I want to be like David in Psalm 57, with my pain leading to praise. I want to love Jesus so deeply that sacrifice pulls me to Him and deepens my knowledge of Him.

—MATT, NORTHERN AFRICAN AND MIDDLE EASTERN PEOPLES

*God,* I JOIN MATT IN PRAYING FOR THE WILL TO SERVE YOU INCARNATIONALLY. LEAD EACH OF US TO BE IN THE WORLD BUT NOT OF THE WORLD; AND WHILE THIS WILL DEMAND SACRIFICE, PLEASE HELP US FULFILL YOUR PURPOSE AND BRING YOU GLORY. *Amen.*

# *Following God's call*

*"Then I heard the voice of the LORD, saying, 'Whom shall I send, and who will go for Us?' Then I said, 'Here am I. Send me!'" Isaiah 6:8 (NASB)*

I've heard people call missionaries "heroes" because of the sacrifices made to serve. But the young men in our church-planting program who have sacrificed to see the unlovable come to God are my heroes. They live by faith for the basic needs of life. They experience opposition in order to start churches, and they meet in rented apartments or run-down cultural centers.

What we and others often forget is the call of God on a person's life. When God placed the missionary call on our lives, we could do nothing else and still have peace, joy, and fulfillment. Leaving our children and grandchildren was difficult, but nothing compares to knowing we are exactly where the Lord wants us.

One church planter and his wife felt that call of God to minister to the Roma people, gypsies in Ukraine. And while many people criticized them for this decision and tempted them with head pastor positions, it is obvious that God has placed them in that community to reach people no one else wanted. This young couple is energized by the work and the obstacles they are able to overcome. The sustaining power of God comes with His call on our lives.

What has God called you to do? Don't be afraid to step out to follow that call.

—MARY ELLEN, EUROPEAN PEOPLES

*Dear Lord,* ARE YOU CALLING ME? I KNOW ALL CHRISTIANS ARE SUPPOSED TO GO AND TO TELL, BUT DO YOU REALLY MEAN ME? NO MATTER THE CALLING, NO MATTER THE DESTINATION, HELP ME RESPOND IN OBEDIENCE, SAYING, "HERE AM I. SEND ME!" *Amen.*

# Unlikely heroes

*"Therefore, since we have so great a cloud of witnesses surrounding us ... let us run with endurance ..."* Hebrews 12:1 (NASB)

Heroes don't just throw passes, record songs, or rescue people. My three heroes are humble and faithful servants of the living God. They are heroes in the kingdom army of the Most High.

"Lazarus" is a pastor in Zambia. Every Sunday, he preaches in two churches. When the rainy season causes the stream to swell and blocks his path to the second church, he waits until the congregation or he can cross the river. Then they worship together and he preaches. It is dark when he reaches home.

"Beatrice" plants a cassava field so she will have something to give to people in need. She helped start a church near her home and gave the land for their building. Her spirit is quiet but strong.

"John" is a pastor whose children have followed in his faith and some in his vocation. Pastor of one church, he has planted another. He has little education but great wisdom and godliness.

These are my heroes, proof of the power of God's Gospel. We are engaged in a dreadful battle, but take heart. God not only has an angelic host; He also has a mighty army of redeemed heroes of the faith. They may not be famous on earth, but they are not forgotten in heaven.

—JOHN, SUB-SAHARAN AFRICAN PEOPLES

*God,* I UNDERSTAND YOU MORE FULLY THROUGH THE HUMBLE SERVICE OF CHRISTIAN HEROES. PLEASE STRENGTHEN THESE CHAMPIONS OF THE FAITH SO THEY WILL NOT GROW WEARY IN THEIR WORK OF LOVE. *Amen.*

## *Thoughts from the trail*

*"Make me know Your ways, O Lord; teach me Your paths. Lead me in Your truth and teach me, for You are the God of my salvation; for You I wait all the day." Psalm 25:4–5 (NASB)*

Walking up a mountain one day, I noticed myself intent on the path before me as I focused on rocks, dirt, and tree roots. While there's nothing wrong with not wanting to trip, when I looked up, my view broadened. I saw the path, but I also saw the beauty around me and what was ahead.

How does God want me to follow the path He has planned for me? Am I to keep my head down, trudging along, focusing on the areas that can trip me up? Or should I lift my head to see more of what's going on in front of me or what He's doing around me? With my head up, I'm still aware of danger spots on the path, but they aren't my main focus. My focal point is the destination, and I am more aware that God is on the path with me, helping me avoid trouble spots and picking me up when I fall.

With head down, it's easier not to step off the path into the un-known and its dangers. With head up, the beauty of God's creation is evident as well as what may be ahead. We may even hold on a little tighter to our Father's hand, knowing that He is the only One who can protect us.

—T.L.C., European Peoples

*Heavenly Father,* I love holding Your hand. Please hold mine tightly as I walk the path with challenges like financial need, heartbreak, or physical health issues all around. Help me stay focused on Your calling. *Amen.*

# The rest of the story

*"I know that all God does will last forever; there is no adding to it or taking from it. God works so that people will be in awe of Him." Ecclesiastes 3:14 (HCSB)*

When "Lin" became a Christian, her outlook on life changed greatly as she found hope and strength to care for her elderly mother. She was anxious to share her faith with her family members, so we gave her a copy of a movie called *Good News* to show her mother.

Watching the movie, the mother's eyes grew wide. She suddenly exclaimed, "I have heard this story before! When I was a very young girl, a foreigner came into our village and told us the story of the Most High God who created the heavens, the earth, and everything on the earth. He came back another time and told us about a flood that covered the entire earth."

Evidently a foreign missionary during the 1940s brought the Gospel story to her village, but then he disappeared forever. The timetable of his visit coincided with civil war, which resulted in foreigners being expelled from the country.

The elderly mother said, "But the foreigner never told me that God had a Son!" At last she had heard the rest of the story and immediately expressed her desire to follow Christ. After 75 years of waiting, this mother joyfully came to faith in Jesus.

Seeds sown by one of the faithful sprouted that day. He is faithful.

—L.M.R., EAST ASIAN PEOPLES

*Lord Most High,* IN AWE I THANK YOU FOR BRINGING SALVATION TO LIN AND TO HER ELDERLY MOTHER. GIVE THEM READY ACCESS TO SCRIPTURAL MATERIALS SO THEY MAY GROW DEEP IN THEIR FAITH. GIVE LIN'S MOTHER BOLDNESS TO SHARE THE GOOD NEWS SHE WAITED SO LONG TO HEAR HERSELF. *Amen.*

# *Seeing the falsehood of cults*

*"Today I have given you the choice between life and death ... Oh, that you would choose life, so that you and your descendants might live!" Deuteronomy 30:19 (NLT)*

An English major in northeast Thailand, "Ken" was excited that a group of native English speakers was willing to teach English at his university. He not only learned English, but he discovered these fun-loving young women had something more important to share.

Ken began to understand that the love present in these volunteers came from God. As he attended Bible studies, he learned about Jesus and what it meant to follow Him. His Christian friends assured Ken they would love him regardless of his decision. After an evangelistic English camp, Ken prayed privately and gave his life to Christ. Unsure if he could now call himself a Christian, he didn't share his decision with others.

Shortly after the volunteers returned home, Ken was invited to a Buddhist retreat. Their claims confused Ken because they distorted teachings about Jesus. The cult leaders were extremely demanding as they pushed him to make a decision to join them. As Ken remembered the unconditional love shown to him by the Christian volunteers, he realized that he wanted to follow Christ completely. Abandoning the ideas of the retreat, he talked with a Christian worker who helped him understand that this simple act of faith made him a Christian.

Reaching out with unconditional love will not be forgotten.

—VALERIE, SOUTHEAST ASIAN PEOPLES

*Your love beckons* PEOPLE FROM EVERY NATION TO FOLLOW YOU, MY SAVIOR AND LORD. HELP ME MODEL YOUR LOVE TO OTHERS. HELP OTHERS LIKE KEN TO REJECT DEATH AND EMBRACE LIFE IN JESUS. *Amen.*

# Doing God's work by His grace

*"[God] who has saved us and called us with a holy calling, not according to our works, but according to His own purpose and grace ..."* 2 Timothy 1:9 (HCSB)

When our family discerned that God was calling us to serve Him internationally, it was a surprise to us and everyone we knew! We're ordinary—no seminary degree or outstanding résumé. We were overwhelmed by the responsibility and wondered how God could use us.

The disaster relief project manager job seemed perfect for my contractor husband. What we didn't know until months later was that God had used that job description to get us where He wanted us, not to define the work He had prepared for us to do in that place. The relief project soon ended, but God led us to opportunities for evangelism and discipleship. Even with no seminary degree, God allowed us to share the Gospel, start house groups, disciple leaders, and help these new believers start house churches.

There have been many times when we've cried out to God, doubting whether we were able to do what He called us to do. But God has been faithful to remind us that He is the One who called us, and through His grace, He accomplishes His own purposes. God's holy call has little to do with our abilities or works. That's why we don't have to worry about what we can and cannot do. He has everything under control.

—D.Y., SOUTH ASIAN PEOPLES

*Sovereign God,* IT'S NOT SO MUCH MY ABILITY THAT YOU ARE CONCERNED WITH AS MUCH AS MY AVAILABILITY TO FOLLOW THE PATH YOU PLACE BEFORE ME. MAY I BE OBEDIENT TO YOUR CALL AS YOU EQUIP ME FOR WHATEVER THE TASK. *Amen.*

# *Praying for boldness*

*"And now, Lord, look upon their threats and grant to your servants to continue to speak your word with all boldness." Acts 4:29 (ESV)*

In the Middle East, I've had several run-ins with the government. I used to pray that God would keep me from harm. But when I studied the example of Peter in Acts, I was convicted. In the face of political threats, floggings, and imprisonments, Peter never prayed for safety. Rather, he cried out to God, asking that these events wouldn't take away his boldness! Peter was more concerned about spreading the Good News than his physical well-being. Hardship continued for Peter as well as imprisonment and beatings. Yet he thanked God for counting Him worthy to suffer for Christ! Warned that proclaiming Christ would result in more punishment and eventually death, Peter continued to speak boldly and passionately.

God answered Peter's prayers. Until his death, Peter faithfully spoke of the One who called him to follow, who ate at his table, who saved him from drowning, who healed his mother-in-law, who was shamefully denied by him three times, and who then extended His own nail-scarred hands in forgiveness.

I can pray for safety concerning governmental threats, or I can step out with faith like Peter, asking that no matter what happens, my boldness in speaking the truth will become stronger. May I be more afraid of being silent than of being persecuted.

—J.L.M., NORTHERN AFRICAN AND MIDDLE EASTERN PEOPLES

*You,* HEAVENLY FATHER, HAVE CALLED ME TO BOLD DISCIPLESHIP, WHOLLY SURRENDERED TO THE POWER OF THE HOLY SPIRIT. HELP ME TO FEARLESSLY PROCLAIM THE TRUTH. *Amen.*

# Following God's call when it's hard

*"And he said to them, 'Truly, I say to you, there is no one who has left house or wife or brothers or parents or children, for the sake of the kingdom of God, who will not receive many times more in this time, and in the age to come eternal life.'" Luke 18:29–30 (ESV)*

I've heard that long ago, missionaries who went overseas would pack their belongings in a casket and say goodbye to loved ones with the thought of never seeing them again. Today, with modern technology, I can speak to my family back home daily if I want. Due to a recent family crisis, a relative said, "Things would be better if you hadn't left." After Hurricanes Katrina and Rita hit my home state, I heard, "This is the absolutely worst time you could be deserting us."

When I heard that another hurricane was possibly heading toward my family again, I was heavyhearted. I walked through our village in Northern Africa and asked God to please send someone to minister to my family. In the background, a *muezzin* from the mosque on top of the hill announced a death. It was a mother with severe stomach pains, possibly from a ruptured gallbladder, an easily treatable ailment in the States. Had I shared the Good News with her? Who will hold her children? Compassion filled my heart as I looked around at my friends and neighbors. They have become my family, too. I can't leave them. The raging storm of spiritual darkness is wreaking havoc, and they have yet to know the One who can rescue them.

—RENEE, NORTHERN AFRICAN AND MIDDLE EASTERN PEOPLES

God, I PRAY FOR RENEE AND ALL MISSIONARIES WHO HAVE LEFT FAMILY FOR THE SAKE OF THE KINGDOM. PLEASE HELP THEM MAINTAIN FAMILY BONDS DESPITE THE DISTANCE. BRING PEACE TO RELATIVES WHO MISS THEM AND SALVATION TO THOSE WHO DO NOT KNOW YOU. Amen.

# Even if I'm not where I thought I'd be

*"Stand firm ... having shod* YOUR FEET WITH THE PREPARATION OF THE GOSPEL OF PEACE.*" Ephesians 6:14–15 (NASB)*

What is the description of my life? A year ago, I would have said my life was like a pitch-black game of laser tag—adventurous, yet uncertain.

We had lived in six different locations in Eastern Europe over a three-year period. Our family of four resided in an attic room in the home of national friends. Bedroom, office, and schoolroom all in one, we were stepping on toes, culturally and literally! This was our holding pattern until we could register in another city. In that environment, it was laughable when I received an e-mail asking me to help with an up-coming conference and lead a small group on the topic: "I can stay on the field even if I'm not where I thought I'd be." What a turning point to realize that God's humor is ever present! If He wanted to use me to encourage others in the midst of my difficult transition, who was I to complain?

These principles have kept me going: (1) Look at the big picture, (2) Do the next thing, and (3) Evaluate myself mentally, physically, spiritually, and emotionally.

In the midst of transition, we can glorify God. There is no need to wait until life becomes normal again; trials in the Christian life are the norm. Our feet can be prepared to maneuver through adventures, one after another.

—DAWN, EUROPEAN PEOPLES

*Prince of peace,* CONDITIONS AROUND ME ARE OFTEN IN PIECES, AND I DO NOT ABIDE IN YOUR PEACE. HELP MISSIONARIES AND ME TO LOOK BEYOND CIRCUMSTANCES AND STAND FIRM IN YOUR PEACE. *Amen.*

# A ministry of interruptions

*"Whatever you do, do it enthusiastically, as something done for the Lord and not for men." Colossians 3:23 (HCSB)*

Bother! The electricity was off again. "Don't open the fridge, kids!" The washing machine was full of clothes after buckets of water had been brought by a man on a bicycle. I couldn't finish the load.

At least we could do homeschool lessons without electricity. "Everybody ready?" I asked. *Knock, knock.* Going to see who was at the door, I saw that it had started to rain. "Kids, run to the clothesline and take the laundry down fast! Grab the buckets to catch the rainwater from the gutters!" On days like these, even the first item on my to-do list is not checked off.

Scenarios like this happen frequently. Between the inconveniences of living in an African village, the needs of family, and the constant knocking at the door by villagers, sometimes I wonder when "ministry" will ever happen.

Yet what am I here for? My idea of ministry may not match God's definition. His goal for me is to bring Him glory in the little things and not just in the big things. Being reminded of this goal has changed my outlook on the interruptions of each day. Each interruption is an opportunity to serve the Lord by loving the people God brings my way.

—CARA, SUB-SAHARAN AFRICAN PEOPLES

*My Rock and Salvation,* IT IS REFRESHING TO KNOW THAT OTHERS FACE THE SAME KIND OF CRAZY DAYS THAT I FACE! PLEASE HELP ME CONFORM MY ATTITUDE TOWARD INTERRUPTIONS WITH YOUR WILL. HELP MISSIONARIES SERVE ENTHUSIASTICALLY, ALWAYS BRINGING YOU GLORY. *Amen.*

# How will they hear?

*"How then will they call on Him in whom they have not believed? How will they believe in Him whom they have not heard? And how will they hear without a preacher?" Romans 10:14 (NASB)*

Suffering from an enlarged thyroid, "Mrs. Sanh" lived with excessive fatigue, fluctuating body temperatures, a racing heart, and swallowing difficulties. This poor, Vietnamese woman, who lived on the river with her family on a small, wooden houseboat, had no hope of receiving medication or the needed surgery. But hope returned when she heard about our medical clinic.

She began to visit the clinic in order to receive medication. During visits, Mrs. Sanh listened to Bible stories, watched the *JESUS* film, and heard a personal testimony from a believer. On her fifth medical visit, I was encouraged to see that the medication was working and that she reported a dramatic reduction in her symptoms. Expressions of gratitude were plentiful. As we ended the exam, I asked her, "Big sister, have you decided to believe God yet?" To my surprise, she responded with a big smile, "Yes, I have believed already." She added, "From the time of my birth until now, I had never heard about God, but now I believe."

Although some days are long and exhausting, what a privilege it is to bring spiritual and physical healing to the lost and hurting. There are many around us who need us to care. Giving hope, helping, and loving, all in the name of Jesus, make a difference.

—ANNA, SOUTHEAST ASIAN PEOPLES

*We bow before You* IN THANKSGIVING, HOLY SAVIOR, FOR THE REDEMPTION OF THIS ONE PRECIOUS SOUL, MRS. SANH. WE PLEAD FOR MORE LABORERS FOR THE GREAT HARVEST YOU HAVE PREPARED AMONG THE NATIONS, DEAR LORD! *Amen.*

## In His care

*"The LORD is constantly watching everyone, and he gives strength to those who faithfully obey him." 2 Chronicles 16:9 (CEV)*

Does God really know my every move, breath, and thought? Is He really my Comforter, an ever-present help in time of need?

During a week of focused prayer for our city, I received a phone call followed by a visit from the police. In this restrictive country, the message was clear: "We know who you are, and we want you to know that we know."

We began to ask ourselves whether we should follow through with the week's activities that would culminate in a weekend of training nationals. The next day, God spoke to me from His Word: "standing firm in one spirit ... in no way alarmed by your opponents" (Philippians 1:27–28, NASB). We proceeded with the plans that had been made and experienced no interference.

Less than six months later, I got a call from a local coworker to say that he could no longer work with us because the police had questioned him. We were being watched again. Why would God allow this? God quickly showed me that I should not be afraid; what can man do to me? I later met with this friend, and he decided to continue working with us.

Again and again we have been faced with similar situations, only to be reassured from God in a very real way. Yes, He does know my every move.

—S.S., EAST ASIAN PEOPLES

*Almighty God,* YOU ALONE SEE MY EVERY MOVE. PROTECT THOSE SERVING IN SENSITIVE LOCATIONS FROM FEAR THAT MIGHT PARALYZE THEIR WORK. MAY THEY LIVE IN YOUR CONFIDENCE AND PROTECTION. *Amen.*

## Seeing good deeds

*"Always let others see you behaving properly ... Then on the day of judgment, they will honor God by telling the good things they saw you do."* 1 Peter 2:12 (CEV)

For several days, our family removed rubble from homes after a devastating earthquake killed a quarter of the people in a Buddhist village. We also taught English classes to the children in a temporary refugee camp.

As we spent hours in the camp, we were frustrated that police watched us constantly. We found out a rumor had been spread that we were journalists coming to write about the deficiencies of the camp. Consequently, we weren't able to share Christ with as many people as we had hoped.

One family at the refugee camp told us how they fled their destroyed village, and we shared the Gospel with them. Afterward, the father said, "I believe that what you have said is true. I have seen that you really have come to help us. The Buddhists are not like that. When the earthquake happened and people were still buried alive in the rubble, instead of helping, the Buddhists ran to the temple to pray for themselves. They and their god did nothing for us. But you Christians are different. I believe your God really does care about us!"

Satan tried to destroy our witness with a rumor, but God's love through us prevailed. People are watching. May we glorify Him always in our Christlike behavior.

—DWAYNE, EAST ASIAN PEOPLES

*Lord,* YOU CARE ABOUT EAST ASIAN PEOPLES AND HEAR THEIR CRIES FOR HELP. BLESS CHRISTIAN WORKERS WITH WORDS OF GRACE AND ACTS OF KINDNESS. HELP ME HONOR YOU THROUGH GOOD DEEDS. *Amen.*

# With you wherever you go

*"Have I not commanded you? Be strong and courageous! Do not tremble or be dismayed, for the LORD your God is with you wherever you go." Joshua 1:9 (NASB)*

"Get on the ground!" the masked men screamed. As our hearts pounded, we climbed out of the van and fell to the ground. "Dollars, dollars," they demanded, pushing guns and machetes in our faces and checking our hands and pockets. Lying facedown on the mountain road, I could see them pulling our belongings out of the van. *Lord, Your promise is to be with us wherever we go,* I prayed. We had been in Guatemala one week exactly.

More vehicles began to come up over the mountain. The thieves robbed them as well but hurriedly sent them on their way. The thieves were obviously getting nervous as the drivers stared at us as we lay helplessly on the roadside. It seemed like an hour but probably lasted no more than fifteen minutes. *Lord, when You said, "Go," we were willing. It's early morning back home—someone's praying! Lord, hear the cries of Your people.*

Finally, the thieves left, carrying our belongings. As we climbed back into the van, I quickly reached under the seat to see if my study Bible was still there. Smiling, but trembling, I turned to the promise in Joshua that He had given us when He called us to missionary service. I know without a doubt that He is with me wherever I go.

—SARAH ANN, AMERICAN PEOPLES

*You are El Roi,* THE STRONG ONE WHO SEES. THANK YOU FOR SEEING SARAH ANN'S NEED AND HELPING HER REMAIN STRONG AND COURAGEOUS IN THE FACE OF DANGER. HELP ME BE MORE AWARE THAT YOU ARE WITH ME WHEREVER I GO. *Amen.*

## *Sufficiently graced*

*"It was for freedom that Christ set us free; therefore keep standing firm and do not be subject again to a yoke of slavery." Galatians 5:1 (NASB)*

Ten years. No results. Not one person in our targeted people group had come to faith through our efforts in a city that is 99.99 percent Muslim. Discouraged can't begin to describe how I felt. We had tried many different ways to reach the people, but there was no interest.

Thoughts of easier locations came to mind. Maybe we should move. I cried out to God, *Why do You want us to live here? Why don't You open the eyes of these people? Please, Lord, move us somewhere else. I can't do this anymore. This is too hard!* Overwhelmed with despair, my heart was broken for these people.

Immediately, the Lord spoke to my heart, *My child, you are not your own. You've been bought with a price. My grace is sufficient.* Realization struck me that I was living out a lesson in freedom. Followers of Christ do not have to make their own plans concerning where they live, what they do, or when they move. Instead, believers live according to the Father's will, which may be difficult; but by His grace, it will bring glory to Him. This truth freed me to keep persevering in His work. Stay put, trust in Him, faithfully proclaim the Word in this dark place, and in His timing and through His grace, His will shall be accomplished.

—T.M., SOUTHEAST ASIAN PEOPLES

*No interest*—OH GOD, HOW CAN A PEOPLE HAVE NO INTEREST IN THE FREEDOM CHRIST OFFERS? I BEG YOU TO OPEN THE HEARTS OF THESE MUSLIM PEOPLE IN SOUTHEAST ASIA. BREAK THE BONDS OF THEIR BELIEF SYSTEM AND CAUSE THEM TO SEEK FREEDOM IN JESUS. *Amen.*

# Worth the sacrifice

*"When the disciples saw it, they were indignant. 'Why this waste?' they asked. 'This might have been sold for a great deal and given to the poor.' But Jesus, aware of this, said to them, 'Why are you bothering this woman? She has done a noble thing for Me.'" Matthew 26:8–10 (HCSB)*

My stomach churned with fear after my husband called. He had been summoned to the police station for the fifth time in two months, accused of distributing Bibles and teaching people about Jesus. We had to ship our belongings to another city and temporarily leave the country. Our hopes for seeing churches planted among a rural, unreached people group were brought to a sudden, crashing halt. Why were we being ousted when there was still so much to accomplish?

*Lord, can't You see us here, spinning our wheels? We're spending money on hotel rooms and eating out. It's a huge waste of time and money!* I prayed. The Lord reminded me of the story of Mary anointing Jesus. Those around asked, "Why this waste?" when Mary broke her expensive perfume on His head and feet. But Jesus said, "She has done a noble thing." That difference of perspective really struck me.

Could it be that what I think is a waste, Jesus sees as a noble thing? I resolved to stop considering this hard time as a waste and instead say, "You are worth this great sacrifice."

—A WORKER WITH EAST ASIAN PEOPLES

*Lamb of God,* WE REJECT ALL SO-CALLED WEALTH THAT ENSLAVES US AND OFFER YOU OUR SACRIFICE OF TIME, OUR PLANS, OUR THINGS. DELIVER THIS EAST ASIAN PEOPLE FROM CAPRICIOUS DOMINION AS YOUR SERVANTS TESTIFY TO YOUR EXTRAVAGANT GRACE. *Amen.*

# Called to those who haven't heard

*"For look, darkness covers the earth, and total darkness the peoples; but the* LORD *will shine over you, and His glory will appear over you. Nations will come to your light." Isaiah 60:2–3 (HCSB)*

"I've never been to that village." That's what one grandmother said to us when we asked her if she knew about Jesus. She thought that perhaps Jesus was a village, unknown to her. But even though we shared about Him that day, she did not understand who He is.

We came to Southeast Asia to share Jesus with those who do not know Him, but we were still surprised to find people who had never heard His name. It's not that they have chosen not to follow Him, rejected Him, or don't understand His love. They have never even heard of Jesus. One friend from the States said to us, "In today's world, with the Internet and Christian television, everyone must have heard of Jesus." But this grandmother does not have access to either, and even if she did, the programming would not be in her language.

There is no church among the grandmother's people group. The Good News must come from someone on the outside. Meeting this grandmother caused us to pray more than ever, "Here we are Lord; send us to them." And we are grateful for those who sent us, pray for us, and support us so that we can go to the unreached.

—G.J., SOUTHEAST ASIAN PEOPLES

*It is hard* TO FATHOM THE DARKNESS, LORD. WE CHRISTIANS CANNOT STAY HOME, COMFORTABLE IN THE SOFT GLOW OF OUR BELIEVING COMMUNITIES. CALL OUT YOUR LABORERS! SEND US TO THE DARKEST PLACES, AND HELP US SHINE BRIGHTLY FOR YOU. *Amen.*

# Faithful to the end

*"For me, living is Christ and dying is gain." Philippians 1:21 (HCSB)*

My missionary family was thrilled when my sister, Theresa, told us that God was calling her overseas as a career missionary. Her love for people and her heart for the nations were fueled by her commitment to follow God. She was ready to be obedient, no matter what.

Little did we know the path the Lord had chosen for her. Just 18 months after moving to Western Europe, Theresa was diagnosed with cancer. The realities of Theresa's diagnosis changed her ministry, but it never changed her focus. She was still determined that her life would glorify God. With our parents' blessing and help, Theresa remained on the mission field to continue serving God while she received her cancer treatments.

Throughout weeks of radiation and chemotherapy, Theresa's quiet and sincere spirit drew people to her. She wanted nothing more than to see the Lord glorified. And was He ever! The hospital became her mission field, and its staff witnessed a life lived in the fullness of Christ.

To the end, Theresa was faithful to God's call on her life. When she had fulfilled her mission, God called her home. She passed gracefully into His presence. Many people have been inspired by Theresa's unwavering commitment to God as she encouraged us all to be faithful to the end, no matter what.

—SHEILA, EUROPEAN PEOPLES

*Thank You,* HOLY SPIRIT OUR COMFORTER, FOR TOUCHING SO MANY HEARTS THROUGH THERESA'S GODLY LIFE. I PRAY FOR THE HOSPITAL STAFF THAT THEY WILL SEEK YOUR TRUTH. PLEASE COMFORT THERESA'S SISTER AND FAMILY AS THEY GRIEVE. *Amen.*

JUNE V

# The Power of the Story

*Who doesn't love a great story?*
*Why do we think Christ used the method so*
*prolifically in His teachings?*

—BETH MOORE

A group of volunteers from the States walked down the dusty, red-dirt paths of a high-density but rural area of Zimbabwe. We were prayerwalking through the area where my husband and I were partnering with a national couple to plant a church. It was the same area where a national woman and I taught sewing and stories from the Bible.

Suddenly, a young woman tapped me on the shoulder. "Mother," she said, which is a common way to address a married woman in Zimbabwe. "Mrs. Mzonza is asking for you." I didn't know who Mrs. Mzonza was, so I asked the girl what this lady wanted. "She has heard that you are talking about a man," she replied. "She wants to know more about this man."

As I stood there swatting the flies from my face, I was in a dilemma. Should I go with this girl to who-knows-where or should I stay with the volunteers who had come all the way from the States to prayerwalk? The whole purpose that day was to prayerwalk. I didn't have to make the decision, however, because my husband said that he would be glad to continue praying with the volunteers and for me to feel free to take my national friend with me to talk with Mrs. Mzonza.

So off we went. My friend and I followed the girl who ran a little ahead, and eventually we came to a hut on a small hill. As we entered the yard, several women came to meet us. In the center of the group was a woman who had been badly burned. Visible scars covered her neck and chest and part of her face. She introduced herself as Mrs. Mzonza, and after all the bowing, clapping, and introductions were complete, she welcomed us into her small, dark hut. We were served tea as we sat on the cool, dirt floor and after some small talk, she asked me who the man was that I had been telling many women about during the sewing class.

"His name is Jesus," I said. I then asked her if she wanted to hear a true story, in fact several stories. She and the others were eager, so with the help of my friend who was translating, I briefly told Bible stories, beginning with creation, the fall of man, the promise of a

Savior, the flood, eventually sharing the story of Jesus from birth to His resurrection.

When the stories and occasional interruptions were finished, perhaps an hour later, I could see the emotion in the dark hut. We invited Mrs. Mzonza and the other women to meet the next day at a new church gathering. We told her that she could accept what Jesus had done for her after she took some time to think about it. But she would not let us leave.

"What you have told me is true. I want to follow Jesus right now," she urgently replied with tears in her eyes. So in that hut, we explained a few more things and then led Mrs. Mzonza in prayer as she surrendered her life to Jesus Christ.

Not only was Mrs. Mzonza one of the first to arrive for the church service the next day, she brought others with her. We learned that she was one of the most influential women in the area. She became a great advocate for our sewing class and for the new church. And she told everyone she met about Jesus.

Hearing God's Word through the stories of the Bible led Mrs. Mzonza to Jesus. Chronological Bible storying is a method used all over the world to reach people with the Gospel. If people don't hear, how will they know? God's Word can't be destroyed, and you will enjoy reading stories this month, including "The unburned Bible" and "A treasured gift from God." His Word stands for all generations.

—*Kim P. Davis*

# A treasured gift from God

*"The kingdom of heaven is like a treasure hidden in the field, which a man found and hid again; and from joy over it he goes and sells all that he has and buys that field." Matthew 13:44 (NASB)*

New believers in an isolated town were ecstatic to each receive a Bible. Only one middle-aged woman already had a copy of God's Word. When my husband's team asked how she alone had a Bible, the woman shared that an evangelism team had previously visited the town. She had believed the Gospel that they proclaimed. However, the visitors left no Bible. So she began asking God to give her one.

One day while visiting the local outhouse, she peered down and saw a book. Curious, she lowered herself into the hole and snatched a Bible out of the filth! She took it home and gingerly wiped off each page. She began to read God's Word at home and at the new church's meetings.

My husband looked at her Bible with its stained, crumpled pages. He offered her a new Bible, but she politely refused. Clutching hers, she explained, "I already have a Bible. I prayed, and God gave me this one."

I was awed by the faith of this convert who, on her own, realized the worth of God's Word and her own God-given Bible. Oh, that we would all desire God's truth and treat the Bible as the living, powerful, life-changing treasure that it truly is!

—SUZANNE, EAST ASIAN PEOPLES

*Father,* YOUR WORD IS A PRICELESS TREASURE. IT IS TRUTH. IT IS LIFE. MAY I NEVER AGAIN TAKE IT FOR GRANTED. THANK YOU FOR THIS WOMAN WHO REMINDED ME OF ITS WORTH. *Amen.*

# The unburned Bible

*"LORD, Your word is forever; it is firmly fixed in heaven." Psalm 119:89 (HCSB)*

Living in a war zone in a North African country, "Omar" and his family relied on food distributions to live. One day, national believers distributed food bags with Bibles in them. Omar's sister received one of these Bibles. When he found her reading it, Omar was enraged. He grabbed the book and slapped her face. Determined to destroy the Bible, he burned it.

That night, Omar had a disturbing dream. In his dream, he saw shining hands take the ashes of the burned Bible and form it into its original state. Then he heard these words in his own language: "This is My Word. I am the One who sent this book to your family so that they might be saved." Omar jumped out of the bed, crying and shouting. His shouts woke his family, so he told them about the dream. Frantic, he ran to the place where he had burned the Bible. Amazingly, he found the Bible lying on top of the ashes, unburned, clean, and new.

Omar's sister told him to go to the Bible distributors and ask them what to do next. Omar found them, and they told him about Jesus. He accepted Christ immediately and then reported everything he learned to his family. I am so thankful for the many ways that Jesus reveals Himself to those He is drawing to Himself.

—J.K., NORTHERN AFRICAN AND MIDDLE EASTERN PEOPLES

*God of miracles,* YOU ASTOUND ME. YOU CAN PART A SEA, TURN WATER INTO WINE, AND EVEN RESTORE YOUR WRITTEN WORD FROM ASHES. MAY OMAR AND HIS FAMILY BRING YOU GLORY BY PROCLAIMING YOUR WORKS THROUGHOUT THEIR COUNTRY. *Amen.*

## His glory in the ordinary

*"I will never forget Your precepts, for You have given me life through them."*
*Psalm 119:93 (HCSB)*

In God's Word, God takes everyday events and people and uses them to bring Himself glory—five loaves and two fishes, water from a well, an ordinary shepherd boy, and a young virgin, just to name a few. "Yosef" had his own experience with God through an ordinary event.

When Yosef ventured into the education center to sign up for an English class, finding Jesus was the last thing on his mind. Like most North African young adults, Yosef deeply desired any educational opportunity he could find.

Enrolled in class, Yosef faithfully attended. Midway through the term, his teacher invited the class to join a "listening club," and Yosef signed up. On Saturdays, he and other students listened to Bible stories on cassette tape in order to improve their English. However, Yosef could not stop thinking about the stories. Suddenly, learning English didn't matter as much because he was captivated by the Bible stories. He was so interested that he asked his teacher if he could have a copy of the stories. He listened to them daily and recognized them as truth.

God's Word transformed Yosef's life, and he asked Jesus to be his Savior. God used a simple English class to glorify Himself.

—J.L., NORTHERN AFRICAN AND MIDDLE EASTERN PEOPLES

*Savior of the nations,* YOUR WORD IS LIFE. THANK YOU FOR SCRIPTURE RECORDINGS ON CASSETTE, VIDEO, AND EVEN PODCAST. IT ISN'T THE MEDIUM, BUT THE MESSAGE THAT CAPTURES THE SOUL. BLESS LISTENERS LIKE YOSEF AS THEY HEAR TRUTH. *Amen.*

# *When the mountains shake*

*"'Though the mountains move and the hills shake, My love will not be removed from you and My covenant of peace will not be shaken,' says your compassionate LORD." Isaiah 54:10 (HCSB)*

Within weeks, three events had turned our lives upside down. First, a teammate was denied reentry into our country, forcing us to say a sudden, painful goodbye to friends who had become like family. Then, days later, I received a call from a former Muslim whom I was discipling. She couldn't tell me much, only that there were "problems with the police" and that I needed to pray. She promised to let me know something when she could, but for over a week, I heard nothing.

While I waited anxiously to hear from my friend, we got more bad news from colleagues. Doctors were afraid that the terrible headaches a coworker was having could be the result of a brain hemorrhage, and they wanted him to return to the States for testing and possible surgery.

Any one of these events would have been traumatic, but together, it was almost more than I could bear. My mountains were shaking. I could barely form the words to call out to God. Desperate for His peace, I began to soak my mind in Scripture about His mighty power, unfailing love, and complete sovereignty. His Spirit slowly took control of my anxious heart and gave His perfect peace.

Regardless of our circumstances, we can always anchor in His life-giving Word.

—HOPE, NORTHERN AFRICAN AND MIDDLE EASTERN PEOPLES

*You are the Anchor* OF MY SOUL. YOU SECURE ME FIRMLY IN YOUR WORD. THANK YOU FOR REMINDING ME THROUGH HOPE'S TESTIMONY. TOUCH HER TEAMMATES WITH YOUR GRACE AS ONE DEALS WITH RELOCATION AND ANOTHER WITH ILLNESS. *Amen.*

# The rich man

*"For the word of God is living and active and sharper than any two-edged sword, and piercing as far as the division of soul and spirit, of both joints and marrow, and able to judge the thoughts and intentions of the heart." Hebrews 4:12 (NASB)*

The stories of God's Word contain such a wealth of everlasting truth that we can spend an entire lifetime mining them. Though seemingly simple, God speaks through Bible stories. And many times, the person He speaks to is the one who is teaching!

Our Bible storying team hosted a weekend training session for a dozen believers from a church outside Guatemala City. Many of them struggle to minister to people who are drug addicts, gang members, or victims of domestic violence. The second morning of our meeting, the pastor told us how overwhelmed his people were that we and another missionary family had opened our homes to house, feed, and train them.

That morning, I told the story of Lazarus and the rich man. Although I did not grow up poor, I had identified myself with Lazarus because I did not see myself as rich. But as I told the story, God changed my perspective and made me see that in the eyes of the group, I was rich. They were the ones grateful for any crumb from my table. I thank God for allowing me to see another facet of this story and changing my attitude about what He has given me in this life.

—Melodie, American Peoples

*Dear Lord,* each time I read Your Word, You reveal truth; however, I'm not always paying attention. Keep me sensitive to the Sword of truth as it wields conviction of sin and instruction in righteousness. May those who hear Your stories today be transformed. *Amen.*

# *Stories change hearts*

*"for God sees not as man sees, for man looks at the outward appearance, but the* LORD *looks at the heart." 1 Samuel 16:7b (NASB)*

Because the Tanzanian constitution allows for religion classes to be taught in public schools on Fridays, we approached the headmaster at the elementary school in a Muslim village. He allowed us to tell Bible stories, especially since the children were not required to attend our class.

The first day, we started with the story of God creating the angels. After we left, the mosque leader approached the headmaster and threatened to have us arrested if we returned. Not knowing this, we arrived the next Friday to tell a Bible story. No one came to arrest us, but several parents did show up to tell the children not to attend our class. One parent even came into the classroom, told his children to leave, and shamed the other children for staying. Over the course of time, however, children listened to the stories.

When time came for us to leave Tanzania, the mosque leader actually thanked us for coming and suggested that other Christians come. We left another missionary couple with the task of continuing the stories. When they told the story of Jesus' birth and said He was God's Son, they later heard that the mosque leader began to ask questions about eternal life and wanted to hear more. At first we saw this leader as an opponent, but God made him an advocate.

—JEFF AND KATHY, SUB-SAHARAN AFRICAN PEOPLES

*"Your word to me,* YOUR SERVANT, IS LIKE PURE GOLD" (PSALM 119:140A, CEV). LORD, YOU SAW THE NEED OF THIS VILLAGE AND SENT PERSISTENT SPOKESMEN. CONTINUE TO DRAW THIS MOSQUE LEADER TO YOURSELF UNTIL THE ETERNAL VALUE OF THESE BIBLE STORIES BECOMES REAL. *Amen.*

# Passing on the Word

*"Wait for the LORD; be strong and let your heart take courage; yes, wait for the LORD." Psalm 27:14 (NASB)*

My husband and "Muhammed" walked together a few times each week. The young man wanted to practice his English, and my husband wanted to practice his Arabic. Yet there was little chance for sharing the Gospel because they were usually joined by other men. If they looked at written material, others gathered around suspiciously. Still, we prayed for witnessing opportunities.

One day, I visited Muhammed's mother. We talked for a while, and then her niece joined us. After small talk, the niece asked me, "What is the difference between Islam and Christianity?" I tried to summarize a main difference between our two religions: Islam teaches that people must earn their way to heaven, but Christians believe God has paid our way. When I mentioned the Bible, she seemed interested. I asked her if she'd read it. When she shook her head, I offered her an Arabic Bible. "But how will I get it to you?" I asked. She replied, "Your husband can give it to Muhammed, who will give it to me." Surprisingly, Muhammed's mother agreed.

I left thankful for answered prayer. My husband gave Muhammed a Bible. I believe that not only will Muhammed's cousin read God's Word, but Muhammed will also.

—K.B., NORTHERN AFRICAN AND MIDDLE EASTERN PEOPLES

*Holy God,* THANK YOU FOR ANSWERING PRAYER! THIS FAMILY NEEDS TO KNOW YOU; AND I PRAY THAT MUHAMMED, HIS COUSIN, AND HIS MOTHER WILL ALL READ AND UNDERSTAND YOUR HOLY WORD. MAY WE REJOICE IN THE DAY OF THEIR SALVATION, GOD. *Amen.*

# Overlooking the undesirable

*"Don't just pretend to love others. Really love them. ... Never be lazy, but work hard and serve the Lord enthusiastically." Romans 12:9, 11 (NLT)*

As I left the woman's house, she invited me to return. I said I would, but as I left, I seriously considered not going back. She had asked me to tell her a story, and I gladly told her about Jesus healing someone. After some discussion, she asked for another story and then a third! But that hadn't changed the fact that she smelled like an old, mildewed outhouse. It was not appealing to talk with her in the least.

As I meandered home, I thought about something Jesus had told His disciples: "From everyone who has been given much, much will be required ..." (Luke 12:48, NASB). Walking out my faith comes with much responsibility. It hit me. *How can I not go back?* This woman wanted to hear stories from God's Word. Here I was, the only Christian in the neighborhood, perhaps the only Christian she even knew. I could be the only person to ever love her with the love of Christ, the only person to ever help her understand God's Word and offer her everlasting life. And I was debating whether I wanted to go back because she smelled bad!

How many others have I passed by because I didn't enjoy being with them? Who am I to choose who will hear His Gospel? I can't "just pretend to love others," but instead, I must "really love them."

—J.M., SOUTH ASIAN PEOPLES

*Lord,* WE ARE ALL SINNERS, NO DIFFERENT THAN THIS WOMAN. EXPAND OUR HEARTS, FATHER, TO CARRY OUT THE GREAT RESPONSIBILITY OF SHARING YOUR LOVE WITH ALL PEOPLES. *Amen.*

## Mentoring along a path

*"Train up a child in the way he should go ..." Proverbs 22:6 (NASB)*

As Gordon and his 8-year-old son, Zach, were walking to the Sudanese market, they encountered another woman headed to the same place. Conversation began, and Gordon found out that she didn't attend church and didn't know about God's love for her. Her life was filled with fear of local spirits and the village witch doctors.

As they made their way to the market, Gordon began sharing Bible stories with the woman while Zach observed. By the time they reached their destination, the woman sat down on a log with Gordon and gave her life to Christ. They then went their separate ways to shop until a short while later when Gordon heard the woman at the other end of the market shouting, "Where's Gordon, where's Gordon?" The woman had her best friend with her and proclaimed, "You *must* tell my friend the same stories you told me." He did and led her to Christ as well.

Situational Bible storying is for anyone, any time, any place. Young Zach was mentored that very day as he watched his father tell stories from God's Word. I have seen and heard Zach tell Bible stories that he now has written on his heart. As we demonstrate sharing His Word in front of our children, they will catch on.

—MARK, SUB-SAHARAN AFRICAN PEOPLES

*Father,* YOUNG CHILDREN ARE SO IMPRESSIONABLE. I PRAY FOR MISSIONARIES TO BE LOVINGLY INTENTIONAL IN MODELING BASIC CHRISTIAN DISCIPLINES OF PRAYER, BIBLE STUDY, AND WITNESSING IN FRONT OF THEIR CHILDREN. *Amen.*

# *God's Word translates*

*"The grass withers, the flower fades, but the word of our God stands forever."*
Isaiah 40:8 (NASB)

Kawengu's heart had been transformed by the Gospel, so he invited me to teach his family. Each week we walked an hour to the village where he and I would tell Bible stories. Two months and numerous Bible stories later, a group of adults believed. Kawengu and I rejoiced! I began praying about which story to tell next.

The parable of Jesus as the Good Shepherd was chosen. I prepared the story and met Kawengu for our weekly walk to his village. Our conversation turned to his cattle, and I was reminded of the parable. Wanting to do my best to communicate the parable later, I began asking him questions. I learned that each cow has a name. He hires a watchman to guard his cattle. At night, his brothers and he join the watchman until midnight when the guard leaves, and they remain until morning to ensure the cattle's safety.

Amazed at the similarities between Jesus' words and Kawengu's life, I was reminded that it is not my clever speech or my understanding of the culture that will change lives, but it is the message of God's Word that speaks to every person, regardless of culture, age, or socioeconomic level. His Word is for me, you, and each person we meet.

—DAREN, SUB-SAHARAN AFRICAN PEOPLES

*I thank You,* GOOD SHEPHERD, FOR GIVING US THE BIBLE. SCRIPTURE STANDS FOREVER WITHOUT FLAW. PLEASE GUIDE MISSIONARIES AS THEY COMMUNICATE BIBLICAL STORIES. HELP THEM SPEAK WITH ACCURACY AND CULTURAL SENSITIVITY. *Amen.*

# God overcomes inadequacies

*"And I was with you in weakness, in fear, and in much trembling. My speech and my proclamation were not with persuasive words of wisdom, but with a demonstration of the Spirit and power." 1 Corinthians 2:3–4 (HCSB)*

I got out of my car to go into the house, but as I looked up, I saw a man. I wondered if he might rob me, but instead, he asked me for a donation for his Quranic studies. I told him that I didn't give money to Quranic schools, but if he was hungry, I could give him some food.

After gathering some items and giving them to "Mahmoud," I asked if he would like to hear a Bible story. He said, "Yes." I told him the story of Peter and John when they met a beggar who couldn't walk. As I got to the miraculous healing in the name of Jesus, I lifted my hands as I described the man leaping, dancing, and praising God. When I asked Mahmoud if he would like to follow Jesus, he eagerly agreed. I prayed for him, and he prayed to commit his life to Christ.

For quite some time, I'd felt very inadequate in speaking the local language. Health problems took time away from language learning. After being challenged to tell stories from God's Word on a daily basis, the focus on these inadequacies have changed to a focus on the wonderful message of Jesus Christ. Now I'm telling stories that are being understood, not because of my fluency, but through the goodness of God.

—RUTH, SUB-SAHARAN AFRICAN PEOPLES

*Holy Spirit,* YOU ARE MY VOICE. YOU GIVE ME WORDS AND COURAGE. THANK YOU FOR SPEAKING THROUGH YOUR CHILDREN. EMPOWER MAHMOUD TO BE YOUR SPOKESMAN AMONG HIS PEOPLE AND DRAW THEM INTO THE FAMILY OF GOD. *Amen.*

# Exchanging a lie for truth

*"You will know the truth, and the truth will set you free." John 8:32 (HCSB)*

The small, one-room house was packed. Men, women, and children were eager to hear God's Word once again. I opened the Bible, and I taught them the best I could, not my thoughts and ideas, but my Father's. A few minutes into the study, an old man came into the room. Some of his children had already made a decision for the Lord and had invited him to come. The only place to sit was on a small stool by the door.

After a few more minutes, the old man stood up. I thought he was going to leave, but he paced and then sat back down. He repeated this process two or three times more during the study. I wasn't sure if he was sleepy or bored.

I ended our time together the way I always did, extending an invitation to come to Christ. To everyone's surprise, this 75-year-old man stood up and said, "I have lived a lie all my life, but not anymore. I have heard the truth tonight. I want to follow Jesus." Then to me he added, "But I don't know how. Can you help me?"

The truth had set the man free! After his conversion, his wife and the rest of his children came to Christ. No one is too old to be transformed by the power of His Word.

—GLORIA, AMERICAN PEOPLES

*Praise You,* WONDERFUL SAVIOR, FOR ADDING THIS FAMILY TO YOUR KINGDOM. MAY I NEVER ASSUME A PERSON IS TOO ELDERLY OR UNINTERESTED TO HEAR YOUR TRANSFORMING WORD. I SHOUT FOR JOY IN THE FREEDOM OF YOUR SALVATION! *Amen.*

# *Eternally important*

*"... rejoice that your names are written in heaven." Luke 10:20 (HCSB)*

"Adam" lives in the city, but when he comes to visit his father, the chief of the Jahanka village, he makes a point to see me. This time, he brought me books that try to discredit Christianity. I spent 40 minutes reading. Once done, I gave the books back and told Adam that the man who had written the books did not understand the Bible. This led to a long discussion.

We discussed whether Jesus is God's Son, whether the Bible was corrupted, and which road leads to heaven. As I shared with him, many others gathered to listen.

Adam considerately tried to bring our discussion to a close by saying, "Even though we are of different faiths, we are basically the same. We both believe in one God." I pointed out that the differences between us are eternally important. My wife then asked Adam, "Do you know if you will go to heaven?" Adam responded in the negative; his faith does not provide assurance. She then asked me the same question. I said, "Yes," explaining that I could be assured because of what Jesus had done for me.

The people were amazed by this statement. A couple of men turned to Adam and commented that what we had said was true. Adam and many others then gathered to hear a lesson from the Word.

—J.N., SUB-SAHARAN AFRICAN PEOPLES

*Jealous God,* YOU WILL HAVE NO OTHER GODS BEFORE YOU. MAY ADAM REJECT THE LIE HE HAS SO LONG BELIEVED AND EMBRACE YOU. BLESS YOU, LORD, FOR GIVING ME AND ALL CHRISTIANS THE CONFIDENT ASSURANCE OF OUR SALVATION. *Amen.*

## Desperate for them to know

*"You shall therefore impress these words of mine on your heart and on your soul ..." Deuteronomy 11:18 (NASB)*

The stars shone bright in the clear, night sky. My teammates and I took our seats on the benches in front of our Muslim friends' village house, and three elderly men took their seats on a straw mat. They had come to share a story from their holy book. Reading by lantern light, one man began singing the story in Arabic, pausing every few lines so the other man could translate into the local language. We understood enough to know they were telling the creation story, but a version different from the Bible. They sang and translated for three or four hours, their strong voices carrying late into the night.

My heart is sad for my Muslim friends, who believe God's language is Arabic and who have been taught falsified versions of Bible stories. That week in the village, we told many people true stories from the Bible in their own language. My teammates and I are desperate for Muslims to know that God is a personal God, and He desires a relationship with them through Jesus Christ.

Through learning to tell these stories in another language, God has taught me much about who He is and how He desires to commune with me. God's Word is timeless, inexhaustible, and powerful enough to change my life and the lives of those around me.

—M.F., South Asian Peoples

*Your words,* Father, guide me. How can Muslims follow You without hearing Your Word? Open their ears and implant the life-giving words in their hearts. *Amen.*

# Adequacy is from the Lord

*"Not that we are adequate in ourselves to consider anything as coming from ourselves, but our adequacy is from God." 2 Corinthians 3:5 (NASB)*

The only adequacy we have in ministry comes from the Lord. My wife and I can barely keep up with nationals in everyday conversation, let alone understand the culture and be effective in making disciples. Still, God is faithful to open doors and use even us to get His Word to those who desperately need the truth.

Our Muslim neighbor, "Roger," brought our kids some ice cream, and I gave him a New Testament in the local language. Although I could barely explain this precious gift to him, he gladly received the book. What a great exchange! We got ice cream, and he got the Word of God. The next day, I found out that he had read the first eight chapters of Matthew.

A couple of weeks later, when Roger was helping me fix a plumbing problem, he told me that he was still reading his New Testament. Not only that, but he wanted one for his Muslim friend who lives down the street. I gave it to him gladly. A few days later, he asked for another New Testament to give to another friend.

God is using Muslims to pass His Word around to one another! Am I adequate? Not now and not ever. My adequacy is from the Lord!

—NICK, CENTRAL ASIAN PEOPLES

*Lord,* YOU ARE THE WORD OF LIFE. I PRAY FOR ROGER AND HIS FRIENDS THAT THEY WILL NOT ONLY DEVOUR YOUR WORD AND FIND SALVATION BUT ALSO BECOME LEADERS IN YOUR CHURCH. MAY WE CLING TO YOU AND YOUR ALL-SUFFICIENT GRACE. *Amen.*

## Aaron's search

*"Do not be afraid any longer, but go on speaking and do not be silent; for I am with you ..." Acts 18:9–10 (NASB)*

"Aaron" is a Muslim who immigrated to the United Kingdom 10 years ago. Like other Muslim immigrants, he has lacked access to the Gospel and has many misconceptions of who Jesus is. Although one-on-one friendships with Muslims take a long time to develop, I began to see signs of hope that Aaron trusted me.

As Aaron has welcomed me into his home, we have had many spiritual conversations lasting hours into the evening. At first, I didn't know what to say, but I knew I had many friends praying for Aaron. Each time we met, it seemed we talked less about the Quran and more about the Bible. He agreed to let me go through the Bible with him and point out the covenants that God made with mankind to save the world through His Son.

Aaron has also been willing to look at Scripture about God's kingdom. His holy book does not discuss heaven, so there's opportunity for me to discuss how we can be a part of the kingdom. He always asks me to pray with him at the end of our time together. I am so thankful to see how God is at work in Aaron's heart, and I pray that one day Aaron will see clearly the way to eternal life through Jesus Christ.

—J.H., SOUTH ASIAN PEOPLES

*Messiah,* YOU ARE WITH ME. I WANT TO SPEAK YOUR WORD WITHOUT FEAR AND WITHOUT CEASING. GIVE CHRISTIAN WORKERS CONFIDENCE IN YOUR INDWELLING PRESENCE AS THEY SPEAK TO OTHERS ABOUT COVENANT RELATIONSHIPS. I PRAY FOR AARON'S SALVATION. *Amen.*

# Overcoming obstacles

*"Sanctify them in the truth; Your word is truth."* John 17:17 (NASB)

When my friend "Nilton" was 15, his cousins began taking guitar lessons. Nilton wanted to learn to play also, but the music instructor told him that his blindness prevented him from learning. Not to be discouraged, Nilton began teaching himself to play the guitar by listening to the radio. He became such an accomplished musician that by the time he reached adulthood, he was making money playing and singing in nightclubs. Yet, he felt empty.

While listening to a new radio station, Nilton heard Christian music. He liked the music so much that he began learning the songs. Realizing these songs were based on the Bible, Nilton wanted to know more. The problem was that he didn't know how to read Braille. Thus, he asked his friends and relatives if they would each record one book of the Bible on cassette tape.

When all was recorded, he eagerly listened and soon decided to follow Jesus. He began attending a church and was baptized. Soon afterward, he felt God leading him to preach. The first sermon he preached resulted in his mother and sister giving their lives to Christ.

God's Word penetrated this young man's heart. God will find a way to speak through His Word no matter the obstacles.

—MONTY AND JANIS, AMERICAN PEOPLES

*Adonai,* YOU LIFT MAN'S SPIRIT THROUGH SONG. THANK YOU FOR USING ALL MEANS TO REACH NILTON AND NOW USING HIM TO REACH OTHERS. MAY THE SONGS OF PRAISE AND WORSHIP OFFERED BY BELIEVERS WORLDWIDE BRING YOU JOY. *Amen.*

# *Yet I will rejoice*

*"Though the fig tree does not bud and there is no fruit on the vines, ... yet I will triumph in the LORD; I will rejoice in the God of my salvation!" Habakkuk 3:17–18 (HCSB)*

I heard him say, "If the Gospel is to spread in this region of China, the way will first be paved with bloodshed." Eighty villagers listened intently as the guest speaker shared from God's Word the true meaning of serving God daily. Many had traveled for hours by bus and by foot in order to participate in a time of fellowship and to be encouraged by God's Word. Over half of them had previously been jailed, fined, or beaten for attending Christian meetings like this one. I had never before heard testimonies of such persecution.

Yet in the midst of these dangerous times, the believers continued to rejoice and faithfully gather. They were hungry for God's Word. Neither the difficulties of the journey nor the threat of further persecution stopped them. They gathered wanting, needing, and expecting to hear God speak through His Word.

What an encouragement their faithfulness was to me as I reflected on my own small faith. I was challenged to examine the source of my own strength. Would I rejoice in the Lord even when everything was dry and barren? Let us learn from these Chinese brothers and sisters to rejoice in our salvation and God's promises, trusting Him to deliver us in the desert days.

—ANNA, EAST ASIAN PEOPLES

*I rejoice in my salvation,* OH LORD, BUT MY FAITH IS SOMETIMES WEAK. UPHOLD ME WHEN I TREMBLE IN THE FACE OF RIDICULE. STRENGTHEN CHINESE BELIEVERS TO STAND FIRM WHEN PERSECUTED FOR THEIR FAITH. YOU ARE WORTHY OF OUR UNWAVERING ALLEGIANCE. *Amen.*

## Working in Danika's heart

*"God saw all that He had made, and it was very good ..." Genesis 1:31 (HCSB)*

When I first met "Danika," she could not tell me her age, birthday, or the number of children she had. Despite her giggle, it was evident that the December 2004 tsunami had traumatized this elderly South Asian.

Her living quarters eventually were upgraded from a donated tent to a tin shack; but when an open sore on her hand became a feasting ground for flies, I worried about her health. God had spared Danika in the tsunami, but she seemed no closer to understanding His offer of eternal salvation. I prayed for her healing and gave her *Our Daily Bread* to read in her language.

The next time I visited, Danika was finally in a new house—two and a half years after the tsunami. Her hand had healed, and her memory was back. Danika unlocked a cupboard and brought out *Our Daily Bread* that she had been reading. Looking at the Buddhist posters decorating her walls, I asked Danika whether she would like a book to read. She nodded eagerly.

At age 90, Danika opened the Word of God for the first time. The next day, she recounted the creation story from Genesis 1 and proclaimed, "And it was very good." Four years after the tsunami, Danika believed the Gospel and professed Christ as her Lord.

God had a plan for Danika all along.

—CHELE, SOUTH ASIAN PEOPLES

*Bread of heaven,* I FEED ON YOUR WORD AND I AM SATISFIED. BLESS YOU FOR SUSTAINING DANIKA AND LEADING HER TO YOUR GRACE. MAY THE THOUSANDS OF DISASTER SURVIVORS NOW DISCOVER THE GOSPEL AND CLING TO YOU. *Amen.*

# Words that speak

*"My life is constantly in danger, yet I do not forget Your instruction." Psalm 119:109 (HCSB)*

One of my best contacts and Christian friends is a former Muslim, an English teacher living in a refugee camp. For the past three years since he believed in Christ, he has faithfully shared the Gospel. Both his mother and oldest sister have become believers through his witness. This sister has also become one of my best friends.

I began studying Arabic with the sister. I hoped to also teach her Bible verses. The first time I went to her house for a lesson, I took my notebook filled with Bible verses. When I got there, however, her husband, daughters, and others were there. I was hesitant to share Scripture, since her family wasn't aware of her beliefs yet.

Finally, I decided to read Scripture verses, no matter the consequences. I got out a paper with John 3:16 written in Arabic. She read it, then her husband and daughters read it, too. Their comments were positive, so I showed them Matthew 6:3. They loved the ideas they were reading about God's love, eternal life, and His kingdom. Before I left that afternoon, they said, "Come every day to study with us!" I left amazed that even though I was hesitant to bring out Scripture due to my own fear, God gave the opportunity to give words of life.

—ANNE, NORTHERN AFRICAN AND MIDDLE EASTERN PEOPLES

*Only begotten of the Father,* YOUR PERFECT LOVE BRINGS DELIVERANCE AND CASTS OUT ALL FEAR. WORK IN THE LIVES OF THIS FAMILY THAT THEY WILL BE COMPLETE IN YOU. MAKE THEIR HOME A BEACON OF LOVE IN THE REFUGEE CAMP. *Amen.*

# Trading revenge for peace

*"I raise my eyes toward the mountains. Where will my help come from? My help comes from the LORD, the Maker of heaven and earth." Psalm 121:1–2 (HCSB)*

Gloom settled over the encampment, and wailing filled the air. "Tragedy has struck our family," a man named "Ibrahim" moaned. "A man from my mother's clan has shot a man from my father's clan. The murder must be avenged, but how can I shoot one cousin while mourning the death of another?" The elders gathered to discuss the problem. Would the murderer accept their judgment, or would a revenge shooting be the next tragedy?

The following month, Ibrahim drove a small herd of goats into town, hoping for a fair selling price at market. He was pleased to meet his foreign friend, "Daniel," a man of prayer who truly loved Ibrahim and his family. They discussed the tragic shooting.

"My cousin refuses to pay the blood price decided by the elders!" Ibrahim stated with anger. "I will avenge the murder and shoot him or a member of his family myself. There is no other solution to our problem."

Daniel shared that he used God's Word and prayer to solve his problems. He read Psalm 121. Ibrahim listened intently as Scripture was read. "This is amazing. This is truth," declared Ibrahim. "I think we should follow this way to solve our problems." Daniel went on to explain God's desire to give peace to Ibrahim and his family.

—M.P., NORTHERN AFRICAN AND MIDDLE EASTERN PEOPLES

*Thank You,* PRINCE OF PEACE, FOR SPEAKING WORDS OF CALM THROUGH DANIEL. YOU, LORD, PRESERVE US FROM ALL EVIL. TEACH IBRAHIM AND THE FAMILIES IN HIS CLAN TO LIVE IN PEACE. *Amen.*

# *Planting a seed*

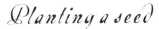

*"But at these words he was saddened, and he went away grieving ..." Mark 10:22 (NASB)*

After I taught the story of the Passover and the death of the firstborn of Egypt, "Daniella" came to me after class and commented, "I don't know anything about the Bible, but what kind of God would kill all those people?" Her question led to a discussion about God's plan from Adam to Jesus and our need for a personal relationship with God through Christ.

The following week, Daniella again asked probing questions about God's character. After class, I invited her to meet with me at my home to read the book of John. Over the next two months, we met several times, eventually reading through the third chapter of John. She had never read in the New Testament about God's love demonstrated by Christ. We spent hours discussing what it meant to be "born again." Each time we talked, she was overwhelmed by what she was learning and eventually considered becoming a Christian. Her husband had no interest in spiritual things, and she was torn between the desire she felt when she read the Word and the desire for the things of the world.

Then one week, she stopped coming to our group. My heart was broken, for I knew Daniella had been confronted with the truth and needed to make a choice. I had to trust God that He would bring the fruit in His timing.

—LINDA, EUROPEAN PEOPLES

*Righteous Judge,* WE TRUST YOU TO WORK IN DANIELLA'S HEART. BUT YOU DO NOT CO-ERCE US TO BELIEVE. PLEASE IMPRESS ON HER HEART AGAIN THAT NOW IS THE DAY OF HER SALVATION. *Amen.*

# Hearing for the first time

*"for we cannot stop speaking about what we have seen and heard."* Acts 4:20
(NASB)

An invitation from her brother who lived in the city caused much speculation for "Kelly." Was her brother crazy? He said that he had something important for her to hear about a living God. Her brother even had invited nine other people to come with her. The trip might be just what she needed. Her husband had been cheating on her, and it worried her so much that she had contemplated suicide.

After arriving at her city brother's home, they listened to a missionary tell stories from the Bible for three days. Nine out of 10 said they had never heard of Jesus, including Kelly. This news surprised the teacher. Listening intently, Kelly was amazed that the true God loved her and could forgive her sin. With hope in her heart, she gave her life to Christ. One of the men who came with Kelly had been a Buddhist monk for 35 years. He also believed along with the other eight friends.

Kelly returned to her village and invited neighbors to her house to hear the Bible stories. Soon, 50 new believers were meeting every day. The former monk also told people that Jesus was the better way. The group was so excited about their new faith that they were called in for questioning by the government. However, this challenge has not dampened their faith.

—VICTOR, SOUTHEAST ASIAN PEOPLES

*Living God,* YOU BRING LIFE EVEN WHEN DEATH SEEMS OUR ONLY CHOICE. PRAISE YOU FOR BRINGING SALVATION TO THESE 10 VILLAGERS. CALL OUT LEADERS FROM AMONG THEM WHO WILL NOT FEAR PERSECUTION AND WILL FAITHFULLY PROCLAIM YOU, THE BETTER WAY. *Amen.*

# A love for the people

*"Therefore do not be ashamed of the testimony of our Lord or of me His prisoner,
but join with me in suffering for the gospel according to the power of God."*
*2 Timothy 1:8 (NASB)*

Receiving an invitation to share Bible stories, "Mrs. T" rode a bus to get as close to the remote village as possible. At the final bus stop and as night approached, she found those who would take her to the village. Because of persecution of believers, the handful of escorts allowed the surrounding darkness to guard their journey up the winding, mountain path. After five hours of strenuous hiking, the small band arrived after midnight.

News of her arrival spread cautiously but quickly. Within minutes, the villagers secretly crowded into a home, where Mrs. T shared God's Word. At daybreak, they quietly filed out.

After a few hours of much needed sleep, Mrs. T was awakened in the late afternoon by someone with food. Presented was a piece of cured meat that was over six months old. It was the only meat in the village. She was hungry, but as she got a whiff of the rancid odor, Mrs. T reflexively gagged. On the meat crawled parasites. With tears in her eyes, Mrs. T received and ate the food gratefully, conveying her love for these people who risked their lives to host her and trusting God to prevent her from getting any diseases from eating the rotten meat.

Very few would risk everything to take His Word to those begging to hear. Would you?

—"COFFEE BEAN," SOUTHEAST ASIAN PEOPLES

*Lord,* YOU SHOW ME YOUR LOVING-KINDNESS EVERY DAY. TEACH ME TO CARE ABOUT THE FEELINGS AND SPIRITUAL NEEDS OF OTHERS THE WAY MRS. T CARED FOR HER HOSTS. IN THEIR COURAGEOUS WALK OF FAITH, ENCOURAGE ALL WHO FACE PERSECUTION. *Amen.*

# People, not projects

*"For the promise is for you and for your children, and for ... as many as the Lord our God will call." Acts 2:39 (HCSB)*

It was a hot, sultry afternoon when I first met "Rachel." Sitting in her house, I prayed that God would plant a new church there. The following week, we began telling Bible stories at Rachel's house. Two of her friends joined us.

One day, my teammate said, "Can we pray that these women will become our friends and not just be a project to us?" So we prayed. Two women eventually came that day and said they were too tired to study since they had attended several weddings the day before. Instead they asked if we would like to visit one of the new brides. Remembering how we had prayed, we said, "No problem." After visiting the bride, the women invited us to a wedding the following Sunday. We felt as if the Lord was saying, "I'm giving you the opportunity. Now go for it!"

Not only did we attend the wedding, but we had outfits made that matched the women in our group. As we left the wedding, we invited several other women to join our Bible storying group. The following week, two more women were there. They were attentive and friendlier than before. Every woman participated in the lively discussion of David and Bathsheba. No longer did we see the group as a project, but as friends.

—Diane, Sub-Saharan African Peoples

*Caring Savior,* You have created us for relationship. I love how Diane prayed for true friendship and not merely seeing these women as a project. Enlarge their group and bring these friends even closer through Christ. Make them family! *Amen.*

# *Light in the darkness*

*"Let your light so shine before men, that they may see your good works and glorify your Father in heaven."* Matthew 5:16 (NKJV)

Zoya was a Communist Party leader who spoke against the existence of God. While at a party meeting in Moscow, Zoya encountered a young, American woman on Red Square who gave her a Bible. Reluctantly, Zoya took it and placed it on her shelf. Soon afterward, Zoya was told that her son was dying. It was in that moment of desperation that she heard a voice telling her to take the Bible and give it to her son because it was going to change his life. This staunch communist did just as the voice said. A week later, she listened as her son told her that he had indeed read the Bible and given his life to Christ. Seeing the dramatic change in her son, Zoya also gave her life to Christ. She now has a vision to plant the first church in her hometown and see many others come to Christ.

In the midst of great darkness, one believer let her light shine on Red Square and changed a life, which now has the potential to change thousands of lives. It may seem improbable, but God uses us in His master plan to change lives all over the world. Let your light shine and share His Word.

—RUSTY, EUROPEAN PEOPLES

*Light of the world,* YOU DISPEL ALL DARKNESS. SHINE YOUR LIGHT IN THE HOMES OF RUSSIA AND FULFILL ZOYA'S VISION OF PLANTING A CHURCH IN HER HOMETOWN. PEOPLE AROUND THE WORLD LIVE WITHOUT ACKNOWLEDGING YOU. ILLUMINE THEIR HEARTS. *Amen.*

# It's that easy

"... 'Go home to your friends, and tell them what great things the Lord has done for you ...'" Mark 5:19 (NKJV)

As the two walked through the Himalayan foothills, the young man asked, "Why are you here?" His question opened the door for the visiting teacher to explain the importance of sharing the Gospel. "I'm illiterate and always thought that I couldn't do much for God," said the young man. The two began to discuss how the young man could share his faith and start house churches, even if he couldn't read or write.

They walked by a village and heard a man yell from his fields, "Come join us for tea." The man, his family, and the two guests sipped hot tea as they talked about the legends of the mountains towering above them. "That reminds me of a story," the visiting teacher said, anxious to share Good News with his hosts and model what he had been describing to his new disciple. The teacher shared a story about how he had experienced God's love. He then asked if he could share a story from God's Word. The family heartily agreed, and when the teacher finished, one listener said, "That's a true story." They prayed and made arrangements to meet again.

As the teacher and his disciple walked away, the young man said, "It's that easy, isn't it?" "Yes," replied the teacher. "It's that easy."

—S.E., SOUTH ASIAN PEOPLES

Lord, I CAN BE SELF-CONSCIOUS, SO I CONVINCE MYSELF IT IS HARD TO SHARE THE GOSPEL. TEACH TIMID PEOPLE LIKE ME TO PROCLAIM THE GREAT THINGS YOU HAVE DONE AMONG THE NATIONS. Amen.

# Ahmed's Desperation

*"As a deer longs for streams of water, so I long for you, God. I thirst for God, the living God ..."* Psalm 42:1–2 (HCSB)

In the dusty, North African town, a group of military officers met together to study the Bible. "Ahmed," one of the officers, couldn't get enough of God's Word.

When Ahmed heard about an upcoming church leadership training conference, he wanted to attend. Bible training was very rare for believers in small towns and villages. Ahmed asked his commanding officer for vacation time so that he might attend. His request, however, was denied.

Saddened by the refusal and desperate for the training, Ahmed began to think of other ways he might be allowed to take leave from his military obligations. When he could not think of another way, Ahmed badly burned his own foot so that he would be able to take medical leave. He then used his time off to attend the conference.

It would be easy to judge Ahmed for the measures he took. But how desperate are we to learn more about God and how to lead others to God? Are we as desperate as Ahmed? These believers desire training. Unless people come out to these hot, dusty, and difficult areas, there will be no spiritual training. When I think about Ahmed, I am reminded not to take for granted the training that I receive from those who are gifted at teaching His Word.

—J.K., NORTHERN AFRICAN AND MIDDLE EASTERN PEOPLES

*Righteous God,* I AM ASHAMED OF MY APATHY. FORGIVE ME AND HELP ME CHERISH EACH OPPORTUNITY FOR TRAINING. I PRAY FOR BELIEVERS WHO WILL GO TO THE DIFFICULT PLACES AND PROVIDE THIRST-QUENCHING SPIRITUAL TRAINING. *Amen.*

# *You see me*

*"So she named the LORD who spoke to her: The God Who Sees, for she said, 'Have I really seen here the One who sees me?'" Genesis 16:13 (HCSB)*

Lozi (LOW-zee), Mbunda (BOON-dah), and Luvale (Lou-VAWL-lay) women walked for hours, carrying bed mats and food for the training sessions. We slept under the stars, sang, and learned stories from God's Word. My hope was for them to learn to share their testimonies and the Gospel through Bible stories.

After learning a story, they retold it in small groups and acted it out. On the last day of the training, we went into a village to practice. Two agreed to share their testimony at the first grass hut, but once there, they were too nervous. So I shared. Later, we came upon a destroyed hut. Sitting against a pole was a frail, elderly woman. Her cloth wrap was in shreds. One woman gave her testimony and then asked me to help tell the Gospel story. After, the old woman began to pray in a shaky voice, "When I was young I had many boyfriends and liked beer very much. Now I have nothing—no husband, no children, and no home. I am alone. I need You, God. Save me." My friends were touched by her honesty, and with tears streaming down their faces, they knelt down beside the old woman, embraced her, and gave her one of their own cloth wraps.

God's story touches the heart. Share it with others.

—SHAWNA, SUB-SAHARAN AFRICAN PEOPLES

*Thank You,* DEAR SAVIOR, FOR BEING OUR BRIDEGROOM. YOU ARE ABLE TO SAVE THIS WOMAN. YOU ARE ABLE TO MEET HER EVERY NEED. MAY THESE LOZI, MBUNDA, AND LUVALE WOMEN BE COURAGEOUS IN SHARING BIBLE STORIES AND HELP ME DO THE SAME. *Amen.*

## No excuses

*"Go ye therefore, and teach all nations ..."* Matthew 28:19 (KJV)

In front of me sat a handful of displaced Zimbabweans. We were studying the Bible together. Living in Botswana temporarily, the Bible brought hope to their lives of upheaval. Even though I knew life for them was hard, I challenged them to go beyond merely hearing God's Word and share what they learned with others. Reminding them of Christ's commands, I encouraged them to tell Bible stories. As we talked about people with whom they could share, my students committed themselves to each sharing with five other people, including friends, neighbors, and relatives. We prayed about this commitment, planning to meet again the next week.

The next day in the grocery store, I saw one of my students, "Basa." He excitedly introduced me to his two friends, saying, "He's my number one, and this guy is my number two!" Already Basa had begun to share with his friends what God was teaching him about Jesus. I felt challenged as I saw my friend obeying Jesus' command to "go." This young man had plenty of excuses not to share: no job, little food, a precarious living situation, and separation from loved ones; but rather than looking for excuses, he looked for ways to share his faith.

Am I sharing what I'm learning? Who is my number one? And who is my number two?

—TIM, SUB-SAHARAN AFRICAN PEOPLES

*Father,* I GO TO BIBLE STUDY AND WORSHIP AND PRAYER MEETING. BUT AM I TEACHING ALL NATIONS? HELP ME THINK OUTSIDE MY REGULAR CIRCLE OF CHRISTIAN FRIENDS. GIVE ME THE NAMES OF FIVE WHO NEED TO KNOW YOUR LOVE. *Amen.*

JULY V

## Lost and Found

*God is working. You can count on it.*

—BETH MOORE

When my husband, D. Ray, and I were finishing our first mission-ary term in South Africa, we and our 3-year-old son, Trevor, went across town to a flea market to buy some curios to bring to the States as gifts. Walking around through the colorful stalls, we overheard an American accent. Immediately we looked around to see where it was coming from. There was a lovely woman speaking near us whom we recognized as one of the television news personalities from our home of Atlanta. We introduced ourselves, and an animated conversation began between the three of us, starved as we were for the company of other Americans.

In the meantime, Trevor ambled away to find something more interesting. We were so busy talking, I hate to say it, but my husband and I didn't even notice he wasn't with us. About five minutes into the conversation, I looked around and asked my husband, "Where's Trevor?"

If you have ever lost a young child, you will know what I mean when I say that my stomach dropped to the floor. My husband and I left our new friend and started shouting Trevor's name. We split up and went to every stall in the flea market. When we didn't find him there, I went to the security office to get help while D. Ray went outside of the market to scan the parking lot. Frantic by this point, we began looking into cars as they exited the market. I had never prayed so hard in my life.

After 30 minutes of searching, we rushed back to the security of-fice to get the city police involved. As we were going over things again with security, D. Ray looked out beyond the market and saw a small hill of dirt. Trevor was smack-dab in the middle of it playing as any boy would.

D. Ray raced to get him, and when Trevor saw his daddy, his face went from happiness to tears of fear as he realized that he hadn't been with his daddy all that time. Trevor didn't even know he was lost until he saw his father.

There is a whole world around us that is lost and they don't even know it. They have not experienced God's grace because they haven't heard the Gospel. They won't know they are lost until they see the Father in us.

In Zimbabwe, my national partner and I taught a sewing class and told the stories of the Bible. A woman showed up one day, obviously carrying the weight of the world on her shoulders. I have never seen anyone who was so bound by condemnation. I learned that two weeks before, she had listened to a witch doctor who had given her instructions to stop feeding her newborn baby. He said that if she did that, her dead grandmother's spirit would be appeased. So this poor woman did what the witch doctor said, and her baby died.

Downcast due to grief and guilt, she began coming to our class. There she heard about Jesus, the One who could free her from all bondage, the One who loved her no matter what. In time, she turned her life over to Christ. The transformation was remarkable. Her old self was gone, and she was made new in Jesus Christ.

This month, you will read about people who didn't even know that they were lost until they saw the Father. God is into the transformation business. The lostness is vast, but He is infinitely bigger.

—*Kim P. Davis*

## Pushing back the darkness with praise

*"Let the high praises of God be in their throats and two-edged swords in their hands ... Praise the LORD!" Psalm 149:6, 9 (ESV)*

Prior to moving to Central Asia, I didn't fully understand the psalmists' prayers concerning their enemies, having never had enemies before. But now I am aware of the spiritual enemy on whose ground I daily walk. The spiritual lostness of our city is so real at times, I can almost physically feel it. We live in a land that has been without witness of God's truth for centuries. The oppressiveness of this spiritual darkness threatens to overtake my joy. Yet I know the omnipotent God reigns over all darkness. And, at times, He chooses to wield His power through us.

In Psalm 149, the psalmist speaks of restraining the nations that are against him and the people of God. How does he plan to inhibit these authorities and push them back? By the power of praise! Praising God and wielding that praise suppresses the darkness around them. Praise filled with the power of His truth penetrates deeply. It is praise that brings His righteousness and honor to His godly ones! Celebrating God powerfully binds the darkness that surrounds me. By singing His praises and choosing to worship Him, I push back the darkness of the enemy who has for so long blinded the people of this place!

Praise Him today!

—JENNI, CENTRAL ASIAN PEOPLES

*All that is within me* PRAISES YOU TODAY, FATHER! I CELEBRATE YOU, FOR YOUR GOODNESS AND LOVING-KINDNESS ENDURE FOREVER! I STAND AGAINST THE ENEMY, IN THE NAME OF JESUS, FOR HE HAS NO POWER OVER ME. *Amen.*

## A smile as your weapon

*"But by God's grace I am what I am, and His grace toward me was not ineffective. However, I worked more than any of them, yet not I, but God's grace that was with me."* 1 Corinthians 15:10 (HCSB)

"Ratko" came to the English club to cause trouble and maybe hurt a few people. But when he arrived, he was met with a powerful weapon—a smile. The teachers welcomed him and answered his questions about God. He didn't know any English, but by the end of the first class, he was able to speak a few phrases. Every weekday for five weeks, he came.

When we met him, Ratko didn't believe that God existed. Yet over the last two years, he has seen God's power. Over and over, Ratko has seen God provide for his needs, protect him from danger, and give him peace during difficult times. Finally, he confessed Jesus as Lord and Savior and was baptized. Now he can't get enough of God's Word, helps lead Bible studies, and witnesses to everyone around him. Once a troublemaker, uneducated, and rough, he is now a peacemaker, wise, and gentle. Ratko identifies with the Apostle Paul. Once out to cause trouble to Christians, he desires all to be saved and to know Christ.

And it all began with a smile. Whose life does God want to transform today through your smile?

—JULIE, EUROPEAN PEOPLES

*Lord and Savior,* TEACH ME TO REACH OUT TO TROUBLEMAKERS WITH KINDNESS. HELP ME SEE THEM AS YOU DO—A PERSON WHO NEEDS YOUR GRACE. GIVE RATKO THE GRACE TO REACH OUT IN KINDNESS TO LOCAL HOODLUMS AND GANG MEMBERS. *Amen.*

## Desperation of the lost

*"Therefore, brethren, since we have confidence to enter the holy place by the blood of Jesus, ... let us draw near with a sincere heart in full assurance of faith, having our hearts sprinkled clean from an evil conscience and our bodies washed with pure water." Hebrews 10:19, 22 (NASB)*

Those who follow the Hindu religion travel from all over the world to bathe in the Ganges River. Vendors ride in canoes hoping to sell "consecrated items" such as flowers and candles to be offered to the gods. Along the shoreline, bodies are cremated and their ashes are scattered in the water. People dip into the water to be cleansed of all their sins.

It was at this river that a local believer encountered a man and his wife who were weeping bitterly. As he tried to console them, the couple shared how they had four daughters, but they wanted a son. They prayed and prayed and finally went to see a Hindu priest who told them that if they wanted a son, they must sacrifice one of their daughters by throwing her in the river to drown. They had just completed this act of sacrifice to their gods.

The believer shared the Good News of Jesus and how He had given His life for all mankind. The man wailed, "Why could you not have told me of this Jesus thirty minutes ago?" The urgency is real, and Jesus does make a difference. Never hesitate to share His love. People are desperate to hear the Good News.

—NINA, SOUTH ASIAN PEOPLES

*In times of heartbreak,* YOU ALONE, LORD, BRING COMFORT. YOU ARE THE LIFTER OF MY HEAD AND YOU ARE ABLE TO RESTORE THIS FAMILY. REVEAL YOURSELF AS THE LIVING WATER. CONVICT ME OF MY SIN, LORD, WHEN I AM SLOW IN SHARING MY FAITH. *Amen.*

## A village transformed

*"And do not be conformed to this world, but be transformed by the renewing of your mind, so that you may prove what the will of God is, that which is good and acceptable and perfect." Romans 12:2 (NASB)*

In southern Romania, not far from the Danube River, lies the tiny village of Valea Mica. This village had a reputation for being the roughest village throughout the area. There was no church.

A Romanian pastor, Laurian, from another town, visited the village and shared the Gospel. Week after week, Laurian traveled difficult roads for two hours to witness in the village. It was all worth it when Viorel, a man with the worst reputation in town, placed his faith in Christ. For two years, Laurian discipled this new convert. Viorel began sharing Christ with his friends, and one by one, they also believed. The entire village was transformed by the power of the Gospel.

The church in Valea Mica now thrives. Every house in the entire village has at least one believer. The men have ceased drinking, and all four bars have closed. There is no more wife or child beating, and the local jail has no business. The county government has sent the police to other localities. There is no longer any crime in Valea Mica.

A village once known for alcoholism and immorality has become a village of godly people who follow Christ. Because one pastor obeyed God, people in Valea Mica have hope.

—BOB, EUROPEAN PEOPLES

*Lord of glory,* MAY YOU BE PRAISED! THANK YOU FOR WORKING A MIRACLE IN VALEA MICA. MAY THESE ROMANIAN CHRISTIANS, ONCE UNDER SOVIET DOMINION, GO TO OTHER VILLAGES AND SHARE JESUS. *Amen.*

# Pointed in the right direction

*"The Lord is ... longsuffering to us-ward, not willing that any should perish, but that all should come to repentance." 2 Peter 3:9 (KJV)*

One afternoon, my daughter and I decided to go to the market. After a long bus ride through crowded streets, we reached our destination. We eagerly got off of the bus and headed down bustling sidewalks filled with shoppers and vendors.

Entering the main market, we spent the morning browsing through an endless maze of booths. When it was time to go home, we could not remember which entrance we had come through earlier that morning. Choosing one that looked familiar, we exited, but it was not where the bus stop was located. Surely our bus stop would be around the next corner! After a while, we were tired and lost. Finally someone pointed us in the right direction.

Because of help, we found ourselves comfortably seated on our bus. As we traveled home, I was reminded that many people around us are spiritually lost. They are looking for a way to experience the peace and joy that only come through a relationship with God. They may believe they can find God through good works, traditions, or empty rituals. But just as my daughter and I needed someone to show us the right way, they are waiting for us to guide them to the Savior. Are we willing to lead the lost to Christ?

—DEBBIE, AMERICAN PEOPLES

*It is so easy* TO GET LOST AND CONFUSED, GOD. THANK YOU FOR TEACHING US RIGHT FROM WRONG IN SCRIPTURE. THANK YOU FOR PROVIDING THE WAY OF SALVATION. BLESS DEBBIE AND HER DAUGHTER AS THEY POINT OTHERS TO YOU. *Amen.*

## *Forgiven much, she loves much*

*"For this reason I say to you, her sins, which are many, have been forgiven, for she loved much; but he who is forgiven little, loves little." Luke 7:47 (NASB)*

There were 11 university students attending a weekly Bible story session at our apartment. They all seemed vibrant and interested, except for one young lady named "Lily," who sat with her head down as though she was on the verge of tears.

After class, Lily slipped me a note that said, "I want to be a Christian. Can you help me?" We invited her to come alone that evening to talk. As soon as she entered our apartment, she started sobbing uncontrollably. She said, "I am terrible. I intentionally cut myself and suck my blood, and I can't stop doing this horrible thing."

Why? Guilt. That was her answer. "No one can help me, and I am so ashamed!" Lily cried. We told her that Jesus could help her. He came to forgive, heal, and love.

Lily prayed from the depths of her heart and laid all her guilt at His feet. As a result of His saving grace, there has been an amazing transformation in Lily. Her smile is now radiant, and she is truly a new creature in Christ. Her friends have noticed her transformation as she praises God. Her love for Him is great, for she realizes how much He has forgiven. He replaces guilt with His inconceivable love.

—C.V., EAST ASIAN PEOPLES

*I have also known* GUILT FOR MY SIN, LORD. THANK YOU FOR YOUR SWEET FORGIVENESS. THANK YOU FOR FREEING LILY FROM CUTTING. LORD, I PRAY FOR OTHER YOUNG WOMEN WHO ARE CUTTING TODAY. BE THEIR GREAT PHYSICIAN AND HEAL THEIR HURTS. *Amen.*

# A question to the lost sheep

*"I tell you, in the same way, there will be more joy in heaven over one sinner who repents than over 99 righteous people who don't need repentance." Luke 15:7 (HCSB)*

As we entered the village, each person put a fist to his mouth, a cultural expression of surprise. Two strangers had walked into their remote village. The village chief asked, "Why would you walk all the way to our village? We are nothing but lost sheep on this mountain."

When we told the story about a lost sheep from Luke 15, these shepherds understood.

They commented that when one of them loses a sheep, looking for it is not an option if it is to be protected from hyenas, the dry heat, or illness. As we told how the shepherd in the story celebrated with neighbors when he found the sheep, the people of this village recalled, "Yes, that is right! We just did that last week!" But when we continued, "There will be more joy in heaven over one sinner who repents than over 99 righteous persons who need no repentance," the villagers became silent and walked away.

I expressed my disappointment to my partner as we walked down the mountain. He replied, "I think that may have been the same response Jesus got when he first told that story." These Muslims are devoted to the law, much as the Pharisees of Jesus' day. They believe, like the Pharisees, that they are the 99 who "need no repentance."

—ROBERT, SUB-SAHARAN AFRICAN PEOPLES

*Great Shepherd,* YOUR VOICE IS CALLING THE 99, BUT THEY ARE NOT READY TO HEAR. PLEASE KEEP CALLING. MANY THINK THEY CAN FULFILL THE LAW AND FIND FAVOR. I PRAY THAT YOUR WORD WILL SHAKE THEM INTO SILENCE AND DRAW THEM BY FAITH TO YOU. *Amen.*

# God is able

*"... If anyone loves Me, he will keep My word; and My Father will love him, and We will come to him and make Our abode with him." John 14:23 (NASB)*

At the Bible study, we introduced ourselves and told about our family, job, and relationship with the Lord. When we got to "Humberto," he said, "I was born and raised in Cuba. I'm an atheist."

Despite his unbelief, Humberto attended the study regularly, always did his homework, and connected well with the group, though he often complained that he didn't understand the context of the verses studied. When we finished that particular study, we began a series of chronological Bible stories. Since all the members of the group were professionals, we would tell the story and then give them a homework sheet, which we discussed the following week.

As the weeks progressed, Humberto decided to read through the Bible from the beginning. He also began meeting with the church body. A few months later, our pastor had a very bad cold and couldn't preach. Instead he divided the congregation into two groups and gave each a set of questions to discuss based on the passage he had planned to use. The last application question said, "In what specific way can I show my love for Jesus?" Before anyone else in the group could respond, Humberto said, "I can show my love for Jesus by asking him into my heart right now."

From atheist to Christian, God can do it.

—HELEN, AMERICAN PEOPLES

*Lord,* YOUR LOVE EVEN REACHES THE ATHEIST. THANK YOU FOR PATIENTLY TEACHING HUMBERTO THROUGH THE STUDY OF YOUR WORD. USE HUMBERTO TO REACH HIS ISLAND WITH YOUR LOVE AND YOUR WORD. *Amen.*

## Following the rules

*"But [Naaman's] servants approached and said to him, 'My father, if the prophet had told you to do some great thing, would you not have done it? How much more [should you do it] when he tells you, 'Wash and be clean?'" 2 Kings 5:13 (HCSB)*

"Jaya" quickly became a friend, welcoming me into her home, taking me shopping, and loving to eat my American cakes. I knew she was a Jain who worshipped 24 deities, and she knew I worshipped only Jesus. During Diwali, the Festival of Lights, she decorates her house so that the goddess of wealth will bless her family.

Jaya listened when I shared with her about how Jesus changed my life and how I have hope. She was particularly interested in my daily Bible study and prayer time. For her birthday, I gave her a copy of the Bible and suggested that she read Matthew, Mark, Luke, and John. She touched the Bible to her forehead as a sign of reverence.

Right before I moved away, we took a walk in our neighborhood park. I told her that because she was my dear friend, I had to tell her one more time how she could have forgiveness and the promise of heaven. She thanked me but said that she still believed if people did good things, surely God wouldn't send them to hell.

There are many who won't listen the first time, but like Naaman, will listen the second time. Will you continue to give people another chance to hear the Good News?

—BREENA, SOUTH ASIAN PEOPLES

*There is none like You,* GOD! JAIN GODS DO NOT COMPARE TO YOUR MATCHLESS WORTH. I PRAY FOR JAYA AND OTHER JAIN FOLLOWERS TO UNDERSTAND THIS TRUTH. I PRAY THEY WILL "WASH AND BE CLEAN." *Amen.*

## *Fulfillment of a dream*

*"A vision appeared to Paul in the night: a man of Macedonia was standing and appealing to him, and saying, 'Come over to Macedonia and help us.'"* Acts 16:9 (NASB)

Wheelchair bound, the man had been ill for several years. One night, he dreamed that a group of foreign medical people came to help him and the villagers. He asked if they came from America. These doctors said, "No. We came from heaven!" They asked the man, "Are you really sick?" The man answered, "Yes. I have been sick for years." The doctors told him, "We could treat your illness. And you will be healed!"

When he woke, he was puzzled about the dream. He shared the dream with his wife, who ridiculed him. One week later, to his and his wife's amazement, a medical team did come to his village! He received treatment, and during a follow-up visit, he heard the Gospel and believed.

After his conversion to Christianity from Buddhism, many villagers came to Christ through his witness. He asked me to tear down a costly piece of paper that was supposed to bring him good luck. He said, "This is useless. I want to follow Jesus and am willing to die for Him."

His confession moved us into tears, and that day, we worshiped the Lord with him for several hours. Sometime later, we learned that he had passed away. He is now healed completely.

—L.C., East Asian Peoples

*You are the Christ,* the Son of the living God. You redeem a soul and nothing is ever the same. Praise be to You! Continue to work through medical teams who labor long hours and faithfully share the Gospel. *Amen.*

# Draped in their beliefs

*"Yes, it is true that I am a family redeemer, but there is a redeemer closer than I am." Ruth 3:12 (HCSB)*

Just a tiny wisp of a girl, she was completely dressed in black. Her mother stood by her side, veiled and gloved, a slender exclamation point above her daughter's small dot.

The child's face was not yet covered, although a scarf was wrapped about her head. She held a brightly colored purse decorated with red and pink flowers and a popular doll. It was a lively flag of individuality raised from the heart beneath. The doll was nearly identical to one I played with as a child, only this one had converted to Islam and wore a long, black burka. My doll had worn a swimsuit. As a girl, I spent hours playing with her colorful outfits and accessories.

The little girl who carried this purse had begun a lifetime of wearing black. Soon the veil will come and with it, the gloves and stockings. On this blackboard, the rules of her life will be written. Endless, unreachable laws will seep into her thoughts and congeal into beliefs. But as I watched her tiny figure disappear, I was reminded of the story of Ruth, a young and beautiful woman who took a journey from Moab to Bethlehem where she unexpectedly met her redeemer. An eternal romance that can be this small girl's story as well.

—SARA, NORTHERN AFRICAN AND MIDDLE EASTERN PEOPLES

*Great Redeemer,* MOST LITTLE GIRLS ACROSS NORTHERN AFRICA AND THE MIDDLE EAST HAVE LITTLE CHANCE TO HEAR YOUR NAME. YOU DO NOT WANT ANY CHILD TO PERISH. SEND THEM DREAMS OF YOU AND PREPARE MIRACULOUS WAYS FOR THEM TO HEAR THE TRUTH. *Amen.*

# *You are Mine*

*"Now rescue your beloved people. Answer and save us by your power. Gilead is mine, and Manasseh, too ..." Psalm 108:6, 8 (NLT)*

"I understand that you are a missionary," said the stranger who came to our gate. "I want to know about Jesus. I have visited many churches, but no one has been able to teach me about Jesus. Do you have a Bible, and will you teach me?"

The Holy Spirit was already at work in this man's heart. He was searching for the truth about God, and I was given the opportunity to introduce him to Jesus. In time, "Relepeli" became a Christian and a strong witness for Jesus Christ. He had been the village drunk who was always in trouble. Now he gave a testimony wherever he went of how God changed his life. He gave up drinking, read his Bible daily, and brought other people to Bible study. Before Relepeli died from AIDS, he helped to plant a church in his home village.

God knew Relepeli and claimed him as His own. He saw His beloved child and said, *Relepeli is Mine.* It did not matter that he had AIDS or a drunken past; He saw Relepeli for who he could be in Christ. Often, we only reach out to those we think have a chance for repentance, but God desires for all sinners to come to Him.

—GEORGE, SUB-SAHARAN AFRICAN PEOPLES

*Mighty Deliverer,* AIDS IS A SCOURGE ON OUR GENERATION. IT DEVASTATES INDIVIDUALS, FAMILIES, EVEN ENTIRE NATIONS. FIND JOY IN MISSIONARIES WHO TEACH "TRUE LOVE WAITS" AND MINISTER TO AIDS SUFFERERS. CLAIM OTHERS LIKE RELEPELI AS YOUR OWN. *Amen.*

# *Losing your life to gain eternity*

*"If you love your father or mother more than you love me, you are not worthy of being mine; or if you love your son or daughter more than me, you are not worthy of being mine." Matthew 10:37 (NLT)*

While shutting the gate outside my house, I heard a familiar voice call my name. I looked across the narrow street and saw Mr. Ganda, the head Islamic leader of the community. He said, "I have been sitting here tonight and wondering how a Christian goes to heaven."

Joining Mr. Ganda on his front porch, I sat down as he began to explain the long process that a Muslim must go through to get to heaven. When it was my turn, I explained the Gospel and then asked him this question, "If I were not a Christian and you were not a Muslim and someone came to us today with these two teachings, which of them would you choose to get to heaven?" Mr. Ganda replied, "I would choose Christianity because you have a Shepherd and a Savior." My heart leaped for joy. I asked, "Mr. Ganda, do you want Jesus to be your personal Savior?" He replied, "I cannot. You might have the best way, but I still have a way. Besides, if I choose Christ, I would have to give up my family, friends, and position in the community." My heart sank. His position and family ties kept him from receiving the Savior that night.

Oh, to see the lost come to Christ!

—D.H., SOUTHEAST ASIAN PEOPLES

*Savior,* PLEASE GRANT MR. GANDA THE FAITH AND COURAGE TO REJECT THE TRADITIONS HE HAS ALWAYS KNOWN. FILL HIM WITH GRACE TO SHARE THIS TRUTH WITH HIS FAMILY. DRAW THEM TO SALVATION TOGETHER SO THAT THEY MAY BE UNITED IN YOU. *Amen.*

# A man and his household

*"... 'Sirs, what must I do to be saved?' They said, 'Believe in the Lord Jesus, and you will be saved, you and your household.'" Acts 16:30–31 (NASB)*

As a volunteer shared a Bible story, one woman replied, "For these women to follow the Jesus road, you must pray for their husbands. Without their husbands believing in Jesus, they will not be able to follow." One husband already had declared that he would beat anyone in his family who chose Christianity.

Wouldn't you know it? God had been leading me to befriend this same violent man. The man had shown great hatred toward Jesus and me. No way did I want to even think about going out of my way to be friendly. He had made his position clear.

But our God is in the "impossible" business. Without explanation, the man began coming to my house to engage in conversation. Another volunteer team came, and he heard God's Word, although he didn't understand everything. When the man heard the story about the jailer and how he and his whole household decided to follow Jesus, he was intrigued. We explained how his whole household could know Jesus. The next morning, he said, "I know the Jesus road is the right road. It will be hard, but I want to follow it, me and my whole household."

God can melt the hardest heart and break through the toughest attitude.

—LORI, SUB-SAHARAN AFRICAN PEOPLES

*I am steeped* IN INDIVIDUALISTIC THINKING, HOLY GOD. I DO NOT OFTEN SEE FAMILIES COME TO YOU, AND I AM CHALLENGED TO PRAY MORE FOR ENTIRE FAMILIES. GUARD THIS FAMILY AS THEY LIVE OUT THEIR FAITH IN A COMMUNITY HOSTILE TO CHRISTIANITY. *Amen.*

# He died for them

*"Yes, to this day whenever Moses is read a veil lies over their hearts. But when one turns to the Lord, the veil is removed." 2 Corinthians 3:15–16 (ESV)*

A high-pitched shrill erupts from a group of university girls. Is someone engaged? Graduating? One girl in a pink scarf sways to music as her friends cheer her on with snapping fingers. I walk through the university center where female students are gathered for breakfast.

My friends are huddled in a shaded breezeway. They greet me in English; I reply in Arabic, making them laugh. After a few more silly exchanges, they comment that my scarf doesn't match my clothes, and the day goes as usual.

As we sit, they talk about how they cannot wait to graduate and get a good job. They dream of studying abroad and working for charity organizations to empower their people. They speak of a time when women of their country will be truly equal and no longer face the horrors of domestic abuse and female genital mutilation.

Properly veiled, they pray five times a day and fast during their holy month. I talk about my Christian faith and my relationship with a God who is love. When I tell them that I'm going to heaven, they don't understand how I can be so sure.

God loves these young, intelligent women for whom He died, but their souls are veiled like the scarves they wear over their hair. I long for the veil to be torn away.

—A.M.W., NORTHERN AFRICAN AND MIDDLE EASTERN PEOPLES

*Lord,* PLEASE TOUCH THE HEARTS OF THESE UNIVERSITY STUDENTS. REACH INTO THEIR LIVES AND TEAR AWAY THE VEIL. REVEAL YOUR GLORY. *Amen.*

## Covering up the damage

*"For the mind set on the flesh is death, but the mind set on the Spirit is life and peace." Romans 8:6 (NASB)*

When the cabinet door fell off, we called a carpenter to repair the damage caused by termites. But when the carpenter examined them closely, he tore out three entire cabinets because all were hopelessly eaten! His evaluation—only the paint was holding them together.

Such extensive damage hidden from the eye is much like sin. One can try to hide it from others, but its destruction on the inside is complete and eternal. Religion is the paint often used to cover up sin, and it seems to hold things together for a while. Only when one honestly admits the hopeless damage inside is he ready to accept the message of salvation.

That's what happened to "Arun," a religious mother who memorized the holy book of her people. Yet she was cruel to her children. She said, "There was no newness in my life; only war, no peace or contentment." When one of her sons found new life in Christ, he began to share with his mother. She didn't want to listen, but she saw the peace her son had. With his help, she became convinced that Jesus could change her life, too. Now she says, "I was a violent mother. Now I am learning to love. I realize that no one can change me but God's Spirit, who takes control of my life."

—D.S., SOUTHEAST ASIAN PEOPLES

*Holy and true God,* WE CRY OUT AGAINST VIOLENCE IN THE HOME. BRING PEACE TO OTHERS AS YOU HAVE TO ARUN. MAY THOSE WHO TRY TO COVER THEIR INNER PAIN WITH RELIGION CRY OUT FOR TRUTH. *Amen.*

# Penetrating the darkness

*"Don't be afraid of them or discouraged by [the look on] their faces, even though they are a rebellious house." Ezekiel 3:9b (HCSB)*

Under God's direction, we desired to see the local witch doctors come to Christ. When we brought Bibles into the village, we unexpectedly were invited to the witch doctors' "office," since they were to see a sick woman. They led us inside a small, thatched hut, and we silently prayed, stooping to avoid the strange things that hung from the rafters.

As my eyes adjusted to the darkness, I saw shelves that held jars of things unidentifiable, candles giving off dim light, and a desiccated frog smoldering on the floor. Several witch doctors sat across from us, and the presence of the evil one was so thick, it was suffocating. The sick woman was helped into the room, too ill to stand, and she sat on the floor beside us. We touched her frail body and began to pray in the powerful name of Jesus. God's strength and light overtook the darkness, and fear vanished as we prayed and later shared the Gospel.

Not long afterward, we began a Bible study about 100 yards from that hut. Each week, without success, we invited the witch doctors to come. Finally, one came and listened. We are confident that God's Word will not return void. Sometimes it's scary, but I know God is unshakable and faithful, whether it is in the darkness or in our own backyard.

—BABS, SUB-SAHARAN AFRICAN PEOPLES

*You, Oh God,* ARE MY STRONG TOWER AND SHELTER FROM MY FEARS! I CALL ON YOU TO BANISH THE DARKNESS IN THIS AFRICAN VILLAGE. I PLEAD FOR THE SALVATION OF THE WITCH DOCTORS. REDEEM THEIR SOULS AND RELEASE THE VILLAGERS FROM FEAR. *Amen.*

# Hearing the prayers of a sinner

*"But the tax collector ... was even unwilling to lift up his eyes to heaven, but was beating his breast, saying, 'God, be merciful to me, the sinner!'" Luke 18:13 (NASB)*

Former heroin addict turned Christian, "Bhanu" knew what it felt like to be desperate. As he looked at the men in front of him at the rehabilitation center he had founded, he loved them as Jesus would and knew that only God's Son could rescue them from their addictions. Getting God's Word to these men would show them the way for hope.

Bhanu asked me to come to the center once a week to teach these men Bible stories. So on Fridays, I shared a Bible story and led a discussion on what was learned. Many of the men wanted me to pray for them before they left.

One week, after sharing another story, seven men repented and gave their lives to Jesus. The next week, God was leading me to encourage these new Christians to pray for others. As the large group of men lined up to pray together, I saw one of the new believers with tears in his eyes. He said, "Until last week, I never thought God would hear the prayers of a sinner like me. And now, here I am, not only praying to God, but praying for others as well."

There is no sinner who can't be saved. And every saved sinner is called to pray for others.

—RICH, SOUTH ASIAN PEOPLES

*God,* BE MERCIFUL TO ME. I AM ALSO A SINNER ADDICTED TO MY SELFISH DESIRES, AND ONLY YOU CAN RESCUE ME. BHANU DEMONSTRATES TRUE HUMILITY. PLEASE BLESS HIM AS HE INTERCEDES FOR OTHERS AT THE REHABILITATION CENTER. *Amen.*

## More powerful than Islam

*"Some boast in chariots and some in horses, but we will boast in the name of the LORD, our God. They have bowed down and fallen, but we have risen and stood upright." Psalm 20:7–8 (NASB)*

As I was reading my morning devotional, I came across a story in 1 Samuel 5 in which the Philistines had captured the ark of God, placing it in the temple of their god, Dagon. The next morning, when they entered the temple, the idol had fallen on its face before the ark. They carefully replaced their god because it could not take care of itself! The following morning upon entering the temple, they not only found Dagon on its face, but its head and hands were also broken off! God is able to protect His glory in all circumstances.

This false god, Dagon, reminds me of the false religion of Islam. Sometimes, we wring our hands and ask how we can make an impact on such a powerful influence. But just as the story in 1 Samuel, God is more powerful and can defend Himself against any false religion. He doesn't need us to bring down the lies of Islam. However, He is giving us an opportunity to be a part of the victory He will have.

Is there a Muslim in your community whom you can befriend? Don't be afraid of the false gods of our day. Place yourself in a position where God can use you to glorify Himself.

—V., NORTHERN AFRICAN AND MIDDLE EASTERN PEOPLES

*Almighty Lord,* GIVE ME COURAGE TO PROCLAIM YOUR NAME, TO STAND UP AND DECLARE YOUR GLORY. HELP ME LOVE MY MUSLIM NEIGHBORS IN MY COMMUNITY. *Amen.*

## *Loving no matter the cost*

*"... be submissive to your own husbands so that even if any of them are disobedient to the word, they may be won without a word by the behavior of their wives, as they observe your chaste and respectful behavior." 1 Peter 3:1–2 (NASB)*

"Aisha" was born into a nominal Christian family. When she was 14 years old, she fell in love with and married a much older Muslim man. Soon after the marriage, Aisha's husband cut off all ties with her family and forced her to become a Muslim.

Many years later, her 8-year-old son became very sick. Desperate, Aisha took her son to a Christian hospital. On the wall in the hospital room, there was a picture of Jesus. Stories she remembered from childhood suddenly flooded her mind, and she began begging Jesus to heal her son. Soon the fever subsided, and Aisha knew that Jesus had healed her son.

Aisha found a Christian church, committed her life to Jesus, and was baptized. When her husband found out, he began beating her, but she continued to submit her life to Jesus. After many years of persecution, Aisha removed herself and her children to another home. However, out of love and respect for her husband, she continued to cook and clean for him while he was at work. The Christian love she showed him caused him to wonder why his wife would continue to treat him with kindness. Eventually, he gave his life to Jesus and was completely transformed.

—S.R., SOUTH ASIAN PEOPLES

*Loving Lord,* YOU HAVE SHOWN AISHA MERCY IN HER SON'S RECOVERY. AISHA DEMONSTRATED MERCY IN SERVING HER HUSBAND. MAY MANY SOUTH ASIAN MEN EXPERIENCE YOUR MERCY AS THEIR WIVES LIVE OUT A PERSISTENT TESTIMONY OF GRACE. *Amen.*

# Under authority

> *"For I also am a man under authority, with soldiers under me; and I say to this one, 'Go!' and he goes, and to another, 'Come!' and he comes ..." Matthew 8:9 (NASB)*

When I answered the phone, "Andrea" was sobbing hysterically and speaking in Mandarin. My mind frantically began to piece together words such as "angry," "hopeless," and "suicide," and all seemed linked to a certain "he."

Andrea was a young Christian, but because of her background of abuse and neglect, her first steps toward Christ were shaky. Her quest for love had been several live-in relationships.

My words calmed her, but she continued on her roller-coaster lifestyle, making confession and then falling back into old habits. As my prayers began to match her desperation, the Lord graciously revealed the necessity of praying with authority.

He said that as long as I held onto habits of rebellion in my own life, I had no authority to pray that Andrea be released from hers. I saw why my prayers for her had been unanswered. It was only to the extent that I allowed the Lord to control my life that I had the spiritual "right" to pray effectively over others. As I prayed, "Lord, change me," He began to change both of us.

Later, Andrea recounted her transformation: "I've exposed to God all my emotions: rage, envy, and lack of forgiveness. All that is in me, I bring to Him. For it is only in Him that I have peace, love, and happiness."

—K.P., EAST ASIAN PEOPLES

*You are my Lord and Master!* I DENY ALL RIGHTS TO MY WILL, LUSTS, AND REBELLION. THANK YOU FOR ANDREA'S EXAMPLE OF SURRENDER AND CHANGE. TEACH ME TO PRAY WITH AUTHORITY FOR OTHERS. *Amen.*

# *Wanted*

*"For there is faithful love with the LORD, and with Him is redemption in abundance." Psalm 130:7b (HCSB)*

Rebellion earned a title for "Ruben": WANTED. Authorities sought him as he aligned himself with rebels, whether communists, local bandits, or other rebel groups living in the mountains. His life of running ended at a church quite unexpectedly. When Ruben was invited to attend technical training at the church, he saw a way to hide out and make a new start. Changing his name, he left the life he had known as a teenager. He received more than training, however, as Ruben learned of God's love. Before long, Ruben repented and began a new life in Christ.

His friendship with a Western Christian brought encouragement for him to return home and share Christ with his own people group, a group unreached with the Gospel. When Ruben returned, he spread the Gospel. It wasn't long before a religious leader heard the story of Jesus and came to faith. The leader and another man were baptized. Ruben continued to share the Word and a few months later, nearly 30 more professed Christ. Now, there are several groups of believers following Jesus in this place that was once without hope.

God is at work turning enemies into brothers, all by the redeeming power of the One who is the way, the truth, and the life.

—A WORKER WITH SOUTHEAST ASIAN PEOPLES

*Thank You, God,* FOR REDEEMING RUBEN FROM A LIFE OF HOPELESSNESS TO ONE OF HOPE AND COMMITMENT. CONTINUE TO GROW YOUR FAMILY OF FAITH AS REBELLIOUS MEN AND WOMEN SURRENDER TO YOUR REDEMPTION. *Amen.*

## Love instead of fear

*"I will give you a new heart and put a new spirit within you; I will remove your heart of stone and give you a heart of flesh." Ezekiel 36:26 (HCSB)*

The first time I saw a woman in full Muslim attire, with face completely covered, I was shopping in a large African mall as a tourist. Shocked, and even frightened, I maintained distance as we passed. What did I possibly have in common with a Muslim woman? Would I ever be able to be friends with women so different?

Ten years later, I walk among such women every day. God used that first encounter to initiate a love for Muslim women that has led me through many books, classes, discussions, questions, and now across an ocean. He has shown me how much we actually have in common. But more importantly, He has shown me how much He loves each of them. The same gentle Father who comforts me in the slightest injury waits to comfort each of them. The same Christ who willingly walked to the cross in my place also walked for every Fatima, Khadija, Aziza, and Maryam in our place of service. The Holy Spirit who guides my days calls them.

That day in an African mall, God began to replace my heart of stone with His heart. He continues to show me how to walk beside these women, to be Him among them. I will no longer cross to the far side of the corridor in the mall.

—J.K., NORTHERN AFRICAN AND MIDDLE EASTERN PEOPLES

*Holy Spirit,* DO NOT LET MY HEART GROW COLD AND INDIFFERENT. OPEN MY EYES AND HEART TO THE MUSLIM WOMEN SHOPPING AT THE SAME STORES I USE. GIVE ME OPPORTUNITY AND COURAGE TO SPEAK PEACE TO THEM. *Amen.*

# Old-age salvation

*"For my eyes have seen Your salvation."* Luke 2:30 (HCSB)

In the second chapter of Luke, Simeon and Anna desired to see the Christ before they died. Anna was most likely over 100 years old, since she had been a widow for 84 years. It seems that most people come to Christ when they're young, but some, like Anna, meet Christ as senior citizens.

In the village of Nata, there lived an old woman we called Mrs. Cherry. She was a tiny Bushman lady whose childhood tribal markings on her face could still be seen. Mrs. Cherry often heard the Bible stories, and one day, she decided to follow Jesus. She often danced and sang to the Lord.

After she had been a believer for four years, she stopped one of our Bible studies to say something important. In her quiet voice, she whispered how thankful she was that she had lived long enough to hear the Gospel. Tears came to every eye when we found out that this sweet saint had become a Christian at age 98, and she was 102. She died not too long after this testimony.

Mrs. Cherry is now praising Him before His throne. Her life is a reminder to me of God's goodness and grace, and just like Anna, she found her redemption through God's Son.

—Brian, Sub-Saharan African Peoples

*Sovereign Lord,* WE CANNOT KNOW THE NUMBER OF OUR DAYS. WHETHER WE COME TO SALVATION AT AN EARLY AGE OR LATE, WE ONLY HAVE THIS MOMENT TO SERVE YOU. HELP US REDEEM THE TIME. *Amen.*

# Sharing with urgency

*"But sanctify the Lord God in your hearts, and always be ready to give a defense to everyone who asks you a reason for the hope that is in you, with meekness and fear." 1 Peter 3:15 (NKJV)*

Transporting the dead body in the back of the truck, I asked the man with me, "Was she a believer? Is she in heaven?"

"No," he said. "She never accepted Jesus Christ as her Savior."

With tears in my eyes as I thought about this wife and mother of four, I was forced to face the hard questions: Had I been diligent to share with those around me? Had I always been ready to give a defense of the Gospel? I did not want to miss any opportunity that God had for me. Although I didn't know this woman, how many people did I know who had died without Christ?

The lady who died lived on the same dirt path as another lady I visit regularly. I keep ending up at this village and each time I do, I ask myself, "What does God have planned for this area? What does He want me to do here?"

Time is short. We do not know when Christ will return, but we do know that God has called us to be faithful in sharing the Gospel with those around us, whether they live in a small mud hut or in a nice mansion.

Whom can I share with today, before it is too late?

—CAROL, AMERICAN PEOPLES

*Rock of salvation,* I CRY FOR THE LOSS OF THIS WOMAN AND FOR THE THOUSANDS WHO DIE DAILY WITHOUT KNOWING YOU. PLEASE GIVE MISSIONARIES EFFECTIVE STRATEGIES FOR REACHING THE LOST. *Amen.*

# *What do Christians look like?*

*"Do not judge, so that you won't be judged." Matthew 7:1 (HCSB)*

"Ernesto" was very anxious for his 17-year-old brother, "Herman," to live with us and get away from the rebellious youth who were becoming his peer group. When he arrived at last, I was doubtful that we would be able to do anything for him. His hair was long and stringy and covered half his face. His left arm had a tattoo of a huge, barbed wire around it, and he dressed only in black.

But God had plans for Herman. After two months of living with us, watching evangelical videos and hearing our testimonies, he decided to follow Jesus. We started him on a simple course about how to live the Christian life, and he went to church with us. But it was obvious that he was uncomfortable at our church. There was another church in town that was filled with young people like him. Their music was a little wild and loud for me, but I remembered that Herman loved that kind of music. So we took him to that church on a Friday night when they had a lot of music and informal interaction between members and visitors. He came home with a glow on his face, and the first thing he said to me was, "They're just like me!"

What do Christians look like? They are filled with the joy of the Lord.

—PAT, AMERICAN PEOPLES

*Thank You, Lord,* FOR PROVIDING A CHURCH BODY THAT WAS A PERFECT FIT FOR HER-MAN. MAY I BE OPEN TO DIFFERENT STYLES OF WORSHIP SO THAT EVERYONE IN MY LOCAL CHURCH CAN TRULY WORSHIP YOU. YOU FILL ME WITH JOY. MAY I SPREAD YOUR JOY TODAY. *Amen.*

# Satan's stronghold

*"… I will never leave you or forsake you. Therefore, we may boldly say: The Lord is my helper; I will not be afraid. What can man do to me?" Hebrews 13:5b–6 (HCSB)*

There is a feeling of darkness in the oppressed areas of Kampala, Uganda, where we work. One particular community is strangled by false teachings and sits in the shadow of a large mosque. Many in this area are seeking truth, yet they fear great persecution if they were to explore Christianity. We have freedom to share the Good News in this country but often face opposition in tangible ways. Days before we were scheduled to show the *JESUS* film, our house was robbed. Although no one was home, my sense of security was rocked to the core. There were many sleepless nights for us and the kids. But finally, we came to realize that Satan wanted to use fear to bind us and keep us from showing the film. We know that we serve a mighty God. What can man do to me?

So instead of hiding away and being bound by fear, we showed the film to over 100 people. God was glorified, and Satan's stronghold began to crumble. Being obedient to His calling and seeking every opportunity to be bold witnesses may not be easy or comfortable, but we know which side is victorious. Satan's stronghold is temporary; God's grace is eternal.

—CHRISTINA, SUB-SAHARAN AFRICAN PEOPLES

*Mighty fortress,* STRONG TO SAVE! NO ONE CAN PREVAIL AGAINST YOU—NOT MAN, NOT DEMON, NOT SATAN. HELPER OF THE HELPLESS, PROTECT YOUR CHILDREN FROM MALICIOUS ATTACK. GRANT THEM CONFIDENCE AND RESTORE THEIR PEACE OF MIND. *Amen.*

# On the right path

*"But the one sown on the good ground—this is one who hears and understands the word, who does bear fruit ..." Matthew 13:23 (HCSB)*

In Matthew 13, Jesus describes seeds sown on different soils. In North Africa, many hearts are hard toward truth, and it doesn't penetrate. Others receive the Good News with joy, but the seed is not able to take deep root. Persecution is certain. For some, it is just too difficult, and they return to Islam. Others are worried they might not be able to marry or get a good job. So like the seed among the thorns, their faith is choked out by worries of life. Yet some of the seed sown falls on good soil.

"Nadia" was good soil. A mother of four, she came to faith through a satellite television program. Her husband, "Mohammed," said he believed in Jesus, but there was no change in his life. He still yelled at Nadia and hit her. She faithfully prayed for her husband. For six months, she was not allowed to leave her house, but she continued to grow in her faith as she read God's Word, watched broadcasts, and received visits from other women believers. The death of Nadia's father-in-law got Mohammed's attention. The next week, he had a dream in which Jesus told him to listen to his wife because she was on the right path. Since that night, God has been transforming Mohammed's life and their home. Nadia testifies, "God has done a miracle."

—BRENDA, NORTHERN AFRICAN AND MIDDLE EASTERN PEOPLES

*Bless You,* GENTLE SAVIOR, FOR YOUR TENDER CARE. GIVE ME PATIENCE WITH BELIEVERS WHO ARE SLOW TO GROW IN THEIR FAITH. STOP ME WHEN I TRY TO BE THEIR "HOLY SPIRIT." HELP ME TO LIVE A GODLY LIFE BEFORE THEM AND TO TRUST THE REST TO YOU. *Amen.*

# Seeking but not knowing

*"I will seek the lost, bring back the strays, bandage the injured, and strengthen the weak ..." Ezekiel 34:16 (HCSB)*

It was our first road trip since arriving in Africa. We were going to visit another missionary family and had been warned that driving after dark was not recommended. Carefully, we planned for enough time to make the drive before nightfall. However, we had not calculated on making a wrong turn and driving 80 to 90 kilometers out of the way. By the time we realized our mistake and contacted our friends who gave us directions, the sun was going down.

Our entire family was extremely quiet and prayerful as we found our way back. Thankfully, a man on a motorcycle appeared in front of us, and he proved to be our guide in the darkness. We trailed the small taillight on the back of his bike. Nearing our destination and safety, the Lord gave us insight into the spiritual condition of many African people. Many earnestly seek after spiritual answers, yet they do not know the truth. Just like our family's experience, they are headed in the wrong direction without even knowing. They are seeking God on the wrong paths—the paths of witchcraft, ancestor veneration, or false religions. Just as our friends helped us find the right way, the Lord reminded our family that we must show people the right way to God.

—JENNIFER, SUB-SAHARAN AFRICAN PEOPLES

*Holy God,* MANY PEOPLE IN MY OWN CITY ARE TRAVELING THE WRONG PATH. THANK YOU FOR REMINDING ME THAT I MUST POINT THEM TO YOU. I AM FOLLOWING YOU, LORD, BUT SOMETIMES I TURN ASIDE IN SIN. CALL ME QUICKLY TO REPENTANCE. *Amen.*

## Soaking up the truth

*"In the day of my trouble I call upon you, for you answer me."* Psalm 86:7 (ESV)

"Vikrum" drives an auto rickshaw for a living. Being new to the city, I needed help learning my way around town and practicing the language. Since he was honest and helpful, he allowed me to live in his house with his family for the purpose of learning the local language. His wife taught me to cook, and his boys taught me to play cricket. I hoped to lead them to Jesus through sharing Bible stories.

One day while I was living with them, the police followed me home and arrested Vikrum for hosting an American, perhaps hoping for a bribe. After much prayer, he was released the same day, but it was still a tense time. I prayed for him, "Lord, let this difficult situation bring You glory. Draw him to Yourself."

A few months later, Vikrum said, "I am ready to pray to only Jesus." I was so excited! I cried when I thought about the hard times with the police and the way in which God had answered my prayers! Vikrum is so excited to learn about Jesus. He is like a sponge soaking up all he can learn. Watching his face light up as he learns more and more will be forever etched in my memory.

—GINGER, SOUTH ASIAN PEOPLES

*Rejoice, oh Lord!* VIKRUM'S JOY BRINGS GLORY TO YOUR NAME. FILL HIS MIND WITH WISDOM AS HE STUDIES YOUR WORD. MAKE HIM A POWERFUL CHRISTIAN WITNESS TO THE POLICEMEN WHO ONCE ARRESTED HIM. *Amen.*

# Recognizing a chicken

*"I am the good shepherd; and I know mine own, and mine own know me."*
John 10:14 (ASV)

The free-range chickens in the village where we live often scratch around, searching for hidden grain. After dark one evening, the chief's third wife, "Kumba," discovered that one of her hens was missing. The boy who fed the horses said that he had noticed a hen roosting in the horse pen. "That must be her," said Kumba. "Go fetch her so that I can keep her with the others for the night." Obediently, the boy went to retrieve the sleeping hen. As he picked her up, the hen clucked loudly. Across the darkened courtyard, Kumba called, "Leave her there. She's not mine."

I was amazed. How could she possibly recognize the cluck of one hen from another, in the dark, across a courtyard? Yet even more amazing, our heavenly Father knows each one of us. Those who hear His voice, obey, and follow Him, He gathers to Himself in safety. Kumba searches for her lost hen, not even knowing that she is the one who is lost. She prays five times a day in a language she does not understand, in need of the Shepherd.

Why are we in the village? Perhaps through us, Kumba and all her family will hear the voice of the One who is calling them by name.

—GAYE, SUB-SAHARAN AFRICAN PEOPLES

*Heavenly Father,* I BOW IN REVERENCE, FOR YOU KNOW MY VOICE. YOU CHOOSE TO KNOW ME PERSONALLY. YOU HAVE CALLED ME BY NAME. I PRAY FOR THOSE, LIKE KUMBA, WHO ARE NOT HEARING YOU CALL. PLEASE OPEN THEIR EARS AND GIVE THEM FAITH TO BELIEVE. *Amen.*

AUGUST V

# Making Him Known

*Witnessing is listed on the divine job description of every single believer no matter what our talents or spiritual gifts.*

—BETH MOORE

Tears splashed into my scrambled eggs as I listened to "Mary" tell her story at the breakfast table. As a teenager living in Nepal, Mary dreamed of going to university overseas, particularly the United States. Her Nepalese father allowed her to apply. Although they were practicing another religion, he decided that his precious daughter should apply to a Christian university so that she would be safe. However, he did not want her to be influenced by Christian beliefs. Mary applied and was accepted to a Christian university where my husband and I are missions mentors.

She brought very little with her besides her enthusiasm to study nursing. When she arrived in the States, not knowing what to expect and without friends or family, university personnel assigned her like all other international students to a local host family. And of course, the host family members were strong believers in Christ who attended a local church.

Mary spent a lot of time with her American family and Christian students. She was also required to attend university chapel services and Bible classes. God began to draw her to Himself through these avenues. But the host family was the key. They loved on her and accepted her as one of their own daughters. She had new "siblings" who shared God's message of love with her. After a year, Mary decided that she wanted to follow the one true God. She became a child of the living God.

It had been three years since Mary left her home country in order to study. She explained to us that God was calling her to go back to share the Gospel with her people group and family. A student team from the university had been organized, and she would go with them at the end of the school year. I watched her dark eyes dance as she expressed gratitude to God that she was going to share Christ. Many had shared the Gospel with her, and she couldn't wait to take the message to her home country.

As we talked, I couldn't help but think of the five Chinese freshmen, whom we call the Five Guys. They attend a local university where we now live. We met two of these students at a Thanksgiving dinner for international students hosted by several churches in our area. One of the guys, who had no idea what in the world to do with cranberry sauce, became my friend that evening. I told him about our Thanksgiving holiday tradition, and he told me about some of his Chinese holidays. We eventually got into a discussion about religion. I asked him if he had ever heard about Jesus. He hadn't. A Chinese pastor was sitting across from me and overheard the conversation. He invited our new friend to his church. I was able to give this student a copy of John's gospel, and my husband and I invited him and four of his friends to our house for supper when they returned for second semester.

On the scheduled date, my husband collected the Five Guys from the university and brought them to our house for one of the most memorable meals we've ever had. Hamburgers, baked beans, slaw, and apple pie with ice cream disappeared in record time. They loved the food! We had lots of fun talking about China and America and answering all their questions. None of them had ever been in an American home.

After several games of Wii and many, many laughs, a relationship was formed that has continued. They call me their "American mom." And I'm thrilled to have these five Chinese "sons." We have never seen them as projects but as people whom we love with the love of God. We have given them Bibles and are sharing and loving, brick by brick.

God's Great Commission is for every last one of us. As you read this month, I pray that you will be inspired to share your faith with your neighbors, internationals, your family, your coworkers, and anyone else you might meet. But we have to meet people and even get out of our churches to do it. Don't be afraid to take a risk. We've got to be where lost people are because most of the time, they are not going to be looking for us believers. Maybe God is calling you to go on a state, national, or international mission trip. Maybe he wants you to be a host family for international students like Mary or the Five Guys. Or maybe He just wants you to share your faith with a coworker. Whatever it is, you can be certain that God is calling you to share your faith.

—*Kim P. Davis*

# Preparing for the harvest

*"Therefore, my dear brothers, be steadfast, immovable, always excelling in the Lord's work, knowing that your labor in the Lord is not in vain."* 1 Corinthians 15:58 (HCSB)

Six months out of the year, the land is frozen where we live. The rocky ground makes it difficult for even a thorn bush to take root in the harsh environment.

We decided to construct several raised garden beds as an agricultural project to assist our community. We soon learned that the project involved much more physical labor than anticipated. The construction of the beds involved filling hundreds of sandbags with dirt and rocks for the first layer. Next, we added good soil and fertilizer. After planting, the hardest task was watering. We bought a gas-powered pump to draw water from the nearby creek, but at times the creek was dry. We carried hundreds of gallons of water from the river.

When high winds threatened to destroy the fragile plants, it seemed like more work than the potential harvest warranted. This feeling changed when we reaped the first vegetables. Suddenly, all those hours of manual labor were rewarded.

Sometimes the labor involved in sharing the Good News is more than anticipated. At times the cost is higher than what we think. Paul admonishes us to be steadfast in our work, knowing that our work is for the Lord. We may not always see the harvest, but we can be assured that our work for Him is not in vain.

—T.M., EAST ASIAN PEOPLES

*Lord,* I PRAY FOR MISSIONARIES WHO ARE STRUGGLING TODAY TO PLANT SEEDS OF THE GOSPEL. ENCOURAGE THEM TO KNOW THAT THEIR LABOR IS NOT IN VAIN. *Amen.*

# Catching fish

*"And He said to them, 'Follow Me, and I will make you fishers of men.'"*
Matthew 4:19 (NASB)

If you live on an island, you think of the sea. One of my favorite pastimes associated with the ocean is fishing. I have to admit, though, I haven't caught a single fish since living here.

Some of the most fertile waters in the world surround this island. I have plenty of good fishing equipment: rods, reels, line, hooks, lures, you name it. I have read books and talked to people about fishing. Good fishing spots are plentiful, and I've watched others catch fish. Why in the world have I not caught a fish then?

As you may have guessed, I have not been fishing yet myself. It is impossible for me to catch a fish unless I get a hook wet. No matter how much I study and talk about fishing, and no matter the money I spend on the best equipment, I will never catch a single fish unless I get out there and go fishing.

Hopefully, this metaphor is clear. In order to seek and to save those without Christ, I must go out, find them, and share the Good News. The lost cannot come to faith unless they hear. How can they hear unless they are told? May I always have a sign up that says, "Gone fishin' for souls."

—VINCENT, SOUTH ASIAN PEOPLES

*Dear Lord,* YOU ARE THE MASTER FISHERMAN. I PRAY FOR WORKERS IN SOUTH ASIA AS THEY DROP THE NET OR CAST THE LINE. GIVE THEM LANGUAGE SKILLS. HELP THEM OVERCOME CULTURAL BARRIERS. SEND THEM FISHING FOR SOULS. *Amen.*

# Prompting from the Spirit

*"For God, who said, 'Light shall shine out of darkness,' is the One who has shone in our hearts to give the Light of the knowledge of the glory of God in the face of Christ." 2 Corinthians 4:6 (NASB)*

Though learning the language was crucial, I cherished my 15-minute break during lessons. I'd dart for the door, heading to the supermarket to give my brain a break. Hoping to recharge for the rest of my studies, I'd pass the supermarket cashiers. One cashier was a young Muslim woman with a beautiful smile. She learned that I was a language student and waited for me every day to help me practice my new vocabulary. Although usually tired, I'd always try to talk with her.

One day as I left the store, the Lord prompted me to go back inside and talk to this woman. I felt awkward, but she was thrilled to talk with me. We made plans to meet later. She told me that she was usually afraid of foreigners, but she could tell from my smile and actions that I was kind and trustworthy.

Now she is my friend. God brings people into our lives from unexpected places. People are watching how we live. If we live daily for the Lord, His light will shine through us and will be noticed. God is always working, drawing others to Himself. In His timing, He will share truth with His people and will use us in the process, if we choose to be obedient.

—B.P., SOUTHEAST ASIAN PEOPLES

*Gracious God,* YOU HAVE CALLED US TO SPEAK YOUR WORD IN SEASON AND OUT OF SEASON. EVEN DURING A 15-MINUTE BREAK, YOU COORDINATED A SPECIAL FRIENDSHIP FOR B.P. STRENGTHEN THEIR BOND, DRAWING THIS FRIEND TO SALVATION IN JESUS. *Amen.*

## *Nothing but Christ crucified*

*"And I, when I came to you, brothers, did not come proclaiming to you the testimony of God with lofty speech or wisdom. For I decided to know nothing among you except Jesus Christ and him crucified." 1 Corinthians 2:1–2 (ESV)*

Living overseas doesn't automatically make you faithful or bold. Even missionaries face the temptation to compromise or simply not talk about the Gospel. We can easily squander opportunities. We can be lazy in prayer and evangelism, while being diligent on secondary things like e-mail, planning, and Internet research. Meanwhile, people die without hearing the Gospel.

The Christian calling is quite simple: tell people the Gospel—the Good News of Jesus' life, death, and resurrection. We often think too hard about security or knowing the culture. For the Christian, disobedience is more painful than rejection. Will we do whatever it takes to reach people with the Gospel? We must ask ourselves, "How many people will hear the Gospel today in my city?"

Do we believe that something that sounds so ignorant, so naive, so simple to some really has this transformational power? Or do we believe we must ask permission to share it or make it "more beautiful," as if that were possible? Jesus has commanded us to go. Our mantra must simply be, "Just tell."

—B.V., EAST ASIAN PEOPLES

*Lord,* I DON'T WANT TO BE LAZY, DISOBEDIENT, OR SQUANDER TIME IN MY CHRISTIAN WALK. MAY I BE FAITHFUL IN TELLING OTHERS TODAY. MAY OUR MISSIONARIES ALSO STAY DILIGENTLY FOCUSED ON THEIR CALLING TO SHARE THE GOSPEL. *Amen.*

# Respecting the neighbors

*"I will plant trees in the barren desert—cedar, acacia, myrtle, olive, cypress, fir, and pine. I am doing this so all who see this miracle will understand what it means—that it is the LORD who has done this, the Holy One of Israel who created it." Isaiah 41:19–20 (NLT)*

When I moved to Southeast Asia, my roommate and I had a tiny yard that was less than attractive. The neighbors had mentioned the garden's condition once or twice, but seeing that neither of us had a green thumb, we did not really pay much attention to their passing comments. As time went on, however, it became apparent that making the yard presentable was important. We had been praying for opportunities to serve, although we did not think it would be in the way of beautifying *our* home. But to gain our neighbors' favor, the garden work began.

There were many neighbors who came by to express their happiness as we worked, bringing us tools we needed and offering advice on landscaping. We weren't quite sure what we had gotten ourselves into, as we didn't know much about gardening, but our yard became the new hangout. We trust that God will remove barriers and will use this experience to allow us to bring the Good News to our neighbors! God is at work and will use even the small things to draw people to Himself. We just have to be sensitive to the needs of others around us and be willing to trust Him with the outcome.

—L.V., SOUTHEAST ASIAN PEOPLES

*Holy One,* YOU FIRST SPOKE TO MANKIND IN A GARDEN; AND IN A GARDEN, JESUS PRAYED BEFORE HIS CRUCIFIXION. ALLOW THIS TINY NEIGHBORHOOD GARDEN TO BE A PLACE WHERE PEOPLE DISCOVER THE RESURRECTED SAVIOR. *Amen.*

# Light shining in darkness

*"Then Jesus spoke to them again: 'I am the light of the world. Anyone who follows Me will never walk in the darkness but will have the light of life.'" John 8:12 (HCSB)*

*Clang-clang-clang!* I awoke in a panic, my heart racing. The darkness of an icy, predawn Arctic morning surrounded me. My watch read 4:30 a.m. I had arrived a few days before, after several hours of hiking, in this remote village of the "Pretty" people group. When I arrived, they were making preparations for the New Year celebration. Today was the day!

Being Tibetan Buddhists, the rituals began early and included chanting mantras to the beating of drums and clashing cymbals, reciting many generations of the family lineage and—beginning about midday—firing guns from house to house. My partner and I were invited into many houses and fed interesting foods. At the end of the day, I was dressed in traditional garb and danced with everyone in a circle around a gigantic bonfire.

The Light of the world, Jesus, made an impact because He joined in the life of the people He came to rescue, attending weddings, funerals, religious feasts, and special dinners while constantly talking about the kingdom. We endured long hikes, bitter cold, and new foods so that the Pretty people could see His Light.

Light is best seen in darkness. What are you willing to do to take His light to dark places?

—Andrew, East Asian Peoples

It is comfortable to stay within my circle of Christian friends, Lord. Yet You have called me to a life of service. Show me where You want me to go, equip me to tackle the challenges, and let me cast Your light. Open the eyes of the Pretty people to see and respond to Your light. Amen.

# The right road

*"... 'Obey My voice, and I will be your God, and you will be My people; and you will walk in all the way which I command you, that it may be well with you.'"*
*Jeremiah 7:23 (NASB)*

To drive where I live, one might as well throw out the rule book. With extreme caution and a massive dose of faith, I get behind the wheel. I expect the absurd, insane, and implausible while on the road. Traffic signals are mere suggestions. Running red lights is normal. Each vehicle at an intersection inches forward until one or the other wins the showdown and scoots across.

Many people prefer motorcycles over cars, which heightens the excitement. These bikes move through traffic like a torrent—often driving the wrong way! Whatever works to get them to their destination is okay. Meanwhile, pedestrians weave and dodge through traffic with unflappable calm, unaware of the threat of death or injury. In fact, in this bubbling cauldron of activity, everyone seems oblivious to danger.

From a spiritual perspective, 99 percent of the people around me are on the wrong road. Some have no idea where they are going. Others think they know, but they don't know where their path ultimately leads. Many seem not to care. As Christians, we know the right road. His name is Jesus. As we point people to Him, we offer peace and hope in the midst of chaos.

—Bill, Southeast Asian Peoples

*You alone, Lord,* are the way. Give missionaries diligence to move forward in Your truth and not yield or be swayed by false doctrine. By Your Word, Your people, and Your Spirit, bring order to the spiritual chaos in Southeast Asia. *Amen.*

# *Taking time for tea*

*"But seek first the kingdom of God and His righteousness, and all these things will be provided for you." Matthew 6:33 (HCSB)*

When we were looking for an apartment, my husband entered the office of a property dealer named "Gaurav." We'd sat in that same room many times before, drinking tea and eating cookies. That day, though, had been long, and we just needed one quick answer. So a friend and I sat in the car to wait while my husband made his inquiry.

Gaurav made my husband sit and asked where I was. Trying to ask the needed question, my husband realized that Gaurav was directing his helper to make tea for a nice, long visit. Eventually, my husband realized he had no choice but to retrieve my friend and me from the car. We all sat together and visited until the tea came. When the refreshments were finished, Gaurav slowly set down his glass, satisfied, and asked, "Now, what is the question?"

Western culture often misses opportunities for relationships because of busyness. But everything Christ did was relational. That day God reminded us that although we were looking for an apartment to begin our "focused" work, we should have been focused first on a person who doesn't know Christ. Now when we intentionally visit with Gaurav, he's not a means to the end of getting a house; he's a man with a need for Christ.

—Daisy, South Asian Peoples

*One day soon,* Lord, I pray that Gaurav will ask a far more significant question, "What must I do to be saved?" Forgive us when we rush ahead with our plans and fail to see another's eternal need. *Amen.*

# An unexpected change

*"Therefore having such a hope, we use great boldness in our speech."*
2 Corinthians 3:12 (NASB)

My local ministry partner called to ask if I could meet him so that we could go to a labor camp where a worship group had started. One of the camp supervisors had given permission for several believers to meet for worship in a trailer. When we arrived, however, we discovered the trailer was living quarters and not empty as we thought. Three believers and 13 Muslim men slept there, and the men, other than the believers, wondered why we were there.

My usually bold partner became nervous, saying we should not teach that night. God prompted me differently; I wanted the group leader to decide if we should teach or leave. When asked, the leader said we could stay. I retold the parable of the 10 virgins, clearly stating that it was a story Jesus taught. I explained that we all must be prepared for Jesus' return, and my partner shared how to be prepared. Two of the men looked disturbed, but almost all of them asked us to come again.

God had closed the door for private worship. He had a different plan. We were sent to declare His message to 13 Muslim men. Boldness is not something that comes easily, but the Holy Spirit is with us as we share the Gospel in impossible situations.

—James, Central Asian Peoples

*"How will they believe* in Him whom they have not heard?" (Romans 10:14b, NASB). Author of salvation, redeeming grace can be found through Bible study. Give workers boldness to teach so the lost can hear. *Amen.*

## A calling, a message

*"So we have the prophetic word strongly confirmed. You will do well to pay attention to it, as to a lamp shining in a dismal place, until the day dawns and the morning star arises in your hearts." 2 Peter 1:19 (HCSB)*

I sat in a bamboo chair under the stars, watching the firelight dance on the faces of the Bambara men and women around me. Their attention was riveted to the Ohio pastor who was preaching. "When we pray, we need to be thankful. Does anyone here want to thank God for anything?" he asked the group.

One man stood up. "For years, something has been drawing me to Christianity," he said. "I just felt like it was the truth, but I didn't know how to become a Christian. I thank God that your group came and told me how." Another stood beside him. "It's been the same with me. Something was drawing me to Jesus, but I didn't know how to find Him until you came." Again and again, it was echoed in the inky, African night. God had been calling them for years, but there was no one to tell them how they could answer until a little church in Ohio sent a handful of volunteers across the ocean.

A year later, a church is flourishing in that village. One man has blossomed into an evangelist, leading others to Christ all across the bush. His wife said, "Just as you came all the way from America to tell us about Jesus, we need to go to other villages to tell them, too."

—SUSAN, SUB-SAHARAN AFRICAN PEOPLES

*One planted,* ANOTHER WATERED, BUT YOU, GOD, GAVE THE INCREASE. WE ASK FOR YOUR BLESSING ON VOLUNTEER TEAMS AS THEY MINISTER TO UNREACHED PEOPLE GROUPS. *Amen.*

# Be strong and contagious!

*"Be strong and courageous, do not be afraid or tremble at them, for the LORD your God is the one who goes with you. He will not fail you or forsake you."*
Deuteronomy 31:6 (NASB)

I was only half listening to my son practice his Bible verse when I heard him say, "Be strong and *contagious*." It was humorous, but when I started to think about it, the statement was profound. Isn't being contagious exactly what we're called to do as we reach out to an unbelieving world? Mission strategy involves living a contagious life as I interact daily with the people God puts in my path. Being a contagious Christian means I smile at every child I see. I give directions pleasantly when I'm asked. I give up my seat on the subway to the older person who comes in after me. I open up my home more than I have in my entire life. I care for my kids and husband in front of my neighbors. In other words, I simply live my life in a way that says, "I'm different. Ask me why." And so far, it's helped me develop more relationships with lost people than I ever imagined.

No matter where I am, no matter what I am doing, I pray that I am living a contagious life, one that affects my lost friends, one the Father uses to draw people to Himself. And as I live out that life, I am not alone. The God of the universe has promised to be with me.

—Kellye, European Peoples

*Lord God,* MAKE MY LIFE CONTAGIOUS! CHALLENGE ME TO LIVE IN SUCH A WAY THAT OTHERS MAY SEE THE GOOD WORKS AND GLORIFY YOU, MY HEAVENLY FATHER. I WANT TO LIVE LIKE KELLYE, SAYING, "I'M DIFFERENT. ASK ME WHY." *Amen.*

## *Two are better than one*

*"Behold, how good and how pleasant it is for brothers to dwell together in unity."*
*Psalm 133:1 (NASB)*

We were as different as could be, and God had put us together to reach a people for His kingdom. Working with a complete stranger was no simple task for either one of us. "Kaye" is an extrovert; I'm introverted. I am a deep feeler; she is rational. She was comfortable living on her own; I struggled. Even our ideas of the "same" thing were different.

Despite our differences, God gave us both one heart and one mind when it came to reaching the Zerma people. When we first began, we would go separately to different villages. After a year, God led us to share Bible stories together in six villages. It doubled the work on each of us, but we found that we were stronger and more effective together. God used our varied gifts and talents to minister to people, and He has blessed His work. We have seen closed places open up to the Gospel. When we are in a spiritual conversation with someone, Kaye and I complement each other, sharing different perspectives and insights. After our term ended, God led us to return to Africa for another two years. He is continuing to show us that the world will know we are His disciples by our unity and love for one another.

—BRANDY, SUB-SAHARAN AFRICAN PEOPLES

*In You, Lord,* WE ARE ONE. MISSIONARIES ARE OFTEN PARTNERED WITH SOMEONE THEY HAVE NEVER MET. MAY THOSE RELATIONSHIPS PROVE FRUITFUL AS MISSIONARIES YIELD THEIR INDIVIDUALISM AND EMBRACE YOUR CREATIVE NEW DESIGN. *Amen.*

# The good Samaritan

*"For He Himself is our peace, who made both groups into one and broke down the barrier of the dividing wall." Ephesians 2:14 (NASB)*

Even though there are many believers in our Southeast Asian country, there remains a wall of separation between them and their Muslim neighbors, a wall built of prejudice and fear.

Amazing things happen when that wall is breached! When the war intensified on their homeland island, "Nadua" and his family fled to the mainland for refuge. As Nadua stood in the street with his wife and children, surrounded by their few belongings, darkness and rain descended. Though many saw the refugees, doors closed tightly. As concern etched Nadua's face, a Christian man approached. He not only invited this Muslim family into his home, but lent them money to build a shelter on his property and a small vegetable store.

One day, the benefactor's son visited and began to talk with Nadua's family about Jesus. Nadua didn't want to hear words from the Bible; he believed the Quran was the only uncorrupted revelation from God. Yet he was ashamed not to listen to this man whose father had helped his family. As he listened, the Spirit opened his heart. After several months, Nadua and his family repented and were baptized. A house group now meets in their home, and he is learning how to share his faith. Ears and hearts are opened when God's love flows through us.

—D.S., SOUTHEAST ASIAN PEOPLES

*Lord,* THERE ARE MANY HOMELESS AND HUNGRY IN MY CITY. BREAK DOWN MY WALLS OF PREJUDICE AND APATHY. HELP ME SERVE THEM. BLESS THE CHURCH IN NADUA'S HOUSE AND THE CARING FAMILY WHO PROVIDED A WAY. *Amen.*

## *The Man of her Dreams*

*"Therefore if any man be in Christ, he is a new creature: old things are passed away; behold, all things are become new." 2 Corinthians 5:17 (KJV)*

"She needs to see the doctor, but she can't walk to your clinic. Will you come to my home?" It was the end of a busy day after seeing over 150 patients in the village. Though tired, the volunteer doctor agreed to see her. He gave the woman medicine for her arthritis but explained there was nothing else he could do. A national believer who had come with us asked if we could pray for her. She agreed, and after we prayed, I told "Marcelina" that I would return soon.

Two weeks later, I returned with my Quechua-speaking friend, hoping the Lord would give us an opportunity to share the Gospel. Marcelina explained how she had been having dreams about a large bird coming into her window at night and attacking her. Through tears, she said she was afraid to die. I shared about a Savior who was greater than the demons tormenting her. The following week I returned, and she again shared her unusual dreams in which a Man in white was guarding her from evil spirits. We explained that the man was Jesus and that He wanted her to trust Him as her Savior.

A new sister was added to the Lord's family that day! Do you know someone who needs to hear about our Savior?

—LINDSEY, AMERICAN PEOPLES

*You, my Lord,* ARE A STRONG TOWER. YOU ARE GOD OVER FEAR. FOR YOU HAVE "NOT GIVEN US THE SPIRIT OF FEAR; BUT OF POWER, AND OF LOVE, AND OF A SOUND MIND" (2 TIMOTHY 1:7, KJV). BLESS YOU FOR TURNING MARCELINA'S NIGHTMARES INTO SWEET AND GLORIOUS DREAMS. *Amen.*

# When I think of pearls

*"Again, the kingdom of heaven is like a merchant seeking fine pearls, and upon finding one pearl of great value, he went and sold all that he had and bought it."*
Matthew 13:45–46 (NASB)

When I think of pearls, I think of my grandmother. I also think of the millions of lost people on our island who sell these treasures. A pearl's value is determined by luster, surface flaws, color, shape, size, and texture. I'm so grateful that I am not valued by my surface flaws, shape, or size!

Pearls are very valuable to Bee because they are her livelihood. I enjoy visiting Bee in her pearl shop to discuss life issues. One day, Bee told me that the Quran mentioned paradise, but she was fearful that she would not enter. It gave me the opportunity to use three strands of her pearls as an illustration: a perfect South Sea, a medium-valued Mikimoto, and an inexpensive freshwater pearl. I asked, "If these three strands represented people, which one would be allowed into paradise according to your Quran?" She quickly responded, "The flawless South Sea strand." I explained to Bee that I was more like the cheap strand, but according to the Bible, I would spend eternal life in heaven since I had been redeemed by Christ. She laughed at first but then asked me how I could be sure. I explained that Jesus saw me as a South Sea pearl, even though I was really like a freshwater one. That's how He sees all His children.

—A WORKER WITH SOUTHEAST ASIAN PEOPLES

*Father,* HALLELUJAH THAT I AM PRECIOUS IN YOUR SIGHT! BECAUSE OF YOUR PLAN OF REDEMPTION, YOU HAVE TAKEN SOMEONE WORTHLESS AND MADE ME INTO A PEARL OF GREAT PRICE. THANK YOU FOR YOUR TREMENDOUS GRACE. *Amen.*

# A Christian's job

*"You have heard me teach things that have been confirmed by many reliable witnesses. Now teach these truths to other trustworthy people who will be able to pass them on to others."* 2 Timothy 2:2 (NLT)

I had not seen "Mrs. Banda" in over a year. She came to Bible study and told me that she had been sick. When she stood up, I was surprised to see that half of one of her legs was missing, and she was using crutches. Doctors had to remove part of her leg, and possibly, she would lose a toe from the opposite leg.

The lesson that day was on 2 Timothy 2:2. When I asked the women how they could apply this verse to their lives, Mrs. Banda replied, "I need to tell my family, my neighbors, and my friends about Jesus. I need to train them so that they can tell others, too." I was surprised by her answer and told her that in her condition, it would be hard for her to evangelize. It was obvious that her disability would make it difficult. Without hesitation, Mrs. Banda gently corrected me: "It is my job as a Christian. I can get along on my one leg. God will help me."

Every time I teach, I learn something in return. Mrs. Banda taught me that no matter what, I should not excuse myself from telling others about Christ. If this woman can share Christ, what is stopping me?

—SUZIE, SUB-SAHARAN AFRICAN PEOPLES

*Merciful Lord,* YOU EQUIP US TO SHARE YOUR STORY. CALL ME TO REPENTANCE WHEN I UNDERESTIMATE YOUR FOLLOWERS, THINKING ANYONE IS LESS THAN ABLE TO CARRY OUT YOUR GREAT COMMISSION. THANK YOU FOR MRS. BANDA'S COURAGE. *Amen.*

# A life redeemed

*"Those who sow in tears will reap with shouts of joy." Psalm 126:5 (HCSB)*

"If only I had listened to your words in Choszczno in 1990, I would not be where I am today." These words began a letter that I received from a Polish prison in 1997. The inmate had attended a crusade in a small, Polish town where I had preached. During the week, the crowds swelled from 30 the first night to over 200 for the last service. A handful repented, but many walked away unmoved by the Gospel. This man was one who walked away unaffected. After years of wrong choices, he was in prison as he penned the letter.

Though we had moved four times since the crusade, he found my contact information. In his letter, he said that he had finally repented as challenged that long-ago night, and he testified to the new life that he now experienced, even behind bars. His only request was for a Bible and Christian literature in his language, which I sent.

Eighteen years after the crusade, I discovered that he was recently released from prison and now attends the church that was started in that small town where the crusade was held. Many years were wasted, but a life has been redeemed, and a believer is serving his King. What a reminder of God's promises and His power. We sow the Gospel seed. He produces the harvest.

—MARK, EUROPEAN PEOPLES

YOUR WORD, RIGHTEOUS GOD, WILL NOT RETURN TO YOU EMPTY. WE REJOICE IN THIS PRISONER'S TRANSFORMATION. IT BRINGS US HOPE. NOW IS THE TIME FOR US TO VISIT THOSE IN PRISON, BUT THE DAY OF THEIR SALVATION IS IN YOUR HANDS. *Amen.*

# *Birthday prayers*

*"Serve only the* LORD *your God and fear him alone ..." Deuteronomy 13:4 (NLT)*

"Margaret" was a witch doctor from a remote village who recently became a Christian. Her heart burned with a desire to return home, four hours away, to destroy her remaining witchcraft relics. I thought about the Israelites turning to God, yet leaving intact the idols, altars, and high places. These became sinful temptations for future generations. What would happen if these evil items from Margaret's past were not destroyed?

We began our long journey to Margaret's home on my birthday, traveling by vehicle and on foot through the rough, overgrown land. Once there, she gathered the relics she had used to call upon evil spirits. Everyone watched Margaret burn the items. Spontaneous prayers, singing, and dancing were offered in praise to Jesus!

Two men passed by who knew Margaret as the community witch doctor, and the Gospel was shared with them. One of them couldn't contain his excitement and wanted his brother to hear this Good News. So off he ran. When he and his brother returned, the Gospel was repeated. The brother simply said, "If my family has come to Christ, then I don't want to be left in the camp of the devil!" They both surrendered their lives to Christ.

Faithful believers around the world were praying for me on my birthday. God answered those prayers by giving me two new Christian brothers.

—MARTHA, FOREIGN CORRESPONDENT IN THE AMERICAS

*God,* HONOR OUR MISSIONARIES' BIRTHDAYS BY FULFILLING THE DESIRES OF THEIR HEARTS. THIS YEAR AND EVERY YEAR, GIVE THEM NEW BROTHERS AND SISTERS IN CHRIST FROM THEIR ADOPTED PEOPLE GROUP. *Amen.*

# God gives the increase

*"So then neither he who plants is anything, nor he who waters, but God who gives the increase." 1 Corinthians 3:7 (NKJV)*

Only one of the three girls coming to the Bible study was a believer. One girl seemed genuinely interested, but the other always wanted to debate. "Emma" had a comeback to every statement, refusing to accept truth. It was frustrating and honestly, I hoped she wouldn't come to our meetings.

One evening, the believer called to tell me that they were running late. She said only two of them were coming. I was holding my breath, hoping it was Emma who couldn't make it, but then learned Emma would be coming.

I was filled with anxiety. I was not in the mood to deal with debating. When the doorbell rang, I prepared for the worst. Emma came in, sat down, and whipped out a tract I had given to her weeks before. Then she excitedly said, "I believe this is true!"

She went on to say that she had begun to pray, and she believed God is real. She insisted we pray with her right then; she was ready to follow Jesus. I was overwhelmed with joy. At the same time, I was convicted. I needed to fall on my face before God to confess my unbelief. What a reminder that I am weak and can do nothing on my own, but He can do anything!

—K., East Asian Peoples

*Precious Lord,* I confess my own selfish attitudes, not wanting to deal with difficult people. Please forgive me. Grant an extra measure of grace to Christian workers who are tired of the debate. *Amen.*

## *Hearing sacrifice stories*

*"This poor man cried, and the Lord heard him and saved him out of all his troubles."* Psalm 34:6 (NASB)

Strategizing to reach a Muslim people group of over 7 million people was daunting. Prayer partners joined me to pray that God would lead us to people who would become catalysts to spread the Gospel.

"Zeke," my national partner, and I made a bold decision to share the Gospel with anyone, anywhere, at any time. Two months later, Zeke met "Tom" at an office. It was a risky place to share the Gospel, but he shared anyway. When Tom showed sincere interest, I met Zeke and Tom at a public park where I shared stories from the Old Testament and about Jesus, the Lamb of God. Each story illustrated the necessity of a blood sacrifice for the forgiveness of sin. Upon hearing the sacrifice stories, Tom responded, "This is good news! I have 50 friends who need to hear these stories." Just a few days later, Tom became a Christian. When "Hardy," Tom's best friend, came to the same park to hear the stories, he could hardly wait to place his faith in Christ.

Tom and Hardy have since led hundreds of people to Christ and have started numerous house churches. Their disciples have done the same. As a result of their willingness to boldly share their faith, despite great opposition, people have professed faith daily.

—Caleb, Southeast Asian Peoples

*God*, I have never seen the Gospel spread so quickly; and where I live, I wonder if it ever will. Help my unbelief. If the Good News can be shared in dangerous places, why can't it happen here? Transform my thinking. *Amen.*

# Little by little

*"At the same time, pray also for us that God may open a door to us for the message, to speak the mystery of the Messiah ..." Colossians 4:3 (HCSB)*

A month before an Arkansas medical team's planned trip, our family investigated the indigenous villages in the Ecuadorian jungle where they would work. We had hoped to share Bible stories, but after the grueling 14 hours by car in jungle terrain and two hours by canoe, we were met with total rejection. The chief was cordial, however, because he wanted health care for his people.

After the visit, I began to worry that the volunteers' time and money might be wasted since there was no spiritual interest among the people. God led me to pray more fervently for the villages and the volunteers who were coming.

The volunteers arrived, the medical clinic began, and there were no patients. Finally, one man came. Little by little, others trickled in. They received medical and dental attention, women received embroidery projects, children enjoyed games and stories, and families received *JESUS* films in their language. The love of Jesus was apparent through the volunteers.

By the end of the week, blank stares had become smiling faces. Children and parents listened intently to the Bible stories, and we were welcomed in their villages! God increased our faith that He could penetrate the hearts of the people when His love is shown through action.

—Kyleen, American Peoples

*Why is it, Lord,* we bathe our projects in planning instead of prayer? On our knees we proclaim, "You are the Lord who goes before us!" May the tentative interest from these villagers in Ecuador soon turn into a passionate faith. *Amen.*

# *Overcoming fear*

*"... 'You of little faith, why did you doubt?'" Matthew 14:31 (NASB)*

My Asian house was surrounded by small stores lit with pink lights. It didn't take long for me to figure out that these "stores" were really brothels under the guise of beauty salons. My heart ached for the young women, who day after day sat in chairs in front of the windows, literally advertising themselves.

My language skills weren't good, and I thought no one would go with me to translate. Those women probably would never talk with me, much less hear the message of salvation. But after almost two years of believing those doubts, the Lord renewed my sense of boldness to approach the prostitutes. I was riding my bike and stopped to take a sip of juice. As I was drinking, I prayed, "Lord, please increase my faith!" When I looked up, a brothel full of girls, all gathered at the window, waved at me with huge smiles.

The women were shocked when I walked in. We covered basic get-to-know-you stuff. Later, I went back with a friend, and we shared the Gospel. They were kind to me, but the owner was not happy that I was there.

When my term of service ended, a national believer took the challenge to witness to the women. They have heard the Gospel, and I pray that they will one day know Jesus.

—RUTH, EAST ASIAN PEOPLES

*Mighty God,* BRING SALVATION TO THESE WOMEN LIVING IN PROSTITUTION. ENCOURAGE THE NATIONAL BELIEVER WHO CONTINUES THE MINISTRY. IT MAKES ME THINK ABOUT THE ROUGH NEIGHBORHOODS IN MY TOWN AND MY RELUCTANCE TO SERVE THERE. FORGIVE ME! *Amen.*

# Passing on the faith

*"Remember your leaders who have spoken God's word to you. As you carefully observe the outcome of their lives, imitate their faith. Jesus Christ is the same yesterday, today, and forever." Hebrews 13:7–8 (HCSB)*

Years ago, we planted a church in a suburb of Tokyo. Sometime later, a middle-aged Japanese lady, "Harumi," began to attend Sunday services. Within six months, her withered heart opened to God's Word, and salvation brought real transformation.

When we returned to Japan for our last term of service 20 years later, word came that Harumi wanted to introduce us to her friend, "Noriko," who believed that if she worked hard enough or was good enough, she would be able to experience similar changes as Harumi.

When we met with the women, we had the opportunity to share the Gospel with Noriko. She refused to open her heart, but her tears confirmed the need. On another occasion, we talked extensively about how Christ transforms lives. Noriko declared that she, too, wanted to repent.

Noriko's transformation has been firm and consistent. She began to witness to her two daughters and helped lead the oldest to Christ. The younger daughter continued to resist but admitted, "I am not a Christian, but I am thankful for the changes that I see in my mother!"

Later, Noriko sent us a note that her young daughter "had received Jesus for real!"

—BURCH, EAST ASIAN PEOPLES

*Eternal Savior,* THE NAMES ARE SO UNFAMILIAR TO MY TONGUE, BUT THEY ARE WRITTEN IN THE BOOK OF LIFE. ALL PRAISE BELONGS TO YOU! MAY THESE WOMEN TURN JAPAN UP-SIDE DOWN BY SHARING THEIR GENUINE FAITH WITH FRIEND AFTER FRIEND AFTER FRIEND. *Amen.*

## Persevering with the Gospel

*"Therefore, do not throw away your confidence, which has a great reward."*
Hebrews 10:35 (NASB)

When I first heard my Muslim friend say to our youngest daughter, "When you are older, you can choose what religion to follow," as a mother, my first reaction was to protect my child. However, the Lord is faithful, and I realized that I could trust Him with my daughter.

My friend "Yassim" came regularly to our house. When the call to prayer sounded from one of the many mosques in our city, she would be excused to say her prayers. Many days, I questioned whether I needed to starve our relationship so that it would gently fade away. But the Lord wanted me to continue the friendship.

Local believers and I shared with Yassim about the Lord, but she was resistant. I nearly gave up. Yet one hot, busy afternoon, Yassim asked to speak with me about Jesus. I couldn't believe what I was hearing. This was not the way I thought it would happen. Yassim received Christ that day and was later baptized.

It wasn't long before she led her sister to the Lord and played a role in our daughter's decision to follow Christ. I discovered again that God calls us to share the Good News, even when it seems overwhelming, impossible, and a waste of time, especially with extremely religious people who follow traditions instead of the Lord.

—CELIA, SOUTH ASIAN PEOPLES

*Righteous One,* NO TRADITION CAN OVERSHADOW YOU! GRANT ME CONFIDENT GRACE
TO TRUST YOU WITH MY FAMILY'S SPIRITUAL WELL-BEING JUST AS CELIA DID. BLESS YASSIM
WITH A FRUITFUL WITNESS. *Amen.*

# Pursuing with love

*"Above all, keep fervent in your love for one another, because love covers a multitude of sins." 1 Peter 4:8 (NASB)*

"Carmen" was a 12-year-old troublemaker in the English class after-school program. One day, I reproached her for something inappropriate that she said during class. In response, she wrote insults about me on the school wall. I was shocked and hurt. It was the day of our first Bible club, and it felt like a direct attack from Satan.

I prayed and considered two choices. I could write her off, or I could purposely pursue her with love. God enabled me to choose the higher road. As part of my plan to show love, I mentioned to the class that I knew who wrote the graffiti, but I forgave that person. Later, after asking permission from her mother, I spent special time with Carmen, talking about the Bible. I invited her to play with my children and to attend Bible club. Slowly, Carmen started changing, the defiant look was gone, and a beautiful smile took its place.

When her mom came to pick her up after she had been with our family, Carmen gave me one of the best compliments: "Mom, when I grow up, I want to be like Mara." I humbly accepted the compliment, praying that I will be one who displays the beauty of Jesus that we, as His followers, should reflect.

—MARA, EUROPEAN PEOPLES

*Father,* YOU ARE FORGIVING AND KIND. THANK YOU FOR GIVING MARA THE GRACE TO REFLECT YOUR CHARACTER TO CARMEN. MAY CARMEN GROW UP IN YOUR DISCIPLINE AND INSTRUCTION TO BE AN INSTRUMENT HERSELF OF YOUR MERCY. *Amen.*

## Reaping in due season

*"Therefore, having this ministry by the mercy of God, we do not lose heart."*
2 Corinthians 4:1 (ESV)

After many weeks of family sickness, cultural irritations, and limited ministry opportunities, I was about ready to call it quits. A few days later, my husband returned home from a trip to a remote village area where we had once focused much of our ministry efforts.

For over two years previously, we had squeezed onto dirty, smoke-filled buses and teetered along cliffside roads in order minister to the people who lived in forgotten mountain villages. We poured our lives out for these indifferent people, loving, serving, and pleading in prayer for their salvation. We shared about Creator God as we ate around the campfire and explained why we didn't need the animistic priests to give offerings to appease local spirits on our behalf. When our term finished, we left heartbroken. Although some had shown interest in God, none had believed.

Returning to Asia, our family situation made it impossible for us to focus our ministry in this area. But now, during my time of discouragement, my husband was finally able to take a trip back to these villages. Our friends were overjoyed to see him. This time, as my husband explained the Gospel, they listened with rapt attention. One even professed Christ! The Lord used my husband's trip to encourage me that seeds sown in His name will bear fruit in His time.

—S.E.B., EAST ASIAN PEOPLES

*Ancient of Days,* YOUR LOVE BRINGS COMFORT WHEN YOU SPEAK INTO OUR DISCOURAGEMENT. LIFT UP THE MISSIONARIES WHO TODAY ARE FEELING DEFEATED IN THEIR LABORS. GIVE THEM A GLIMPSE OF THE HARVEST YOU ARE PREPARING. *Amen.*

# Retrieving a tract with a trunk

*"The point is this: whoever sows sparingly will also reap sparingly, and whoever sows bountifully will also reap bountifully." 2 Corinthians 9:6 (ESV)*

Enjoying a safari of looking for rhino while riding on elephants, my colleagues and I suddenly heard the scream of a bull elephant. I saw an elephant carrying four of my friends chasing away another elephant, which also carried four other friends.

This conflict between elephants started when a colleague was sharing the Gospel with the *mahout*, the person "driving" the elephant. The other *mahout* saw him looking at the Gospel tract and asked to see it. After he got it, he would not give it back to the first driver. That is when the first *mahout* steered his elephant into the other elephant, causing it to scream and chase his own.

Angry that he had to give back the Gospel tract, the driver threw it on the ground. The offended *mahout's* elephant picked up the tract with his trunk and handed it to his boss. That incident started a joke circulating among us that even the elephants were sharing the Gospel along with us. During that time together, we shared not only with those men but also with all the people living around the camp. Seven people believed and were baptized, and a house church was launched.

Sometimes, going out in groups is the key to witnessing. In this case, we also had the help of God's creation!

—B.B., SOUTH ASIAN PEOPLES

*Creator God,* YOU OPENED THE MOUTH OF BALAAM'S DONKEY AND ALLOWED IT TO SPEAK. AND YOU ARE ALSO ABLE TO USE ELEPHANTS IN SHARING THE GOSPEL! PLEASE NURTURE THIS HOUSE CHURCH. *Amen.*

# *Sensitive to His leading*

*"Now everything is from God, who reconciled us to Himself through Christ and gave us the ministry of reconciliation."* 2 Corinthians 5:18 (HCSB)

While working with a volunteer team, we had an incredible opportunity to see God work, a profound reminder of His faithfulness when we are sensitive to His leading and obedient to His commands.

The team gathered information from those who passed by as they considered adopting an area for a church plant. When they were prompted by the Spirit, they talked to individuals. Talking with an older lady, a woman ran down the hill with a big smile on her face. We assumed that she was coming because she was curious. But as the older woman showed disinterest, the woman, Maria, continued to talk and acted as though she expected the conversation to lead to something very important. Noticing this, one of the volunteers shared the Gospel with her. Maria listened intently, often shedding tears. At the conclusion, she asked if she could follow Christ. After praying, Maria explained that she had been troubled, knowing something was missing in her life. When she saw us, she said that she just knew that we had the answer.

Beyond doubt, God had prepared Maria's heart to receive the Gospel and the answer for her troubled heart. And He was faithful to send the answer to her through the obedience and sensitivity of these volunteers.

—FLETCHER, AMERICAN PEOPLES

*Faithful Lord,* PRAYER IS CRUCIAL TO EFFECTIVE VOLUNTEER MINISTRY. RAISE UP MULTITUDES OF VOLUNTEERS AND CHURCHES WHO WILL EARNESTLY SEEK YOU AND BE READY TO REACH THE MARIAS OF THE WORLD. *Amen.*

# The timely arrival

*"You enlarge my steps under me, and my feet have not slipped." Psalm 18:36 (NASB)*

One hundred and 20 miles and backpacks full of Scripture! Three men took the challenge to walk through the remote African bush to give out 350 Scripture portions during their 10-day journey. At home base, we prayed and tracked their progress using a GPS and satellite phone. One trekker got sick and could not continue. At that point, another trekker went with a local Fula man to meet the other two continuing the journey. The goal was to find each other and then meet a truck that held supplies to replenish their stock.

Along the road, the truck carrying supplies had its own problems. One rear shock broke, and with the rocky terrain, progress was extremely slow. It would be well after dark before the truck would arrive at the rendezvous point.

The men and the truck would eventually meet. But circumstances were such that only two men could cross the border. After facing many obstacles, God gave these two men the strength and perseverance to walk the final 10 or 15 miles into the targeted village. Upon their arrival, the chief started praising God. He had dreamed the foreigners would return, although they had not been there for five years. A handful of believers, discouraged in their faith, were encouraged that they had not been forgotten.

—BOB AND AMY, SUB-SAHARAN AFRICAN PEOPLES

*My God,* FORGIVE ME FOR GIVING UP ON PEOPLE I CONSIDER TO BE IMMATURE BELIEVERS. OPEN MY EYES TO THEIR HURTS AND CHALLENGES. HELP MISSIONARIES PERSEVERE AS THEY GO TO THE END OF EACH ROAD TO REACH THE LOST AND ENCOURAGE BELIEVERS. *Amen.*

# The back burner

*"Don't abandon your friend ..." Proverbs 27:10 (HCSB)*

A good five-bean soup needs time for the beans to cook and the seasonings to "get married," as a friend of mine always said. But as it cooks, if not watched, it could bubble up and over the pot, making a huge mess as it burns on the stove top.

Just like a good soup, it may also be necessary for an evangelistic relationship to sit a while and be put on the back burner. We had been meeting with a Kurdish family once a week for a while, but the relationship seemed to be going nowhere. We decided to allow them time to think through what we had been sharing and wait until they called us before meeting with them again.

Time went by, and we did not hear from them. We thought about them but never called. Two weeks before we were leaving the country for a year, we received a call from the man who asked if we could go on a picnic. We shared a wonderful time, and all deeply regretted that our family was leaving.

Rethinking the "back burner" relationship idea, we realized our mistake. We had put this couple on the back burner and left them to burn up. A relationship, like soup, takes time, but it also needs tending. You have to stir the pot now and then.

—TARA, CENTRAL ASIAN PEOPLES

*Even missionaries* MAKE MISTAKES, LORD JESUS. THANK YOU FOR REDEEMING THIS FRIENDSHIP. PLEASE CONTINUE TO DEVELOP THIS RELATIONSHIP. MAY THIS KURDISH FAMILY GROW IN RELATIONSHIP TO YOU AS THEIR MOST FAITHFUL FRIEND. *Amen.*

# Not giving up

*"And do not neglect doing good and sharing, for with such sacrifices God is pleased." Hebrews 13:16 (NASB)*

"Just taste it!" I pleaded with my son when trying to expand his diet from mostly peanut butter, macaroni and cheese, and an occasional pizza. I tried every way I knew how to convince him to try the Mediterranean food. I let him watch me enjoy it and then gave him a morsel of bread dipped in the hummus. He looked completely repulsed and clammed up tight. As much as I wanted him to taste and enjoy it as his daddy and I did, I couldn't force him to eat it.

Nor can I convince someone to believe in Jesus. Several times, we have visited with a certain family dear to us. It concerns us greatly that their lives are filled with hardships concerning health, family, and unemployment. The father believes in his head many of the truths of the Bible. However, no matter how hard we try to convince him to follow Jesus, he still rejects Christianity.

One morning, I had a wonderful time of prayer and worship with the Lord on a nearby mountain. I thought about that family and desperately desired that they experience a relationship with Christ. Just as it is important for me to be creative and try to get my son to eat healthy foods, I also must continue to share the Gospel with my friends.

—TARA, CENTRAL ASIAN PEOPLES

*Persistent Father,* I LOVE THAT YOU NEVER STOP TEACHING ME. IN MY IMMATURITY, YOU PATIENTLY TRAIN ME. HELP ME BE PERSISTENT, TOO, AS I SHOW YOUR LOVE TO OTHERS. PLEASE GRANT THIS FATHER FAITH SO THAT HE MIGHT BELIEVE IN YOU. *Amen.*

SEPTEMBER

---

# Lessons from the Young

*A person doesn't have to turn 20 for the Lord to use him
in ministry. Why not make a point of encouraging a
young servant through a note, a call, or a pat on the back?*

—BETH MOORE

I was stunned that so many of the 650 stories missionaries submitted for inclusion in *Voices of the Faithful, Book Two* were about children—missionary kids, student volunteers, or national children. It became clear that God was inviting children to be part of His kingdom work and that the young were teaching the old many spiritual lessons.

Unlike adults, children seem to have no inhibitions in matters of faith. In fact, we adults sometimes unknowingly squash the faith of children because of our own unbelief. "But Jesus said, 'Let the children alone, and do not hinder them from coming to Me; for the kingdom of heaven belongs to such as these'" (Matthew 19:14, NASB).

Before my family got serious about going overseas as missionaries, I remember one particular missionary couple we invited to our home to enjoy a meal with us. Our oldest son, Paul, who was 3 or 4 years old at the time, was very excited about hosting this couple. Over the course of the next few days, we noticed him looking around the house and in the cars. When the missionaries arrived at our home later that week, he enthusiastically and immediately took out a bulging pocketful of coins and proceeded to dump the change into Mr. Thomas's hands. "This is to help you do your missionary work," he said with a smile.

We learned a lot from our son that night. Not only did he give the missionary couple a blessing, but he taught his parents a lesson about offering everything we have to follow God's call in our lives. Two years after this event, we were missionaries in Africa. Our children were part of our ministry from the start. We never had to drag them to the village because they couldn't wait to go. While I taught sewing and Bible stories and my husband visited with the men, our kids ran all over the place with bare feet, big smiles, and dirty clothes just like the African children. They learned the art of making a soccer ball with newspaper, plastic bags, and rubber bands or string, as well as what to do with the ball after it was made. We had to make them go home with us at the end of the day. And, we never knew if they would come home with their flip flops or all their clothes because often they would give away their stuff to a child who needed it more. They were a great asset to our ministry, and their African experiences made them who they are today, years later.

There is something to be said about missionary kids (MKs) and their unique perspective on life. Most of them never meet a stranger. Most can live without television because they grew up reading books. Most see people's hearts, not their skin color or their traditions. And that's why they are involved in their parents' ministry. They love people.

Interviewing MKs is one of my favorite things to do. No matter their ages, the many I've talked to are actively involved in telling others about Jesus. They pray for their friends. And they often teach their parents what it means to accept and love those around them.

There's another group of young people who have a heart for the lost—the many high school and university students who go on mission trips. They go with complete abandon. They try different foods, they share their faith, they help out with children, they do manual labor, they serve others, and their lives are changed. Some of our dear friends brought their teenage children with them on a mission trip to help us in our work, and their four kids pitched in just like the adults. We were all blessed by their participation and love for the people.

You may need to pull out your tissues this month. You will laugh until you cry and cry when you have been inspired. If you are a parent reading this book as a family devotional, your children will love these stories. You will be forever changed by what you learn. And hopefully this will include a renewed ability to approach Jesus with the humility and faith of a child.

—*Kim P. Davis*

# Touched with God

*"As far as the east is from the west, so far has He removed our transgressions from us." Psalm 103:12 (NASB)*

Many people have never heard the Good News of Jesus Christ and God's redemptive love. Sam, our 6-year-old son, powerfully reminded us of this truth one night during family devotion time.

We were talking about sin and how it can destroy us and those around us unless we regularly confess, ask for God's forgiveness, and repent. During this discussion, Sam bowed his head. He was obviously having an urgent discussion with the Lord.

After he finished praying, his mother asked, "Sam, do you have sin?" "No," Sam said with confidence. His older sister immediately launched into an exposition of Romans 3:23 saying, "All have sinned, Sam." Sam looked at her and said, "But I just touched with God, and He made my sin to be zero!"

Simple, childlike faith is all it takes to be saved. If the lost peoples of the world can be led to "touch with God" through Jesus, He will make their sin to be zero! That is Good News to proclaim to people all around us who need to hear.

We rejoice to see God at work in our children. We expect to see God do the same work among our unreached people group as we labor to help them understand what Sam learned about God's forgiveness and love.

—TIM, SOUTHEAST ASIAN PEOPLES

*I confess that* I HAVE WRONGED YOU AND OTHERS BECAUSE OF MY SIN. FATHER, I AM CONFIDENT THAT YOU ARE FAITHFUL TO FORGIVE MY SIN. THANK YOU FOR YOUR REDEEMING WORK IN MY LIFE. *Amen.*

# Surrendering your children

*"But Jesus said, 'Let the children alone, and do not hinder them from coming to Me; for the kingdom of heaven belongs to such as these.'"* Matthew 19:14 (NASB)

Coming to the mission field was not easy. I knew without a doubt that God desired for us to follow Him overseas, but I also had good excuses: three children, a great life, and established ministries. But how could I not obey? I became willing to surrender to God's will. Still, I was anxious about surrendering my children, even knowing that God would work things out for them.

We had been in our host country for two months when I heard neighborhood children yelling, "What is your name? What is your name?" in their broken English. They were simply using what English they knew, but in my mind, they were being obnoxious toward my babies. My mother nature went into overdrive as I went to rescue them. By the time I had made it outside, the neighborhood children had left.

About 30 minutes later, I heard it again: "What is your name? What is your name?" That was enough! I marched outside saying, "Time to come in, kids." My son ran around the house and said, "Just a minute, Mom. I am waiting on Sissy." I looked to see my precious daughter lovingly handing the "ringleader" a flower through the fence. It was a beautiful picture of God telling me, *They are just fine, Mom; I have them in My hands!*

—KRISTEN, EUROPEAN PEOPLES

*How many times* HAVE I FAILED TO SURRENDER TO YOUR WILL, LORD, BECAUSE I DO NOT TRUST YOU WITH MY FAMILY? FORGIVE ME. I KNOW THAT YOU ARE MORE CONCERNED WITH MY FAMILY THAN EVEN I AM. HELP ME FOLLOW YOU WITHOUT RESERVATION. *Amen.*

# Sometimes we fall

*"For the moment all discipline seems painful rather than pleasant, but later it yields the peaceful fruit of righteousness to those who have been trained by it." Hebrews 12:11 (ESV)*

My son is a climber. Although we have told him repeatedly not to climb walls or doors, we turned around one day and saw "Mason" reach a ledge on the wall of a local restaurant and continue climbing up like Spiderman. Another day at a friend's house, someone said, "Do you care if Mason climbs out the window?" I did care and put an end to it.

With all this climbing, he seldom falls. His brother, however, often gets hurt. As "Aden" tried to shimmy up a doorway, he lost his grip about four feet up and crashed onto his tailbone. After recovering, he informed me that it wasn't a good idea to climb doorframes, and I shouldn't have let him. I agreed that it wasn't a good idea for him to climb, but would he have believed me without the pain of a bruised tailbone?

I learn much about how God parents me from these experiences. Sometimes He spares me much deserved pain because of His unmatchable grace. Sometimes He allows me to fall so that I can understand more fully that His rules are in place to protect me. Thankfully, He often spares me from pain and blesses me with gentle chastisement rather than the full consequence of my actions. Following my heavenly Father's instructions keeps me from much unnecessary pain.

—KATIE, NORTHERN AFRICAN AND MIDDLE EASTERN PEOPLES

*Father,* I CONFESS THAT SOMETIMES I DON'T LISTEN TO YOUR INSTRUCTIONS. THANK YOU FOR YOUR GRACE AND YOUR REBUKE WHEN I FALL. MAY I WALK BY THE SPIRIT SO THAT I WILL NOT CARRY OUT THE DESIRES OF THE FLESH. *Amen.*

## Remembering what God has done

*"So remember your Creator in the days of your youth: Before the days of adversity come, and the years approach when you will say, 'I have no delight in them.'"*
*Ecclesiastes 12:1 (HCSB)*

Training our three small children in the ways of God goes on throughout the day, but at bedtime, we are able to focus on the Bible and prayer. After reading a story from the Bible, we talk about what we have learned and then we take turns praying. When my husband wasn't feeling well, our 4-year-old son prayed for him to feel better. He prayed for several days until Daddy felt better and then we thanked God.

A few days later, our son was playing, and he fell and hit his head on the wooden floor. The result was a huge knot! So of course, we began praying for his boo-boo. Our little girl prayed for a week for her brother. Finally, he said, "Sister, I am already better, remember? God already heard that and put my boo-boo back in my head!" After I reminded him that she was only 2 years old, I told him that sometimes we forget what God has done.

My kids are forming a godly foundation of remembrance because they are being raised in a Christian home. Most children are growing up without any foundation or knowledge of God. Ecclesiastes 12:1 reminds us to remember God in our youth. How can they remember what God has done if they don't know who He is?

—P.T., SOUTH ASIAN PEOPLES

*Creator God,* FORGIVE ME FOR THE TIMES THAT I HAVE NOT HELPED BUILD A FOUNDATION FOR THOSE YOU HAVE ENTRUSTED TO ME, BUT INSTEAD HAVE DESTROYED THE FOUNDATION. I COMMIT TO YOU TODAY THAT I WILL INTENTIONALLY ASSIST IN BUILDING FIRM FOUNDATIONS. *Amen.*

# Jesus loves you

*"May God be gracious to us and bless us; look on us with favor so that Your way may be known on earth, Your salvation among all nations." Psalm 67:1–2 (HCSB)*

Truth be told, I panicked when we were sure that God wanted us to enroll our twins into the local school. They had grown up in our host country since infancy, but how would they adjust to such a major cultural transition on a daily basis? Would they hate us for making them go? Would the small buds of faith blooming in their tiny hearts be strangled by the prevalent religion?

Our daughter cried a lot at first, and our son both gave and received his fair share of punches. I volunteered in the classroom, helping with activities, field trips, and even mopping the floor. Gradually, our children began to learn the language and make friends. I was also able to befriend some of the mothers. We sensed that we had done the right thing.

One night, our decision was confirmed. As I put my daughter to bed, I asked her what she wanted to pray about. Immediately, she said, "My friends because they don't know anything about Jesus." She grabbed a small piece of paper and pencil and asked me to write "Jesus loves you" in the language so she could take it to school in her pocket. Not only was the Lord giving us a chance to meet neighbors, but He was doing a mighty work in the hearts of my children.

—A worker with Central Asian Peoples

*"Jesus loves me,* this I know." What a powerful truth to be told to the nations! Father, give missionaries in Central Asia opportunities in school settings to share Jesus. *Amen.*

# God's intervention

*"So the poor have hope, and injustice shuts her mouth." Job 5:16 (ESV)*

Our team resides in a desert outpost just outside of Timbuktu and shares Bible stories with the villagers. It is the setting of fables, but we have come to offer truth in this Islamic stronghold.

"Kathy," our village hostess, and her family of seven live across the sandy alley. Two of her children are severely physically and mentally handicapped. Healthy, strong people have a hard time living in the desert. Imagine the challenge of daily life for them! Their youngest is so cheerful that she earned the nickname of "Happy Baby" from our team. At 24 months old, she had yet to walk. She scooted on the ground impressively, but that did not help her future quality of life. When I asked about her progress, her tired mother hopelessly replied, "She is feeble."

I shared with Kathy about our God of hope. She gave me permission to pray in Jesus' name for the baby to be able to walk and be healthy. After we finished praying, I excused myself so that I could cry privately.

Having to leave the village for a few months, my team enthusiastically reported that "Happy Baby" was up and running! I had forgotten my prayer. Our God of hope doesn't forget. He remembers those tucked away in the desert or the remote jungles and reaches out to all.

—JUDY, SUB-SAHARAN AFRICAN PEOPLES

*Dear Lord in heaven,* BRING THOSE IN THIS MUSLIM DESERT AREA TO A SAVING KNOWLEDGE OF YOU. BE WITH THESE TEAMS WHO ARE LIVING IN REMOTE PLACES TO BRING YOUR WORD TO MANY. *Amen.*

# God uses our children

*"Tell of His glory among the nations, His wonderful deeds among all the peoples."*
*Psalm 96:3 (NASB)*

Sitting on the sidelines watching his father play sports in a planned outreach event, my 6-year-old son immediately found someone to talk to. The young man was in his early 20s and seemed nice, so instead of intruding, my husband instead kept a close watch. The two seemed to be having a great time laughing and talking to one another.

Almost two hours later, the sports event was over, and our family was going to meet some friends for coffee. As we were getting ready to leave, our son said, "I invited my friend, Shawn, to come with us." My husband, a little frustrated, could only agree as the invitation was on-the-spot. As we walked to the coffee shop, my husband introduced himself to Shawn but realized very quickly that our son had done a thorough job of telling this young man all about our family and why we were in Serbia.

Our visit with Shawn that day was the beginning of many friendly conversations. With his interest aroused for spiritual things, Shawn has started coming to Bible study. His first question every time we meet with him is still, "Where is your son and how is he doing?" These little ones can be God's ambassadors, many times better than we.

—KRISTEN, EUROPEAN PEOPLES

*Father God,* I COMMIT MYSELF TODAY TO REACH OUT IN THE NAME OF CHRIST TO SOMEONE I DON'T KNOW. GIVE ME THE BOLDNESS OF A CHILD TO NOT BE AFRAID. GROW SHAWN'S INTEREST IN THE WORD. *Amen.*

# Formed by Him

*"Your hands made me and fashioned me ..."* Psalm 119:73a (NASB)

The room felt small and hot as the doctor gave me the news. "You should consider terminating the pregnancy. Your body is not going to be able to support it," the doctor said grimly.

I was 21 weeks pregnant with our second son. While my first pregnancy had been a breeze, this one had been fraught with difficulties. I'd already faced threats of miscarriage, position of the placenta, and bed rest. Now there was another problem possibly preventing from me carrying this baby to term.

Ending our baby's life was, of course, not an option. I was scared, but I knew that God had created this life for a reason. The doctor was chagrined, knowing the certain jeopardy. I spent most of the rest of my pregnancy on bed rest and stayed in the hospital for several days when I went into early labor at 30 weeks. But finally, at 41 weeks, our perfectly healthy son was born into the world.

Every time I look at our infant son, I am filled with thankfulness to the Father. He forms us. He knows us intimately. He alone creates the miracle of life in each of us. He alone gives and takes away life. Through this ordeal, God showed Himself good and sovereign, not only to our family but also to the doctors and nurses.

—ELIZABETH, EAST ASIAN PEOPLES

*Merciful God,* THANK YOU FOR THE LIFE OF THIS CHILD. USE HIM TO FULFILL YOUR PURPOSES. GRANT MISSIONARY FATHERS AND MOTHERS, WHO ARE AWAITING THE BIRTH OF A CHILD, A DEEP AND ABIDING PEACE THAT YOU ARE IN CONTROL. GLORIFY YOURSELF THROUGH THEIR LIVES. *Amen.*

# Eager to tell

*"Then go quickly and tell His disciples, 'He has been raised from the dead ...'"*
Matthew 28:7 (HCSB)

"Fei" knew this would be her last opportunity to teach biblical truth to her class of wiggly 5-year-olds before summer break. She asked God to help her clearly teach Jesus' resurrection.

Telling the resurrection story simply in her Chinese-accented English, she repeated, "Jesus is alive! Children, this summer, you can tell five people that Jesus is alive!" Five-year-old "Jin" raised his hand and asked, "Teacher, can I tell ten people?" Fei said, "More is better; tell ten people." Jin excitedly asked, "Can I tell twenty people?" His teacher responded, "Yes! Tell twenty people."

As towels were placed on the floor for the children during quiet time, Jin plopped down and asked, "Can I tell thirty people?" Fei nodded, "Yes, Jin, you can tell many people." Lying still and looking his teacher fully in the face, he asked, "Can I tell forty people?" Fei lay down on the floor beside Jin and patted him on the chest to quiet him. She said, "Jin, so many people. It seems impossible, but nothing is impossible with God." To her surprise, Jin asked, "Miss Fei, will you pray for me?" Fei prayed, "Dear Lord, you hear Jin's prayer. He needs your help to tell forty people that your Son Jesus is alive!"

Do you have such eagerness to tell others that Jesus is alive?

—A.F.B., EAST ASIAN PEOPLES

*Heavenly Father,* THANK YOU FOR YOUR SON, JESUS, WHO WAS RAISED FROM THE DEAD! PLEASE GIVE ME OPPORTUNITIES THIS WEEK TO TELL AT LEAST FIVE PEOPLE THAT JESUS IS ALIVE. *Amen.*

# Children praise Him

*"You have taught children and infants to give you praise."* Matthew 21:16 (NLT)

It has always been my prayer, as a missionary parent, that my children would be an active part of sharing Christ's love with friends in their community. I believe that each person in our family plays an important role in God's plan to bring light to the nations. My young boys have befriended neighborhood children, helped women grind coffee, conversed in the national language, and eaten meals with families of our community. When our family takes a walk, store owners and elderly men call out our boys' names in greeting. They have created avenues of friendship and given us many opportunities to tell people the Good News of Jesus.

On one particular rainy afternoon, the boys were playing inside with Ali. The sounds of drums beating, music playing, and loud singing came drifting from their room. A team volunteer and I decided to sneak beside their door to observe without being noticed. What we saw was a beautiful sight—one child playing drums, another clapping his hands, and the third child singing a worship song at the top of his lungs. And then, in the middle of the song, my son said to his unbelieving friend, "Ali, this is how you praise the Lord." I realized that God even uses children to accomplish His purposes and be His ambassadors.

—J.L., NORTHERN AFRICAN AND MIDDLE EASTERN PEOPLES

*Thank You, Father,* FOR CHILDREN WHO PRAISE YOU. MAY MISSIONARY CHILDREN IN NORTHERN AFRICA AND THE MIDDLE EAST HELP TO BRING CHILDREN LIKE ALI INTO THE KINGDOM OF GOD. *Amen.*

# The Father knows best

*"Many plans are in a man's heart, but the LORD's decree will prevail."* Proverbs
19:21 (HCSB)

Adjusting to a new culture requires change, but one of the most heart-breaking challenges was the adjustment our children had to make. As a mom, I often try to bargain with God and say, "Spare my children. Do whatever you want to me. Just spare my kids."

Before we moved overseas, our kids attended a private Christian school. Putting our kids into British schools was a huge change. While our daughter had academic struggles, our son was bullied. At the end of the school year, our son's teacher suggested that our son needed professional counseling. We wondered why God wasn't protecting our children.

I began to pray more earnestly than ever before for our kids. God showed me through His Word that I needed to be specific about my prayers. Since the struggles of that first year, each year has become a more positive experience. Now both kids are doing great!

I have wondered if I would ever put my kids through a year like that again. I would not choose to. But God is teaching me that although the kids went through a horrible year in my eyes, God is using all of their experiences to build them into the people He wants them to be.

—KERIE, EUROPEAN PEOPLES

*Father,* YOU KNOW WHAT IS ULTIMATELY BEST FOR MISSIONARY CHILDREN. THEY ARE IN YOUR HANDS. BE WITH MISSIONARIES TODAY WHO ARE HAVING A HARD TIME TRUSTING YOU WITH THEIR CHILDREN. *Amen.*

# *Boldness of a child*

*"I promise you this. If you don't change and become like a child, you will never get into the kingdom of heaven. But if you are as humble as this child, you are the greatest in the kingdom of heaven." Matthew 18:3–4 (CEV)*

Tact. It's an art. One that our 5-year-old son, Micah, is apparently still learning.

As Micah was getting his hair cut, the owner's wife conversed with him. She asked if he liked living in Southeast Asia. Returning here had been hard for Micah. We explained to him that we came back to tell people about Jesus. So now, in his mind, all we need to do is tell everyone about Jesus and then we can return to America. So he told the owner, "We've come to teach people about Jesus. God wants you to stop worshipping idols and worship Him."

I didn't know what to do, so I pretended to be engrossed in reading the newspaper. I was torn between wanting to cause a diversion and not wanting to interrupt Micah's first witnessing encounter. She wasn't offended, and the subject quickly changed when Micah got hair in his mouth. Later, she took him next door to get candy, and as I sat in the chair, I realized that in the three years we've known this couple, I'd never once told them about Jesus. Micah's approach wasn't tactful, but at least he felt no fear—more than I could say for myself.

Tact is never an excuse for not sharing the Gospel. Because of Micah's boldness, this couple is more interested in Christianity with each successive visit.

—Kyle, Southeast Asian Peoples

*Lord,* grant me the boldness of this child. May I never hide behind tact as an excuse not to share. Give courage to the workers in Thailand, and bring this hairdresser into the kingdom. *Amen.*

## Anna's prayers answered

*"As it is my eager expectation and hope that I will not be at all ashamed, but that with full courage now as always Christ will be honored in my body, whether by life or by death." Philippians 1:20 (ESV)*

Our daughter, Anna, was like any other 9-year-old girl. She loved horses and liked to dress up. She danced, sang, and played the piano. But most of all, Anna loved her Lord Jesus Christ and wanted others to know Him as well.

Even though her language skills were limited where we lived in Asia, it did not stop four little Muslim girls from approaching Anna and asking if she would be a member of their club. Although Anna was very shy, she gathered her courage to join these new friends. For one week, the girls went on walks, played in rice fields, and picked leaves from trees. Although she had a good time, Anna was disappointed that she could not communicate the Gospel with them. She began praying and asking others to pray that God would help her to share God's love.

The next week, Anna was killed in a tragic bicycle accident. Although unable to speak further with her friends herself, the four friends came to a memorial service held at our home. They heard the Gospel preached in their own language. Anna's prayers were answered, but in a way that neither Anna nor anyone else expected. What a privilege to have been entrusted with a daughter whose heart belonged to Jesus.

—TODD, SOUTHEAST ASIAN PEOPLES

*Compassionate Father,* MAY YOU COMFORT THIS FAMILY WHO LOST ANNA. THANK YOU FOR ANNA'S DESIRE FOR THESE FOUR FRIENDS. MAY THESE FOUR LITTLE GIRLS COME TO KNOW YOU. IN THE NAME OF JESUS, *amen.*

## *Angels in green T-shirts*

*"Save us, O LORD our God, and gather us from among the nations, to give thanks to Your holy name and glory in Your praise." Psalm 106:47 (NASB)*

A group of teenagers from Texas waited for instructions. How could God use inexperienced volunteers to reach Muslims? For many of the youth, it was their very first mission trip; they were eager but nervous. "Okay, girls. You speak to ladies. Let Jesus do the talking!" With courage, the teens surged forward into the waiting crowd, ready to be used by God.

"Marsha" had recently arrived in the UK from her Central Asian country. She had wondered about Christianity, but it was forbidden. Curious, however, she cautiously entered the gathering. I noticed a huddle of teenagers in green T-shirts, swaying ponytails, and hand gestures. Giggling Southern accents surrounded Marsha, who was seated in the middle of the teenage volunteers. The girls talked, hugged, and even stroked her hair. *They'll scare her,* I thought. I rushed to rescue the wide-eyed newcomer, but the girls, all talking at once, cheerily introduced her. "Doesn't she have beautiful hair!" said one of the girls.

Unafraid, Marsha prayed to the Father. "You have brought me here to find the truth, God. These are angels from You. Look at Your light shining from their faces! Thank You for sending them to me! I didn't know angels wore green T-shirts!" Marsha received the truth of Christ into her heart. These Texas "angels" could be heard hollering praises to Him!

—JODY, CENTRAL ASIAN PEOPLES

*Thank You, Lord,* FOR TEENAGERS WHO PARTICIPATE IN MISSIONS. CALL THEM TO BE MINISTERS OF THE GOSPEL. MAY YOU CONTINUE TO STRENGTHEN THESE TEENS FROM TEXAS TO FOLLOW HARD AFTER YOU. *Amen.*

# A simple faith

*"If you abide in Me, and My words abide in you, ask whatever you wish, and it will be done for you." John 15:7 (NASB)*

When our son was very little, he would ask us about the idols that could be seen frequently where we live in East Asia. Somewhere along the way, he began praying for the idol worshippers whenever he saw an idol.

One day as we passed by a shop displaying a large idol, my son exclaimed, "They still have the idol! I have already prayed for them to know the one true God." I explained to him that sometimes we must pray for a long time, but I was convicted that it also takes sharing the Gospel. We can't just pray and hope that somehow they turn from idol worship to God. We have to pray *and* obey.

God's Word makes some astonishing promises. With simple faith, my son was praying for people's salvation. He was shocked when he saw the idol still in the shop the next time he passed. It made me question my own faith in God's Word. Do I share in a way that demonstrates a simple trust that God meant what He said? He said that the Gospel is "the power of God unto salvation" (Romans 1:16, KJV). He said that "all things are possible" with Him (Mark 10:27, KJV). He said, "Greater is he that is in [me] than he that is in the world" (1 John 4:4, KJV).

I want to be guilty of a simple faith.

—H.C.P., EAST ASIAN PEOPLES

*Father,* HELP ME TO HAVE THE SIMPLE FAITH OF A CHILD AND TO ACTIVELY PARTICIPATE IN SPREADING THE GOSPEL. I TRUST YOUR PROMISES FOUND IN YOUR WORD. *Amen.*

# A pretty cool God

*"The LORD is near to all who call upon Him, to all who call upon Him in truth. He will fulfill the desire of those who fear Him; He will also hear their cry and will save them." Psalm 145:18–19 (NASB)*

I never expected to get my dream job. Yet I am in the middle of Central Asia teaching kindergarten to missionary kids of five nationalities.

One day, there were so many prayer requests that I asked the children to pray for each other. By the time we were finished, "Kyum" had prayed in Korean, "Emily" had prayed in English, and "Musajan" had prayed in Russian. "Lisa," a Uighur (WE-ger) student, said, "So you're saying, Miss Elise, that God understands Korean, English, Russian, *and* Uighur?" "Yes, and He understands Chinese, French, Italian, Spanish, German, and all the other languages as well!" I responded. "Lydia's" eyes got big and she whispered, "Do you think He speaks in them, too?" Laughing, I said, "Yes. There is not one language in the world that our God does not speak and understand." Lydia replied, "Wow. He is a pretty cool God!"

I might not be able to get my class to stay in a line. But on this day, I watched a child catch a glimpse of how awesome our God is. This makes every trial worth it. No matter how much I struggle with the language and how excruciating it is to communicate God's love in that language, God knows these people, and He speaks their language.

—ELISE, CENTRAL ASIAN PEOPLES

*Thank You, Father,* FOR MISSIONARY KIDS AND FOR THEIR SPECIAL CONTRIBUTION TO MINISTRY. LET THEM EACH PERSONALLY UNDERSTAND WHAT A "COOL" GOD YOU ARE. *Amen.*

# A godly generation

*"No one should despise your youth; ... be an example .... Do not neglect the gift that is in you ..." 1 Timothy 4:12, 14 (HCSB)*

As young parents in the States, we tried to pass on a godly heritage. But as we lived in the fast lane, we began to notice how our convictions got swallowed up in living life. Our children were busy, too, and often we returned home weary from all the activity, which ruled out family time in the Word.

Now we live in an area where only 0.2 percent of the population knows Jesus. The way we trained our children had to drastically change. Though we had many national disciples, at the top of that list had to be our children. Later, after our son led a third person to Christ, I pondered how warped our mentality can be when it comes to teaching our children. We invest in their education and their athletic or musical talents, which is good. But what about training them spiritually?

To God's credit, I have seen my youngest children live in a way that prompted their Buddhist Montessori teachers to comment, "There is something different about them." I have listened to my 7-year-old practice his testimony to share with others. I have seen my teenager use e-mail to speak truth into lives of friends.

Training children to be His disciples is one of the greatest things we can do. It requires commitment, prayer, and constant guidance from the Father.

—SYDNEY, SOUTH ASIAN PEOPLES

*Loving God,* MAY I PROVE FAITHFUL TO SPIRITUALLY TRAIN THE CHILDREN YOU HAVE PUT INTO MY LIFE. MAY THESE YOUNG ONES GROW PASSIONATE ABOUT WINNING THE LOST FOR CHRIST. *Amen.*

## *You came, you loved*

*"but whoever keeps His word, in him the love of God has truly been perfected.
By this we know that we are in Him." 1 John 2:5 (NASB)*

"Come to our school," invited the principal who surprisingly gave us complete freedom in what we taught at our English camp. American volunteers joined us, with fear and anticipation, and when we arrived at the school, a small group of mothers greeted us, saying, "Praise God!" A little dumbfounded after that welcome, the principal explained that 25 percent of the students were Christian, 25 percent were Buddhist, and 50 percent believed in the spirits.

The next three and a half days were amazing. We taught Christian songs, shared the Good News in every class, but most of all, we loved them. These children of refugees were some of the poorest we had seen in that mountainous area. In general, they looked unclean and unkempt. But we truly loved them with the love of God.

On the last day, tears flowed in abundance; the children and the volunteers were hugging and crying. In the cards that they had made for us, the recurring theme was, "You came and you loved us—even though we are poor and dirty—you loved us." One little boy had drawn a map of his country and a map of America with a beautiful cross between the two countries. In truth, the cross of Christ, God's expression of love, is what connected us.

—Pam, Southeast Asian Peoples

*Father,* may Your love in me draw others to a saving knowledge of You. May I be a disciple who loves greatly. Thank You for Your unconditional love. *Amen.*

# Am I like a child?

*"Instead, just as we have been approved by God to be entrusted with the gospel, so we speak, not to please men, but rather God, who examines our hearts."*
1 Thessalonians 2:4 (HCSB)

My language teacher, "Anne," who is a strong believer, is bringing up her 5-year-old son to love Jesus. This action doesn't sit well with Anne's mother, who is very much against her daughter's conversion to Christianity. She spends every phone call and visit begging them to return to Islam.

When Anne and her son arranged to visit her mother in the home village for four days, she resolved to show love rather than argue. Her son, being a natural evangelist, talked about Jesus continuously during the visit. The grandmother didn't like it, but how upset can you get at a grandson? Anne's son continues to share with visitors and friends and encourages them to pray to Jesus in their time of need.

When I heard this story, I was greatly encouraged to hear how the younger generation is growing up to love and share Jesus, but I was also greatly challenged. How openly and easily do I share with others about Jesus? If I believe Jesus is the answer for all people, why am I not telling everyone that I see? Am I too worried about what other people will say or how they react? This little guy completely trusts Jesus and wants to share Him. Should I be any different?

—JULDUZ, CENTRAL ASIAN PEOPLES

*Forgive me, Lord,* FOR MY INHIBITIONS ABOUT SHARING THE GOSPEL. GIVE ME THE BOLDNESS OF ANNE'S SON. CONTINUE TO USE THIS LITTLE BOY TO BE A DYNAMIC WITNESS FOR YOU. *Amen.*

# *Children are partners in ministry*

*"Share with the saints in their needs; pursue hospitality."* Romans 12:13 (HCSB)

"Would you like to come over?" My sunny-tempered 4-year-old was eager to make friends in our new neighborhood. She had already invited herself into other neighbors' homes, so of course, she wanted friends at her house, too. At the time, I was thinking about the stuff I needed to do and that she should have asked permission before inviting. But I had to consider that people are more important than tasks.

As the neighbor's child played with my children, the mother began to ask if I went to church every Sunday. She had seen us leave and assumed our destination. She then told me that her mother and brother were Christians. "My mother used to think about sad things all the time, but now she is happy. She really likes the Christian people," she said. We talked a little more about the joy the Lord brings, and then I asked her if she was a Christian. "Not yet," she replied, "but maybe one day I will become one."

After she left, I praised God for what had taken place. People are usually more reserved about spiritual matters in our Southeast Asian country, but I believe that the hospitality of my daughter enabled this mother to feel open to talk with me. God uses the friendliness of little ones to bring honor to His name.

—R.A., SOUTHEAST ASIAN PEOPLES

*Lord,* HELP ME TO BE MORE HOSPITABLE TO MY NEIGHBORS. PEOPLE ARE MORE IMPORTANT THAN TASKS. I DEDICATE MY HOME TO BE OPEN FOR YOUR PURPOSES. *Amen.*

# *No matter what happens*

*"... she gave birth to a son; and she named him Samuel, saying, 'Because I have asked him of the* Lord.*'"* 1 Samuel 1:20 (NASB)

Before becoming missionaries, my wife and I tried to have children, but we suffered several losses. After tests, we were told that nothing was medically wrong, but we still were unsuccessful. After arriving in Costa Rica for language school, we learned that my wife was pregnant again. We prayed that God would be glorified through this pregnancy and that everyone would know that He was in control, no matter what the outcome.

At 36 weeks, God answered our prayer. While connected to a fetal monitor, the placenta began to detach, and the baby's heartbeat dropped drastically. After notifying the only nurse on duty at the time of the problem, she pressed the panic button in a feeble attempt to solicit help. Most of the doctors had left for lunch or meetings, or so we thought. To our amazement, each of my wife's doctors came rushing in, reporting that their plans were canceled or delayed for one reason or another. The doctors took my wife to perform an emergency cesarean, and within minutes, I was holding our healthy newborn, Samuel.

God was in control of the situation. If my wife had not been at the hospital connected to the fetal monitor at that moment with her doctors still around, our son would not be here today. No matter what happens, we can trust Him.

—John, American Peoples

*Sovereign God,* You are worthy of my trust in all situations. I'm not even aware of all the events You control! I trust You today with my own worries and concerns. *Amen.*

# A teenage witness

*"And you will testify also ..." John 15:27 (NASB)*

Sports ministry opens doors among immigrants in our city. When we requested a volunteer team to help us, "Marjorie" answered our request and said she could assemble a team of adults to lead a camp for softball, soccer, football, and volleyball instruction.

Later, Marjorie asked if she could bring her 15-year-old son on the trip. "He has been on mission trips before, is a strong witness, and plays both football and soccer." We had no objections. In the following weeks, she asked if she could also bring a 16-year-old softball pitcher and a 10-year-old Little League baseball player. What was God planning for this sports camp?

A prayerwalking team prayed throughout the city as they distributed fliers advertising the camp. The sports team came, and 30 to 50 kids participated each day. Bible stories were told between the sports instruction, and the kids listened attentively. The three "kids" on our team shared what Jesus meant to them and how they had become Christians.

The final evening, we allowed the parents to participate with their children. A total of 11 boys and three adults decided to follow Jesus. My husband meets weekly with these boys for Bible study. What kind of results would there have been if these three kids hadn't come? We'll never know, but God used these kids to share their faith.

—J., EUROPEAN PEOPLES

*Heavenly Father,* THANK YOU FOR USING FAITHFUL CHILDREN IN YOUR KINGDOM WORK. STRENGTHEN THE 14 WHO CAME TO CHRIST THAT WEEK, AND USE THEM TO CONTINUE TO SPREAD THE GOSPEL. *Amen.*

## God preserves and provides

*"The name of the LORD is a strong tower; the righteous runs into it and is safe."*
Proverbs 18:10 (NASB)

Thousands of miles away from our college-age son, we received a call that a tornado had ripped destruction through the Union University campus. I clung to the words, "All our missionary kids are safe." Not having access to television coverage of the devastation, I had no idea of the danger that threatened my son. God preserved. We phoned, amazingly getting through to our son. He and others were huddled together as they waited through a second storm wave.

Later, hearing that the Woman's Missionary Union provided funds to help missionary kids replace damaged possessions, I wrote a thank you note. A couple of days after, I received this message: "I was in Jackson, Tennessee, on Friday with the MKs. I spent some time with your son at lunch. It was so great to meet him. He seems to be doing really well! He, like all the other MKs, is more concerned with other students than himself. I was able to pray with him and give him a couple of hugs! I thought that you would like to know I loved on your son for you!"

This Christian sister stood in the gap and loved on my child because I couldn't be there. God's protection and provision go far beyond what we can imagine.

—DEBBIE, SUB-SAHARAN AFRICAN PEOPLES

*Father,* YOU ARE MY STRONG TOWER. THANK YOU FOR PROTECTING AND PROVIDING FOR THESE STUDENTS. HELP ME TO KNOW THAT YOU ARE WITH MY CHILDREN, EVEN WHEN I'M ABSENT FROM THEM. MAY I BE REMINDED TODAY THAT YOU ARE THE ONE I RUN TO FOR SAFETY. *Amen.*

# The late lamb

*"I know the LORD is always with me. I will not be shaken, for he is right beside me." Psalm 16:8 (NLT)*

In some parts of Africa, the term "late lamb" is used to describe a child born in the autumn of one's life. Whatever you call him, mine is continually used by God to instruct me in His ways. As I watched our preschooler run ahead down the dusty road, I thought of his freedom and naiveté. It was a wonderful feeling to see him seek such simple pleasure with complete abandon. He enjoyed his surroundings and my company while embracing the moment.

Our gate appeared and as he neared it, I was struck by the vastness of the world that opened up beyond it. He took no notice of the enormous panorama. He was working only to conquer the piece of ground directly in front of him. While I could see the large expanse of mountains, cattle, goats, and thorn trees, he was content to plow ahead with minimal caution. If he falls, he believes that I can make it all better.

Sometimes Joseph tests his limits to see how fast he can go. Sometimes he chooses to grab my hand and walk with me. He has many questions. Some of them I can answer, but sometimes they require a response that is too complex for him to understand. Either way, he continues to trust me enough to put his hand in mine.

—SANDRA, SUB-SAHARAN AFRICAN PEOPLES

*When I run* WITH COMPLETE ABANDON OR FALL HEADFIRST, YOU ARE THERE TO HOLD MY HAND, FATHER. THANK YOU FOR YOUR WATCH-CARE AND LOVE. KEEP ME CLOSE SO THAT I WON'T STRAY. *Amen.*

# In the fog

*"Consider what I say, for the Lord will give you understanding in everything."*
*2 Timothy 2:7 (HCSB)*

As the maintenance men were spraying for mosquitoes, Sarah walked with her mother and brother, trying to dodge the toxic fog. Suddenly, she said, "I think God just changed my heart."

The night before, our 8-year-old Sarah had used half a box of tissue to dry her tears when I told our children that we were moving to another country. I knew that it wouldn't be easy since we had lived in our current home for five years. We prayed together, but when it was Sarah's turn to pray, she pleaded, "God, I don't want to move." My wife assured her that it was okay to pray like that.

When Sarah made the comment a day later about God changing her heart, her mother asked, "How so?" She replied, "When I looked at the fog around our building, I thought about the people in the country we are moving to. They are in a fog, and they don't even know it. That is why we have to go and tell them about Jesus."

Isn't it wonderful that we serve a God who still changes hearts? God gave a child spiritual insight and an open heart willing to make sacrifices to tell the lost about Jesus. He makes a way to clear the fog.

—T.K., SOUTHEAST ASIAN PEOPLES

*Father*, HELP MISSIONARY KIDS ADJUST TO MOVING. MAY THEY BE CONTENT IN YOU AND IN THE SECURITY OF BEING WITH THEIR FAMILIES. BLESS THEM WITH NEW FRIENDS AND OPPORTUNITIES FOR MINISTRY. IN THE NAME OF JESUS, *amen.*

# Inviting the bullies

"LORD, You will establish peace for us, since You have also performed for us all
our works." Isaiah 26:12 (NASB)

It was early on the first day of Holiday Bible Club in an older South
African neighborhood. I felt like the pied piper as a clown and I led a
group of children down the sidewalk singing at the top of our lungs.
Ahead, we saw some older boys smoking and blocking the walkway. The
clown grabbed my arm in warning, but I decided to approach them.
"Hi, guys. We are having a Holiday Bible Club. You are welcome to
come."

When we got back to the church building, the clown told the teachers that I had invited a bad gang. Afraid that the gangsters would cause
trouble, the teachers decided to pray long and loud for God to give
them courage.

The morning stayed sunny, and many children arrived, including
the "bad" ones. We had planned for 80, but 140 came when they heard
we were providing lunch. I prayed for a miracle. After classes when it
was time for lunch, I broke each bun in half, and we starting ladling out
soup. There was enough for everyone, including the workers. When
the older boys tried to take soup cups from the smaller children, we offered second helpings instead of recriminations. They grew quiet and
polite. I guess when Jesus said to let the children come, He meant the
bullies, too.

—JERRY, SUB-SAHARAN AFRICAN PEOPLES

Lord, I ADMIT THAT I DON'T ALWAYS WANT TO REACH OUT TO UNDESIRABLES. I'M SURE
MISSIONARIES FEEL THAT WAY, TOO. SHOW US THE ONES WHO NEED OUR LOVE. AND FATHER,
PLEASE DRAW THESE YOUNG BULLIES TO YOURSELF. TRANSFORM THEM INTO SERVANT LEADERS.
Amen.

# *Speaking the truth in love*

*"but speaking the truth in love, we are to grow up in ... Christ."* Ephesians 4:15 (NASB)

Starting each day with prayer, our kids had recently been praying for the salvation of their playmates. One day while playing outside, one of our five children accidentally stepped on a friend's chalk drawing of one of their gods. The young artist was upset that an image of his god was violated. Our children apparently tried to tell them that Jesus is the one true God, which made the playmates angrier! Strong words of attack were shouted at our children, and one of our kids got slapped. Another's arm was twisted.

After the incident, when they reported to me what happened, our children kept saying, "We were only trying to tell them the truth!" Though it was hard for the younger ones to understand why others don't care about Jesus, we realized that this had been a small dose of reality for our children.

In the end, there was certainly no long-term damage and no extreme persecution, by any means. Our kids handled it fine and even went back to playing with the same playmates. As their parents, we were silently thankful for this incident. It was an opportunity for our kids to see that they will need to stand together for what's right, for the truth, and for Jesus while at the same time showing love and compassion to the lost.

—LACY, SOUTH ASIAN PEOPLES

*Father,* STRENGTHEN MISSIONARY CHILDREN ALL OVER THE WORLD TO STAND IN THE TRUTH. MAY THEY SHOW LOVE FOR OTHERS WHILE BEING A COURAGEOUS WITNESS FOR YOU. *Amen.*

## Teenage examples

*"For this is the will of God, your sanctification; that is, that you abstain from sexual immorality."* 1 Thessalonians 4:3 (NASB)

Two engaged, college-age couples had made a pledge to each other and to God to stay sexually pure until marriage. With premarital sex and AIDS being such huge issues in Zambia, I asked these youth to come from the States to teach on sexual purity in a rural village. When they came, we stayed in the village for three days, sleeping in tents at night and teaching during the day.

One morning, we were allowed to speak at a local school. The volunteers spoke about their promise of purity to God and to each other, how it wasn't always easy to keep, but how God blessed them because they did. They shared from God's Word His command for purity and the blessing that would follow. Later that evening, the schoolteacher, "Moola," asked us how he could be saved. The Holy Spirit had used the Word and the testimonies of these students to reveal what was missing in his life. He wanted the same hope and strength.

Moola has been growing in his faith, but he is often slandered by others because of it. Even though it can be difficult to follow Christ, Moola is faithful. The example he saw in these four students made an eternal impact that he will never forget.

—MELISSA, SUB-SAHARAN AFRICAN PEOPLES

*Faithful Lord*, I PRAY SPECIFICALLY FOR _____ TO REMAIN PURE UNTIL MARRIAGE. RAISE UP GODLY YOUTH TO COMMIT TO SEXUAL PURITY. STRENGTHEN YOUNG SHORT-TERMERS WHO ARE TEACHING "TRUE LOVE WAITS" IN SUB-SAHARAN AFRICA. *Amen.*

# God takes care of the little things

*"Your faithfulness is for all generations; You established the earth, and it stands firm." Psalm 119:90 (HCSB)*

As we drove away from the church building in Texas, I heard my son ask, "Mama, we're going to come back here in a few years, and Daddy will be my youth minister, right?" My wife replied, "No, son. God wants us to go to Ukraine for many years. But don't worry. God will do something wonderful for you." Trying to be brave, our 10-year-old bowed his head to hide his tears.

When we visited the States six years later, our son was fluent in Russian and had a new view of the world. While our family attended a conference, our son participated in activities with other youth. One day, they passed out Vacation Bible School advertisements for a new church nearby. Our son prayed that God would use him. After knocking on one door, an elderly lady answered saying, "No English." Recognizing the accent, our son began speaking in Russian. She conversed with him and his partner for 30 minutes, and she heard the Gospel in her language for the first time. Returning to the conference, he said, "Dad, I know that I was the only person at that place, at that time, God could use for His purposes. That's what I want in my life!"

Now he is leading a youth ministry in Russia. God did something wonderful for him.

—MICK, EUROPEAN PEOPLES

*You have a plan* FOR MY CHILDREN AND GRANDCHILDREN, FATHER. DO NOT LET ME HINDER WHAT YOU ARE DOING IN THEIR LIVES. TRAIN THEM TO BE WORKERS FOR THE GOSPEL IN WHATEVER MANNER YOU CHOOSE. *Amen.*

## The small sheep

*"I assure you: Whoever does not welcome the kingdom of God like a little child will never enter it." Luke 18:17 (HCSB)*

It was the day of our first Bible club! I had sent invitations to parents, explaining that I would teach the Bible to their children, just the way I teach my own children. Not sure who would respond, I was pleasantly surprised when children started arriving. My couches were full of the expectant faces of children! What if they didn't like it? What if they were offended? What if they left when I mentioned God?

I started with a simple prayer and explained briefly how to pray. It was a first for many of them. The Bible story was about Jesus, the Good Shepherd. I displayed a large picture of Jesus with open arms and gave them little sheep. One by one, each child placed his sheep by the picture of Jesus. They were not hesitant. They had no questions. In their minds, Jesus was the Good Shepherd, and they were the sheep who needed Him. Their responses were so different from the responses we had seen from some of their parents. Why is it so hard for adults to express such a simple and genuine faith in God? Why can't we become as these trusting, little children?

Jesus reminds us to come into the kingdom like a little child. Simple and innocent faith is what it takes.

—MARA, EUROPEAN PEOPLES

*Gracious Lord,* GIVE _____ SIMPLE AND CHILDLIKE FAITH SO THAT HE/
SHE WILL COME INTO YOUR KINGDOM. MAY I BE PATIENT AND SENSITIVE AS YOU WORK.
*Amen.*

# From Adversity to Triumph

*The church of Jesus Christ in the latter days
will doubtless experience the worst of times and the best of times.*

—BETH MOORE

It's strange how your life can unexpectedly but purposefully inter-twine with other lives. Bob had been a wealthy homebuilder, and he and his wife, Susan, had a beautiful lake house, new cars, boats, and two wonderful children. They had lots of things, but nothing made them truly happy. For years, their marriage struggled and counseling didn't seem to help. Finally, a marriage counselor suggested that they move to a new city to start over.

They moved to Decatur, Texas, and things did seem to improve. Four months later, they returned to their former town, just 30 miles away, to participate in a Christmas parade. On the day of the event, Susan and their oldest son, Matthew, were riding on the back of a large wagon in the parade when, unnoticed, he fell off and was run over by the wagon wheels. What started out as hope for the future turned into great sadness and grief.

Bob and Susan had always handled things in their own strength, but on the way to the hospital, Bob remembered calling out to God for help for the first time in his life. When their son died shortly after the accident, they returned to a house void of Matthew's laughter in a town where they had no real friends. The first person to come to their doorstep was the local pastor from the church where their two children had attended day care. Bob recalls, "I don't remember much of what he said to us that day except, 'God loves you and He will see you through.'"

Bob and Susan clung to that hope in the midst of tragedy. They began to attend church and were drawn to God. After many discus-sions with the pastor, they both accepted the love and personal rela-tionship that Jesus had to offer.

We met Bob and Susan at seminary before going out as mission-aries. It was a little uncanny how they were going to be missionaries as well, and in fact, they had taken the job opening in Angola that we had first accepted. Later we were asked to take a different position in South Africa. To this day, we feel a special connection to Bob and

Susan because of our shared missions calling and journey. They are dear friends.

Their son would have been 30 years old now. Do they wish he was still with them? Absolutely. But God took this terrible tragedy and brought new life out of it. Bob and Susan became Christians, they have three beautiful children who serve the Lord, and they are still missionaries reaching lost Africans with the Gospel.

Most of us can quote Romans 8:28, "And we know that God causes all things to work together for good to those who love God, to those who are called according to His purpose" (NASB) and Jeremiah 29:11, "'For I know the plans that I have for you,' declares the LORD, 'plans for welfare and not for calamity to give you a future and a hope'" (NASB). Bob and Susan are living out these verses.

We all have stories concerning things that the enemy meant for evil, but God meant for good (Genesis 50:20). Our experiences may not be as life-changing as Bob and Susan's, but nevertheless, God has proven His faithfulness and love to us by making things turn out for our good. You will read stories this month of losses that turned to gain and destroyed plans that resulted in God's perfect plan. May your heart be filled with praise for our all-wise, all-powerful, loving Father as you are daily reminded that even in the difficult, stormy times, God has your welfare in mind.

—*Kim P. Davis*

## Making sense of my past

*"You saw me before I was born. Every day of my life was recorded in your book. Every moment was laid out before a single day had passed." Psalm 139:16 (NLT)*

Years ago, I was greatly remorseful concerning bad life choices and felt unworthy of God's love. As I observed other Christians, I wondered whether my life could be effectively used for Him.

Thankfully, God's great mercy helped me to make sense of my past. There is a lady who owns a shop at the market. On a hot day, I went to the shop with two of our summer volunteers and engaged in conversation. Life had not been kind to her either. Her parents separated when she was a child, and she grew up not knowing her father. She endured unhealthy relationships, worked grueling jobs, and made unwise choices.

As it turned out, our life stories were so similar that God allowed us to connect. Neither of us knew enough of the other's heart language, but God worked through our communication using bits and pieces of three languages and hand gestures. I was able to share with her how He had forgiven my sins and made me whole again. God used my past life to show this woman how far He had brought me up from the pit.

I am recognizing daily that God can and will use me, even in this imperfect state. There are many who need to hear about His redeeming love from someone who used to be like them.

—O.C.L., NORTHERN AFRICAN AND MIDDLE EASTERN PEOPLES

*My Redeemer,* YOU HAVE BROUGHT ME OUT OF THE PIT. THANK YOU FOR YOUR LOVE AND MERCY. HELP MISSIONARIES AND ME, WHO MAY FEEL UNWORTHY, TO REMEMBER THAT OUR MINISTRY COMES FROM YOU. YOU HAVE MADE US NEW. *Amen.*

# Remembering "Black Sunday"

*"Then you will go safely on your way; your foot will not stumble. ... Don't fear sudden danger or the ruin of the wicked when it comes, for the LORD will be your confidence and will keep your foot from a snare." Proverbs 3:23–26 (HCSB)*

I was cutting out a newspaper article about the events in our city when our daughter asked, "Why are you doing that?" I told her, "Because I want to remember." I wanted to remember the day we had to flee our city, when we weren't free to worship, when churches were attacked and burned, and believers were beaten because they loved Jesus. I wanted to remember how our children reacted when we had to leave our national brothers and sisters behind and how they cried for them. I wanted to remember our family and friends back home who appealed to God and asked Him for our protection. I wanted to remember that God had been enough.

If I had been allowed to erase that hard day, I would have missed God's faithfulness. Even though I was afraid, I felt protected at the same time, safe in the palm of His hand. I realized that I would rather die for something than live for nothing.

I still do not understand why believers suffer. I don't like it, but I do trust my Father more than ever. If I couldn't trust Him with every detail of my life, where would I be? Being content to do it His way instead of mine is a lesson I'm learning.

—CATE, SOUTH ASIAN PEOPLES

*Thank You,* BLESSED FATHER, FOR SCARS THAT RECALL WOUNDS INFLICTED DURING THE BATTLE FOR SOULS, WOUNDS THAT WERE HEALED BY YOUR LOVING TOUCH. I'M GREATLY BLESSED. *Amen.*

## The extra mile

*"And if anyone forces you to go one mile, go with him two." Matthew 5:41
(HCSB)*

Sometimes, you have to go the extra mile—literally. Every Sunday evening, we drove our truck on a dirt road to get to a trail that led up to the Quechua mountain village where we told Bible stories. As the rainy season came, landslides made the road impassable. That meant that we would have to walk over four miles to reach our destination. It also meant a long walk back down the dark, muddy road.

The first Sunday after the landslide, several villagers who had been shopping in town wanted to ride to the village with us for Bible study. "What about the landslide?" we asked. "You will have to park your truck and walk," they replied. So we loaded up and off we went.

During the long walk, we soon saw how God was working good out of the landslide. We had been frustrated for some time by a feeling that the villagers had not accepted us. As we walked along the road, God gave us an opportunity for extended conversation with the community leader. We laughed together as we slogged through the mud. Over several weeks, a new appreciation for each other was gained and a deeper friendship was formed. Hearts were opened to receive the message of truth from God's Word.

The extra miles? They were well worth the effort.

—SHERRI, AMERICAN PEOPLES

*Merciful Father,* PLEASE FORGIVE ME FOR TURNING BACK WHEN THE GOING BECOMES DIFFICULT. HELP ME TO CATCH A GLIMPSE OF YOUR HAND AT WORK, READYING THE WAY FOR CONTINUED MINISTRY TO THOSE IN NEED. *Amen.*

# The rainout

*"I declare the end from the beginning, and from long ago what is not yet done, saying: My plan will take place, and I will do all My will." Isaiah 46:10 (HCSB)*

It was the second time that my husband and I had tried to show the JESUS film in the squatter camp. The first time the generator had failed to work, but this time we were determined to succeed. Zatu and I walked through rows of tin shacks announcing the film with a loudspeaker. Meanwhile, my husband and his friend Esau readied the equipment.

Suddenly, black storm clouds gathered overhead. As drops of rain began to fall, we prayed that it would stop. Even as lightning struck around us, we asked God to intervene. Finally, we told the faithful few who were still waiting to go home. With nothing else to do, I asked about a sick baby I had seen the day before. The women said the mother had taken him to the clinic but had received no help. So we decided to walk through the pouring rain to find the mother and sick child.

We found the baby very dehydrated, and I realized that he could die by morning. With mother and baby in tow, we sloshed back through the mud to our truck. With some difficulty, we made it to the hospital in town. Hours later, the baby was given IV fluids and immediately responded. Now, every time I see this baby's smile, I praise God for the storm that interrupted our plans.

—J.S.P., Sub-Saharan African Peoples

God, when adversity comes, I often focus on the problem rather than Your good plan. Lord, help me to know when to let go and trust completely in You for a new and better plan. Amen.

# Outbreak gives opportunity

*"For God has not given us a spirit of fear, but of power and of love and of a sound mind." 2 Timothy 1:7 (NKJV)*

"Ebola! You've got to be kidding me," I said when news came of the outbreak in a neighboring area 30 miles away. All I could think about was my 7-month-old baby until God's Spirit reminded me of 2 Timothy 1:7. Many times in our African journey when I was scared of living in Uganda, this verse had ministered to me. So what should we do now?

The more we prayed about it, the more my husband and I felt that we should stay. On the radio, Ebola was incorrectly broadcast as an airborne disease. There was so much false information stirring the Batooro people into panic mode. We gathered facts and got a plan together so that we could educate our friends and neighbors. As we gave out more than 8,500 fact sheets about Ebola, we took the opportunity to share Bible stories from creation to Christ's resurrection. People needed hope, and we had access to both the facts and the peace that surpasses all understanding. They were so excited to have the truth.

God used a deadly disease to get His Word out and validate us in the community. Yes, we were afraid, but God is bigger than our fear. He protected us, and gave us power, love, and a sound mind to follow His will.

—BRANDI, SUB-SAHARAN AFRICAN PEOPLES

*Thank You, God,* FOR YOUR LIBERATING TRUTH. THROUGH IT, I AM FREED TO CONFRONT THE TRIALS OF EACH DAY BY YOUR INNER PRESENCE, FREED TO BOLDLY PROCLAIM THE TRUTH OF THE GOSPEL BY YOUR EMPOWERING SPIRIT, AND FREED TO GAIN VICTORY OVER DEATH THROUGH YOUR RESURRECTING POWER. *Amen.*

## *Making the most of a situation*

*"For it is God who is working in you, [enabling you] both to will and to act for His good purpose."* Philippians 2:13 *(HCSB)*

"There is no reason that your daughter can't get on that plane tomorrow," the surgeon told my mother in 2004. I had a cyst removed the day before going on a mission trip to Central Asia. Reluctantly, Mom put me on the plane. Three years later, I moved to Central Asia as a two-year worker. I had no idea that the cyst, which almost kept me from coming in 2004, would return. Once again, God would use it for good.

I should have been terrified about having surgery in a foreign country performed by a doctor who could not speak my language. But God gave me peace. My roommate was out of town, so a national friend stayed with me while I recovered. We spent a lot of time reading the Bible, praying, and sharing stories. Christian friends brought food and prayed over me. My friend was able to see what the body of Christ looked like.

At the end of the week, my friend wrote out a prayer in her language and told me that she had asked God years ago to bring someone to her to explain truth. She believed God had answered her prayer. Praying with me, she turned her life over to Christ.

God can use anything, even an unwanted cyst, and anyone to bring a new child into His family.

—MALLORY, CENTRAL ASIAN PEOPLES

*Lord,* USE MY INFIRMITIES FOR YOUR GLORY. TAKE WHAT IS IMPERFECT IN ME TO COMMU- NICATE THE MESSAGE OF YOUR PERFECT LOVE TO THOSE IN NEED OF TRUSTING CHRIST AS SAVIOR AND LORD. *Amen.*

# Bonded by tragedy

*"As for you, you meant evil against me, but God meant it for good in order to bring about this present result, to preserve many people alive." Genesis 50:20 (NASB)*

"Lord, please start a church in this village," we cried out to God concerning a Mexican village where many had become Christians, but the enemy was making it difficult to bring them together. We invited a medical missions team to offer their services to the village and prayed that somehow God would use this event to unite these new believers as they helped us organize.

As the women worked to cook a meal for the doctors, our 4-year-old daughter fell into a large washtub filled with boiling salsa, causing second-degree burns on 22 percent of her body. The trauma affected everyone. After spending a month at a burn center in the States for our daughter's recovery, we returned home to Mexico and found that the new believers had bonded as a result of this tragedy.

On average, 25 new believers now meet to hear the Bible. Since our daughter's accident, four new people have come to Christ, and a church has been planted. I never would have chosen for God to allow the accident; however, He used the situation to unite His people. We praise Him that He chose to use a tragic situation for His glory. We also praise Him that our daughter's injuries were not more severe. To God be the glory!

—MELISSA, AMERICAN PEOPLES

*I don't understand* WHY THIS LITTLE GIRL HAD TO SUFFER, BUT I THANK YOU FOR YOUR HOLY SPIRIT'S UNIFYING PRESENCE AMONG THIS GROUP OF BELIEVERS. THANK YOU FOR NEW LIVES IN CHRIST, FOR THE CHURCH BORN DURING THIS TRAGEDY. MAY YOU CONTINUE TO HEAL THIS MISSIONARY CHILD. *Amen.*

## God works in mysterious ways

*"also we have obtained an inheritance, having been predestined according to His purpose who works all things after the counsel of His will." Ephesians 1:11 (NASB)*

Shortly after I moved, I met five young girls sunning in front of my apartment complex. After talking, I asked if they wanted to study English. We agreed to meet the following week.

When I went to the same place the following Saturday, the girls weren't there. Instead, two apartment security guards approached me and started asking about where I lived, why I had come to the city, and so forth. Then neighbors started asking me questions and treating me harshly. Upon returning to my apartment, more people came to my door to yell at me, and a few minutes later, the police came. They asked to see my identification. In the midst of all of this, I amazingly felt peace.

Three days passed. I was called to the police office and took a Christian interpreter with me. One of the policemen, who had come to my apartment, politely helped me complete the forms. He admitted that when he first met me, he sensed that I had a good heart. He also told me that if my neighbors bothered me again, he would talk to them. Surprisingly, before I left, he even asked me to teach English to his daughter.

I didn't understand at first why all this happened until I heard the policeman's request. God works in mysterious ways!

—A WORKER WITH EAST ASIAN PEOPLES

*Your ways,* OH LORD, ARE FOREVER PERFECT AND LIFE-GIVING. WHEN TRIALS COME, I REJOICE IN THE ASSURANCE OF YOUR MIGHTY PRESENCE. ALL PRAISE TO YOU. *Amen.*

# My weakness, His strength

*"for when I am weak, then I am strong." 2 Corinthians 12:10b (NASB)*

Intestinal ailments do not make pleasant conversation, so I hesitate to mention it. But they are common in South Asia. When such trouble sets in—nausea, pain, cramps, no appetite—a trip to the local lab is a good idea. A particular bout I had was really discouraging. I didn't feel like talking or being kind; I just wanted to sulk.

As I sat waiting at the lab, God's Spirit prompted me to talk to the lab assistant. I countered back, *Do I have to talk with him while feeling like this and right after he examined my stool sample under a microscope?* But the Spirit kept prompting. So I began asking the technician about life, happiness, death, eternity, and Jesus. The young man had never heard of Jesus. He listened attentively and asked questions. Before leaving, I gave him some Gospel tracts and my phone number if he wanted to talk more. I left the lab feeling better—at least in spirit!

Time passed. One day, the technician called and wanted to meet. He asked for a Bible. In the following weeks, we met for Bible study. Not long after, he decided to follow Jesus. On our front lawn, this young man gave his life to Christ.

By that time, God had healed my stomach, but more importantly, He healed a young man's heart.

—MALCOLM, SOUTH ASIAN PEOPLES

*Dear Lord,* I REJOICE THAT YOU USED ILLNESS FOR YOUR GLORY WHEN MALCOLM WAS ABLE TO SHARE CHRIST WITH THE SOUTH ASIAN LAB TECHNICIAN. STRENGTHEN THE FAITH OF THIS NEW BELIEVER AS HE CONTINUES IN YOUR WORD. USE MALCOLM AND HIM TO REACH OTHERS FOR CHRIST IN SOUTH ASIA. *Amen.*

# A bend in the road

*"The Lord will guard your going out and your coming in from this time forth and forever." Psalm 121:8 (NASB)*

Traveling in an unfamiliar area of Mozambique, the back end of my truck fishtailed as I came around a sharp curve. Dodging an approaching motorcycle, I swerved and went off the road, which caused the truck to flip and roll several times until it came to a stop on its side. Shaken, I unstrapped my seat belt, kicked out what was left of the door, and noticed lots of my blood.

People in the nearby village rushed to the scene. Several villagers insisted that I sit down and asked me where I wanted to go. A Muslim man, "Mussa," said that he would take me, so I climbed on the back of his motorcycle. After several stops for gasoline, we finally arrived at the house of missionaries who took me to a bush hospital and allowed me to recover at their house.

Mussa came to check on me many times. I was surprised, but it gave us an opportunity to build a friendship. When I recovered, I visited him at his house and met his family. After six months of visiting him each Saturday, the opportunity finally came to discuss God's Word. Then for three months, I taught Mussa and several of his friends from God's Word. Eventually, Mussa decided to follow Jesus.

Beginning with the accident, God set in motion Mussa's conversion.

—Jimmy, Sub-Saharan African Peoples

*Great and mighty God,* thank You, not only for preserving Jimmy's life but also for bringing Mussa to his aid. Thank You that good can come out of unplanned trials. Help Mussa to become an effective instrument of Your grace among His people. *Amen.*

# Forced to move

*"So I gave my attention to the Lord God to seek Him by prayer and supplications, with fasting ..." Daniel 9:3 (NASB)*

After 15 years in a city, we moved to a village in order to focus on a people group of 9 million. The people in the village were friendly and must have thought we were great entertainment. As far as we knew at that time, there were no other Christian workers among them.

We were at a loss as to how to begin, so we decided to pray and fast for a period of time, not eating during daylight hours. We wanted to find people who would open the doors for our ministry. About a week into the fast, the religious matriarch of the area turned against me. She stirred up religious leaders and students who were ready to burn down our house. The mob told our landlord that we had to leave, or they would cause more trouble in the future. At first we thought our land-lord and neighbors would stand up against these threats, but they didn't, and we were forced to move. We felt disappointed and discouraged.

In the following days as we were forced to leave, the Lord brought several believers into our lives who were looking for ways to share the Gospel there, too. We were able to encourage one another in reaching the lost millions around us. God turned this event into one that glori-fied Him.

—MARY, SOUTHEAST ASIAN PEOPLES

*Thank You, God,* FOR THE JOY AND ENCOURAGEMENT I RECEIVE FROM MY BROTHERS AND SISTERS IN CHRIST. HELP US TO ENCOURAGE ONE ANOTHER TO REACH OUT TO THE LOST IN OUR COMMUNITY AND AROUND THE WORLD. TO YOUR PRAISE AND GLORY. *Amen.*

# For something eternal

*"So we do not focus on what is seen, but on what is unseen; for what is seen is temporary, but what is unseen is eternal." 2 Corinthians 4:18 (HCSB)*

For over a year, my husband and I tried to become pregnant with our first child. After many doctors' appointments, we had no explanation for the lack of success. As others had babies, I tried to remind myself that God's plan is perfect, yet I was disappointed. Some days it hurt so much that I began to doubt God's goodness. I thought, *Haven't I done everything You've asked of me, Lord? Here I am in a foreign country serving You. Why would You withhold this from me?*

I met "Yuki," a neighbor, and was stunned to find out that she had been trying to have children for 10 years. Through our common experience, the Lord gave me a unique opportunity to share my testimony. As we studied God's Word, I shared that my struggles are only temporary, but in God, I have hope for eternity. She said, "After talking with you, I am thinking differently about my life." She asked if we could study the Bible again.

God brought Yuki and me together, not only so that she could hear the Gospel, but also to remind me of His goodness. Nothing I had been through had been in vain; in fact, He had been preparing me to meet Yuki. He has allowed me to experience temporary pain for the sake of something eternal.

—LINDSEY, EAST ASIAN PEOPLES

*Father,* YOUR GOODNESS OFTEN OVERWHELMS ME. EVEN WHEN I BEGIN TO QUESTION YOUR GRACIOUSNESS TOWARD ME, YOU QUICKLY REMIND ME THAT YOU'RE WORKING TO DRAW THE LOST UNTO YOURSELF. I PRAY FOR YUKI'S SALVATION. *Amen.*

# Flight change

*"In time to come you will understand it clearly." Jeremiah 23:20b* (HCSB)

Not too many people fly to a country and never leave the airport before making their return trip, but that is what I did. Immigration officials refused to honor my valid visa and put me right back on the plane from which I had just disembarked.

My spirit crushed, I fought tears as I reboarded the airplane, only to discover that I would be in a middle seat between two men. *Why me, God?* I asked silently while sighing. I had to pull myself together because tears would only make my fellow passengers uncomfortable. I resorted instead to interviewing the men beside me.

One was married with children, the other a recent college graduate. I chatted with both extensively, but my heart went out to "Aseem," the graduate. This young man was leaving his family and country for the first time in order to begin graduate studies.

By the end of the flight, the Lord had answered my silent question. I knew why I had been returned to that plane. Aseem needed someone to listen and someone who would remember his name and his need for Christ. We keep in touch by e-mail, have spiritual discussions, and I pray for him.

Why me? God always has a purpose.

—CHELE, SOUTH ASIAN PEOPLES

*Gracious Father,* YOU CLOSE DOORS, AND YOU OPEN DOORS. HELP ME TO WALK THROUGH NEW OPPORTUNITIES WITH YOUR EYES. I PRAY FOR ASEEM'S SALVATION. CONTINUE TO DRAW HIM, AND LET HIM SEE HIS NEED FOR YOUR SON, JESUS. *Amen.*

# Checkpoint

*"not paying back evil for evil or insult for insult but, on the contrary, giving a blessing, since you were called for this, so that you can inherit a blessing." 1 Peter 3:9 (HCSB)*

After an awesome week of sports camps, we stood in the airport to watch our volunteer team file through security. We began to joke about which member of the team might look "suspicious" enough to be searched. It wasn't long before Keith was chosen. Decked out in his newly purchased, handmade Colombian hat, Keith smiled like he'd just won a prize.

As the officer inspected his suitcase, he found a folding box that illustrated the Gospel visually. Using basic Spanish and the cube, Keith explained to the security officer about man's sin and separation from God; Jesus' death, burial, and resurrection; and the choice to accept God's free gift of forgiveness. To our utter amazement, the officer listened to every word. Keith gave the cube to the officer along with a Spanish-English New Testament.

As Keith rejoined the team, the officer took the cube and repeated what he had heard to other officers. Then he took the cube to show more officers at the next checkpoint. About 30 minutes later, we saw the same officer walking through the airport, Bible and cube in hand.

Divine placement of those two items and Keith's boldness to share in a language he barely knew turned an inconvenient security check into what this officer needed to find everlasting security.

—SARAH, AMERICAN PEOPLES

*I praise You,* GOD, FOR ENABLING KEITH TO SHARE THE GOSPEL WITH THIS SECURITY OFFICER. MAY HE AND HIS FELLOW OFFICERS FIND ETERNAL SECURITY BY PLACING THEIR FAITH IN JESUS AS SAVIOR AND LORD. *Amen.*

# All things work together

*"We know that all things work together for the good of those who love God:*
*those who are called according to His purpose." Romans 8:28 (HCSB)*

Have you ever wondered what possible good could come from an especially challenging experience? I certainly did when I was interrogated
several times in one week by police. They wanted to know why I was
evangelizing, distributing Bibles, and training believers.

These interrogations were the result of police bugs planted in our
home and the many times they had followed me and my family. We
loved our work of two years among these unreached people, but we
were forced to move. Leaving people we had come to love was agoniz-
ing. What possible good could come of this?

After moving, a catastrophe hit a city near us. We immediately
went there to be involved in relief efforts. Because of having contacts
with national businessmen, we were able to help many victims with
daily necessities and share the Gospel. We also trained local brothers
and sisters in evangelism techniques, which are still producing fruit to
this day.

The Lord used the circumstances of police pressure to move us to
another city where our skills could be used for those most in need. So
the next time you are wondering what good could come from a difficult
situation, be patient and have faith because Jesus will be glorified.

—A WORKER WITH EAST ASIAN PEOPLES

*Thank You, Father,* FOR TAKING EACH SITUATION IN MY LIFE, BOTH THE GOOD AND THE
BAD, AND USING THEM FOR YOUR GLORY. GIVE ME SPIRITUAL EYES TO SEE YOU AT WORK AND
A PATIENT HEART TO WAIT UPON YOU. *Amen.*

## *Loss turns to gain*

*"This is good, and it pleases God our Savior, who wants everyone to be saved and to come to the knowledge of the truth."* 1 Timothy 2:3–4 (HCSB)

Most of what we do for Christ here on earth will only see its reward in heaven; still, we pray for a glimpse. After the death of my husband and daughter seven years ago, I have continued to serve as a missionary in Mexico. I've watched the leaders of a church I planted come to Christ, be baptized, grow, and become the men of God they are now.

As I was leaving the pastor's house after a visit with his family, "Margarito" said, "Please forgive me, but I have something to tell you." I had no idea what he was going to say. He continued, "If your husband and daughter would not have died, you would not be here, and my family and I would not have known about God's Word."

I quickly said goodbye, and as I was driving home, I had two different reactions to the pastor's words. First, I thought that if God would have given me a choice, I would have chosen my husband and daughter over Margarito's family. But just as that thought came to mind, I also marveled that our sovereign God's plan is perfect, and His love was far-reaching on the day I lost my loved ones. Even on that day, God had Margarito's family and me in mind.

—GLORIA, AMERICAN PEOPLES

*Sovereign God,* THERE ARE TIMES WHEN I DON'T UNDERSTAND TRAGEDY. BUT KNOWING YOU GETS ME THROUGH ANY DIFFICULTY I FACE. MAY GLORIA DRAW FROM YOUR STRENGTH AS SHE MINISTERS TO THOSE AROUND HER. *Amen.*

# The ones God sent

> "Many, O LORD my God, are the wonders which You have done, and Your thoughts toward us; there is none to compare with You. If I would declare and speak of them, they would be too numerous to count." Psalm 40:5 (NASB)

It all started with a food box and a sore throat. Although I had cancelled language lessons with my tutor, by the time "Andrew" asked me to distribute food in a poor community, my throat was feeling a little better. I agreed to go with him, and Andrew and I asked God to direct our steps before we left.

When we reached the community, we were welcomed into one home. They served us coffee, and if I heard correctly, invited us to attend their daughter's wedding. We gave them a box of food, sharing that we were giving it in the name of Jesus. Later, we did attend the daughter's wedding.

After a few weeks, Andrew and I returned to give our new friends the *JESUS* film. We had prayed that they would at least watch it at some point. Upon arrival, our friends proudly introduced us to their guests as "the ones God sent to us." The moment we gave them the film, they responded, "Let's watch right now!" Not only the family, but many friends also watched. God opened the way for a whole community to hear truth through a food box and a sore throat. We continue to share and pray with the family.

—VIRG, CENTRAL ASIAN PEOPLES

*All glory to You,* HEAVENLY FATHER, THAT YOU BRING UNEXPECTED OPPORTUNITIES FOR MINISTRY. MAY THIS FAMILY EXPERIENCE SALVATION IN CHRIST JESUS AND BECOME WITNESSES IN THEIR COMMUNITY. *Amen.*

# *Becoming a child of God*

*"But to all who did receive Him, He gave them the right to be children of God, to those who believe in His name." John 1:12 (HCSB)*

"Can you do a funeral in English?" In 33 years of French ministry in Guadalupe, that request was a first. "Anick's" husband, who was from Trinidad and England, had died. His grown children from England were coming to the funeral and did not speak French.

We met with Anick and her family and planned the funeral service. I presented a simple funeral message about the assurance of eternal life, as Anick's husband was part of an evangelical community in London. God was working in the hearts of people that day, and some of Anick's family expressed an interest in knowing more.

Learning that her husband had sometimes gathered her family for Bible study, I asked Anick if she would like for me to continue that practice. She agreed, and a date was set. Anick, her two grown daughters, and seven other family members met for Bible study. In the following weeks, the group became smaller but more interested. Eventually, Anick and two of her sisters decided to follow Jesus. One sister, upon learning John 1:12, responded, "My religion taught me that I am a child of God; I did not know that I had to *become* one!"

Though Anick lost her husband, she found her heavenly Father and became God's child.

—AL, AMERICAN PEOPLES

*Gracious Lord,* I REJOICE WITH THIS MISSIONARY WHO RECOGNIZED THE OPEN DOOR OF MINISTRY THAT LED TO THE SALVATION OF A GRIEVING WIDOW AND TWO OF HER SISTERS. CREATE IN ME A DISCERNING HEART TO CAPITALIZE ON THE MANY LIFE-GIVING MINISTRY OPPORTUNITIES YOU PLACE BEFORE ME EACH DAY. *Amen.*

# Complaining or content

*"I have learned to be content in whatever circumstances I am."* Philippians 4:11 (HCSB)

Our family of three lived in one room of a hostel. We went weeks without water or electricity, or both. Trying to take care of a newborn in this situation was complicated. Since we didn't have a car, we truly felt like we were dropped in the middle of nowhere.

In spite of everything, God had called us to work in this location to share the Gospel. We knew that He had a plan for us, although we didn't particularly like the circumstances. He was still in control. Although the situation was ripe for plenty of complaints, and maybe even to place blame, how could we? God had greatly blessed us. He had given us everything we needed—a place to live, food to eat, His presence and protection, and the opportunity to be His witnesses. If we complained, we realized we would be complaining against God. We would be saying that we weren't satisfied with the great opportunities that He had chosen for us.

God used these first several months to teach me about being content. He is still teaching me this lesson while He takes care of me. It's a matter of trust—trusting Him in the middle of the good and the difficult times.

—SONIA, AMERICAN PEOPLES

*Almighty God,* HELP ME LIVE IN AND FULLY ENJOY THE PRESENT, WHATEVER JOYS OR PROBLEMS COME ALONG. BE WITH MISSIONARIES AS THEY FACE INCONVENIENT SITUATIONS. MAY YOU USE THESE TIMES IN THEIR LIVES TO STRENGTHEN THEIR DEPENDENCE ON YOU. *Amen.*

## *God has a plan*

*"For I know the thoughts that I think toward you, says the LORD, thoughts of peace and not of evil, to give you a future and a hope." Jeremiah 29:11 (NKJV)*

It was dusk as we approached the tram track in our car. My husband and I both saw nothing coming on the track. Suddenly, however, something hit us and began to drag our car. As the car was crushing in, I remember saying, "When is it going to stop?" I thought we were going to die, but fear never came. Finally, we came to a stop, and where we sat in the car was the only place untouched.

Smelling gasoline and seeing electrical wires dancing, we had to somehow get out before the car caught fire. Some bystanders saw our dilemma and rushed to help us by breaking a window and pulling us out like feathers. By this time, hundreds of Romanians had gathered at the scene, and witnesses reported that the tram had been without lights. We moved away from the car, but seeing the condition of it, my body starting shaking uncontrollably. It was evident that God had been our only protection from the crushing and twisting metal.

God received the glory that night as people asked, "Where are the people from that car?" They would see us and immediately start praising God. They knew it was God and God alone. We walked away knowing that God had a plan and that He wasn't finished with us yet.

—FREDA, EUROPEAN PEOPLES

*Merciful Father,* I, TOO, PRAISE YOU FOR YOUR PROTECTIVE HAND ON THIS MISSIONARY COUPLE. YOU ALONE GAVE THEM LIFE AND SAVED THEIR LIVES. HELP ME TO REST IN THE ASSURANCE OF YOUR LOVING CARE AND TO TRUST IN YOU FOR ALL MY TOMORROWS. *Amen.*

# God's presence

*"In my distress I called upon the LORD, and cried to my God for help; He heard my voice out of His temple, and my cry for help before Him came into His ears."*
Psalm 18:6 (NASB)

A former prostitute of 20 years, "María" chose new life in Christ when she heard the Gospel. Having to find a new job for her new life, she found one as an onion cleaner, even though the hours were long and wages low.

One day while at work, tears of anguish poured down her cheeks as she sensed an overwhelming urgency to pray for her 13-year-old daughter. At that moment, without María's knowledge, her daughter was being forced at knifepoint by her boyfriend's brother to go to a motel. Only miraculous intervention by God gave the daughter strength to escape. She was able to get to the front desk of the motel, where an employee called the police. All day, her mother had been praying for her daughter.

María later shared that in the midst of her intense praying, she had never felt closer to God. Her gratefulness for God's protection was beyond words. And she experienced something else. For the first time, she did not respond in vengeance according to her old way of life but rather forgave the victimizer and placed her trust in a just God. Although the young man has been faced with consequences, María's response to life's injustices brought peace and God's presence.

—BARBARA, AMERICAN PEOPLES

*Dear Lord,* THANK YOU FOR WORKING IN MARÍA'S LIFE. THANK YOU FOR PROTECTING HER DAUGHTER. THANK YOU THAT YOU TOTALLY TRANSFORM LIVES. *Amen.*

# Is God there?

*"If only I knew where to find God, I would go to his court." Job 23:3 (NLT)*

Being one of five foreigners in our city of 1 million, my husband and I are often asked to teach English. One older woman demanded that I teach her, and she would not take no for an answer. I felt like I had nothing left to give.

We waited a month before finally going to her house. She insisted that we eat, and even after we were full, she made us eat more. During our visit, we discovered that her son had become a Christian a year before. Although this mother didn't agree with his conversion and did not want to discuss it, she had not kicked him out. I didn't think building a relationship with her would go anywhere, but I reluctantly decided to give it a try. Because she liked to cook, we began teaching each other new recipes.

I had been experiencing a dry time in my spiritual life and was desperate to feel God's presence. One night while I was half-asleep, God brought this woman to mind. I realized a change had occurred in me because I didn't want anything to do with her at first, but almost a year later, she was like a mother to me. It was proof that God was there. And I know that He will bring this woman to Himself.

—CANDICE, SOUTHEAST ASIAN PEOPLES

*Father,* FORGIVE ME FOR EVER DOUBTING YOUR PRESENCE IN MY LIFE. AS I REFLECT ON DIFFICULT DAYS, YOUR SPIRIT SHOWS ME HOW YOU WERE NOT ONLY PRESENT BUT ALSO ACTIVELY ORCHESTRATING EVENTS THAT WOULD ACCOMPLISH YOUR MOST PERFECT WILL IN MY LIFE AND IN THE LIVES OF OTHERS. YOU ARE AN AWESOME GOD! *Amen.*

# Letting Jesus in

*"But from there, you will search for the LORD your God, and you will find [Him] when you seek Him with all your heart and all your soul." Deuteronomy 4:29 (HCSB)*

Although "Freda" had heard the Gospel for many years, her beliefs in Buddhism kept her from giving her heart to Jesus. She tried to add Christianity to Buddhism, but that didn't work.

With her young daughter facing another brain surgery, she felt helpless. In her desperation, Freda prayed to all gods, including God, to protect her daughter during surgery. Freda even prayed to a Buddhist goddess. She asked if I would pray to my God.

I explained to her that she shouldn't pray to other gods and God because God is jealous and will not share His glory. At her wit's end and getting no peace from her false gods, she despaired. Dejected, she left the hospital.

On her way home from the hospital, she stopped at a bookstore. Glancing at a Christian book, she began to read stories of other people's struggles. God used these stories to captivate her heart. She decided to allow Jesus into her own heart.

Although her daughter didn't live long after the surgery, Freda's faith in God has grown steadily. It has not been easy, but she acknowledges God's hand even in her daughter's death. It was this death that moved her to receive eternal life.

—K.C., EAST ASIAN PEOPLES

*Thank You,* GRACIOUS LORD, FOR THIS REMINDER THAT YOU DRAW PEOPLE TO FAITH IN JESUS. YOUR AMAZING LOVE IS OVERWHELMING. HELP FREDA TO GROW IN HER FAITH, AND COMFORT HER IN THE LOSS OF HER DAUGHTER. *Amen.*

# "Sing with those people"

*"... break forth into a shout of joy, you mountains, O forest, and every tree in it; for the LORD has redeemed Jacob and in Israel He shows forth His glory."*
Isaiah 44:23 (NASB)

"Lisa" eagerly waited for her family to go to bed so that she could sneak out to where her friends huddled in a boat. They had planned to escape the country the night before, but the winds were not right. Would they ever find freedom? As her family lingered longer than usual, finally the boat left without her. Disappointment overwhelmed Lisa.

The next morning, bodies washed up on the shore. The boat with Lisa's best friends had capsized in the stormy seas. Terror filled Lisa as she thought about her friends and what should have happened to her. She became so despondent that others noticed. One day a store owner told her, "You need to be around happy people. Why don't you go to the church on the corner and sing with those people; they seem happy." Curious, Lisa passed by the church several times, but she didn't enter.

One desperate day, Lisa thought, *I'm going to kill myself, but before I do, I will go and hear the happy music.* The same day, she entered the church and heard the Good News of Christ. Within a few months of attending, she committed her life to Jesus. Lisa's sadness turned to joy, and she found true freedom.

—YVONNE, AMERICAN PEOPLES

*Gracious Lord,* YOUR MESSAGE IS ONE OF HOPE. YOUR PRESENCE IN OUR LIVES REPLACES TEARS OF DISCOURAGEMENT WITH THE JOY OF BRIGHTER TOMORROWS. THANK YOU FOR BRINGING LISA TO YOURSELF. *Amen.*

# Taking the Gospel to killers

*"Indeed, all who desire to live a godly life in Christ Jesus will be persecuted ..."*
*2 Timothy 3:12 (ESV)*

On June 16, 1976, 10,000 youth protested against South Africa's apartheid government. Many students were killed as they incited violence as a means to stop an oppressive government. Pastor Bonani's son, "Jonas," was a youth leader during that turbulent time, and he questioned his teacher for using the Bible to justify violence. Because of this, he was labeled a traitor. His continued refusal to participate in violence led to his untimely death. A mob came to the pastor's house and wiped the blood from their machetes on the front steps, warning that they would return for the rest of the family.

The day Jonas was buried, the mob bombed the pastor's house with his family inside. Even though the house was engulfed in flames, the room where the family was trapped did not burn. For three years, this family moved from place to place, fearing for their safety.

Over 20 years later, Pastor Bonani stopped beside a graveyard and began to pray. He was too afraid to enter the location, known as Barcelona, because this was where his son's killers lived. Eight years later, this pastor and his wife serve in a church in Barcelona and foster 21 children. God has been glorified!

—MIKE, SUB-SAHARAN AFRICAN PEOPLES

*God,* WITH THE ECHOES OF "CRUCIFY HIM" STILL RINGING IN THE AIR, YOUR SON LOVINGLY RETURNED TO THE PEOPLE WHO CALLED FOR HIS DEATH. SIMILARLY, THIS PASTOR RETURNED TO BE YOUR TOUCH OF LOVE IN THE COMMUNITY THAT BRED DEATHLY HATE. MAY I BE EQUALLY MOVED BY YOUR SPIRIT. *Amen.*

## Sharing Christ's sufferings

*"He who believes in Me ... out of his heart will flow rivers of living water."* John 7:38 (NKJV)

As I waited at the airport for a volunteer team to arrive, I received a frantic call from my national partner, Anna. "Lonya has had an accident at work; I don't know whether he is dead or alive!"

I learned that Anna's husband had fallen under the wheels of a moving train. His leg had been severed, and because of infection and shock, he was in critical condition. With hospital care being very basic, drugs, meals, patient care, linens, and other supplies had to be provided by family and friends. For three weeks, Anna and her four children took care of Lonya.

After his recovery, Lonya shared, "I am a common laborer. I provide for my family and love the Lord. When I became a broken man, God made me popular. The men sharing my hospital room were astonished that my wife and children cared for me. An American lady frequently brought supplies. The men concluded that I was a special man! Co-workers and the director at work visited. So the men were convinced that I was famous!"

Paul rejoiced in his suffering because he was given the opportunity to be a testimony to others. Lonya and Anna saw their trial as a way to minister to those observing them.

—B.B.H., EUROPEAN PEOPLES

*Father,* YOUR MERCY IS AMAZING. THANK YOU FOR NOT ONLY SPARING LONYA'S LIFE, BUT FOR TOUCHING OTHERS THROUGH HIS SUFFERING AND THE VISIBLE TESTIMONY OF A LOVING FAMILY AND CHRISTIAN COMMUNITY. MAY THE SEEDS SOWN REAP ETERNAL FRUIT IN THE LIVES OF THESE MEN. *Amen.*

## Saved for a purpose

*"Before I formed you in the womb I knew you, ... I have appointed you a prophet to the nations." Jeremiah 1:5 (NASB)*

April 17, 1975—a day Cambodia will never forget. I was 7 years old when my homeland fell into the hands of the Khmer Rouge communists. My parents were taken away to work in labor camps. For four years I lived as an orphan, left behind to care for my 4-year-old sister.

The communists fed us only one spoonful of rice per day. To supplement our diet, I searched for insects and dug up roots. The saddest day of my life came the next year when my sister succumbed to starvation. I cried myself to sleep night after night, asking, "Why?"

Following the end of Khmer Rouge rule, my parents returned and we escaped from Cambodia to the United States. Attending a Baptist church in Tennessee, my Buddhist family heard for the first time how Jesus died and rose again for our sins. We were convicted of the truth of the Gospel and gave our lives to Christ.

My life was spared to be a spokesperson to the nations. Like Jeremiah, we have all been given a message of hope to share with the world. When I shared my story with an atheist university student recently, she gladly embraced the Good News. God uses our testimony of His faithfulness for a purpose.

—Sarahn, Southeast Asian Peoples

*Dear Lord,* I'm so grateful for this reminder that we are all saved for a purpose. My story might not be as moving as Sarahn's; nevertheless, it chronicles the precious miracle of spiritual transformation in my life. I pray that I will be faithful to share it with others. *Amen.*

# Refuge in the storm

*"God is our refuge and strength, a very present help in trouble."* Psalm 46:1 (NASB)

Over a period of two years, volunteer teams came to Santa Catarina for a construction and evangelism project. The staff of the community center built by these volunteers rejoiced that they finally had a place to help people obtain documents, learn job skills, have Bible studies, and offer day care for children.

And then came the rain. A downpour began one morning and flooded most roads, closing accessibility. Families fled homes being washed away by torrents of muddy water from the overflowing river. Their desperate search for higher ground led to the community center and a nearby public school. At the center, workers struggled to help hundreds of people who were seeking shelter. God provided in miraculous ways throughout that week as staff and volunteers fed over 600 people three times a day and distributed food staples and disaster relief supplies to the homeless. The building that volunteers prayed would become a source of hope became more than they ever imagined.

In the months since the storm, opportunities have continued for missionaries, staff, and volunteers to share the Gospel with hundreds of people who personally experienced God's love in action in this place of refuge. God truly is our refuge and strength during trouble.

—LORETTA, AMERICAN PEOPLES

*Redeeming Lord,* THEY CAME HUNGRY, THIRSTY, AND TIRED. THEY LEFT FILLED, REFRESHED, AND RESTED. THEY CONTINUE TO COME HUNGRY, THIRSTY, AND TIRED. THEY LEAVE HAVING TASTED THE BREAD OF LIFE AND LIVING WATER. THANK YOU, GRACIOUS ONE. *Amen.*

# Reaction during the storm

*"Then He said to them, 'Why are you fearful? Do you still have no faith?'"*
Mark 4:40 (HCSB)

While a university student, I participated in a mission trip to Honduras. I felt like God was saying to me, *If I ever call you into overseas missions, I will take care of you and your children.*

A year after I married, my husband and I came to Malta as two-year workers and later as career missionaries. We grew to love our neighbors and felt at home. Then our landlord informed us that we had to move because he sold our apartment. I was upset at losing the home we had lived in for over nine years. I pleaded with God to let us stay. Then I read the story of Jesus calming the storm. His Word challenged me, "Why are you so afraid? Do you still not have faith in me?" God also reminded me of the promise He gave me in Honduras.

Choosing to finally trust Him, God led us to our new flat a few blocks away, and it was much more suitable for our three children. As a daily reminder of His goodness, I can look out my kitchen window and see our first flat. I pray for my former neighbors as I look out while washing dishes.

During storms, I have to choose how I respond. Next time, hopefully I will remember that God is in control!

—ROBIN, EUROPEAN PEOPLES

*Thank You, Master,* FOR THE STORMS IN LIFE THAT CAUSE ME TO TRUST YOU MORE. HELP MISSIONARIES TRUST YOU WHEN THEY ARE FORCED TO MOVE UNEXPECTEDLY AND FACE DIFFICULT CIRCUMSTANCES. MAY THEIR FAITH INCREASE. *Amen.*

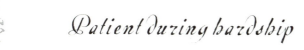

## *Patient during hardship*

*"Strengthened with all power, according to His glorious might, for the attaining of all steadfastness and patience ..."* Colossians 1:11 *(NASB)*

Burdened for a nomadic people group, Walmiy took a job in an extremely hot area. He built relationships and worked hard. The people began to trust him as he helped them work more efficiently. It wasn't long before they also listened to him as he shared his faith and life lessons from the Bible.

During oppressive heat at night, sleeping outdoors on the sand was the best option. One night as Walmiy and the people slept outside, the wind began to blow fine dirt, which eventually covered those who slept. Walmiy awoke, brushed the dirt off, and went back to sleep. Then again, he awoke covered in dirt, brushed off, and fell back asleep.

The third time he awoke covered in dirt, he got up and went inside his room. "Do you see me, God?" he said. "Are you going to bury me alive in this sand? I can't continue to live like this or work at this job any longer!" He dropped on his bed and fell asleep in the stifling heat.

Before dawn, Walmiy arose and looked out his door to see the people still sleeping and covered in dirt. God filled his heart with compassion and impressed him that he must be patient with the conditions. As he asked God for strength, he thanked God for allowing him to see.

—JULIE, NORTHERN AFRICAN AND MIDDLE EASTERN PEOPLES

*Forgiving Father,* GIVE ENDURANCE TO CHRISTIAN WORKERS OVERSEAS. ALLOW THEM TO IDENTIFY WITH THE PEOPLE WHOM THEY SERVE. HELP ME TO ENDURE THINGS OUT OF MY COMFORT ZONE IN ORDER TO MINISTER EFFECTIVELY. *Amen.*

# Brokenness

*"The sacrifice you desire is a broken spirit. You will not reject a broken and repentant heart, O God." Psalm 51:17 (NLT)*

There are some lessons that I thought I had learned previously in my Christian walk. Yet once on the mission field, I was hit square between the eyes with truths not mastered. Brokenness became my state of mind. God brought me to a point of depending on Him alone. Stripped of all things familiar—language, food, family, and friends—no longer could I depend on my own good efforts, pride, or strength. With my need to be dependent solely upon Him revealed, He led me to brokenness over sin and self.

Sometimes pain is well worth it. When I confessed my inadequacies and sin, God revealed areas in my life where He was at work or wanted to work. Humbling yet freeing, He taught me to be thankful for brokenness. When God breaks down pride and self, He is also building a continued sense of dependency upon Him and deeper, personal faith.

Since then, my heart's prayer is no longer "Lord, change my circumstances," but "Father, show me how I can honor You in any and every circumstance." A broken spirit delights God. It's the kind of spirit that says, "Yes, Lord, I will depend on You, no matter what happens."

—MELANIE, EUROPEAN PEOPLES

I, TOO, AM QUICK TO CRY OUT FOR A LIFELINE TO PULL ME OUT OF DIFFICULT CIRCUMSTANCES. FATHER, HELP ME TO EMBRACE MY BROKENNESS AS AN OPPORTUNITY TO COMPLETELY TRUST IN YOU. SHOW ME HOW I CAN HONOR YOU IN EVERY CIRCUMSTANCE. *Amen.*

# NOVEMBER

## Be Encouraged

*That we care is still the loudest Christian creed
the world around us will ever hear.*

—BETH MOORE

"If you can't say something nice, don't say it at all," my mother said like a broken record to my brothers and me when we were growing up. That statement, however, is a good motto to tuck into our minds and practice.

The Bible talks a lot about how words either damage or heal. Proverbs 16:24 says, "Pleasant words are a honeycomb, sweet to the soul and healing to the bones" (NASB). My grandfather's hobby was beekeeping. I can remember him suiting up in his "bee" outfit, a baggy white garment topped with a pith helmet and attached netting that protected his face and neck. The grandkids had to maintain a safe distance when he collected the combs but close enough to watch as he pulled out trays of dripping, golden honeycomb from the hives. Then he would gently place the honeycomb in a bucket and bring it over to us so that we could have a taste of the delicious product made by hardworking bees. Oh, was that honeycomb good! That first taste of the sweet liquid was heavenly. We'd almost be sick from eating our fair share, and we were definitely sticky.

Words of encouragement are a lot like that honey. We look forward to receiving them, and we can certainly anticipate giving them. Sweet words build others up, especially when they are timely. Missionaries are no different than the rest of us. They need to know that they are loved and prayed for, especially on the days when they just don't think they are going to make it.

Because most missionaries live such transient lives, they aren't always sure where their physical home is any more. Sometimes, they can despair or get cranky when they lose their visas, get kicked out of their apartment, or are asked to transfer "just one more time." When our young family was in the process of preparing to go to the mission field for the first time, we sold our house, moved into someone's basement, visited relatives, moved to seminary for a few months, visited more relatives, and spent seven weeks in missionary orientation before finally leaving for Africa!

Our 2-year-old daughter, Emily, was fed up with the instability.

After seven months of seminary, we drove across the country for five weeks to see family before our training, spending hours upon hours in our blue minivan. Emily whined from the get-go. About three weeks into these final stateside travels, Emily cried, "I want to go home." I'm not proud of it, but frustrated as well, I replied firmly, "Emily, we don't have a place to call home. This car is your home right now." A week later at an aunt's house, Emily had a meltdown. She was inconsolable, wailing her head off. I mean *wailing*! Her daddy said, "Emily, what's wrong, honey?" And she shouted out between pitiful sobs, "I want to go to my car!"

Missionaries just want a familiar place to lay their heads, too. But when that isn't possible, an encouraging word can make all the difference in the world. I can't tell you how many times when I was ready to throw in the towel that a timely good word or an unexpected act of kindness helped me get through another day. Then another.

God encourages us through His Word and answered prayer, too. You will read stories this month that will help you get through the day. As one missionary couple put it, "There are days that discouragement threatens to overtake us. On those days, God never fails to send along a neighbor or an encouraging e-mail from a friend. Maybe He brings to mind a favorite verse or song ... God reminds us that we are where He wants us to be."

As you read this month's stories of encouragement, I hope they will encourage you to spread a little of that sweet honey around. As my mother used to say, "What goes around, comes around."

—*Kim P. Davis*

# Encouragement for the discouraged

*"Count it all joy, my brothers, when you meet trials of various kinds, for you know that the testing of your faith produces steadfastness. And let steadfastness have its full effect, that you may be perfect and complete, lacking in nothing."*
James 1:2–4 (ESV)

Without the intense winds, the hot temperatures of summer would be unbearable. Unlike most cities in our Central Asian country, we have reliable electricity, which allows us to run fans and our swamp cooler on really hot days. The whip-you-around winds take the edge off the heat. When they blow, however, they also leave a thick coat of fine, desert dust on everything.

It seems that at times, a season of discouragement can settle on our family. The novelty of foreign life quickly wears off. Language difficulties and the lack of depth in friendship dishearten us. Inconveniences and cultural restrictions chew us up and spit us out. Like the dust after the much-needed winds, frustration can surface as we're refined and stretched.

Nevertheless, there is great benefit in the grueling process of learning perseverance. When we don't think we can make it, God gives us a glimpse of how He is growing our faith and character. It is faith to believe He is working when we don't see it, to trust He will equip us to minister, and to know He is moving in the hearts of people when it feels slow and tedious. The challenge is to fix our eyes not on the "dust of discouragement," but on the Great Encourager.

—Jenni, Central Asian Peoples

*My Comforter,* my Friend, I praise You for the trials I face. Thank You that You are refining me to be more like You. I pray that You will encourage missionaries today in the ways in which they need it. *Amen.*

## *Encouraging others*

*"And let us consider how to stir up one another to love and good works."* Hebrews 10:24 (ESV)

I've never liked to run, but by His infinite wisdom and great sense of humor, running was a part of our missionary training. Every day, I woke up early with the sun and struggled out from under mosquito nets in order to run through the hot, wet jungle.

Most of the other trainees were indigenous believers who barely weighed over 100 pounds. I normally lost sight of them about two minutes into the run. We looked like 10 squirrels and one elephant, and you can guess which one I was.

Javier, a former trainee and national believer, taught some of our physical endurance classes. He wasn't obligated to run with us, but one morning, I noticed him stretching. Javier patted me on the shoulder and said, "Let's go, brother. I'm going to run with you." As we neared the end, I noticed that he was limping a little. I found out that his shoes were too small and his feet had blistered.

The next morning, Javier ran with me again. The third morning, he wasn't wearing shoes. "Javier, you can't run on a gravel road barefoot for five miles," I said. He insisted on running with me. What a blessing it was to watch this man do whatever it took to encourage his brother. It is important to encourage the body of Christ even though it's hard work.

—TRENT, AMERICAN PEOPLES

*Thank You, Father,* FOR THE ENCOURAGEMENT I'VE RECEIVED FROM MY BROTHERS AND SISTERS IN CHRIST DURING DIFFICULT DAYS. PLEASE HELP ME TO BE MORE SENSITIVE TO THE NEEDS OF OTHERS. HELP ME TO BE THEIR ENCOURAGER, TO BE YOUR TOUCH OF LOVE. THANK YOU FOR JAVIER'S EXAMPLE. *Amen.*

# Their dreams, my dream

*"Worry weighs a person down; an encouraging word cheers a person up."*
Proverbs 12:25 (NLT)

When I asked the teenagers in my class if the earthquake had damaged their homes, I found out that they were living in tents. For the first time, I was glad that I wasn't going to leave that evening and go to a hotel. That day we discussed their dreams, and they had many, including becoming a soccer player, a singer, and an actress. A couple of guys wanted to join the military. "Bob" wanted to be an artist.

I encouraged all of them to work hard, keeping their dreams in focus. Bob went back to his tent that evening and drew a picture for us on damp paper, a difficult feat. He stayed up until 2 a.m. to complete the artwork and then returned to the camp the next morning to present a drawing of a panda sitting in a bamboo forest.

I was touched by his gift and continued to encourage him. He was pleased and for the first time, we saw a little smile. And because the other teachers also wanted a picture, he spent the rest of the day drawing. His dream was coming alive.

Bob is in my prayers, and my dream is that he will someday come to know our Creator, the one true God.

—N.M., EAST ASIAN PEOPLES

*Merciful and gracious Father,* I LINK MY HEART AND PRAYERS WITH THIS MISSIONARY. AS BOB DRAWS PICTURES OF YOUR CREATION, I PRAY THAT YOU, THE LORD OF ALL CREATION, WILL SPEAK INTO HIS HEART, REVEALING THE TRUTHS OF YOUR GOSPEL. *Amen.*

## Bearing up under the load

*"Blessed is a man who perseveres under trial; for once he has been approved, he will receive the crown of life which the Lord has promised to those who love Him." James 1:12 (NASB)*

My grandfather had been diagnosed with cancer a year before I moved to South Asia. As I prepared to leave America, the possibilities of seeing this dear man again were slim. Although I had surrendered this possibility to the Lord, five months later when I got a phone call saying he had passed away, I didn't know how to deal with it emotionally.

My teammates were there to encourage me. They even arranged a small memorial service so that I could share about my grandfather with them, since I was unable to travel to the funeral held in the States. God encouraged me to persevere. In spite of everything, the Father was using this event to draw me closer to Him. There were times when I felt like giving up, but I knew that I needed to hang in there. Perseverance is bearing up under the load. It doesn't mean coming out of a trial or being freed from the load, but it's continuing to walk and trust while under the load. God was faithful to provide the strength for me to stand back up again.

Persevere, friend. Listen to Him and other Christians as they encourage you. You will make it by His strength, compassion, and love.

—S.F., SOUTH ASIAN PEOPLES

*Compassionate Father,* WHEN THE CARES OF THIS WORLD WEIGH ME DOWN, YOU SEE ME THROUGH TO A NEW DAY. I PRAISE AND THANK YOU FOR YOUR HOLY SPIRIT, WHOSE ENCOURAGEMENT INSPIRES ME TO PERSEVERE THROUGH DIFFICULT EXPERIENCES. *Amen.*

# The blessing of fellowship

*"Set your minds on what is above, not on what is on the earth."* Colossians 3:2
(HCSB)

Setting my mind on God and what's important to Him goes a long way when I'm trying not to let outward circumstances determine personal joy and contentment. Practical application was provided by God when my family stayed with an elderly couple, former Muslims who now follow Jesus.

We had determined to be thankful, and the Lord used our four days with this couple to see how serious we were. They live on the fifth floor of an old Soviet apartment block. Water pressure was weak, so the water didn't make it to their floor. The electricity was off about 50 percent of the time, making it uncomfortable to sleep in the heat. Odor from raw sewage was overpowering since the system had leaked into the basement.

Despite all of this, the fellowship with this elderly couple was so sweet and inspiring. Polio-stricken, the wife served us as best she could with no use of her left arm. The husband rose at 5 a.m. to carry buckets of water up five flights of stairs so that we could wash and use the toilet each morning. They had absolutely no complaints about their living conditions but rather were grateful for their salvation out of Islam. Their joy in the Lord was infectious, and we left them feeling blessed and encouraged.

—FRED, CENTRAL ASIAN PEOPLES

*Father,* WHY DO I OFTEN EQUATE BLESSINGS WITH COMFORT, HEALTHFULNESS, AND PLEASANT CIRCUMSTANCES? I SO WANT TO COUNT AS BLESSED THE DIFFICULT MOMENTS AND HAPPENINGS AS WELL. THANK YOU FOR THIS GENTLE REMINDER OF CONTENTMENT THROUGH THE EXAMPLE OF THIS COUPLE. BLESS THEM, FATHER. *Amen.*

## The text message

*"For he will bring our darkest secrets to light and will reveal our private motives. Then God will give to each one whatever praise is due."* 1 Corinthians 4:5b (NLT)

They come and quickly go. Sometimes we don't know when or where. Teaching English to Muslim refugees, ones not welcomed in this European country, is an opportunity to show God's love and share the Gospel during their temporary situations.

One day, a student called me from another city to announce his soon departure. I appreciated that he made an effort to let me know that he was leaving. I sent him a text message, thanking him for his call and wishing him well. He responded to me with the following text message: "Takyotovirmachmautichar."

At first, I thought it might be in his heart language, but as I studied it, I realized that it was English. I added spaces to his message to separate out different words: "Tak yo to vir mach mau tichar." When I adjusted the spelling, the translation was: "Thank you too very much my teacher."

Even though his English proficiency was low, I was grateful for his simple expression of appreciation. This text message reminded me that our work is making a difference. Even though we don't often receive overt thanks, we could find it if we were to look closely enough. Regardless, our final reward will not come in this world but in the coming kingdom.

—Tracy, European Peoples

*Father,* help missionaries as they minister to refugees in Europe. May Your Holy Spirit draw refugees toward a longing for You. Encourage these missionaries today. *Amen.*

## Needing confirmation

*"He said, 'But I will be with you ...'" Exodus 3:12 (ESV)*

The stress of moving, shopping, and settling into a new place with three kids was just about to take its toll as we waited for promised deliveries and installation of air conditioners. When workers left after six hours with their jobs still incomplete, I went for a walk and prayed, *Lord, I really need some encouragement that this is where we are supposed to be.*

I began to look around me. There was a banana tree, a papaya tree, and a mango tree. *We sure don't have trees like this in Kentucky!* I thought. Then a neighbor drove by with a smile and a wave. Now that was just like back home. Around a corner, I met a man who was grilling and selling hamburgers. We conversed, and it was just like I could hear the Father whispering, *This is why you are here.*

There are days that discouragement threatens to overtake us. Let's face it. It would be easier to live in our home country. On those days God never fails to send along a neighbor or an encouraging e-mail from a friend. Maybe He brings to mind a favorite verse or song. When discouragement comes like the rain, God comes like the rainbow to remind us that we are where He wants us to be.

—C. AND A., SOUTHEAST ASIAN PEOPLES

*Arms linked,* FINGERS ENTWINED, WE'VE TRAVELED TOGETHER, LORD. YOU HAVE PERMITTED ME TO EXPERIENCE THE JOY OF YOUR PURPOSEFUL, PROMISING PRESENCE. HELP MISSIONARIES IN THEIR HOMESICKNESS TODAY. *Amen.*

## Feeling His encouragement

*"But godliness with contentment is a great gain."* 1 Timothy 6:6 (HCSB)

It was a homesick, lonely day. Not feeling up to taking the crazy taxi ride across town, being stared at, or being called "foreigner" once again, I had to force myself since I had promised "Lilian," a national friend, that I would meet her for lunch and shopping.

So off I went feeling emotionally drained. The moment Lilian saw me, she linked arms with me and started walking. It was as if the Father said, *I love you. I know you are missing home, but I am here wrapping my arms around you through this Asian girl whom I love.*

Feeling His presence brought tears to my eyes, and I was able to take the attention off of myself.

As we walked around and shopped, Lilian could tell that something was wrong when she first saw me. I told her that I missed my family, but I was so glad that she had wanted to hang out. God gave me a friend. As I focused on her, I was able to share how the Father loves her so much, that He sent His only Son to die for her, and that she could have a personal relationship with Him. He encouraged both of us that day. He is faithful to meet our needs.

—Joy, East Asian Peoples

*Heavenly Father,* I ask that Lilian would seek You. May she one day have a personal relationship with You. Thank You for Your encouragement by giving us special friends. *Amen.*

## Inflation woes

*"And Abraham called the name of the place, The-LORD-Will-Provide; as it is said to this day, 'In the Mount of the LORD it shall be provided.'"* Genesis 22:14 (NKJV)

Global inflation. Because of the quick and drastic economic changes worldwide, how was I going to make $100 stretch to feed our family of eight for a week? Usually relaxed about finances, I began to be concerned about my husband who felt pressure to provide sufficiently for us in the struggling South African economy. One day, he came home very anxious about the immediate future of our family budget.

But on the same day, God had something to teach us. We heard a knock at the door, and upon answering it, we found our unemployed neighbor. Her husband makes very little money, and they struggle financially to make enough to support their family of four. That day, our neighbor was standing there with a huge bag in her arms filled with potatoes, vegetables, and even some cookies. She said that her mother was trying to get rid of leftovers from a big dinner party, and their family couldn't possibly eat all of it. We could not believe it!

My husband was overwhelmed with how God supplied immediately. He needed that timely encouragement to build his faith and trust in God to provide. We were reminded that God is not limited by circumstances, and He can provide through unexpected people.

—Vicky, Sub-Saharan African Peoples

*Gracious Father,* Your goodness is overwhelming. Your provision arrives; my faith strengthens. Your love is amazing, Jehovah Jireh, our Provider. *Amen.*

## *Holding the arms*

*"While Moses held up his hand, Israel prevailed, but whenever he put his hand down, Amalek prevailed. When Moses' hands grew heavy, ... Aaron and Hur supported his hands ... so that his hands remained steady until the sun went down." Exodus 17:11–12 (HCSB)*

Reflecting on Moses, I'd have to say that his life is similar to what we've seen happen with the church in our location in Central Asia. As God birthed His church, we felt like the midwives of Egypt, running interference from those trying to kill it! Like baby Moses, the church needed protection and nourishment. We came alongside, much like Miriam, offering sources for growth and maturity. As it grew, the church became more independent, and God gave the leaders the vision to see people reached for Him. They would often feel inadequate, and like Aaron, we've come alongside them in the tasks.

Through persecution, the church is flourishing. We've wondered about our roles as foreigners. Is it time to leave now that the church has grown up? A friend told us, however, "Our arms still get tired." In the heat of the battle against Amalek, when Moses lifted up his arms to lead the people, the Israelites prevailed. But when he lowered them in weariness, the battle would swing the other way. So Aaron and Hur, his trusted fellow laborers, came to his aid, holding up his arms. That's our role now: to humbly hold up their arms, encourage them in the battle, and be there to listen.

—Dana, Central Asian Peoples

*Lord,* there are many times a brother or a sister in Christ has encouraged me. Please strengthen church leaders in Central Asia as they suffer hardship, even persecution, for their faith. *Amen.*

## Praise breaks the bonds of discouragement

*"Now therefore, our God, we thank You, and praise Your glorious name."*
1 Chronicles 29:13 (NASB)

Praise breaks us free from the shackles of discouragement. I listened in amazement to my friend "Akim" as he praised God and expressed incredible faith. He professed, "You know, my store is so small, but with God it is so big!"

A young father of eight, four children of his own and four from his deceased sister, Akim provides for his family by running a small "tuck shop" in the local market. When he invited us to his home for a meal, we did not want him to feed us with so many other mouths to feed, but he insisted. As the meal was prepared, we asked Akim how things were for his family. That's when he had nothing but praise for our Father who provides for him. I smiled and nodded but couldn't help thinking about his poverty. When I see poverty, I want to make life easier for people. However, I could rob a person from growing spiritually when I try to rescue people from all circumstances. I don't want people to rely on my resources instead of God's miracles! I am thankful for the encouragement God provided to me through Akim because I struggle with how to help those around me. I remember that it was during the "famines" in my life when God became the most real to me.

—Denise, Sub-Saharan African Peoples

*Father,* I pray for Akim and his family. Provide all their needs. Use this family to be a strong testimony of Your goodness and faithfulness. *Amen.*

# A different perspective

*"and lo, I am with you always ..."* Matthew 28:20b (NASB)

Absolutely nothing was like our expectations. Our assignment and location changed three times, we struggled with culture, and we were completely alone. My initial excitement and optimism had slipped away, leaving me depressed. As the cold wind blew and the freezing summer rain poured, it became hard to get out of bed.

A preplanned prayerwalking team came to help us for a few days. Their first ministry location was a beautiful town where the people were friendly and where we were supposed to have lived. Having the team distracted me from depression, but each night in bed I was filled with anxiety, frustration, and fear. I worried about the team coming to our community because it was ugly, unfriendly, and horribly cold.

On the day in our community, the prayerwalkers expressed how much they loved it and the beautiful people. I will never forget hearing one guy say, "It is such a relief to come here, and I believe that God is working." As I listened to each person share their observations, God showed me that I had been looking at my community through my own expectations and perspective. I had not fully trusted that He will never leave me. Instantly, the depression lifted, hope presented itself, and I had a new love for my community. I will not forget the lesson of that night.

—W., EUROPEAN PEOPLES

*Thank You,* MERCIFUL GOD, FOR SPEAKING INTO THE HEART OF THIS MISSIONARY THROUGH THE PRAYERWALKERS. AND THANK YOU FOR THE REMINDER THAT EVEN IF I DON'T FEEL YOUR PRESENCE, YOU ARE INDEED WITH ME, WATCHING OVER ME, DRAWING ME CLOSER UNDER THE SHADOW OF YOUR WING. *Amen.*

# At the well

*"... 'If anyone is thirsty, let him come to Me and drink.'" John 7:37 (NASB)*

Can you imagine having to walk one mile to get your water for cooking, bathing, drinking, and washing clothes and dishes? It's hard for us to relate to this way of life in many South Asian villages. "Yacob," a believer and village resident, wanted to do something about it in the name of Jesus. So he came to us to see how we might partner in a project. At that time, we had a group of college students from Georgia helping with our work. One of the students was burdened with the need, and through our organization, he and his friends sponsored a well in this community.

After the monsoon time, Yacob contracted to have the well drilled by his father's tiny home. When it was complete, the women were thankful to be able to draw water close by. The college student was able to visit the community and gave testimony of God's faithfulness and love.

When the weather became extremely hot, wells across the area began to dry up, except for this well. People walked from all over to use this particular well. When they asked Yacob's father why it had not dried up like the others, he explained that the one true God had kept this well overflowing with water. He then shared about Jesus, the Living Water. Many came to know Jesus as a result.

—NELLIE, SOUTH ASIAN PEOPLES

*Lord Jesus,* HELP PEOPLE IN SOUTH ASIAN VILLAGES NOT ONLY TO HAVE A SOURCE OF PHYSICAL WATER, BUT SHOW THEM JESUS, THE LIVING WATER. THANK YOU FOR COLLEGE STUDENTS WHO HAVE A BURDEN TO WIN THE LOST FOR CHRIST. *Amen.*

## *Being optimistic*

*"I also say to you that you are Peter, and upon this rock I will build My church; and the gates of Hades will not overpower it." Matthew 16:18 (NASB)*

"This is not a bad thing," said my friend who was a former Muslim but is now a Christ follower. I had just commented about the new, elaborate mosque built in our city and asked her what she thought about it. I wasn't sure that I had heard her correctly and asked her what she meant. "People will go there trying to find God," she stated, "but they will not have success because He is not there. Then they will come to the believers and will find Jesus, the Messiah, as the true God."

Here were a woman and her husband who were not only former Muslims but also former communists. Her optimism surprised me; despite living in a place where believers are greatly outnumbered, she had complete faith that Jesus was building His church in her city and the gates of hell would not prevail against it. They were excited about the opportunities the Lord was giving them to share the Gospel in a place that is dominated by Islam and the pursuit of material wealth.

There seems to be a lot of pessimism about the state of the church today and how it will stand up to the twin threats of secularism and Islam. Do we believe that as part of God's kingdom, we are always winning? May we have optimistic faith.

—FRED, CENTRAL ASIAN PEOPLES

*Your kingdom, Lord,* IS ADVANCING THROUGHOUT THE WORLD. MAY MORE PEOPLE GROUPS IN CENTRAL ASIA HEAR YOUR WORD, ACCEPT YOUR TRUTH, AND TELL OTHERS ABOUT JESUS. *Amen.*

# *Generation after generation*

*"The boundary lines have fallen for me in pleasant places; indeed, I have a beautiful inheritance." Psalm 16:6 (HCSB)*

It's not every day you meet a fourth-generation believer from Lottie Moon's church. The government-registered, nearly century-and-a-half old church still has an active congregation. I was privileged to have coffee with a young believer whose great-grandmother, grandmother, and mother had all come to faith through the ministry of this church. Although she never knew her great-grandmother, she had heard stories about her and the early days of the church.

She told me of her faithful grandmother, who made sure she attended church every Sunday, and her atheist mother, who had been part of China's Red Guard during the years of the Cultural Revolution. At her grandmother's funeral, she began to understand her grandmother's relationship with Jesus. She knew something was missing in her life and fell to her knees, asking Him to be her Lord, too.

The loving church family and an English teacher helped her grow as a Christian. And then, her mother came into the family of faith. Four generations of women in her family belonged to Jesus.

Just an hour before my coffee visit with this young woman, she had led someone to Jesus. How similar to Miss Moon she seemed to be! I was encouraged by God's faithfulness.

—G.L.S., EAST ASIAN PEOPLES

*Great is Your faithfulness,* FATHER. MAY YOU CONTINUE TO MAKE GENERATIONS OF DISCIPLES FROM THIS VERY CHURCH WHO WILL SHARE THEIR FAITH AND BE EXAMPLES OF YOUR SAVING GRACE. *Amen.*

# *God is in control*

*"And my God will supply every need of yours according to his riches in glory in Christ Jesus." Philippians 4:19 (ESV)*

Not believing my eyes, we walked to our vehicle that was completely surrounded by police. With our shopping bags in hand, we learned from the police that a lady, who had been kidnapped at gunpoint, insisted that our vehicle was her stolen car. Apparently guilty until proven innocent, my husband and I were taken to jail, fingerprinted, and separated.

As the jailer took me to the women's side of the prison, I felt a tear running down my cheek and prayed silently, *God, please help me.* When we reached the small cell, there were seven other women incarcerated. "I am putting you with the nice ones," said the jailer. I was scared but knew God was with me. The inmates invited me to sit on the floor, and I explained that we were falsely accused of stealing a vehicle and were in this country to share God's Good News. One lady helped me with my incorrect Spanish. Another lady told me that she prays to God, but He never answers her. God was working, despite my Spanish, so I shared with her that God hears us, but sometimes He answers my prayers in a way that I didn't expect.

God is faithful to be with us every step of the way.

—DEBBIE, AMERICAN PEOPLES

*Merciful Father,* WOULD YOU DRAW THESE WOMEN IN PRISON TO YOURSELF? THANK YOU THAT ALTHOUGH THIS MISSIONARY HAD TO BE TEMPORARILY INCARCERATED, YOU USED HER TO BE THE LIGHT OF CHRIST TO THESE PRISONERS. STRENGTHEN MISSIONARIES TODAY WHO HAVE PRISON MINISTRIES. *Amen.*

# *God's forgiveness is complete*

*"But God demonstrates His own love toward us, in that while we were yet sinners, Christ died for us." Romans 5:8 (NASB)*

"So you see, I've hated my son for all these years." The woman looked at me with deep hurt, waiting for help in making sense of her guilt. I had just shared a lesson from Matthew 18 about the need to receive God's forgiveness, so that we could freely wipe away the debts others owe us. Sixteen years before, she had tried to abort her son but failed. Her son was born and grew to be incredibly bright, loving, and tender. The fact that he was so unusually gifted only made her feel worse—she had tried to kill him! Because of guilt, even the sight of him was painful, and her hatred had grown. Of course, the son had no understanding of this and tried hard to win his mother's approval.

Before she had heard of Jesus, God demonstrated His love for her. I gently shared God's grace with her. I encouraged her to see her son, not as a reminder of her guilt, but as a reminder of God's love for her. He forgives even though we do not deserve it. He gave His only Son for us while we were yet sinners, and He gave her a special son as a reminder.

She left that night a changed lady. How incredible to see the simple truth of God's Word change lives.

—DANA, CENTRAL ASIAN PEOPLES

*Heavenly Father,* I PRAY FOR THE RELATIONSHIP BETWEEN THIS MOTHER AND SON. MAY YOU RESTORE THE YEARS THAT WERE LOST. MAY YOU SURROUND BOTH OF THEM WITH YOUR EVERLASTING LOVE. *Amen.*

## Hope anchored in a promise

*"Before you were born I set you apart and appointed you as my prophet to the nations." Jeremiah 1:5 (NLT)*

While rising, I felt a strange sensation come over me. I walked into the room where my wife was and said, "Honey, I do not feel good." At that moment, I started to black out and collapsed. My cell phone fell out of my hand and slid across the room. My wife rushed to feel my pulse and said, "Your heartbeat is not normal. I need to go for help."

Lying on the cold, tile floor and fighting to stay conscious, I began to pray, *Lord, if You take my life today, I am ready to meet You. You know how much I love my family. Please be with them. I believe You have called me to be a spokesman to the nations. If You continue to give me life, I will dedicate my existence to that cause.* When I finished my prayer, a strange thing happened. My cell phone beeped as it received a text message. I could not reach the phone, but later at the hospital, I read the earlier text. The words of Jeremiah 1:5 were there. My soul was uplifted with that promise from God. Many people doubted that I would be able to continue overseas service, but I had hope. I had a promise from the great I AM, and He does not break His promises.

—D.H., SOUTHEAST ASIAN PEOPLES

*A timely word,* A HOPEFUL WORD, A PROMISING WORD, A PROPHETIC WORD, A BLESSED WORD, AN ENCOURAGING WORD, A HEALING WORD—YOUR WORDS, OH LORD, ARE A BALM FOR MY SOUL. THANK YOU. *Amen.*

# I have never, but He is able

*"Therefore He is always able to save those who come to God through Him, since He always lives to intercede for them." Hebrews 7:25 (HCSB)*

I have never spent weeks living in a tent made from rice sacks. I have never waited for relief goods to arrive, my stomach gnawing with hunger. I have never been afraid to go home. Yet thousands of displaced people experience these difficulties as a way of life. Can a few kilos of rice, a can of sardines, a bar of soap, and some noodles impact their hopelessness? It can and it did. When others said, "You won't be able to get past the barricades," a small group of believing servants delivered not only the relief goods but also the message of Good News to people who had never heard. He is able to bring spiritual abundance to destitute places through the story of Jesus.

Can clothing and shoes given to help meet the needs of refugees make a difference? Yes. When others questioned why such people should be helped and denied them assistance because of their ethnicity, a group of young students spent a week abundantly giving to the needy. Others interceded while some believers took a step of faith and courage to bring gifts of love and the message of salvation. And the receivers wept.

I have never, but He is able.

—I., SOUTHEAST ASIAN PEOPLES

*Fairest Lord Jesus,* USE CHRISTIAN BELIEVERS TO REACH OUT TO REFUGEES AFFECTED BY NATURAL DISASTERS OR WAR. WITH PHYSICAL FOOD OFFERED, GIVE THE BREAD OF LIFE AND LIVING WATER. *Amen.*

# A child's testimony

*"... I have called you friends, for all things that I have heard from My Father I have made known to you. You did not choose Me but I chose you, and appointed you that you would go and bear fruit, and that your fruit would remain ..."*
John 15:15–16 (NASB)

As a two-year worker, I have the privilege of teaching missionary children. Perhaps that doesn't seem to be a very important or glamorous job, but I soon began to see how important it was. By teaching the kids, I was giving their parents the chance to learn the culture and share the Gospel. There were challenges. Teaching several grade levels and working with kids during periods of culture shock is not that simple. The kids weren't the only ones learning. The kids taught me much. I was amazed at how much they loved God and knew His heart. Every morning when we would pray together, most of the children would pray for their local neighbors to follow Jesus.

Unexpectedly, one of my students had an asthma attack during class and had to be taken to the hospital. Tragically, after a week of setbacks, she died. It was as if we had lost our sister. But God has been our rock during the storm.

In one of her last papers, Anna wrote, "I don't know how I could ever repay God for doing so much." Already, people have come to Christ because of her story. Because of Anna's love for Christ, the fruit from her short life will continue to spread for many years.

—ALANA, NORTHERN AFRICAN AND MIDDLE EASTERN PEOPLES

*Thank You,* GENTLE FATHER, FOR TOUCHING OTHER LIVES THROUGH ANNA. CONTINUE TO EXTEND OUR CHRISTIAN FAMILY THROUGH THIS YOUNG GIRL'S STORY. EMBOLDEN AND EMPOWER ME TO SHARE MY STORY WITH THE LOST AROUND ME. I TRULY WANT MY LIFE TO COUNT FOR YOU. *Amen.*

# Still standing

"and he will stand, for the Lord is able to make him stand." Romans 14:4c
(NASB)

Our years in Africa have not been easy. The difficulties have not been
electricity going on and off, dirty water, or difficulty in shopping and
cooking. True difficulties have come from postpartum depression and
being away from close friends and family. I cannot say how many times
my prayers were sent up to heaven through the groaning of the Holy
Spirit. I felt like I wasn't standing up to the trials or fighting valiantly
against the odds.

Through it all, God was my constant companion. Even when it felt
like He wasn't there, I *knew* He was. I knew that when my pain was so
great that I couldn't even form thoughts, the Holy Spirit was crying out
on my behalf. Sometimes just "hanging on" is standing. Crying out to
God is standing. Trusting God to be in charge is standing. I did not do
these things myself. God made me stand by helping me to hang on, to
cry out, and to trust.

There are some struggles in which we can feel God stiffening our
spine, making us stand. There are many struggles that require spiritual
hindsight in order to see how God's hand was at work. Even though we
feel we are weak, if we are hanging on to God, we are still standing.

—Nicole, Sub-Saharan African Peoples

*Mighty God,* You are my Rock, standing tall in turbulent waters. For missionaries experiencing dark days, strengthen them today with Your mighty power.
*Amen.*

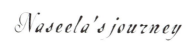

# Naseela's journey

*"Yet even now I know that whatever You ask from God, God will give You."*
John 11:22 (HCSB)

Ten years ago, "Naseela" moved to Europe as a pregnant, 19-year-old bride. When her abusive marriage ended, she was left alone in a foreign culture. Desiring a better education and life for her son, Naseela decided to apply for a visa to remain. Her applications were repeatedly denied. After seven years of visa struggles, I reassured Naseela, my friend of four years, that if the Lord desired for her to live here, He would make a way.

Soon after, her lawyer's appeal for the visa was once again denied. Worry mounted. Naseela and her son feared that they would soon be deported. I continued to pray with her often. One day, the Lord spoke to my heart, assuring me that when her lawyer appealed the next time, the visa would be approved. I felt that God wanted me to tell this to her. I was hesitant. What if these were just my own hopeful thoughts? If her visa was denied, what kind of witness would this be for God? But the Lord continued to nudge me, so I told her. Naseela was still unsure but appreciated my prayers. The day of the court hearing arrived and by God's grace, Naseela's visa application was finally approved! Not only was Naseela amazed, but my faith increased beyond measure.

I learned a lot about trusting His voice that day.

—SUE, EUROPEAN PEOPLES

*I hear many voices,* LORD, AS I SILENTLY WAIT BEFORE YOU. ARE THEY MY OWN IDLE, MUDDLED THOUGHTS? OR ARE THEY THE FRUIT OF YOUR SPIRIT'S PROMPTINGS ON MY HEART? HELP ME TO WALK CLOSER TO YOU SO THAT I'LL CLEARLY RECOGNIZE YOUR VOICE. *Amen.*

# One of them

*"strengthening the hearts of the disciples by encouraging them to continue in the faith, and by telling them, 'It is necessary to pass through many troubles on our way into the kingdom of God.'" Acts 14:22 (HCSB)*

"The women in my Bible study group want us to get matching outfits," a new missionary shared. "Does this mean they have accepted me?" I answered, "You are no longer an outsider."

I later thought of this conversation when walking into the church building wearing a black skirt and white blouse. As I placed a blue scarf around my neck and sat beside my friends with the same outfit, the pastor commissioned us to teach a Bible study that we had just completed. Our goal was to disciple 20,000 women between the large group of trained women.

Thinking about the early days of this church, which coincided with my first days as a missionary, I remembered the struggles of the older and wiser missionary women who began the first women's Bible studies in the new church. In those early days, there were more disappointments than joys, but I was seeing the fruit of their work.

Still sitting in the crowd, I began to wonder what my role was now. God is using Kenyans to do His work. I then remembered the unique opportunities God gave me to strengthen and encourage Kenyan Christians in the past week. This is what God is calling me to do. I am no longer the leader, but the encourager.

—Bert, Sub-Saharan African Peoples

*Thank You, Father,* for the pioneering work of female missionaries. Their perseverance and reliance upon You continues to bear fruit even today. All praise and glory to You. *Amen.*

## *Running the race*

*"Do you not know that those who run in a race all run, but only one receives the prize? Run in such a way that you may win." 1 Corinthians 9:24 (NASB)*

We never dreamed God would call us to live and work in Guatemala. "Welcome!" our church members cheerfully shouted when they greeted a group of stateside volunteers. As one of the Guatemalan ladies in the church grabbed a volunteer's hand, we saw a look of amazement on the volunteer's face. Tears filled his eyes as he stared at the words on the Guatemalan woman's shirt: "Eric Griffin Memorial Run." Calling his uncle and cousin over, who were also stateside volunteers, we saw the same reaction on their faces. As the volunteer team circled around, staring at the shirt, this Guatemalan woman was unaware that the T-shirt she had purchased secondhand bore the name of the volunteer's brother.

Eric Griffin was born with Down syndrome and had touched many lives. A race had been named in Eric's memory when he passed away in 1992. Each year, T-shirts are printed with his name, and one providentially made it all the way to Guatemala. Only God could have put that particular T-shirt on that lady that day. And only God could bring that particular team thousands of miles away from their home and then have Eric's brother, uncle, and cousin be right there at that moment in time! God encouraged us that we have a race to run for Him, and we are to run in a way that brings victory.

—SARAH ANN, AMERICAN PEOPLES

*Thank You* FOR THE ENCOURAGEMENT YOU GAVE THIS FAMILY, LORD. CONTINUE TO USE THEM IN YOUR KINGDOM WORK. ENCOURAGE VOLUNTEERS TODAY WHO ARE SERVING ALL OVER THE WORLD. *Amen.*

# A Thanksgiving surprise

*"In Him, you also, after listening to the message of truth, the gospel of your salvation—having also believed, you were sealed in Him with the Holy Spirit of promise." Ephesians 1:13 (NASB)*

Olgerd faithfully came to English class to improve his English. Each week, he eagerly conversed in English with his fellow students during conversation practice. However, during comprehension time, when Bible verses were read and discussed, "Olgerd" consistently pulled a Russian newspaper from his briefcase to read. From time to time he peered around the edges of his paper, but for the most part, Olgerd remained entrenched behind his newspaper fortress.

I became increasingly frustrated in his lack of interest in the Bible. When the semester was over, his English had improved dramatically, and we moved to another city.

On Thanksgiving Day, my cell phone rang. "Don, this is Olgerd, your English student. I know that today is your American holiday of Thanksgiving. I wanted to say thank you. Thank you for teaching me about Jesus. Recently, I repented and am following Jesus. I will be baptized this weekend, and I am a greeter at church."

All of my earlier frustrations melted. God was working in Olgerd when we didn't see it. As we continue to teach English, I keep my eyes open for the other Olgerds God sends our way. We may not think they are listening, but they are.

—DON, EUROPEAN PEOPLES

*Your Word*, OH LORD, IS ABLE TO PIERCE THROUGH WALLS OF DISINTEREST, UNBELIEF, EVEN HOSTILITY, INTO THE HEART OF MAN. HELP ME TO TRUST IN THE MIGHTY POWER OF YOUR GOSPEL TO TRANSFORM LIVES. USE OLGERD TO BE A BOLD WITNESS FOR CHRIST. *Amen.*

# *Where two or more ...*

*"For where two or three have gathered together in My name, I am there in their midst." Matthew 18:20 (NASB)*

Typical for our family on Saturday mornings, we packed everyone in the truck and headed to one of the villages to meet with believers of the church we planted four years earlier. The church had struggled with not having a national leader and with constant social pressure from others not to follow the way of Christ.

As we arrived that day, we weren't expecting many people to be at the designated place, but we were surprised when only two men were present. There were plenty of excuses for why they were the only two and why the other believers had not come, but we felt a bit discouraged.

My husband decided to go ahead and lead a short, informal service for those of us present. We sang some familiar Aymara hymns and kneeled together to pray. Then my husband began to share from the book of Philippians. As our family and these two faithful men sat outside on the hill, listening to God's Word, I felt the Lord reminding me that He was receiving just as much honor and glory from our little gathering as He would from a large group having a formal service. What truly matters is that God receives glory from His children.

—KELLY, AMERICAN PEOPLES

*Thank You, Father,* FOR THIS REMINDER THAT BIGGER ISN'T BETTER NECESSARILY. YOU SEEK HEARTS THAT ARE WHOLLY TURNED TO YOU. DRAW MANY AYMARA PEOPLE TO YOURSELF. *Amen.*

# Showing His love

*"And the King will answer them, 'I assure you: Whatever you did for one of the least of these brothers of Mine, you did for Me.'" Matthew 25:40 (HCSB)*

The stench of urine and unwashed bodies flooded my nostrils as I entered the orphanage for the first time. Dirty faces turned toward the noise of the metal door slamming shut behind me. Some of the small faces displayed cleft lips or mental disorders. Some of the little bodies were twisted by cerebral palsy. Immediately, tiny hands stretched out with the plea, "Auntie, hold me!" Eyes lit up as I pulled toys from my bag. Laughter echoed as I held one child after another.

After a year of frequent visits, I am amazed at the changes that have occurred in the orphanage. A preschool for the older children holds daily classes. A Christian teacher introduces praise songs, and the sound of innocent voices singing to God encourages me. Four women now work hard to keep the rooms clean and the children well-fed.

When the "foreign aunties" walk into the room, the children run to us with arms outstretched or sit in their wheelchairs and clap for joy. Once cooped up inside those four dirty walls, the children now make occasional excursions to the park or to the lawn outside their doors. While we do not know what will happen to these children once they become adults, at least we can make sure they know that they are loved by God and Christians during their childhood.

—R.C., East Asian Peoples

*Merciful Father,* I casually pass by scores of closed doors every day. What special need is waiting for me to fulfill just on the other side? Bless these orphans and surround them with Your unending love. *Amen.*

# *Letters*

*"Then Moses said to the LORD, 'Please, Lord, I have never been eloquent, ... for I am slow of speech and slow of tongue.' The LORD said to him, 'Who has made man's mouth?' ..." Exodus 4:10–11 (NASB)*

Walking to the gate, I noticed another note tucked into the corner nearest the fragrant honeysuckle. Like an excited schoolgirl, I unfolded the letter. "Candy, I'm happy you wrote me back. I'm very lonely. I have no friends or family here. I cannot understand why you want to be my friend, but thank you. Sorry my English no good and my spelling bad. Thank you for giving me your Bible and showing me where to read. Please write back. Your friend, 'Eve.'"

For a year, I prayed that God would use me to reach my neighbors with the Good News. Like Moses, I wondered why God would choose me. I told God that I am a writer, not a talker.

One day, a neighbor's child came to my door with a note requesting an English novel to read. After praying, I sent a Janette Oke novel in which two ladies leave notes for one another. After loaning this book, I received the first note tucked into my front gate that asked if Eve and I could exchange notes, just like the fictional ladies.

Thus began a friendship. First through letters, then by meetings, we wrote and talked about forgiveness, love, and the Gospel. Telling God that He could not use me was ludicrous. He has a purpose for each of us.

—CANDY, CENTRAL ASIAN PEOPLES

*I, too, loving Lord,* DESIRE TO REACH MY NEIGHBORS WITH THE GOOD NEWS OF JESUS CHRIST. MAY YOU BRING SALVATION TO EVE. MAY YOU BRING SALVATION TO MY NEIGH-BORHOOD. *Amen.*

# Turning pain into triumph

*"The* Lord *gives, and the* Lord *takes away. Praise the name of the* Lord*."*
Job 1:21 (HCSB)

God meets us in our disappointments and joys, many times turning our disappointments into joys if we let Him. A year ago, I wrote to a dear, wise friend who always knows how to encourage. I expressed disappointment in my infertility. She sent me a book about having a calm heart, and it was just what I needed for God to remind me that He was in control.

Reading the book, I felt led by God to share it with ten women where I serve. Worriers by nature, these women have gone through many challenges. Discovering that the book had been translated into the local language, I could hardly wait. Encouraged, I started a women's Bible study although my language ability was limited.

Some of these women were studying the Bible for the first time in their lives. Each week we met, it seemed that my circumstances got harder, but my trust in God grew. Toward the end of the study, I had a miscarriage, a hard thing to endure. However, God used my heartache to relate in a small way to the hurt these women had faced. Had I not gone through this lengthy struggle, there would have been no need for my friend to send me the book. Ten women would not have been touched by its message. Praise the Lord!

—Amy, European Peoples

*Sovereign Lord,* the tears that I shed often water the harvest field about me. Open my eyes that I may see Your Spirit at work and join You in introducing hearts to the River of Life. *Amen.*

## An amazing adventure

*"... diligently watch yourselves, so that you don't forget the things your eyes have seen and so that they don't slip from your mind as long as you live."*
Deuteronomy 4:9 (HCSB)

As we dropped our guest off at his hotel, I noticed that I was feeling more encouraged than I had in months. My husband and I had spent the evening with a stateside visitor and had shared stories from our time overseas. The hours had passed quickly as we, through much laughter and occasional tears, recounted our amazing adventure in the Middle East.

I could hardly comprehend all that God had done. My heart soared in gratitude as I remembered His faithfulness toward us—the countless demonstrations of His presence, the amazing acts of protection and provision, the perfectly orchestrated divine appointments, and His sustaining grace through the darkest of days. Through challenges, there was no mistaking the gracious hand of God. Every victory was a sweet gift from above, a reminder that God can use even humble servants like us to glorify His name.

What a powerful exercise "remembering" can be! In our work, the pressure is great, and the temptation to allow circumstances to overwhelm us is constant. But the antidote God prescribed for the Israelites centuries ago is just as effective today. When we are diligent to remember God's faithfulness of yesterday, we will find confidence in His sufficiency for today.

—HOPE, NORTHERN AFRICAN AND MIDDLE EASTERN PEOPLES

*Forgive me, Father,* WHEN I DON'T PAUSE LONG ENOUGH TO RECOUNT VICTORIES WON BY YOUR POWERFUL HAND. ENCOURAGE MISSIONARIES TODAY THAT THEIR WORK IS NOT IN VAIN. THANK YOU FOR ALL THESE STORIES THIS MONTH ON ENCOURAGEMENT. *Amen.*

# DECEMBER

## Hope for the World

*We're meant to be like multicolored Christmas lights attached to one electrical cord called the Holy Spirit and strung strategically all over the earth. Yep, millions of lights on one cord, with the guts to shine more brightly because we know the others are there.*

—BETH MOORE

I will never forget my first Christmas as an international missionary in 1992. Our young family was living in a village in what was formerly a homeland called Bophuthatswana, South Africa. Being in the southern hemisphere, it was hot in December—so hot that you had to take a cold bath, lie on the cement floor, and point a fan at yourself to get relief in our un-air-conditioned house.

We brought one Christmas decoration with us, knowing that we would still be in language school during the season. It was a ceramic Christmas tree that my sister-in-law made, the kind you plug in and a lightbulb shines through tiny colored bulbs on the outside of the tree. But when we unpacked it, we heard jingling—lots of jingling. Opening the package, I found the ceramic tree broken into many tiny pieces. I sat at my kitchen table, with sweat pouring down my face, and cried my eyeballs out.

Then I got up and announced to my two small children and husband that we were going to glue it back together because *this was our only Christmas tree*. My husband went to the nearest South African town and bought the closest thing to super glue that he could find, which turned out to be model airplane glue. He picked up some green, white, and black model airplane paint as well.

That night, the painstaking process began of laying out the tiny, ceramic pieces like a jigsaw puzzle and gluing them together. I wasn't sure what kind of tree we'd have when it was finished, but we were all determined. After two weeks of piecing, gluing, and painting, it was time to plug it in. Supper was over, the dishes were washed, and we turned out the lights. My son plugged the cord into the transformer. Voila! The tree was illuminated, never mind that we could see the light shining through every single crack!

That tree and the intense heat were unforgettable, but even more unforgettable was our fellowship with local Christians who met in a classroom at the primary school. They helped us that Christmas to focus on Jesus more than anything else. We didn't have family, old friends, snow, lots of presents, or turkey, but we had Jesus and these vibrant new friends. It was one of the best Christmases ever.

This month's stories end the book well. They are a beautiful reminder of where our focus should be this month and every month—Jesus Christ! When everything normal is stripped away, it is not difficult to see the evidence of what really matters. Christmas is about what God did for us when He gave us the greatest gift, His Son. We can get wrapped up in the shopping lists, the holiday parties, and the decorations, but those things don't last. Jesus lasts forever!

*—Kim P. Davis*

# Are you a Christmas?

*"... nations who do not know you will run to you. For the* LORD *your God, even the Holy One of Israel, has glorified you." Isaiah 55:5 (HCSB)*

December was upon us, but there was nothing to signify that Christmas was just around the corner. There was no snow heralding the change of seasons in the desert landscape of our village. No shopping malls with Christmas wares or jingling Salvation Army bells to remind us that the celebration of the birth of our Savior was fast approaching. It was odd that it should be this way since we live in the region where He was born so long ago. It was as if Christmas had been wiped off the calendar.

Seeking to meet people, my husband entered a restaurant. There he began a simple conversation, using limited language skills, with a man who was waiting on his order. At the end of the conversation, the man asked, "Are you a Christmas?" Surprised by the error of the man's question, my husband was able to share who a Christian really is, salvation, and redemption.

My husband later related to our family what he had asked. What a powerful question: Christmas is here in this village! It is alive in the hearts of our family. Christmas is not just a seasonal holiday; it is a change of life. It is the presence of God's love shown through "Christmases" serving all over the world. Am I a Christmas? You'd better believe it!

—BARBARA, NORTHERN AFRICAN AND MIDDLE EASTERN PEOPLES

*Heavenly Father,* LET THE SAVIOR SHINE THROUGH ME. GIVE MISSIONARIES AND ME OPPORTUNITIES TO SHARE THE STORY OF CHRISTMAS WITH MUSLIMS, HINDUS, BUDDHISTS, ATHEISTS, AND OTHERS WHO MAY BE CURIOUS ABOUT THE SEASON. THANK YOU FOR THE GIFT OF YOUR SON. *Amen.*

## *Doing what's necessary*

*"I do all things for the sake of the gospel, so that I may become a fellow partaker of it."* 1 Corinthians 9:23 (NASB)

"My friends want to take you to the banya," Roma said after Bible study. "When can we go?" was my enthusiastic response. I had never enjoyed this experience, but since it was a social event, I was keen. All I knew was that it included ice and freezing water.

Arriving at the deserted village on a crisp, December morning, we began to cut wood for a fire. No problem! I had done this as a child on an Alaskan homestead. Yet the vigorous workout and thin, cold air caused me to pass out temporarily. A red streak on my forehead from falling was not going to keep me from the experience.

A short hike brought us to a small hut. With the traditional felt cap and sandals, I wanted to prove that I was no wimp. My friends immediately gave me lessons in swatting my body with softened tree limbs that had been placed in a basin of hot water. Next, we went to a hole cut in the frozen pond. I looked down, and a friend's head bobbed on the frigid water's surface. My turn was next. The cold plunge was shocking; my face must have revealed the pain. The men grabbed my hands, rescuing me from the icy water.

I determined that day that I could do what it took for the Gospel.

—RANDY, EUROPEAN PEOPLES

*I acknowledge, Lord,* THAT SOMETIMES IT IS NOT CONVENIENT AND EVEN PAINFUL TO BE YOUR WITNESS. GIVE MISSIONARIES AND ME THE STRENGTH TO "DO ALL THINGS FOR THE SAKE OF THE GOSPEL." *Amen.*

# A work in progress

*"Love not the world, neither the things that are in the world. If any man love the world, the love of the Father is not in him." 1 John 2:15 (KJV)*

"There is nothing magical about an airplane ride across the Pacific Ocean that will make you into a missionary." Those wise words were heard at my missionary training. The person I was in the States upon my departure was the same person 20 hours later at my arrival in East Asia.

I thought giving up everything in America was enough. I gave up a good job. I had forsaken holiday times, especially Christmas with family, and given up watching Sunday afternoon football on TV. When I got to Asia, I thought I was finished sacrificially giving up things, and in fact, I acted as if I was entitled to receive. I turned into a more self-absorbed, unlovely version of myself.

Nothing I left behind was evil, but loving these things of the world had become so deeply imbedded in my soul that they were crowding out my love for God. Extricating those things from my heart has been painful but necessary and freeing.

Arrival on the field is just the beginning of the sacrifices one has to make, not the end of them. I have a long way to go until God is finished making me into what He intends for me to be. Getting overseas just gave me the eyes to see it more clearly.

—A WORKER WITH EAST ASIAN PEOPLES

*Lord,* I CONFESS THAT THERE ARE THINGS THAT I PUT BEFORE YOU SUCH AS _____ I RELEASE THOSE THINGS TO YOU. I WANT TO LOVE YOU ABOVE ALL ELSE RATHER THAN BEING SELF-ABSORBED. IN THE NAME OF JESUS, DO THIS WORK IN ME. *Amen.*

# The Christmas tree at Easter

*"So when He was raised from the dead, His disciples remembered that He said this; and they believed the Scripture and the word which Jesus had spoken."*
John 2:22 (NASB)

It was Easter Sunday. As I was listening to everyone singing about the resurrection of our Lord, I looked over into one of the corners of the church building and noticed that a Christmas tree was still up, fully decorated. Thirty-three years from Jesus' birth to resurrection were represented in that room.

The day continued to be unique. I went to town to purchase a gift. When I found what I wanted, I began to barter in true African fashion over the price. Finally, the Muslim shopkeeper said, "You would treat a vendor like that with such a low price on Easter?" I laughed and asked him, "Do you even know what Easter is about?" He said, "Of course. It is the birth of Jesus." I grinned, thinking about the Christmas tree, and began to share the Gospel from creation to the resurrection.

After we talked, this Muslim prayed and committed his life to Christ. I found out that he had been reading the Bible lately because he could not understand the Quran. God had been drawing him.

Christmas and Easter—two great seasons with the two best gifts of all. I was determined to think of the two together from then on.

—KATHY, SUB-SAHARAN AFRICAN PEOPLES

*Praise You, Father,* THAT THE BABY JESUS IS OUR RESURRECTED LORD! MAKE THIS MUSLIM MAN A COURAGEOUS TESTIMONY OF YOUR GRACE SO OTHER MUSLIMS IN WEST AFRICA WILL FOLLOW YOU. *Amen.*

# Christmas every Sunday

*"Thanks be to God for His indescribable gift!" 2 Corinthians 9:15 (NASB)*

We knew our first Christmas in Uganda would be celebrated differently, but we were shocked at how different. Where were the Christmas carols and special Christmas services in the churches? Worship on Sundays during December was just like all other Sundays. The same Ugandan praise songs with many repeated verses, testimonials, greetings, and sermons were present, but all with no mention of the advent of Christ.

*But Lord,* I complained, *how can they not sing carols? How can they celebrate Christmas without singing "Silent Night" or sharing from Luke 2 or hanging red and green decorations?* But they did! Mamas with babies on their backs, men, and children worshipped God with eyes closed, hands lifted in praise, and faces tilted upward with sweet smiles of adoration for their God. The Ugandans were celebrating the birth of Christ every Sunday. Christmas wasn't defined by expensive pageants, huge Christmas gift exchanges, or even cherished traditions. It was focused joy in Christ. The ravages of war, HIV/AIDS, life in refugee camps, poverty, disease, and a short life span had taught these believers the indescribable Gift given to them in Jesus. As I experienced worship with our Ugandan brothers and sisters, I was challenged to focus on Jesus, the Savior of the world.

—CLAUDIA, SUB-SAHARAN AFRICAN PEOPLES

*I admit, Lord,* THAT I CAN GET CAUGHT UP IN THE TRADITIONS, THE BUSYNESS, AND THE COMMERCIALISM OF CHRISTMAS. THIS CHRISTMAS SEASON, TEACH ME HOW TO FOCUS MY ATTENTION ON YOUR SON, JESUS. *Amen.*

# The perfect gift

*"For the wages of sin is death, but the free gift of God is eternal life in Christ Jesus our Lord."* Romans 6:23 (NASB)

It was a balmy day in early December. Children and curious parents crowded together on a grassy field beside the lake near our home in Madagascar. Each person was fixed on what they were going to get from the foreigner. Few realized the real gift we wanted them to have.

I began to share a Christmas message with our Malagasy neighbors. "It's almost Christmas, and all the children are thinking about gifts. I want to tell you about a gift unlike any other—the greatest gift of all. Some gifts wear out and get old, but this gift never does. Some gifts don't fit or are not what we want, but this gift is the perfect one. It is free to all who will receive it, but it cost Someone dearly—He paid for it with His life. The gift I'm talking about is eternal life in Jesus Christ, the One whose birth we celebrate at Christmas."

After the message, our kids helped distribute items my sister had sent us: "Jesus loves you" pencils, pencil bags, and other similar items. Everybody wanted to make sure he got something. In the midst of the chaos, we prayed that there would be those in the crowd who would finally understand and receive the real Gift of Christmas.

—MATT, SUB-SAHARAN AFRICAN PEOPLES

*Your Son* IS THE REAL GIFT OF CHRISTMAS, FATHER. MAY I BE MORE FOCUSED ON GIVING THE FREE GIFT OF ETERNAL LIFE THAN GIFTS UNDER A TREE. THANK YOU FOR THE PERFECT GIFT OF SALVATION. *Amen.*

# Grateful

*"In any and all circumstances I have learned the secret [of being content]— whether well-fed or hungry, whether in abundance or in need." Philippians 4:12b (HCSB)*

Stepping across the open ditch, we entered the pastor's tiny house. Our eyes slowly adjusted to the dim light. Half the dwelling was the congregation's meeting space, and the other half was the cramped living quarters for the pastor's family. Two rustic beds and a crib took up most of the space at one end of the room. The kitchen and living area made up the rest of the single-room parsonage. The lone bathroom served the family and the congregation!

A small bookcase caught our attention. "You seem to have several books," we commented. The pastor's wife, bouncing her baby on her hip while watching their two preschoolers, proudly showed us their theological library of about 20 books. Then a big smile broke across her face as she said, "We are truly blessed. God has given us so much. We are very fortunate to have so many wonderful books to read and study."

We saw the cramped, living quarters and the lack of creature comforts and felt compassion. The pastor's wife saw the luxury of having a library and counted her blessings. The ability to be content, no matter what life brings, is indeed a blessing. Even in bleak circumstances, especially when we're stressed about affording Christmas presents, God gives blessings other ways.

—Joe, American Peoples

*Help me* to notice Your blessings, Father, and help me to be content no matter the circumstances. You have indeed blessed me so much. You are worthy to be praised! *Amen.*

## God's beauty

*"And let the beauty of the LORD our God be upon us ..."* Psalm 90:17 (NKJV)

Today was the day! We were on our way to Romania for the beginning of our missionary adventure. Following a frazzling check-in of 12 bags, we settled into our plane seats. We looked at each other, and the tears flowed. Many had asked why we would do this upon retirement, especially with a grandbaby due later that year. I confess in that fleeting moment, I, too, asked, "Why?" The answer? "God is beautiful."

The move, language acquisition, and culture shock brought a flood of emotions, yet the thought of God's beauty persisted. I asked God to help me find what He wanted me to learn, and my research began. Later, my research concluded with this truth: It is in salvation that God's beauty is wonderfully manifested.

My husband and I serve a people group that has no point of reference for God's beauty. Their faith tradition does not teach about a loving God who magnificently demonstrated His beauty by sending His Son, our reason for celebrating Christmas. Whether it is telling an abandoned child that Jesus loves him or praying in Jesus' name, I thank God for each opportunity to share about His beauty.

As you follow the Lord's leading in your own life, do you find yourself asking, "Why?" Think upon God's beauty, for He is truly beautiful!

—CHARLOTTE, EUROPEAN PEOPLES

*Holy God,* BEAUTIFUL SAVIOR, YOU HAVE AN ANSWER FOR ALL MY "WHYS." REMIND ME OF YOUR BEAUTY TODAY IN WAYS I LEAST EXPECT. I WILL BE WATCHING. I DESIRE TO BE A SWEET AROMA TO YOU TODAY. *Amen.*

# Priest and water

*"Brothers, do not grow weary in doing good." 2 Thessalonians 3:13 (HCSB)*

Our first encounter with the local Orthodox priest was at a Christmas concert. He stood in the hall, discouraging people from attending and handing out propaganda about cults. His black-robed figure was a fixture at every event we planned. During children's camp, he told parents to pull their children out of the camp. He even called the police to verify the camp's license. Fortunately, the parents and police supported our ministry. The priest persisted in his vendetta for years while we continued to pray.

Recently, the priest built a home across the road from the camp. One day, the priest came hesitantly to the office to ask if he could get drinking water from the camp property, as his place did not have water. Then he said, "I apologize for my previous behavior toward your group. I was wrong to do what I did. I didn't know anything about you and thought you were here to cause trouble. Please forgive me."

This man who had been persecuting us was now apologizing. Over the years, we had been wearied by the priest's constant abuse, but we continued to pray for him. Now our hearts overflowed with thanksgiving and rejoiced as the priest allowed his son to attend our next children's camp.

—ROBIN, EUROPEAN PEOPLES

*As thousands* PRAYED FOR THIS PRIEST IN THE FIRST *VOICES OF THE FAITHFUL*, WE SEE HOW YOU ANSWERED PRAYERS FOR THIS MAN. THANK YOU, GOD, THAT YOU ARE SOVEREIGN AND DRAW PEOPLE WE PRAY FOR TO YOURSELF. CONTINUE TO WORK IN THIS MAN'S LIFE AND IN THE CHILDREN WHO ATTEND THESE CAMPS. *Amen.*

## *Spiritual sacrifices*

*"You also, as living stones, are being built up as a spiritual house for a holy priesthood, to offer up spiritual sacrifices acceptable to God through Jesus Christ."*
1 Peter 2:5 (NASB)

We challenged the new believers to secretly hand out as many Christmas party invitations as possible to friends and coworkers. On the day of the party, more than 220 seekers attended.

The whole Christmas program was focused on sharing the Gospel. As local believers shared the eight Gospel stories from creation to Christ, the listeners clearly caught the essential concepts of the Gospel and were moved. Then "Sister Yang," a CEO of a company, shared her testimony. Even though she is very busy, she uses all her time, except working and sleeping hours, to share the Gospel. In one year, she led more than 100 people to Jesus Christ, and 15 new churches were started.

Passionate for God, she offered the equivalent of one year's salary to support the Christmas party. That night, 69 nonbelievers gave their lives to Jesus.

On the day after Christmas, she met with Christian leaders at a restaurant to encourage the new believers to attend small groups. She treated them with noodles that cost the equivalent of 25 cents because she had only $4 in her pocket. She had sacrificed all. Her coworkers started offering their time and money to share the Gospel with seekers as she had done.

—A WORKER WITH EAST ASIAN PEOPLES

*Father,* THIS WOMAN'S SACRIFICE ASTOUNDS ME! LORD, CONTINUE TO GIVE HER COURAGE AND PROVIDE FOR HER NEEDS. GUIDE AND EMPOWER THIS GROUP OF YOUNG BELIEVERS, MULTIPLYING BELIEVERS AND CHURCHES THROUGH THEIR MINISTRY. *Amen.*

# The Christmas open house

*"Go therefore to the main highways, and as many as you find there, invite to the wedding feast." Matthew 22:9 (NASB)*

"How can we get to know our neighbors when they live behind high walls?" I complained to my husband. "If I ring their doorbell, I only get to talk with the maid. I couldn't even pick them out of a police lineup! When they leave their house, all I see is a car with darkened windows."

As I prayed that morning, the Lord gave me the idea of having a Christmas open house. When I mentioned it to our national pastor, he promised his support. "But don't be disappointed if no one comes," he warned, "as this is not cultural."

For two weeks, I made peanut brittle, cookies, and other goodies. I went door-to-door, introduced myself, and handed out invitations. My husband and I also gave invitations to the people we saw on a regular basis as we walked in the mornings.

Finally, the Christmas tree was up, manger scenes were assembled, and everything was ready. The morning of the event, our doorbell rang. A neighbor stood with a beautiful poinsettia. "Thank you for the invitation. I would love to come, but I have a wedding this afternoon." My stomach was in knots as the hour approached. Would anyone show? Then the doorbell began to ring. Before the afternoon was over, 60 people had come and new friendships were begun.

—Helen, American Peoples

*Father God,* as missionaries host parties during the Christmas season, bring those who are lost and seeking. Reveal to me if having an open house for my neighbors is something that I can do for Your glory. *Amen.*

# *What Christmas means to me*

*"... you shall name Him Jesus. He will be great and will be called the Son of the Most High; and the Lord God will give Him the throne of His father David; and He will reign over the house of Jacob forever, and His kingdom will have no end." Luke 1:31–33 (NASB)*

Christmas markets, carol singing, cold days and nights with maybe a dusting of snow, an abundance of fresh-cut evergreen trees, and unique decorations come to mind when I think of the 16 Christmases spent in Germany. What a thrill to experience the festive sights, the smell of spices and wood-burning fires, and the sounds of Christmas music through a different cultural lens. But a most meaningful aspect of the Christmas season has been spending time with friends.

Missionary families, a journeyman, an American study-abroad student, and a Senegalese young woman have eaten or stayed with us. Hosting someone from a Muslim background has caused a renewal in me of the significance of Christmas. Jesus' birth began something in history that has changed my life forever. What a refreshing experience to examine the meaning of Christmas from a new perspective so that it can be shared with others! I didn't get to have pork sausage in my stuffing last year due to our Muslim guest, but I was blessed by God who gave me the opportunity to share His Son.

What is God saying to you about the meaning of Christmas and how it applies to your everyday life? Does it make a difference?

—LAURA, EUROPEAN PEOPLES

*Giver of life,* GLORIOUS GOD, THE GIFT OF CHRISTMAS HAS CHANGED MY LIFE! REFRESH MISSIONARIES IN THEIR COMMITMENTS TO YOU AND MAKE THIS CHRISTMAS SEASON A TIME OF RENEWAL. *Amen.*

# Amid change, He never changes

*"You will keep in perfect peace the mind [that is] dependent [on You], for it is trusting in You." Isaiah 26:3 (HCSB)*

Christmas was memorable. The rains were good, the river was full, and a lone hippo rested in our stretch of the river. Fellow missionaries were with us as were my parents. We even had a football game on video to watch after dinner! But most of all, we were enjoying the celebration of the birth of Jesus.

In the back of my mind, I knew big changes were coming, but I did not want to think about it. I wanted to enjoy this last Christmas in my Zambian home and not think about the changes of the New Year. In just a few weeks, we were to move from rural Zambia to a city in Botswana. God was clear in His call, but the changes coming were big: exchanging 4x4 driving for highways, boats for traffic lights, homeschooling for regular school, and gardens for grocery stores. God's Word helped me to recognize that I could trust in the One who never changes.

Since our move, I have experienced and seen God's faithfulness in new ways. The time is appropriate for us to be in Botswana. I was reminded of this today when I met Mma Usedi (mah oo-SED-ee), a terminally ill lady who bowed her head with me in her front yard and trusted in Jesus. Praise Him, for He never changes.

—SHAWNA, SUB-SAHARAN AFRICAN PEOPLES

*Unchangeable God,* IN THE MIDST OF CHANGE IN MY LIFE, YOU ARE THE FIRM ANCHOR AND ROCK. THANK YOU THAT I CAN CLING TO YOU SO THAT I WON'T BE TOSSED ABOUT. BE WITH MISSIONARIES TODAY WHO ARE IN THE MIDST OF ASSIGNMENT CHANGES. *Amen.*

## Hearing, seeing, and more

*"The shepherds went back, glorifying and praising God for all that they had heard and seen, just as had been told them." Luke 2:20 (NASB)*

As the members of our small group walked into our apartment and smelled the potpourri simmering on the stove, they asked, "What is that odor?" They had never *smelled* Christmas. Once inside, they began looking at all the Christmas decorations. They closely examined each piece in our Nativity and wondered why animals were included. They had never *seen* Christmas.

We gathered around our table filled with my traditional Christmas goodies, such as the Hawaiian cheese ball, Swedish meat balls, ding bats, and chocolate peanut butter balls. This was their first time to *taste* Christmas. Then my husband and I asked our Chinese friends to help us decorate the tree. They acted like delighted children as they placed the ornaments on the tree. They had never before *touched* Christmas.

Lastly, we all sat in a circle, sang traditional carols, and my husband read the Christmas story. This was the first time they had ever *heard* Christmas.

We will never forget the joy felt that night as we shared the wonder of Christmas with new believers who had never experienced it before. The Holy Spirit bonded us together. Not because of traditions, but because of Jesus.

—C.Y., East Asian Peoples

*Loving Father,* hearing that You sent Your Son into the world and seeing the transformed lives of Your followers make a difference in people's lives. Give missionaries unique opportunities to share the experience of Christmas with the people around them. *Amen.*

# *Sketching the story*

*"then whoever calls on the name of the Lord will be saved."* Acts 2:21 (HCSB)

In mid-December, I traveled to a Buddhist mountain kingdom, a land known for tales of dragons. It was like experiencing an adventure from a historical novel. Although the people have some modern conveniences, they remain untouched by the world.

Being an artist, I searched for sketching opportunities and people to meet. At a town square, I began to sketch and noticed two young men watching me. I started a conversation by asking them if they could tell me any stories about their country. When they couldn't, I asked them if they had heard of Jesus. One had heard the name, but it was from some frightening movie. The other young man had never heard of Jesus. Both were interested.

I began to sketch an illustration while sharing the Gospel. Another young man came up and wanted to hear the story. Happily, I started again. The third young man told me that his aunt had become a Christian and had talked with him about following Jesus. He said that he didn't want to become a Christian because it was not accepted in his country.

I was glad to have this unusual opportunity to share God's Word in a remote place. It was a great way for me to celebrate the Christmas season. I pray that God will use this encounter to change three young lives.

—BRYSON, SOUTH ASIAN PEOPLES

*Dearest* AND PROFOUNDLY INTERESTED GOD, I PRAY FOR THESE THREE MEN. CAUSE THEM TO THINK ABOUT WHAT THEY HEARD ABOUT JESUS. BRING THEM EACH A COPY OF YOUR WORD. STRENGTHEN THE AUNT WHO IS SURE TO FACE PERSECUTION FOR HER FAITH. *Amen.*

# *"Good morning, Mary!"*

*"Glory to God in the highest, and on earth peace, good will toward men." Luke 2:14 (KJV)*

I will never forget my first Christmas in Africa. Christmas Day fell on a Sunday. When we arrived at the church building, we could feel the excitement. After wonderful, joyous singing, the Christmas story was presented in true African style through a youth-led drama.

Running down the aisle, a young man held a sheet so that it billowed out behind him. As he approached the front, a young woman was kneeling there as if in prayer. The first words out of the "angel's" mouth were not, "Greetings, Mary, favored one of God," but instead, "Mangwanani!" or "Good morning" in Shona! (I had never imagined the angel speaking anything but English.)

In that moment, the universal message of God coming to man struck me anew. Maybe the angel did not speak that long-ago day to Mary in Shona, but neither did he speak to her in English! God's message is for all people for all times. As the rest of the drama unfolded, God spoke to my heart about His eternal love message for the world. And even though that first African Christmas Day had some moments of homesickness, I was overwhelmed that God had called me to share His Good News in a far-off place.

May we be as eager as the angel to share the Good News!

—CHARLOTTE, SUB-SAHARAN AFRICAN PEOPLES

*Lord,* MAY I BE LIKE THE ANGEL BURSTING TO TELL THE GOOD NEWS OF JESUS, THE SAVIOR OF THE WORLD. I PRAY FOR OPPORTUNITIES THIS WEEK TO SHARE THE CHRISTMAS STORY. *Amen.*

## Showing kindness

*"Yes, you will be enriched in every way so that you can always be generous. And when we take your gifts to those who need them, they will thank God."*
2 Corinthians 9:11 (NLT)

Families lost nearly everything in the earthquake. "Margarita" lost virtually all her possessions, but her five turkeys survived. When I asked Margarita about her turkeys, hoping to get information to develop a community project for raising turkeys as a source of food and income, she enthusiastically told me about her birds.

A few weeks later, Margarita came to see me and offered to give me one of her turkeys, so we could have a turkey for Christmas dinner. In her big, black bag was a live, male turkey.

Because Margarita could not afford the turkey feed, three hens had died. She couldn't provide food for the remaining two, so she gave me the male. I expressed sincere gratitude and made a deal with her. Since my home wasn't a good place to raise a turkey, I asked if she would continue to care for it until Christmas and in exchange for her labor, I would provide feed for both turkeys. Margarita cried tears of joy.

We returned to the community to take turkey feed, food for the children, and vitamins for the elderly. Margarita gave her heart to Christ. I will always be humbled by the generosity of one who had so little.

—WAYNE, AMERICAN PEOPLES

*Heavenly Father,* SHOW ME WAYS THAT I CAN REACH OUT TO THE NEEDY WITHOUT BEING OFFENSIVE OR DESTROYING THEIR CONFIDENCE. ENCOURAGE THESE VILLAGERS IN THIS PARTICULAR COMMUNITY BY PROVIDING A MEANS TO SUPPORT THEMSELVES. ABOVE ALL, MAY THEY FIND ETERNAL LIFE IN YOU. *Amen.*

# Motherly neighbors

*"In everything give thanks; for this is God's will for you in Christ Jesus."*
1 Thessalonians 5:18 (NASB)

Life in our country involves moving often. With each move, God has provided me with a motherly neighbor who takes pity on me and helps me understand the culture. One neighbor's mothering left me considering whether I should be irritated, thankful, or just highly amused.

"Gul" walked in my home one day and insisted that I was cooking my meal incorrectly. Never mind that it was an American dish that was unknown to her. She finally brought some frozen peas to supplement the dinner that she was sure would be a disaster. My personal favorite is when Gul came for tea and scolded my husband because part of his T-shirt was untucked and showed beneath his polo. "Young man, in our country, we consider that *underwear!*"

To be fair, though, her mothering was a huge blessing. As queen bee of the apartment complex, she made sure the tenants befriended our family. She invited me to every ladies' tea. She taught me to cook local food. And when we had to move, Gul expressed genuine sadness.

I am learning to welcome each friendship God brings with thankfulness, receiving the frustrations along with the blessings. God sometimes chooses the most unlikely people to be a part of our lives.

—JOY, CENTRAL ASIAN PEOPLES

*Father,* BRING PEOPLE INTO THE LIVES OF MISSIONARIES WHO WILL NURTURE THEM IN CULTURAL ASPECTS. LORD, I THANK YOU FOR THE PEOPLE YOU HAVE BROUGHT INTO MY LIFE. HELP ME TO BE THANKFUL FOR THE FRUSTRATIONS AS WELL AS THE BLESSINGS. *Amen.*

# The comfort of the Christmas story

*"But Mary treasured all these things, pondering them in her heart."* Luke 2:19
(NASB)

Our daughter called to tell us that our son, Kris, and his girlfriend, Rebecca, had been in a terrible accident. Crying, Megan asked how quickly we could get to the States. A short time later, she called again with the tragic news that our son had not survived.

We had served in the Philippines for 15 years before transferring to South Asia. Our children graduated from Faith Academy in Manila and were now attending Southwest Baptist University. Kris was to graduate in December with a degree in criminal justice. Ironically, Kris had served 14 months in Iraq with the army reserve before returning to finish his college degree. He would have turned 27 three weeks after the accident.

The Christmas holidays that followed were filled with shock and grief. Christmas morning, we asked Megan if she wanted to read the Christmas story. No answer came. Her eyes reflected only sadness. I cried, said the simplest of prayers, and opened to Luke 2. Verse 19 about Mary spoke to me like never before. I started thinking about our past Christmases, especially remembering our family reenacting the Christmas story, with Kris narrating, when the children were young. God comforted me, much like Mary, with wonderful memories that I can treasure in my heart forever.

—PAM, SOUTH ASIAN PEOPLES

*Sovereign Lord,* COMFORT THIS FAMILY THAT STILL GRIEVES THE LOSS OF THEIR SON. ALSO, COMFORT THOSE WHO HAVE LOST A LOVED ONE THIS YEAR. MAY YOUR TENDER HAND OF COMPASSION ADMINISTER GRACE IN THEIR LOSS. *Amen.*

# Snow for Christmas

*"For He says to the snow, 'Fall to the earth,' and the torrential rains, His mighty torrential rains." Job 37:6 (HCSB)*

When God sent me to serve in Mexico, I left 10 grandchildren scattered among California, Arkansas, and Spain. When my Mexican neighbors came to my house to have a prayer time, 10-year-old "Germancito" asked me about the photos on my bookshelf of my grandchildren playing in snow. This gave me an opportunity to tell how God answers prayer.

Before leaving Mexico for my Christmas vacation, I asked all my national friends to pray for snow in the California mountains where I was going because my grandchildren from Spain wanted to see snow when we were all together. The night after Christmas, a snowstorm did come through, and we were able to drive from the valley up into the mountains to play in the fresh snow. We found a good place for sleds, and the children had great fun.

God not only provided enough snow for sledding, but He delighted us when it soon began to snow beautiful, big flakes. My grandchildren were even able to see it snowing! We took lots of pictures, and now I have them displayed in my living room in Mexico. When Germancito asked at our prayer meeting, I was able to tell him the beautiful story of how specifically and wonderfully God answers the prayers of His children.

—JERRI, AMERICAN PEOPLES

*Thank You* FOR ANSWERED PRAYER, FATHER, AND THAT YOU LOVE TO DELIGHT YOUR CHILDREN SPECIFICALLY AND WONDERFULLY. HEAR THE REQUESTS OF YOUR SERVANTS ON THE MISSION FIELD TODAY AND THRILL THEM WITH YOUR ANSWERS. *Amen.*

# A cultural Christmas

*"And the angel said unto them, Fear not: for, behold, I bring you good tidings of great joy, which shall be to all people." Luke 2:10 (KJV)*

An eggless cake for my vegetarian Hindu friends. Avoiding pork for my Muslim friends. These were some of the challenges of hosting a Christmas party in South Asia. As my language tutor served us a rice dish, the electricity suddenly went off with 35 people in my apartment. I scurried around for candles, and some of my friends graciously went to find people who could restore the power. Forty-five minutes later, the power returned, just in time to begin decorating the tree.

Persuading my friends to put on the lights and garland before the ornaments was a losing battle. Some ornaments ended up on light fixtures and curtain rods. Before I knew it, my living room and tree were decorated in a very unique way. Though different, the room looked nice.

Then we turned the lights off—voluntarily, this time—and admired the tree. One of my colleagues began to tell the story of God, who created the world and loved it so much that He gave His one and only Son that we might have abundant life in Him. Once we accept this news, he said, God expects us to go and tell it, just like the angels did after Jesus was born.

Who needs to hear the Christmas story from you this season?

—ETHAN, SOUTH ASIAN PEOPLES

*Father,* HELP ME TO BE SENSITIVE TO YOUR SPIRIT AS YOU LEAD ME TO THOSE WHO NEED TO MEET THE CHRIST OF CHRISTMAS. AS I ATTEND OR HOST GATHERINGS THIS SEASON, MAY I BE A WITNESS FOR YOU. *Amen.*

# *The birthday paper*

*"She will give birth to a son, and you are to name Him Jesus, because He will save His people from their sins." Matthew 1:21 (HCSB)*

The day before Christmas, I found myself frantically searching through our small North African town for wrapping paper to wrap Christmas gifts for my workers, friends, and neighbors. I had failed to bring Christmas paper with me from the States. After a fruitless search through five local stationery shops, I felt my frustration level rising. There was no Christmas paper to be found—only birthday, congratulations, and a wide assortment of floral patterns.

How could this be true? Orthodox Christians celebrated Christmas here. There were plenty of shops with miniature Christmas trees and Christmas cards. I continued my search through another five shops and finally had to settle for "happy birthday" gift paper. As I sat behind the steering wheel of my car, I tossed my purchase into the seat beside me. How could this town not have one shop with Christmas gift wrap? Just at that moment, I felt the Lord say, *This is my Son's birthday. Why don't you celebrate Him?*

That day as I wrapped gifts, I hoped someone would ask me, "Why the birthday paper?" Then I could share the joyous occasion of Jesus Christ's birth. I challenged myself to use birthday gift wrap for future Christmas gifts as a means of telling the Christmas story.

—L. Lee, Northern African and Middle Eastern Peoples

*Father,* may I focus on the birthday of Your Son rather than the tinsel and gifts. Forgive me when I lose sight of this wondrous occasion. Use me to bring about true celebration of Your Son's birth this season. *Amen.*

# The Christmas present

*"... the Son of Man did not come to be served, but to serve, and to give His life—a ransom for many." Matthew 20:28 (HCSB)*

On Christmas Eve in Guatemala, the streets are empty except for some who are headed to church or to the house of a family member. Women are preparing the traditional meal of tamales, pork roast, black beans, lots of tortillas, and a hot fruit drink called *ponche* (PAHN-chay). The festivities begin around 11 p.m. and continue until early morning. Dinner is at midnight as well as lots of fireworks. After midnight, presents are opened and families spend time together.

Growing up in Texas, I worked with my dad at his drug store until 8 p.m. wrapping gifts for last-minute shoppers on Christmas Eve. We celebrated Christmas Day by waking up early to open presents. The day was spent relaxing and having fun with family.

Different cultures, different traditions, but one celebration. Some celebrate because it is tradition; some celebrate because they love Jesus and want to celebrate His birthday. He came to give us the biggest gift of all—Himself. Does it matter that our Christmas traditions are different around the world? Not really. What really matters is receiving that one big gift that will last for eternity.

—Janet, American Peoples

*Father,* thank You for the gift of Jesus. As I observe Christmas traditions this year, may I be mindful of the gift You gave me. Use missionaries to give the gift of Your Son to the lost today. *Amen.*

## Christmas Dreams

*"Where is the newborn king of the Jews? We saw his star as it rose, and we have come to worship him." Matthew 2:2 (NLT)*

"My sister-in-law, 'Holly,' will be visiting from my country. She is having dreams about Jesus. May I bring her to the play?" My wife and I looked at each other as "Alan," one of our Middle Eastern English students, mentioned the upcoming Christmas Eve event. We had invited our entire class to attend the children's Nativity play at a local church. Knowing that Muslims often dream about Jesus when God's Spirit is working in their lives, we replied, "We would love that!"

While waiting for our friends to arrive on Christmas Eve, we perused the program. Instead of a traditional story in Bethlehem, the play was set in the American Old West. Would this be confusing for our friends? When Alan and his family came in, we saw Holly stop abruptly. She then spoke quickly, using sweeping hand motions. She pointed to the altar, where a manger was placed. Alan translated, "This is the exact location of her dream. She walked down this aisle. She saw Jesus standing there, with His arms open for her. She bowed to Him there." Alan pointed to the manger.

We gave Holly a Bible, and she hugged it to her heart. We needn't have worried; juggling chimpanzees could have been in the play, and Holly wouldn't have noticed. She sat smiling, reading her Bible the entire time—a dream come true!

—TIM, CENTRAL ASIAN PEOPLES

*Thank You, Father,* FOR DRAWING MUSLIMS TO YOURSELF SO THAT THEY CAN FIND JESUS. DURING CHRISTMAS, I PRAY THAT YOU WILL USE DREAMS TO SPARK INTEREST ABOUT JESUS AMONG MUSLIMS. *Amen.*

# Ding's Christmas

*"Give yourselves to the gifts God gives you. Most of all, try to proclaim his truth." 1 Corinthians 14:1b (MSG)*

When I called "Ding" to invite him to Christmas dinner, he seemed reserved. But when I mentioned that I also had a gift for him, he continued laughing until we hung up. It wasn't until the day of the meal that I discovered why.

Ding is one of the "lost boys" from southern Sudan. After fleeing the ravages of the civil war, he spent many years in a refugee camp in northern Kenya. I first met him when he and three other young Sudanese men, just graduating from our Baptist seminary in Kenya, asked if I could help them get back into Sudan to work with their people. They were able to return to bring God's message in an indigenous way.

When he came for his first ever Christmas meal, Ding was his usual cheery self. I had purchased a memory stick for him to transfer information on his computer. When I gave him this gift, Ding started laughing again. He said, "I have heard about the Westerners' tradition of giving gifts at Christmas time, but I have never received one." His laughter was simply his way of expressing joy over receiving his first Christmas gift ever. I pray that God will continue to use Ding as a "gift" to his people in southern Sudan.

—MARK, SUB-SAHARAN AFRICAN PEOPLES

FATHER, I AGREE WITH THIS PRAYER THAT YOU WILL USE DING AND OTHER SUDANESE CHRISTIANS TO SPREAD THE GOSPEL IN SUDAN. THANK YOU THAT THESE YOUNG MEN ARE NOT LOST, BUT SAVED BY GRACE. Amen.

# *Opportune flight delay*

*"Making the most of the time, because the days are evil." Ephesians 5:16 (HCSB)*

Returning to South Asia after Christmas, I arrived at an airport after nine hours on a plane and headed to the gate of my connecting flight, only to discover that the flight was significantly delayed. Frustrated, I sat down, and soon after, a German man asked to sit by me. I was taken off guard, but I agreed, remembering that Europeans do not follow the same rules as South Asians.

We began a conversation, which soon turned to religion. He was a former Catholic who was traveling to India to find God. He left his job to go on this spiritual quest. As he quoted Gandhi, Muhammad, and even Jesus, I asked him if he had ever read the Bible. He told me no. Having a Bible in the bag beside me, I pulled it out and asked him if he would like to have it. He took the Bible gladly and promised me that he would add it to his meditation.

I don't expect to ever see this man again, but neither do I expect our lives to be quite the same. I only pray that he kept his word and was changed, not by the spirituality of his Asian pilgrimage, but by the living words of Jesus found in God's Word.

—KARI, SOUTH ASIAN PEOPLES

*Thank You, Father,* THAT THIS MISSIONARY MADE THE MOST OF HER FLIGHT DELAY. I PRAY SPECIFICALLY FOR THIS MAN TO FIND THE ANSWER HE DESIRES IN JESUS CHRIST. DRAW HIM TO YOURSELF THROUGH THE LIVING WORDS OF THE BIBLE GIVEN TO HIM. *Amen.*

# The blessing of giving

*"And God can give you more blessings than you need. Then you will always have plenty of everything—enough to give to every good work." 2 Corinthians 9:8 (NCV)*

In Zambia, each day is one of survival for many. Trying to find enough food to make it through the day is common. People live year by year hoping for a good crop so they can make it to the next year. In spite of these difficulties, Zambians are a giving and charitable people.

This past year had not been good for growing corn, the staple food, because there was too much rain. In many places, flooding wiped out entire fields. As I talked with a local pastor, I asked how his fields had fared. He only expected to harvest about five 40-pound bags of maize. When asked how many bags he needed to get his family through the year, he said about 20. With a heavy heart, I began to leave. Before I got into the truck, he asked me to wait. I was stunned when he presented me with 10 cobs of fresh maize from his field. These were obviously the best he had, the first fruits.

I was humbled and blessed. I seriously considered refusing and telling him that he needed it more than I, but in reality, he desired the blessing of giving—not giving from his abundance but giving from his abject poverty.

—Kevin, Sub-Saharan African Peoples

*Jehovah Jireh,* I pray that You will provide for the needs of believers in Zambia. Let their fields produce unusually well this season as a testimony to Your goodness. May Your name be glorified in this country. *Amen.*

# *Where I've been; where I'm going*

*"Then Samuel took a stone and set it between Mizpah and Shen, and named it Ebenezer, saying, 'Thus far the LORD has helped us.'" 1 Samuel 7:12 (NASB)*

"Come Thou Fount of Every Blessing" is one of my favorite hymns. The reference to Samuel raising a memorial that he called "Ebenezer" makes me take stock of where I have been and where the Lord has brought me. Without these mental stones of remembrance, it would be easy to become discouraged. Russia in the winter is gray and cold. We miss our family and friends. We often make awful mistakes with the language.

But if those problems become the focus, I must remember God who called us and says, "Do not fear, for I have redeemed you; I have called you by name; you are Mine!" (Isaiah 43:1, NASB) He is here, just like He was there with Samuel and the Israelites. We see His hand as we think of the Russian friends whom God has given us to love and disciple. If I pay close attention, His fingerprints are on every aspect of my life. In fact, I clearly see that He has left His mark all around me. If I look with eyes of faith, I must proclaim with the songwriter, "O to grace how great a debtor daily I'm constrained to be!"

Whether it's through an easy time in life or a difficult time, He's at work. Raise your Ebenezer today, praising God for bringing you this far.

—KELLYE, EUROPEAN PEOPLES

*I praise You,* AWESOME GOD, FOR BRINGING ME THIS FAR. THANK YOU THAT YOU ARE WITH ME AND THAT YOUR GRACE IS LAVISHED UPON ME. I AM YOURS! PRAISE YOUR BLESSED NAME! *Amen.*

# Giving first

> "'Bring the full 10 percent into the storehouse so that there may be food in My house. Test Me in this way,' says the LORD of Hosts. 'See if I will not open the floodgates of heaven and pour out a blessing for you without measure.'" Malachi 3:10 (HCSB)

Church leaders in our area were discouraged that no matter how often they asked church members to give tithes and offerings, the amounts collected were very small. So we decided to instruct 30 national pastors, leaders, and evangelists on biblical giving.

As an illustration, I displayed a plastic container, Ping-Pong balls, and a tennis ball. The seminar participants named family expenses, such as food, clothes, shelter, shoes, school tuition and uniforms, medicine, and other items. Ping-Pong balls would represent each of these things. The tennis ball represented tithes and offerings. When we placed the Ping-Pong balls in the plastic container first, then added the tennis ball on top, the lid wouldn't fit on the container. But when the tennis ball was placed in the container first, all the Ping-Pong balls fit, and the lid closed! The illustration showed that we should give tithes and offerings first, then watch to see how God would supply all our needs. We challenged the participants to do the same.

These national leaders began encouraging their people, mostly poor farmers or laborers, and tithes and offerings increased substantially. You can't out give God.

—SHIRLEY, SOUTH ASIAN PEOPLES

When TIMES ARE TOUGH ECONOMICALLY, Father, USE THIS ILLUSTRATION TO REMIND ME TO GIVE TO YOU FIRST. I CAN TRUST YOU WITH THE NEEDS OF MY FAMILY. YOU ARE JEHOVAH JIREH, GOD WHO PROVIDES. Amen.

## *Our choice or His*

*"Instead, God has chosen the world's foolish things to shame the wise, and God has chosen the world's weak things to shame the strong." 1 Corinthians 1:27 (HCSB)*

When we met "Natalia," she shared her tragic story as a Lebanese refugee with a husband who had severe mental problems. This wasn't someone I imagined would someday become an evangelist but rather a desperately hurting woman who needed the Lord and caring friends.

Over the years, my friend Demi and I kept up with Natalia's family as the government relocated them from small apartments to hostels. We prayed with her through many health issues, the birth of a child, the breakdown of her marriage, and the loss of her extended family. She came to depend on those prayers.

Then one day, she called from a hostel housed with new immigrants. "God is using me to pray for these people! You cannot believe it, these are Muslim people who love Jesus and want to know more about Him." Her heart was bursting with joy and a sense of privilege to be used by the Lord to pray for the very people group that had shattered her world in her home country.

We often are attracted to the most "put-together" person, yet our Lord most often chooses the "most broken" to channel His love and blessing. God chose Natalia to reach out to many refugee women because she knows their pain.

—BARBARA, EUROPEAN PEOPLES

*Father,* OUR COMFORTER, YOU TAKE OUR PAIN AND USE IT FOR YOUR GLORY. SHOW ME HOW I CAN REACH OUT TO ANOTHER IN THE COMING YEAR WHO IS EXPERIENCING THE SAME PAIN I'VE ALREADY GONE THROUGH. MAY YOU USE ME TO BRING YOUR HEALING TOUCH. *Amen.*

# Always prepared

*"Watch! Be alert! For you don't know when the time is [coming]." Mark 13:33 (HCSB)*

Moving into the nomadic community meant that we would live in a traditional felt-wrapped tent structure that had a wooden door. We were soon to find out that the local nomadic culture views doors quite differently than our Western culture does. Neighbors and strangers walked into our house at any time without warning.

Living in a one-room house, I quickly learned that it was important to always have my house in order and myself presentable, or else be embarrassed when someone suddenly entered. So we're in a constant state of readiness for visitors, being always prepared to serve them food and drink when they arrive unannounced.

God asks the same of our lives. We are always to be ready for His return, and you and I are to live in such a way that we are prepared to be a reflection of Christ in our lives. We don't know when others may be watching us or when the opportunity will arise for us to share His love and His Word with those around us.

Are you ready for Christ's return, and are you ready to minister to those He will bring into your life in the coming year? Be prepared so that you do not miss these precious opportunities to be a servant of the Lord.

—T.M., EAST ASIAN PEOPLES

*Dear God,* HELP MISSIONARIES LIVE IN A CONSTANT STATE OF PREPAREDNESS TO HOST OTHERS. MAY I LIVE LIKE THIS, TOO, SO THAT MY DOORS ARE OPEN TO ANYONE WHO DROPS BY. *Amen.*

# INDEX

## MARCH: DIVINE APPOINTMENTS

AUGUST: MAKING HIM KNOWN

## OCTOBER: FROM ADVERSITY TO TRIUMPH

## November: Be Encouraged

# INDEX

# HAVE YOU HEARD GOD'S VOICE?

God loves you and wants you to experience peace and life. But it's just not any life He has in mind for you; it's life that's abundant and eternal.

But there's a problem. Because of our nature, we humans disobey God and go our own ways; we are separated from God. The good news is that the problem has an answer: Jesus Christ. He died on the cross for our sins and rose from the grave. In this way, Jesus bridges the gap between God and people. When we trust Jesus Christ and receive Him into our hearts by our personal invitation, we begin experiencing God's peace and the abundant, eternal life He planned for us.

### HOW TO RECEIVE JESUS CHRIST
1. Admit your need for forgiveness and peace.
2. Commit to turn from your sins, believing that Jesus Christ died for you on the cross and rose from the grave.
3. Through prayer, invite Jesus Christ to forgive your sins and accept Him as Savior and the Lord of your life.

Once you've trusted Christ as Savior—or if you are still struggling with that decision—please quickly get involved with a Bible-teaching church. Building relationships with other Christians and hearing God's Word taught will provide invaluable encouragement and accountability.

# A Message from the International Mission Board

When Jesus commissioned us to make disciples of all nations, the terminology He used did not refer to geopolitical boundaries but to all the *ethnos* or peoples of the world. We live in a world without borders when it comes to people groups. For example, massive numbers of Chinese are found all over the world. Why should a strategy to reach the Chinese be focused exclusively on East Asia? Europe has become a melting pot of Africans, Arabs, and Asians. To see reaching Europe as a witness to only Europeans is to overlook the realities of our modern world.

One way to reach a borderless world is to view people by affinity groups. Affinity groups are large groupings of related peoples who share similar origins, languages, and cultures. They act as a lens through which missionaries view lostness and focus strategy to share the Gospel. The affinity group strategy is based on reaching specific groups of people rather than individual nations or geographic areas. The IMB has identified eight primary global affinity groups that encompass all of the world's 11,000-plus known people groups. The devotionals in this book were written by missionaries who are bringing the Gospel to one of these affinity groups: American Peoples (Central and South American people groups), European Peoples, Northern African and Middle Eastern Peoples, Central Asian Peoples, Sub-Saharan African Peoples, Southeast Asian Peoples, South Asian Peoples, and East Asian Peoples.

The International Mission Board is part of the Southern Baptist Convention, the nation's largest evangelical denomination, claiming more than 42,000 churches with nearly 16 million members. In 2008, 5,000-plus IMB missionaries and their Baptist partners overseas reported more than 565,000 baptisms—each representing a life changed by the Good News of Jesus. I'm reminded of the words of Jesus in Matthew 24:14: "This good news of the kingdom will be proclaimed in all the world as a testimony to all nations. And then the end will come" (HCSB).

We don't know when that end will come, nor do we fully understand God's criteria for completing the Great Commission; however, it is evident that those words of Jesus are being fulfilled. Our mission task remains focused on the vision of John in Revelation 7:9 and that day when there will be "a vast multitude from every nation, tribe, people, and language, which no one could number" (HCSB) gathered around the throne, worshipping the Lamb of God!

—JERRY RANKIN, PRESIDENT
INTERNATIONAL MISSION BOARD, SBC

---

TO LEARN MORE ABOUT THE INTERNATIONAL
MISSION BOARD, PLEASE VISIT IMB.ORG

TO LEARN MORE ABOUT VOICES OF THE FAITHFUL
RESOURCES, PLEASE VISIT VOICESOFTHEFAITHFUL.COM

---

# How to Pray for International Missionaries and People Groups

Throughout this book you've come heart to heart with international missionaries—and probably realized they're not much different from you. They need your prayers. By daily voicing prayers for specific missionaries, you'll become a key instrument in God's design for strengthening His workers throughout the world. If you don't know any missionaries by name, start by choosing missionaries who have written these devotionals. Though you don't know the missionaries' full names, God does.

These ideas will get you started in praying for missionaries as the Holy Spirit guides you:

1. Pray that missionaries will love God with all their hearts, souls, and minds and will love all others as themselves.
2. Pray for protection from the evil one and for good health.
3. Pray for wisdom and attentive spirits to God's direction and leadership.
4. Pray that missionaries will deny themselves and follow Jesus anywhere.
5. Pray for moral purity in thought, sight, word, and action.
6. Pray that missionaries will have courage, boldness, and strength in the Lord. Pray they will have favor with local governments.
7. Pray that family relationships will be filled with love, respect, and honor. Pray that single missionaries will find strong relationships to strengthen their walk with the Lord.
8. Pray that the Gospel will spread rapidly throughout the people group the missionaries are working to reach.
9. Pray that relationships with missionary colleagues and local believers will reflect Christ.

10. Pray for daily needs to be met: safe drinking water, nutritious food, housing, and transportation.
11. Pray for the building of strong prayer networks among local and stateside partners. Pray for good connections to stateside churches.

Pray the following for the people groups of the world:

1. Pray that the light of Christ will replace the darkness in the lives of the lost.
2. Pray for the breaking down of religious barriers, for freedom from spiritual bondage, and for people to experience dreams and visions pointing them to the truth of Jesus Christ.
3. Pray that the Gospel will penetrate the hearts of the people via every means possible, such as radio, television, tapes, videos, e-mail, the Internet, drama, and medical clinics.
4. Pray for the translation of Scripture—both written and oral stories—for each people group, asking for protection and accuracy for translation teams. Intercede for the careful and strategic distribution of Christian literature so that people will be drawn to the Word.
5. Pray for the development of training materials as well as praying that biblical, theological, and leadership training be accessible for emerging church leaders.
6. Pray that as people come to Christ, they will catch the vision of the Great Commission and boldly share their faith, leading to a church-planting movement among the people.

FIND INTERNATIONAL MISSION BOARD PRAYER
RESOURCES AND REQUESTS AT PRAYER.IMB.ORG

# Your Church's Role
## in Missions

Has God touched you through these stories? Wondering what to do next? God has made your church unique, with its own combination of people, talents, and resources to be used to help fulfill the Great Commission. Use the suggestions below to start exploring God's missions plans for your church.

Start in God's Word. Lead your church through Scripture so the entire congregation will share God's heart for all nations to worship Him (Revelation 7:9).

Develop a strategy. A comprehensive strategy follows Acts 1:8, encompassing local, state, national, and international missions. That strategy should include knowing, praying, giving, and going. Organize a missions team of leaders who have a burden for missions.

Love. Expose your church to needs across the globe. Jesus felt compassion for the multitudes. Compassion compels Christians to get involved. Communicate with missionaries and allow their passion for the lost to overflow into your church.

Know. Educate church members about how they can be involved. Invite missionaries to speak or conference them into a worship service. Establish a missions center with literature, videos, and other tools to use in multiple settings. Resources may be ordered at imbresources.org. (Free resources are available to Southern Baptists.)

PRAY. Design a prayer strategy. Ask missionaries who have visited your church to send you regular prayer requests. Find other missions prayer resources at pray.imb.org.

GIVE. Keep the missions challenge before your congregation and provide opportunities to give. Let your church know how their giving makes a difference. For more information, go to give.imb.org.

GO. Serve alongside missionaries on a short-term project. Then report and celebrate God's work when you return. Learn about volunteer opportunities at volunteer.imb.org. To learn more about going as a long-term or short-term Southern Baptist missionary, go to going.imb.org, or call (888) 422-6461.

If your Southern Baptist church would like personal coaching to assist you, call the Church Services Group of the IMB at (800) 999-3113 or go to churchservices.imb.org.

# ABOUT BETH MOORE AND LIVING PROOF MINISTRIES

God captured Beth Moore's heart at a very young age. Her first love was a man with long, dark hair, tan and weathered skin, and loving eyes. When she saw a picture of His face tacked onto the wall in Sunday School, she knew Jesus would be the love of her life. Like many children brought up in church, she learned about the Bible, His love letter to her. Beth's love for Jesus Christ grew over the years, and at the age of 18, she committed her entire life to God.

The Lord is using Beth Moore to encourage women through her Bible studies and conferences not only to stand on the Word of God, but to know what it says. In 1995, the Lord led her to establish Living Proof Ministries to guide women to love and live on God's Word.

Living Proof is committed to fanning the flame in others for God and His Word. Every message, program, tape, book, or product offered through this ministry is diligently directed toward this goal. Living Proof Ministries was founded upon Hebrews 4:12: "For the word of God is living and effective and sharper than any two-edged sword" (HCSB).

Beth and her husband, Keith, not only have a passion for the Word, but for missions as well. They have ministered to missionaries in many parts of the world. They have two daughters, Amanda and Melissa; two sons-in-law, Curt and Colin; and two grandchildren, Jackson and Annabeth.

---

FOR MORE INFORMATION ABOUT BETH MOORE AND
LIVING PROOF MINISTRIES, SEE WWW.LPROOF.ORG.

---

440

# ABOUT KIM P. DAVIS

Practically growing up in the church in the Deep South gave Kim Davis a love for Jesus as a girl. As a college freshman at the University of Georgia, she committed her life to follow Him completely. With a degree in journalism and a love for God, writing has been a joy. She has held such jobs as news journalist, editor, and author.

Kim and her husband, D. Ray, served as International Mission Board missionaries in Southern Africa for 13 years, and D. Ray continues to serve on staff at the IMB. She led Bible studies with ladies in South Africa and told stories of the Bible and taught sewing skills to women in Zimbabwe. Born out of her passion for missions, Kim was the compiler of best-selling *Voices of the Faithful* and author of *My Life, His Mission*. She speaks all over the country, sharing God's heart for the nations.

Currently, Kim and D. Ray reach out to university students. As missions mentors at a Christian university, they help students explore God's calling on their lives. They also enjoy opening their home to international students from a local university in order to show them the love of Christ in action.

She and her husband have three children, Paul, Emily, and Trevor, and one funny dog, Elle. They reside in Richmond, Virginia.

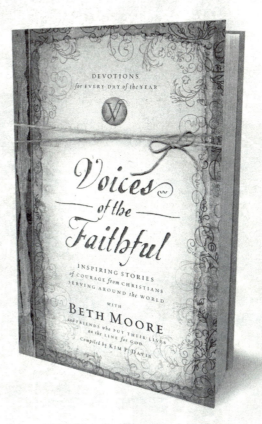

American Peoples